Architecture, Ritual and Cosmology in China

Drawing on the author's extensive fieldwork in the Dong areas in southwest China, this book presents a detailed picture of the Dong's buildings and techniques, with new insights into the Dong's cosmology and rituals of everyday life meshed with the architecture, and the symbolic meanings. It examines how the buildings and techniques of the Dong are ordered and influenced by the local culture and context.

The timber bridges and drum towers are the Dong's most prominent architectural monuments. Usually built elaborately with multiple roofs, these bridges and drum towers were designed and maintained by the local carpenters who also built the village suspended houses, in an oral tradition carried down from father to son or to apprentice. They were funded entirely by the local people, and the bridges tend to be built in places without great pressure of traffic or another bridge already existing close by. Why does such great expense go into the Dong's buildings with elaboration? How were they built? And what do they mean to their users and builders?

This book is an anthropological study on the Dong's architecture and technique, and it aims to contribute a discourse on the interdisciplinary research area. It is suitable for graduate and postgraduate readers.

Xuemei Li holds a PhD in Architectural History and History from the Architectural School at Sheffield University. Her research on the vernacular architecture and traditional techniques of the Dong community has been published in the *Journal of Landscape Research*, the *Journal of Architecture*, the *Journal of the Society of Architectural Historians* and the *Journal of Architectural Research Quarterly*. She has taught Architectural History and Theory, and Architectural Structure courses in the universities of America, Canana and China. She was Visiting Scholar in Graduate School of Architecture, Planning and Preservation, at Columbia University, and Associate Professor in He Xiangning College of Art and Design at Zhongkai Agricultural University.

Routledge Research in Architecture

The *Routledge Research in Architecture* series provides the reader with the latest scholarship in the field of architecture. The series publishes research from across the globe and covers areas as diverse as architectural history and theory, technology, digital architecture, structures, materials, details, design, monographs of architects, interior design and much more. By making these studies available to the worldwide academic community, the series aims to promote quality architectural research.

Architecture and Affect
Precarious Spaces
Lilian Chee

Modernism in Late-Mao China
Architecture for Foreign Affairs in Beijing, Guangzhou and Overseas, 1969-1976
Ke Song

The Spatialities of Radio Astronomy
Guy Trangoš

The Ambiguous Legacy of Socialist Modernist Architecture in Central and Eastern Europe
Mariusz E. Sokołowicz, Aleksandra Nowakowska, Błażej Ciarkowski

Architecture, Ritual and Cosmology in China
The Buildings of the Order of the Dong
Xuemei Li

For more information about this series, please visit: https://www.routledge.com/Routledge-Research-in-Architecture/book-series/RRARCH

Architecture, Ritual and Cosmology in China
The Buildings of the Order of the Dong

Xuemei Li

LONDON AND NEW YORK

Cover image: Xuemei Li

First published 2023
by Routledge
4 Park Square, Milton Park, Abingdon, Oxon OX14 4RN

and by Routledge
605 Third Avenue, New York, NY 10158

Routledge is an imprint of the Taylor & Francis Group, an informa business

© 2023 Xuemei Li

The right of Xuemei Li to be identified as author of this work has been asserted in accordance with sections 77 and 78 of the Copyright, Designs and Patents Act 1988.

All rights reserved. No part of this book may be reprinted or reproduced or utilised in any form or by any electronic, mechanical, or other means, now known or hereafter invented, including photocopying and recording, or in any information storage or retrieval system, without permission in writing from the publishers.

Trademark notice: Product or corporate names may be trademarks or registered trademarks, and are used only for identification and explanation without intent to infringe.

British Library Cataloguing-in-Publication Data
A catalogue record for this book is available from the British Library

ISBN: 978-1-032-13355-3 (hbk)
ISBN: 978-1-032-13356-0 (pbk)
ISBN: 978-1-003-22883-7 (ebk)

DOI: 10.4324/9781003228837

Typeset in Times New Roman
by codeMantra

Contents

Preface vii
Acknowledgement ix

1 The Geography of the Dong   1
2 The Cosmology of Separation and Reunion of the Dong   27
3 The Drum Towers as the Cosmological Centre of
   Separation and Reunion   74
4 Wind and Water (*fengshui* 风水) in Shaping the Dong
   Villages   109
5 The Traditional Building Techniques of the Dong   153
6 The Rituals which Accompany the Construction of
   Dong Houses   196
7 Conclusion: Symbolic Meaning, Ritual and
   Architectural Order   238

   Bibliography   255
   Index   267

Preface

Inspired by the anthropological discourse of the 1960s, this is an exhaustive study of the ritualistic tectonic culture of the Dong civilization; a people living since time immemorial in a land-locked, mountainous region in the southwest corner of the vast Chinese continent. However inadvertently it is a seminal contribution to the anthropology of building, a field pioneered by Pierre Bourdieu's study of the micro-cosmological coding of the Berber house; his essay the *Berber House of the World Reversed* of 1969 and by a number of young German scholars who, throughout the 60s, established the discourse through their research into primordial Japanese landmarking signs and agrarian renewal rites; the architects Gunter Nitschke and Guadenz Dominique and the etymologist, Josef Trier. Although this independent study makes no reference to these precedents it nonetheless deals with deeply rooted Chinese building culture in a similar anthropological manner not only in regard to cosmological survival but also with respect to the specific relationship obtaining in Dong society between built form and ritualism, particularly in relation to the quixotic forces of nature, as much prone to gratuitous destruction as to the provision of a beneficial environment.

The most revealing and compelling aspect of this study is the manner in which the Dong have occupied their mountainous and river inundated territory and above all else the ritualistic role played in their society by two prominently, monumental timber structures; the tiered, vertical form of the drum tower and the contrasting horizontality of the so-called, "Wind and Rain" bridge, this last often spanning across a river to link the aggregation structures serves to announce and accommodate the public space of the society, the wind and rain bridge not only affords a crossing over an otherwise impassable river, at an auspicious site determined by the divination processes of Feng shui, but also simultaneously affords a mythical rite of passage through which souls may pass from this world to the next and vice versa. In retrospect it is remarkable how two such highly sophisticated and expensive structures would be invariably built and maintained in at least every other village, sometimes creating a time-honoured cosmos for as little as 300 people within a regional population that today stands at 25 million.

The second half of Xuemei Li's remarkable study is not only devoted to the apotropaic rites accompanying the construction of ordinary Dong houses, auspiciously sited in accordance with the dictates of the Fengshui compass, but also to the detailed morés of the Chinese dynastic building tradition in wood, as first documented by American trained Chinese architect, Liang Sicheng and his wife in the 1930s along with the important discovery of the Song Dynasty building manual, the Ying Zao Fa Shi which not only stipulated standard timber sizes by also established an hierarchy range of house types in terms of their size and the complexity of framing according to the social status of the occupant. Perhaps in the last analysis the most extraordinary aspect of this complex tradition is not only the prescribed statistical and buildable function of all the various components, the complex brackets, over-hanging eaves, beams, stepped framing, mortices and terms from which the whole elaborate form is assembled but also the specific naming of every conceivable element, thus not only establishing a linguistic cosmos, bordering on the mythical, but also extending to the nomenclature of every tool used in process of fabrication and erection, above all the indispensable but also slightly varying Lu Ban rule deployed by every master carpenter in the construction of the work. Herein every part, and manipulative gesture serves to engender and maintain a mythical cosmos wherein building is inseparable from language and vice versa.

Ultimately inspired by Amos Rapoport's path-breaking study *House Form and Culture* of 1961 and Mircea Eliade's *The Sacred and the Profane* of virtually the same date, this exemplary and enriching anthropological study is the result of years of painstaking hands-on, field research within the time-honoured but still insufficiently studied aspect of traditional Chinese cosmological culture and as such it establishes a new port of entry into the infinite complexities of building anthropology.

Kenneth Frampton
The Ware Professor of Architecture at the Graduate School of
Architecture, Planning, and Preservation at Columbia University

Acknowledgement

The seeds of research on the Dong's vernacular architecture were sown in 2000, when my father took me to the Dong areas on his business trip to build a new school for the village. I was so intrigued by the timber cover bridges built by the Dong, I brought the idea of researching on traditional techniques of the Dong's architecture to my supervisor Peter for my PhD study in the Architectural School at Sheffield. Instead of directly encouraging or discouraging my research proposal, Peter passed a book to me, The Rites of Passage written by Arnold Van Gennep. Since then, I have been fascinated by anthropology and involved in a journey on the cross-disciplinary study of anthropology and architecture over 20 years. I have worked with a number of professionals and local carpentry masters in the Dong. During my fieldwork in Sanjiang county, I met Wu Hao, an expert in Dong research, where he introduced many books on Dong customs, narratives, songs and mythologies that inspired me to study the Dong's vernacular architecture through an anthropological viewpoint. Every time I did fieldworks I would visit Yang Shenren, who was a builder and master of the Dong bridges. Each time, he kindly explained to me about the structure and materials in the Dong buildings, and showed how the models and carpentry rules work in building up the architecture. I would also like to express my appreciation to his brother, master Yang Shiping, who made a customized physical model of three pavilions of the bridge for me to bring to the UK for my study. I am extremely grateful to have cooperated with Kendra in Ryerson University, who provided valuable opinions to polish my research topics and encouraged me to publish them in peer-reviewed journals. I hope to contribute this book to memory my father Li Lin, late professors Peter Blundell Jones and Kendra Schank Smith, and masters Yang Shanren and Yang Shiping.

I own a special debt of gratitude to all those Dong acquaintances who provided help in the research field, particularly my friends and informants for my fieldwork the Dong villages. No doubt for the people that I thank here have not included everyone that I should. I am grateful to the genius of indigenous builders of the Dong, specifically to the late master Yang Shanren's sons Yang Nianlu, Yang Shiyu and his grandson Yang Quanjing, who provided valuable information to support the closer collaboration between the two disciplines of anthropology and architecture, and to confirm that the built forms, within which the rituals enacted, are rooted in the traditional cosmology. My debt also goes to my friends, Li Weiye, Shu Zuoxi and Mo Shihua, because my fieldwork could not have been so productive without their sustained and generous support and organization. My thanks go particularly to Professor Wu Shuoxian and Xiao Dawei in the State Key Laboratory of Subtropical Building Science at South China University of Technology, which offered me its hospitality as a Visiting fellow and a research grant for my study. I would also like to thank to Professor Albert C Smith in Ryerson University and Dr. Klass Ruitenbeek, for their enthusiasm and inspiration to share their research and knowledge on the western and eastern measurement to this subject. I am grateful to Li Changjie, the expert of Dong architecture, and Professor Ronald G Knapp, for their contribution of some of the images in the book. Most generous of all is Professor Kenneth Frampton, for his strict criticism, fertile ideas, and contribution of a preface to this book.

Above all those, I am forever grateful to my family, my mother Lin Ruifang and my daughter Huilin Zhang, for their unfailing support, and constantly inspiring me throughout my research.

1 The Geography of the Dong

In March 2001, when we drove for the first time across Sanjiang and Longsheng counties, an instant impression flashed past us—the drum towers and timber bridges in the Dong villages (Figure 1.1). The drum towers are impressive with their huge roof combined with many layers of eaves, and the bridges are covered and crowned with pavilions, scattering among the mountain landscape on the rivers or grain fields near the Dong villages, both identifying the Dong communities with their neighbours. These bridges are well-known as Wind and Rain bridges in the world, which are extremely striking for their elegant forms and the elaborate skills of the structures. They are called Wind and Rain bridges in the poetry of Guo Morou, since they are often conceived for providing passage for the villagers across the

Figure 1.1 The Yanzhai village, drum tower, and the Wind and Rain bridge, Sanjiang, 2011.

DOI: 10.4324/9781003228837-1

2 The Geography of the Dong

river, and the shelters for protecting them from the wind and rain in the humid and wet weather. Our questions consistently came forward: why are so many drum towers and timber bridges built in the adjacent villages, and so elaborately? And what are the origins?

The Typology, Language and Custom of the Dong

In Southern China, in the mountainous regions of Guizhou, Hunan and Guangxi, live the Dong minority, long cut off from the rest of China by a difficult topography that leaves eighty percent of land as mountainside, ten percent river and the final ten percent fields (Figure 1.2).[1] According to the Fourth National Census in 1990, most of the Dong reside in these three provinces, with a total population exceeding 2.5 million.[2] Villages of the Dong are normally composed of two or three hundred homes on average and sometimes with a thousand or more in the largest settlement, or only ten or twenty in the smallest. The tadeonal Dong homelands occupy the basin region surrounded by mountains and rivers.[3] The remarkable topography of the Dong areas is complicatedly comprised of mountains, rivers and basins

Figure 1.2 Map of rivers and townships in Sanjiang county (from Annals of the Nationalities in Sanjiang county, 2002. Redrawn by author).

among the mountains. The description in Chinese as 'basin land holed under sky' (*dong tian pen di* 洞天盆地) appropriately marks the special characters of topography: the valleys are settled on the basin land and are surrounded by mountains, the views are blocked by the mountainsides, and people can only see the sky when they look up.[4] The famous mountains include: Xuefeng Mountain, which lies in the east of the Dong region of Hunan province, and extends from south to north; Miaolin Mountain chain, sitting in southern Guizhou; Wulin Mountain, ranging along the edge of north-western Hunan, Hubei and Guizhou; Jiuwan Mountain, mainly locating in northern Guangxi and extending to the south of Guizhou; Yuechenlin Mountain, which is a branch of Wu Mountain, and extends from the north-east of Guangxi into south-west Hunan within 200 km; and Shanshenpo Mountain, which is adjacent to the areas of Hunan Province, Guizhou Province and Guangxi Province. The tallest one is Yuanbao Mountain, which is adjacent to Jiuwan Mountain and to Congjiang and Rongjiang county, which has an altitude over two-thousand meters.[5]

There are over five-thousand rivers, meandering through the Dong areas under the foot of the mountains. The famous ones are Qushui river, Wushui river, Qingshui river, Yuanshui river, Xun river, Duliu river and Qing river, with a total length of about twenty-thousand kilometres, covering about fifty-thousand square kilometres of the area, and carrying a rate of water volume of more than 90-billion m^3 per year. The largest Dong settlement plain is found near Rongjiang county, which extends about 20 km in length and 2.5 km in width with over thousands of households inhabited. With the particular topography, the Dong villages actually are protected from the strong winds and, as a consequence, they enjoy a warm and humid weather with an average temperature of twenty degrees, offering a mild climate and habitable regions for the Dong to plant and cultivate.[6] The main crop is rice, although they also grow cotton for textiles, China fir timber for buildings and boats and all necessary food.

More intensive agriculture is practiced based on artificial irrigation, thus the flat areas with plenty of water and forests are planted with rice; and mountainsides are covered with fir, pine and fruit trees. Cotton, tea bushes and vegetables are grown on small terraces on the hillsides.

So remote were they until a few decades ago that people a mere five kilometres away were total strangers, and in their isolation, they retained their own language, which lacked any form of script until 1958. A distinct language binds the people of this region and acts as one of the critical features in distinguishing it from other societies. The population of the Dong widely extends over mountain valleys in different regions and contact is maintained with other ethnic groups of diverse cultures, such as Miao, Yao, Zhuang, Molao, Shui, Buyi and Tujia.[7] The language spoken in the Dong belongs to the Kam-Tai family of Sino-Tibetan languages, which includes four families: Chinese, Tibeto-Burman, Kam-Tai and Miao-Yao. The Kam-Tai family is divided into two main branches: Kam-Shui and Tai.[8] The Kam-Shui branch

4 *The Geography of the Dong*

contains Dong, Mulao, Shui and Maonan, and the Tai branch contains Zhuang, Buyi, Dai and Thai. The Dong people used to name themselves Kam, which in the Kam language means to 'cover, conceal, defence, and protect', particularly identifying them as the kind of people who 'hide' and 'settle' in the remote isolated areas for self-preservation.[9] Thus the typical topography of the Dong means being surrounded by mountains and forests with the basin lands in the middle for planting, and the villages are protected by artificial defence from the intruders or wild animals. *Kam* also means 'tilt-hammer', which is found in all traditional *Kam* homes for hulling rice. The stone grinding for hulled rice is circular, with a dip in the middle. One theory is that the *Kam* people started to use *Kam* as an autonym because the grinding stone resembles the shape of the mountain valley in which most Kam villages are located.[10] According to *Gui Hai Yu Heng Zhi* and *Song Shi,* the Dong areas were separated into prefectures, which were composed of counties, and the Dong is one branch of the ethnic groups belonging to these counties. 'Dong', the name given by other ethnic groups, then came to be used in the Sui (581–618) and Tang (618–907) dynasties to refer to the people living in south and southwest China, as the name for an administrative unit.[11] Between 1911 and 1949, three different Chinese characters (洞, 侗) but all with the same pronunciation *dong* were used as the Dong's name, all of which were associated with wild animals, 'hole, cavity', and 'cave, cavern'. After 1949, these three former original names were replaced by the current Dong (侗) without carrying any pejorative definition.[12]

Villages are traditionally occupied by people of the same surname and paternal line, depending on a strict marriage system relying on exchange of women with other local villages. The formerly independent political system involved an elected headman with quasi-religious powers who made administrative and judicial decisions with the help of a handful of elders. Before 1949, the Dong communities are administrated by their social groups called *kuan* (款) institutions. The Dong people have a long tradition of self-government administrated via *kuan*, which is a set of strict rules or laws set up and obeyed by the Dong. According to the record of Sanjiang gazette, a person accused of theft crimes, either valuable or invaluable, must be punishable by death by the assembly in the drum tower without getting permission from the local government. Therefore, nobody risks stealing, and the livestock, such as cows and sheep, are shepherded freely and never lost. Over the centuries the *kuan,* managed by the village heads and elders, have played essential roles in organizing and governing the Dong communities.[13]

Based on their distinct historical and cultural background, the community usually chooses a certain way of life for the distinguished ascription to other ethnic groups. The Dong's agricultural calendar is filled with particular customs involved in almost every aspect of their daily life. The 1st month is occupied by the ceremonies for Chinese New Year and Stepping on the Singing Stage; the Sweet Rice Cake and Worship the Bridge festivals are held in the 2nd month; in the 3rd month, there are Sowing Seeds,

The Geography of the Dong 5

Fireworks Day and Tidying the Grave ceremonies; celebration of the Water-Buffaloes' Birthday, Planting Cotton and Girls' Day are in the 4th month; Dragon Boat Festival is in the 5th month; ceremonies for Washing Water-Buffaloes and Zong ba (Eating sweet rice cake) Festival are held in the 6th month; Eating New Rice festival is in the 7th month; the ritual of *lu sheng* Day, Mid-Autumn Festival, Pumpkin Day and Cultivating New Land ceremonies are performed in the 8th month; and the rest of time prepare for the coming of new year.[14] During these festivals, the villages pay visits to each other, with the ritual performance of singing, dancing and sharing of a community meal. The Dong people, who are tied with their own special language and custom, build up their unambiguous social and distributional boundaries with their cultural identity, and separate themselves from other communities.

The Drum Towers and the Wind and Rain Bridges

The typical village is found on the low hillside above the river to keep from flooding and to avoid wasting rice-growing land (Figure 1.3). It consists of timber *ganlan* houses on stilts tightly disposed about narrow winding lanes, surrounded by a perimeter of vegetable gardens and with defined gates at every exit to the outer world. The village centre is a public square with an adjacent opera stage for the song performances for which the Dong are famous and which are involved in many social rituals. Standing adjacent,

Figure 1.3 The drum tower, *ganlan* houses and the rice-growing field in Yanzhai village, in Sanjiang, 2011.

6   *The Geography of the Dong*

and marking the village's ceremonial and administrative centre from afar, is the drum tower. These multiple eaves of pagoda-like structure traditionally contained a drum calling villagers to assemble, and in its base lies the village hearth. As ceremonial and symbolic focus, it was meant to be visible from every house. Apart from a few small shrines and the singing stage, there is only one other kind of ceremonial structure to compete seriously with the drum tower: the Wind and Rain bridge sited on the village periphery.[15]

Chinese architecture has been dominated by carpentry for at least two millennia, its major monuments consisting essentially of open fields of columns supporting an elaborate overhanging roof, perimeter and partition walls being secondary, added as cladding. This meant that traditional building in China, especially for monuments, is largely a question of making a roof, which involves preparing and assembling a complex framework of pre-cut and pre-jointed timbers.[16] The dimensions would be modular and carefully controlled, and the building would be preconceived by the carpenter in terms of applied layers in a strict logical sequence. In the Dong areas timber is plentiful and carpentry is, even more than in other parts of China, the dominant building discipline. Buildings are designed and constructed by master carpenters but assembled by communal effort. A local carpenter's mention of the traditional illustrated text Lu Ban jing suggests dependence on centralized Chinese culture,[17] though the work also has a strong regional flavour. A drum tower or a bridge is exceptional: something a Dong carpenter would only do once or twice in a lifetime.

Most of the time the Dong carpenters' work is the building of houses following the standard Ganlan type, that is with tree-trunk stilts and suspended floors. Gable ends of interlocking horizontal and vertical members follow standard Chinese principles, and the whole assembly depends on interlocking mortice and tenon joints secured with timber pins. Making a house frame requires first deciding on numbers of bays and bay sizes, then accurately prefabricating the elements with their jointed ends. A special ruler is prepared before the beginning of each construction to regulate not only the general dimensions but also the sizes of the joints. The whole process is accompanied by elaborate rituals, starting with the propitiation of spirits at the felling site and ending with the lighting of the first fire in the hearth.[18] That the culminating moment of the entire sequence should be the placing of the ridge beam, a special performance by the carpenter and ritual specialists followed by a feast, underlines the fact that the roof is the defining element of the house.

If a house is a roof and a drum tower or a bridge is a kind of big house, they have their striking counterpart with the roof and the structural style, which are mentioned as the special building types for the Dong that both represents community and stands as the pinnacle of the master-carpenter's art. The Dong tradition of marrying out by finding wives from other villages involved organized communal visits for courtship and betrothal including much singing and dancing, and these festivities also took place at the centre of each village next to the drum tower. Like a European belfry with its bells, its raised position both increased its acoustic radius and made it visible as the crown and centre-point for the village.[19] This special ceremonial purpose is marked by the most extreme form of multiple roof, amounting in the case of village drum towers. The oldest drum tower is Ping Zhai old drum tower in Ping village, which is humble with one floor main hall, supported by some columns and closed with half-opened solid walls and pillars (Figure 1.4). Although located in the neighbouring village of Ping village, the drum tower of Yan zhai village was originally built in 1909. However, in 2005, the village decided to build a new drum tower based on the original one, to be an icon of the village, where the new building is about 30 meters high, supported by four main columns and 12 additional columns, and crown with a huge roof of fifteen eaves (Figure 1.5). Similar to the Yan zhai drum tower, the Batuan drum tower is the tallest building in Batuan village, built with a roof of eleven eaves (Figure 1.6). The drum tower and the bridge are also sites of spiritual presences and ritual observances, the major difference being that the drum tower is central to the village rather than the bridge's peripheral and transitional.[20] The drum tower and the bridge constitute a complementary pair, and their relative positioning is crucial.

Figure 1.4 The old drum tower in Pingzhai village, Sanjiang, 2011.

8 *The Geography of the Dong*

Figure 1.5 The Yanzhai village drum tower, Sanjiang, 2018.

Figure 1.6 The Batuan drum tower and houses, Sanjiang, 2011.

The Wind and Rain bridges are the Dong's most prominent architectural monuments, usually built of timber and with multiple roofs. They are locally also called 'bridges of good fortune'.[21] Many have now become tourist attractions, but they were until a couple of decades ago entirely local both in their production and in their significance.[22] These bridges, and the drum towers with which they share a reciprocal role, were not the work of architects, but were designed and are maintained by local carpenters who also built the village houses, in an oral tradition extending back indefinitely, carried down from father to son or to apprentice. They were funded entirely by local people, who attributed to them an importance far beyond the practical business of crossing rivers, sometimes building them in places where there was no great pressure of traffic or where another bridge already existed close by. The covered wooden bridges, known across the world as Wind and Rain bridges, are one of the architectural landmarks of the Dong community that grace the area's many rivers and streams, which form perhaps the most frequent and widespread bridge type.[23] Particularly, situated in the special geographical circumstances, the Dong villages, which are typically one or two kilometres away from the other, are separated from one another by mountains and rivers meandering through, and as a result, journeys between villages become impossible without their Wind and Rain bridges.

In the Sanjiang county of northern Guangxi Province, there also exist over hundreds of notable Wind and Rain bridges. The most famous one is the Chengyang bridge built on the Linxi river in Ma'an village, which is known as one of the largest and most elegant bridges in the Dong areas (Figure 1.7).[24] This bridge is built in 1912, about seventy meters long and four meters wide, constructed with the Dong traditional skills. It is supported by five piers, built up with large stones outside, making sharp angles, each about 30°, facing the flowing water with gravel filling. The distance between two piers is about eighteen meters, and the timber foundation of the bridge is piled up in two layers of large connected timber logs, with nine logs in each layer, suspended off the piers by two meters. Another two layers of timber logs are piled up on the foundation between two piers, with the load of pavilions and passages resting on both ends of the upper logs. The beams and columns of the bridge are connected and tied with tenons and mortises, without nails. The waist eaves (*yao yan*腰檐), projecting outside the bridge's main body about one and a half meters, are added on the top of the timber foundation to protect the timber logs from damage caused by rains, creating a sense of elegance of the whole bridge. The long beams are resting on the projecting beams and are loaded by pavilions on both ends in an elaborately balanced structure, while the short beams rotate around the piers in the middle, helping the piers to support the long beams and reducing the suspended spans.

Apart from the famous Chengyang bridge, Batuan bridge is another striking bridge because it is combined by two separate passages for humans

10 *The Geography of the Dong*

Figure 1.7 The Chengyang bridge in Ma'an village, Sanjiang, 2011.

and animals (Figure 1.8). It is located on the Miao river of Batuan village, about forty kilometres away from Sanjiang county. It was built in 1910, and the total length is fifty meters. The dimensions of the two passages are different, and they are set at different heights, the animal one set with its floor about one and a half meters lower. The passage for pedestrians is four meters wide and two and a half meters high, while the animal passage is just one and about half meters wide and two meters high, again lower than the pedestrians' passage. The bridge is supported by three piers, and the three half-gable pavilion roofs on each pier are raised to the same height, about six and a half meters. The three pavilions follow the same style with three layers of eaves, and the east pavilion is combined with a pitched roof as the village entrance. The entrance for animals lies on the south, parallel with the longitudinal axis of the bridge, but the axis of the main entrance has an offset of 80 degrees to the main bridge's axis and is oriented instead to the north approached by a long staircase, which is possibly associated with the legend of Sa Spirit of the Dong, who is conceived to come from the north and thus to enter the village through the north village gate. The treatment of the animal passage is elaborated: because the level of the animal passage is lower than the main passage and its total height is reduced, it provides a good view and ventilation to the main passage and changeable elevation in façade. The elegant gate roof, combined with the main body of the bridge pavilion, exhibits the posture of a dragon's head with his mouth

Figure 1.8 The Batuan bridge in Batuan village, Sanjiang, 2011.

open. The bridge roof is celebrated by curving the motif of vane plants on the end of roof ridges, and the whole bridge gate postures a warm welcome to the guests to the rural area in remote mountains.

Distinguished from other Wind and Rain bridges by its long stone rod piers instead of solid piers, Jielong bridge is located in Mengdong village of Pingdeng county, built across the Mengdong river in 1919 (Figure 1.9). The whole bridge is built of timbers with five stone piers, each of which is constructed of two long stones about 380mm by 750mm in section and four meters long, standing slightly sloped to produce a stable foundation, and reducing the risk of being carried away by the torrential stream. Because of the slim stone rod piers, the three pavilion roofs on top couldn't be built too heavily. Thus the middle pavilion is covered by two layers of eaves, and raised five and a half meters high, with the hexagon pavilion roof topping the square eaves underneath; the other two quadrilateral pavilion roofs beside it have only one layer and rise four and a half meters high; while the remaining two pavilion roofs are larger than the others, about five and a half meters high with three layers of eaves and a hexagon pavilion roof crown on top of the two square eaves underneath. The total length of the bridge is about sixty-five meters and it is three and a half meters wide. The five pavilions on top are connected by the passage, giving a sense of lightness and transparency. Even in gaps between fields and villages, many Wind and Rain bridges have appeared. For instance, Helong bridge, located in the Yanzhai village of Sanjiang county (Figure 1.10), and Wanshou bridge

12 *The Geography of the Dong*

in the adjacent neighbouring Pingzhai village (Figure 1.11).[25] It spans a gap between the village houses and fields, where there is only water at times of flood. It consists of three large pavilions, all covered with three layers of eaves and connected by short passages. From all these facts, it is apparent that the genius of the covered bridges lay in a subtle combination of the rational with the aesthetic as well as highly structural skills; as Needham puts it, "no Chinese bridge lacked beauty and many were remarkably beautiful".[26] The elegance of the covered bridges constructed by the Dong shows that the builders explored the possibilities of the simple method up to the maximum strength of the strongest natural material available. Although the Dong's covered bridges, made with elaborate combinations of triangles in trusses, are found in some parts of the world, they never achieve the sense of elegance, lightness and simplicity when compared with Wind and Rain bridges. The construction of a bridge, a drum tower or a timber house is a rare event that the author was unable to witness, but the carpenter master Yang Shanren interviewed by the author confirmed that the rituals are essentially elaborate versions of the Dong architecture, again with the emphasis on completion of the roof.[27] Yang Shiping provided a model of a bridge structure with simplified versions of the joints to show in three dimensions its geometry and the logic of its assembly process (Figure 1.12).

Figure 1.9 The Mengdong bridge in Longsheng county, Longsheng, 2004.

The Geography of the Dong 13

Figure 1.10 The Helong bridge in Yanzhai village, Sanjiang, 2011.

Figure 1.11 The Wanshou bridge in Yanzhai village, Sanjiang, 2011.

14 *The Geography of the Dong*

Figure 1.12 The model of the pavilions of Chengyang bridge, 2005 (model made by Yang Shiping).

A glimpse of this model shows how much more appropriate to the process and way of thinking it is than any number of drawings.

Ganlan (干栏) Structure in Southern China

Evidently, the pile buildings (*Ganlan*) existed in southern China from the primitive times (Figure 1.13). As early as 2000 B.C., China's inhabitants perceived themselves as being in the middle of the world, surrounded by ethnic groups speaking other languages and practicing different cultures. Before the Qin dynasty (221-206 B.C.), the aboriginals in southern areas of China were named barbarians (*man* 蛮), whose names were related to insects and snakes. It is mentioned in *Han Fei Zhi*:

> In primitive time, the number of beasts was more than that of people, and people failed to conquer beasts, insects, and snakes. A sage constructed a hut on a tree with timber, which was similar to a bird's nest, to protect people from beasts.[28]

In the myths and legends, the great sages introduced the basic techniques for building dwellings, teaching their people how to build a pile-built structure so as to protect themselves from the wind and rain, escaping the cold and heat, and to keep beasts, insects and snakes away. Many minorities in southern China today claim that they descend from the *man* people, which

Figure 1.13 The model of bronze granary of *galan* structure, 1978 (from the archaeological collections in Guangxi museum).

includes the Dong, Zhuang, Buyi, Miao and Yao ethnic nationalities, and they enjoy the timber structures like birds' nests built on trees.

According to historical records, ancient *yue* and *liao* people generally lived in pile-built huts.[29] In the Qin (221-206 B.C.) and Han dynasties (206 B.C.-220 A.D.), the name of *man* of southern minorities was replaced by the name *yue*, and there were many groups among the *yue* settling in such a wide range of areas that they were often named Hundred Yue (*bai yue* 百越). In the early years of the first millennium A.D., the name *liao* began replacing *yue*. Almost the whole of southwestern China, including today's Sichuan, Guizhou, Hunan, Guangxi and Hubei provinces, was under the domain of the *liao*. Further strong evidence of the descent of the Dong from the *liao* is found by comparing *liao* language data with words from the present-day Dong language.[30] *Bei shi·Liao zhuan* is one of many descriptions of the *liao* people:

> The liao people, who are descendants of the southern *man*, live in the remote mountains and dense forests of the south, and use huge logs to build their homes. People live upstairs with pigs, buffaloes and goats

locked on ground level. This kind of home is called Ganlan...Liao people use bamboo to make lu sheng. At festival times everyone gets together and plays...Liao people make their own cloth, and like to raise dogs.[31]

Most customs of the *liao* people, such as making *lu sheng* (musical instruments) with bamboo, getting together and playing *lu sheng* at festival times, and weaving their clothes themselves, are still practiced in present-day Dong communities. The Dong people are believed to be descendants of the southern *Chu Jung*, who then developed into the tribes of Ti Shun in the Xia dynasty (2070-1600 B.C.), and formed one branch of hundreds of *yue* (*bai yue*) ethnic groups in the late Zhou dynasty (475-221 B.C.).[32] Accordingly, the Dong's history could be dated back to ancient China, almost two millennia before the Christian era, during which time the earliest historical civilization of China was created under the Three Dynasties, Xia (2205-1766 B.C.), Shang (1766-1122 B.C.) and Zhou (1122-256 B.C.).[33] In the record of Lu You, who is one of the famous Chinese ethnographers of the 1100s, he made a journey through Dong areas in 1170 A.D., in which areas occupied by present both by Geling and Gelan people nowadays. Geling and Gelan are thought to be transcriptions of the Kam autonym of that time: Klam. He particularly recorded their custom: young men wear hats with pheasant feathers in the festivals of slack-farming season; and one or two hundred villagers join hands, dancing and singing, to be guests in another village with *lu sheng* players leading the way.[34] Obviously, the Dong is one of the original ethnic groups which live with the *Ganlan* structure.

The earliest *Ganlan* structure has been found in the archaeological evidence from southern China, offering some proof of a Neolithic development of pile buildings in China. According to the excavated archaeological evidences of the Hemudu Culture, which dates back to the fifth and fourth millennia B.C. and originates from the south of the Yangzi river, timber pile-built houses were found (Figure 1.14). The site of this important culture was excavated between 1973 and 1977 at the village of Yuyao county in northern Zhejiang Province. As Chang's account claims:

> At the fourth layer from the top, the remains of a pile-dwelling village were found. Wooden posts and planks were found from a concentrated area, and in the same layer were unearthed huge quantities of animal and plant remains, potsherds, and food residues. At least three buildings were reconstructable in the excavated area. They were built on piles; their length was over twenty-three meters and the depth about seven meters. A frontal bay ran along the length of the houses, about 1.3 meters wide. The floors constructed of planks and probably paved with mats, were 0.8–1 meter above the ground. The garbage was dumped directly under the floors, probably into the water of a pond or river, along the shore of which the houses were built. The timbers are still

The Geography of the Dong 17

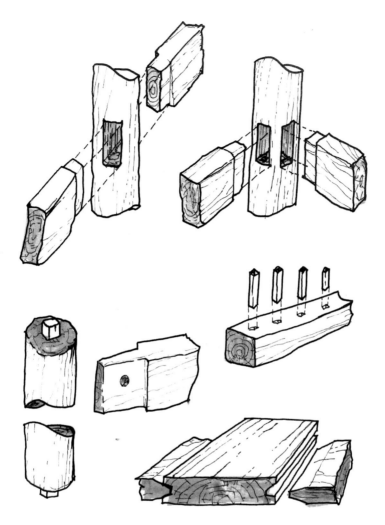

Figure 1.14 The remains of tenons and mortises in the building site (redrawn by Jie Zhou after Zhang 2000:8-9).

well preserved, showing rather advanced joinery for the construction of houses.[35]

It is by far the earliest timber pile-built structure that has been found and excavated in China. The style of buildings in south China share many features of this pile-built structure, which can still be seen today. The skills of wooden structures are elaborated in the areas around the Yangzi river and the influence of Homudu Culture is profound.[36] The unique cultural and geographical environment of ancient China had produced an architecture which not only gave them an identity in the rest of the world, but which also had been sustained through thousands of years, although the form and construction of buildings have only minor changes throughout such a long period.

According to the proofs found in about the fifth and fourth millennia B.C., the ancient people in the areas south of the Yangzi river were already cultivating rice in the fertile plains.[37] From the garbage debris throughout the site of Yuyao county, also in Chang's report, vast amounts of plant and animal remains were collected and identified, such as straw, ears and husks, such as domesticated rice. A number of trees with subtropical broad-leaf of deciduous forest could be identified, indicating a warmer and moister climate. The animal species identified from the bones were consistent with such environmental characteristics, including monkeys, sheep, and deer. Among the animal bones are also those of the dogs, pigs and water buffalos, which were possibly domesticated. To agricultural societies granaries were very important, and possibly the pile-built structures were initially developed for the purpose of raising livestock and storing rice.[38]

In her account of the development of gable-roofed pile structures from pit dwellings in Japan, Waterson considers that it might be associated with the late-Neolithic and early-Metal Age that Yayoi people linked with an archaeological site in Southwest Honshu, where remains of this culture were first excavated. The Yayoi people are thought by Japanese scholars to have been immigrants who reached Japan perhaps via Taiwan from a homeland somewhere in southern China, bringing with them knowledge of rice cultivation. The development of pile-building may have been intended originally for the construction of granaries, which would thus have provided improved storage conditions for grains, where they were always being attacked by rats and mould. While analysing an 'Austronesian' style of pile-built architecture in Southeast Asia, Waterson quotes Domenig and also stresses the potential importance of southern China as a source of cultural influence in both Japan and South-East Asia, with much of her evidence drawn from the work of Japanese archaeologists on the Neolithic and early Bronze Ages in Japan.[39] According to Domenig, the origins of 'Chinese' (Han) culture are to be sought in the valley of the Yellow river in northern China. However, as Domenig points out, the Neolithic cultures of southern China, concentrated around the Yangzi river basin, are better regarded as the contribution to the influence on the world of Southeast Asian, and the peoples of this region likewise began to be strongly influenced by northern Chinese culture in the Han period (206 B.C.-220). Domenig presumes that pile-building might have developed in southern China during the Neolithic period. He notes that this area is also possibly a key region in the development of rice cultivation, and that it had an important influence not only on the subsequent Bronze Age Culture of Dongson in North Vietnam, but also on the developments in Japan.[40]

It is interesting that, moving into the early Bronze Age, clear representational images of pile-built structures, accompany people in rituals, appear on the bronze drums.[41] The engraved images with pile structures and saddle roofs on bronze drums of the Dong Son Culture are defined as an 'Indonesian-type' house by archaeologists, and according to Peter S. Bellwood, the heartland of bronze drum culture was found in North Vietnam.[42] However, antecedents' sites with bronze drums have recently been excavated by Chinese archaeologists, and the number of bronze drums altogether is 1386 found in Yunnan Province of Southern China by 1980, many more than the numbers found in Vietnam. This suggests a central role for the region of Yunnan, which is the original site of Dian Culture (滇文化), in the development of bronze metallurgy. Most of these bronze drums are large with elaborately carved images on their surfaces, such as pile-built houses, musicians and dancing figures with feathers on their heads, called *yuren* (feather man 羽人). According to Ting Yu Jiang, through trade contacts and movements of people the bronze drum culture originated in the areas of western Dian of Yunnan Province, extended to Vietnam following the Red river about 300 B.C. while the skills were integrated with the bronze-making skills of Vietnam, they resulted in the famous Donson bronze drums.[43] A striking example is Kaihua Drum from southern Yunnan, which shows people with feathers on their hats performing rituals with dancing, and between them, there are two pile-built structures with peacocks on top (Figure 1.15).[44] These houses have the ground floors occupied by animals—a pig, two cocks and a dog—the main floor by humans, and a partitioned attic containing what appear to be valuables (a chest and a drum).

Although the pile-built houses shown in these engraved images are simplified with only one storey, the most interesting feature is that the buildings have more functions than shelters for people as residence and as granary for store of food and livestock, where they are related to daily life rituals. In traditional Chinese cosmology, the human body is a combination not only of its flesh but also of a soul, which is believed to dominate a person's thought and activity. In this view, when a human is dead, it means his flesh is dead but its soul continues to exist in the world. It is believed not only to attach to the corpse, but also involves the survivors' lives in the world with its supernatural power. So the 'corpse' must be worshipped, usually appearing as the representation of the soul to accept the offerings and prayers from the survivors, and in return, if the soul is entertained by its descendants, it would bless and protect them from evils; but if it is unkindly treated, the family could invite trouble from the disturbing spirit. The belief in the supernatural power of souls thus makes the burial rituals very complicated. A number of bronze models were found in the second–first century B.C., centring on Shizhai Mountain in Yunnan, which were often converted by the rulers to make lidded chests for the

20 *The Geography of the Dong*

Figure 1.15 The image on the top of the Kaihua drum (from Jiang 1999: 185).

storage of coins with the engraved images of scenes of people and houses (Figure 1.16).[45] In a bronze container with a ratified ritual scene on the top, the fragments of engraved pictures on the top of the lid are decorated with an elaborate three-dimensional bronze model of a pile-built house structure, surrounded by people and drums on a raised open platform with a saddle-roofed enclosed upper storey.[46] In the Qin dynasty (221-206 B.C.), the ritual with the scene shown clearly in the figure curved on the top of the containers is called *shili* (worship corpse ritual 尸礼). In the ritual, a man, named *shi* (corpse), appears as an ancestor behind a mirror frame, he accepts the offerings on behalf of all ancestor spirits. At the end of the ceremony, after the *shi* (corpse) has been satisfied and worshipped, the offerings would be shared by the participants. It symbolizes that the ancestor spirit has accepted the offerings and the prayers from the descendant and would bless the people with good fortune and wealth.[47] So what do these

The Geography of the Dong 21

Figure 1.16 The image of *ganlan* structure and people performed in the ritual on the top of the container of Shizai mountain (from Herbert Plutschow, in Anthropoetics XIV, no. 1 Summer 2008).

archaeological collections mean to the Dong architecture and building techniques, and how are they relevant?

Conclusion

Although attempts have been made to explain the symbolism of the decorative features, the conventional architectural historian's tools of stylistic and technical analysis scarcely begin to penetrate this question. The Dong's bridges and drum towers are only mentioned in passing in western general studies on Chinese architecture, and there are only some general books in

Chinese about techniques of vernacular construction.[48] A work by Li et al., about local vernacular architecture of the northern Guangxi Province, contains many useful measured plans and other drawings, but without getting to grips with the social meaning of the Dong's architecture.[49] Better in this respect is a book of essays specifically edited by Zhang Zhezhong, particularly the contributions by Wu Hao on stories about the bridges and drum towers, and by Li Xi on their fengshui aspects.[50] This source confirmed the need to go beyond architectural studies to engage more deeply with the people and their culture, their beliefs and their habits: their anthropology.

For political reasons, western anthropologists were for a long time denied access to China, and the development of the discipline by the Chinese was delayed, so coverage of the continent has remained patchy. Relatively little published fieldwork has come directly out of the area concerned, but the linguist D. Norman Geary and his local group of Chinese experts conducted much valuable research in the 1990s which is rich in information about the society, if surprisingly thin about the Dong's architecture.[51] Among further Chinese sources of help are the extensive local reports about politics, economics, culture and customs officially kept by each province, part of a reporting and archival system that persisted unbroken from imperial times until the mid-twentieth century, and which has been reinstated since.[52] It is particularly in these records that are found the songs of the Dong, the substantial vehicles of myth and legend which traditionally play a central role in their ritual occasions.[53]

The story that follows has been compiled drawing on and translating such sources in combination with fieldwork by the author, who visited the region and conducted interviews with local people including building carpenters.[54] Inevitably it is also necessary to draw on general texts about Chinese culture, such as the fifteenth-century carpenter's manual *Lu Ban jing*,[55] Ernst Boerschmann's *Chinesischer Architektur* of 1925 based on his Chinese tour from 1906 to 1909[56] and Joseph Needham's immense and still unrivalled *Science and Civilization in China*.[57] It has been impossible to draw a distinct borderline between local Dong beliefs and values and the more general Chinese cultural background, particularly regarding the pervasive Daoism.[58] The fact that the Dong's language has no script until half a century ago, on one side, has also meant a lack of means to record the precise chronology of events, however on the other side, helped to preserve their oral narratives and customs intact, particularly their famous cycles of songs, and a tendency to fall back on mythical time.[59] It was beyond the scope of this book to engage the chronological dimension either in terms of charting historical development or in terms of the modernization now sweeping the region. The meanings of the Dong's architecture are obviously changing, but the book's concern has been with discovering what they meant traditionally, within living memory but before the substantial intrusion of the modern world, i.e, about forty years ago.[60]

Notes

1 Cf. Rossi, Gail and Lau, Paul 1991. *A Hidden Civilization: The Dong People of China*. Singapore: Hagley & Hoyle; Xian, Guangwei 1995. *Dongzu Tonglan* 侗族通览 (A General Survey of the Dong Nationality). Nanning: Guangxi Minzhu Press; and Geary, D. Norman, *et al.* 2003. *The Kam People of China: Turning Nineteen*. London: RoutledgeCurzon.
2 The data is from Census Office of the State Council (1991). *Zhongguo Disici Renkou Pucha De Zhuyao Shuju* 中国第四次人口普查的主要数据 (Data from the Fourth Population Census in China). Beijing: Zhongguo Tongji Press. About 1,400,344 inhabit Guizhou, 757,130 in Hunan, 295,673 in Guangxi, and Hubei with 54,798.
3 See Xian, Guangwei 1995. *Dongzu Tonglan* 侗族通览 (A General Survey of the Dong Nationality). Nanning: Guangxi Minzu Press. Most of them settling on the counties named Congjiang, Rongjiang, Liping, Jinpin, Tianzhu, Jianhe, Sanshui, Zhenyuan, Chengong, Yupin, Shixian, Jiangkou, Wanshan, Tongren, Shongtao, Lipo, Dushan and Dujun of Guizhou Province; Xinhuang, Zhijiang, Huitong, Jianzhou, Tongdao, Chenbu, Shuining, Dongkou and Qianyang of Hunan Province; and Sanjiang, Longsheng, Rong-an, Rongshui, Luocheng, and Donglan of the North of Guangxi Province.
4 Geary, D. Norman, *et al.* 2003. *The Kam people of China: Turning Nineteen*. London: RoutledgeCurzon, p. 43.
5 Xian, Guangwei 1995. *Dongzu Tonglan* 侗族通览 (A General Survey of the Dong Nationality). Nanning: Guangxi Minzu Press, pp. 9–12.
6 *Ibid.* pp. 12–16.
7 Xian, Guangwei 1995. *Dongzu Tonglan* 侗族通览 (A General Survey of the Dong Nationality). Nanning: Guangxi Minzu Press, p. 1.
8 Geary, D. Norman, *et al.* 2003. *The Kam people of China: Turning Nineteen*. London: RoutledgeCurzon, p. 31.
9 Zhang, Min (ed.) 1985. *Dongzu Jianshi* 侗族简史 (A Concise History of the Dong Nationality). Guiyang: Guizhou Minzu Press, pp. 9–10; Xian, Guangwei 1995. *Dongzu Tonglan* 侗族通览 (A General Survey of the Dong Nationality). Nanning: Guangxi Minzu Press, p. 32; and Geary, D. Norman, *et al.* 2003. *The Kam people of China: Turning Nineteen*. London: RoutledgeCurzon, p. 3.
10 See Xian 1995: 32; and Geary, D. Norman, *et al.* 2003: 3.
11 *Ibid.*
12 See Xian 1995: 33–4.
13 See Compilation Group of Annals of the Nationalities in Sanjiang county 2002 (first published 1946). *Sanjiangxian Minzuzhi* 三江县民族志 (Annals of the Nationalities in Sanjiang county). Nanning: Guangxi Minzhu Press, pp. 60–1; and Geary, D. Norman, *et al.* 2003. *The Kam people of China: Turning Nineteen*. London: RoutledgeCurzon, pp. 62–76.
14 Cf. Compilation Group of Local Gazette of Guangxi Province 1992. *Guangxi Tongzhi Minsuzhi*, 广西通志: 民俗志 (General Gazette of Guangxi Province: Custom Section). Nanning: Guangxi Renmin Press; and Geary, D. Norman, *et al.* 2003. *The Kam People of China: Turning Nineteen*. Curzon, London: Routledge, pp. 209–13.
15 General information found in Geary, Norman, *et al.* 2003. *The Kam People of China*. London: Routledge.
16 See Ssu-cheng, Liang 1984. *A Pictorial History of Chinese Architecture*. Cambridge, MA: The MIT Press. (The trivial-sounding title is deceptive but correctly reflects the dominance of some crucial drawings. Liang Ssu-cheng [or Sicheng] was the leading pioneer in Chinese architectural history in the 1930s,

decoding ancient texts and measuring many buildings. His story is told in Wilma Fairbank, Liang and Lin 1994. *Partners in Exploring China's Architectural Past.* Philadelphia: University of Pennsylvania Press).
17 Interview with Yang Shanren by Xuemei Li on 30th July, 2002, in Sanjiang County.
18 The whole sequence of house rituals is recorded in Yu, Dazhong, Dongzu Minju 2004. 侗族民居 [The Dwellings of the Dong]. Guiyang: Huaxia Wenhua Yishu Press, pp. 108–38.
19 As discussed in R. Murray Schafer's essay on acoustic space in, Seamen, David and Mugerauer, Robert (eds) 1989. *Dwelling, Place and Environment: Towards a Phenomenology of Person and World.* New York: Columbia University Press.
20 The drum tower, its functions and its symbolism are described in Xing Ruan 2006. *Allegorical Architecture: Living Myth and Architectonics in Southern China.* Honolulu: University of Hawaii Press, 2006.
21 The original name of the Wind and Rain bridge in the Dong dialect is 'Jiu', which means fortune, as it represents fortune to the village: oral information from Wu Hao gathered by Xuemei Li, 01/02/05.
22 Dating is often difficult, as bridges are frequently repaired or rebuilt and when a date is known it is often late nineteenth or early twentieth century, but Longjin Bridge in Zhijiang County is said to date from 1591.
23 Cf. Li, Changjie (ed.) 1990. *Guibei Minjian Jianzhu* 桂北民间建筑 (Vernacular Architecture in Northern Guangxi). Beijing: Zhongguo Jianzhu Press; Rossi, Gail and Lau, Paul 1991. *A Hidden Civilization: The Dong People of China.* Singapore: Hagley & Hoyle; and Geary, D. Norman, *et al.* 2003.
24 See record in Compilation Group of Survey of the Sanjina Dong Autonomous County 1984. *Sanjiang Dongzu Zizhixian Gaikuang* 三江侗族自治县概况 (Survey of the Sanjinag Dong Autonomous County). Nanning: Guangxi Minzu Press; and Compilation Group of Annals of the Nationalities in Sanjiang County 2002 (first published 1946). *Sanjiangxian Minzuzhi* 三江县民族志 (Annals of the Nationalities in Sanjiang County). Nanning: Guangxi Minzhu Press.
25 From my fieldwork in 2004, Sanjiang County.
26 Needham, Joseph 1971. 'Civil Engineering and Nautics', in *Science and Civilization in China*, Vol.4: Physics and Physical Technology, Part 3. London: Cambridge University Press, p. 145.
27 Interview with Yang Shanren by Xuemei Li 12th August, 2004, in Sanjiang County.
28 Quoted from Zhang, Yuhuan *et al.* 1985. *Zhongguo Gudai Jiangzhu Jishushi* 中国古代建筑技术史 (The History of Chinese Traditional Architecture and Technique). Beijing: Ke Xue Chuban Press, p. 7. The author's translation. *Han Fei Zi* (Book of *Han Fei*) is a work of political philosophy from the early third century B.C.
29 Cf. Compilation Group of Annals of the Nationalities in Sanjiang County 1989 (first published 1946). *Sanjiangxian Minzuzhi* 三江县民族志 (Annals of the Nationalities in Sanjiang County). Nanning: Guangxi Minzhu Press, pp. 48–9; and Xian, Guangwei 1995. *Dongzu Tonglan* 侗族通览 (A General Survey of the Dong Nationality), Nanning: Guangxi Minzhu Press, p. 31.
30 Xian 1995: 29–32.
31 Quote from Geary, D. Norman, *et al.* 2003. *The Kam people of China: Turning Nineteen.* London: RoutledgeCurzon, p. 2.
32 The *baiyue* (hundred *yue* 百越) was divided into *dongou* 东瓯, *minyue* 闽越, *nanyue* 南越, *xi-ou* 西瓯, and *louyue* 骆越. See Xian, Guangwei 1995. *Dongzu Tonglan* 侗族通览 (A General Survey of the Dong Nationality). Nanning: Guangxi Minzu Press, p. 29.
33 The Three Sovereigns are Fu His (the First Man), Sui Jen (or Chu Jung, the inventor of fire) and Shen Nung (the inventor of plant husbandry); and the Five

Emperors are Huang Ti (the celebrated Yellow Emperor, the initiator of civilization), Chuan Hsu (the emperor in whose hands heaven was separated from earth), Ti Ku, Ti Yao, and Ti Shun. See Chang, K. C. (Kwang-chih) 1983. *Art, Myth, and Ritual: The Path to Political Authority in Ancient China.* Cambridge, MA: Harvard University Press, pp. 1–2. In *Shan Hai Ching,* the four God's agents of four directions, which are known as Kou Mang of eastern China, Ju Shou of western, Chu Jung of southern and Yu Chiang of northern, bring messages back and forth between heaven and earth by the help of dragons and snakes. See Wang, Hongqi 2003. *Jingdian Tu du Sanhai Jing* 经典图读三海经 (The Visual Pictures of *Sanhai Jing*). Shanghai: Shanghai Chishu Press, pp. 136–73.

34 Cf. Zhang, Min 1983. *Qiantan Dongzu Yu Geling He Ling* ('A Brief Discussion of the Relations between the Dong and the Geling and Ling Nationalities'), in *Guizhou Minzu Yanjiu* (Journal of Guizhou Nationality Research), vol. 1, pp. 86–93; and Geary, D. Norman, *et al.* 2003. *The Kam People of China: Turning Nineteen.* London: Routledge Curzon, p. 2.
35 Chang (Kwang-chih) 1983: 209–11.
36 Pan, Guxi (ed.) 2001. *Zhongguo Jianzhushi* 中国建筑史 (Chinese Architectural History). Beijing: Zhongguo Jianzhu Gongye Press, p. 15.
37 Chang (Kwang-chih) 1983: 208–12.
38 Waterson, Roxana 1990. *The Living House: An Anthropology of Architecture in South-East Asia.* Singapore: Oxford University Press, pp. 16–17.
39 Waterson, Roxana 1990. *The Living House: An Anthropology of Architecture in South-East Asia.* Singapore: Oxford University Press, p. 15.
40 Quoted from Waterson 1990: 15.
41 Jiang, Tingyu 1999. *Gudai Tonggu Tonglun* 古代铜鼓通论 (Research of Ancient Bronze Drums). Beijing: Zhijincheng Press, pp. 33–6.
42 Bellwood, Peter S. 1978. *Man's Conquest of the Pacific: The Prehistory of South-East Asia and Oceania.* Auckland: Collins, p. 193.
43 Jiang 1999: 35–8.
44 *Ibid.* pp. 184–5.
45 Cf. Bellwood, Peter S. 1985. *Prehistory of the Indo-Malaysian Archipelago.* Sydney (N.S.W.); Orlando, Fla.: Academic Press, p. 189; Waterson, Roxana 1990. *The Living House: An Anthropology of Architecture in South-East Asia.* Singapore: Oxford University Press, p. 18; and Jiang, Tingyu 1999. *Gudai Tonggu Tonglun* 古代铜鼓通论 (Research of Ancient Bronze Drums). Beijing: Zhijincheng Press, p. 185.
46 Wu 1999: 148–52.
47 Wu, Zhao 1999. *Dianguo De Yinyue Yu Jisu* 滇国的音乐与祭俗 (Retracing the Lost Footprints of Music). Taiwan: Dongfang Press, pp.148–52.
48 Zhang, Yuhuan, *et al.* (eds.) 2000. *Zhongguo Gudai Jianzhu Jishushi* 中国古代建筑史 [The Techniques of Chinese Traditional Architecture]. Beijing: Kexue Press. (The technical development of Chinese traditional architecture, including earth structures, timber structures, brick and stone structures, decoration, conservation, town planning and the rganization of landscape. The chapter on stone structures includes a section on stone bridges from 475 BC to1840 AD discussing techniques in piers and spans).
49 Li, Changjie (ed.) 1990. *Guibei Minjian Jianzhu* [Vernacular Architecture in Northern Guangxi]. Beijing, Zhongguo Jianzhu Press, 1990.
50 Zhang Zhezhong (ed.) 2001. *Dongzu Fengyuqiao* [The wind and rain bridges of the Dong], Guiyang: Huaxia Wenhua Yishu Press.
51 Geary *et al.*, The Kam People of China, op. cit. Kam is an alternative designation to Dong. The presence of the bridges is duly noted along with some remarks about the symbolism of their decoration, but they are not treated in proportion to the social and economic effort obviously invested in them. Geary's primary specialization was linguistics.

26 *The Geography of the Dong*

52 Minzuzhi, Sanjiangxian 2002. 三江县民族志 [Annals of Sanjiang County]. Nanning: Guangxi Minzu Press: copy of the version of 1945, which was compiled by Jiang, Yusheng, et al. (eds.) (Ten volumes: vol. 1 concerns the topography of Sanjiang County; vol. 2 the nationalities, the language and the customs of the society; vol. 3 concerns the polity, including institutes and schools; vol. 4 concerns the economy; vol. 5 education; vol. 6 local organizations; vol. 7 records of important events; vol. 8 famous local people; vol. 9 is an appendix and vol. 10 contains references.) See also Minsuzhi, Guangxi Tongzhi 1992. *General Annals of Guangxi Province: Custom Section*. Nanning: Guangxi Renmin Press. (The same kind of work for Guangxi Province, was compiled by Zhang, Youjuan, et al., in 1992, with 7 chapters: Chapter 1 concerns working customs; Chapter 2 domestic customs; Chapter 3 social customs; Chapter 4 rituals; Chapter 5 festivals; Chapter 6 religion; and Chapter 7 research into customs).

53 Their nine-tone language had no written form until the 1950s, but all kinds of events and festivities were accompanied by group singing, often in antiphonal style between a host and a guest village and alternating between men and women. The content and form of the songs was highly conventionalized, with rhythm and music aiding their memorability. They provided both a ritual structure and a major vehicle for the cultural transmission of mythology. See Geary, *et al.*: 2003, op. cit., Chapter 9, and also Wu Hao, Sanjiang gezhu minge [Sanjiang County Nationalities Songs], Zhong guo geyao jicheng guangxi fenjuan, Sanjiang dongzhu zhizixian zhiliaoji (3) (Sanjiang: Sanjiang County santao jicheng bangongshi press, 1989), pp. 12–13.

54 Fieldwork was conducted in the Dong areas north of Guangxi province by Xuemei Li. In the spring of 2001, for the first time, she carried out a short-term survey of Wind and Rain bridges in Sanjiang county, and she returned to Ma'an village of Sanjiang County to measure the Chengyang bridge in the summer of 2002. Then in the summer of 2004 she visited the Dong areas in northern Guangxi again for the follow-up field survey.

55 Ruitenbeek, Klaas 1996. *Carpentry and Building in Late Imperial China: A Study of the Fifteenth-century Carpenter's Manual*, Lu Ban jing, 2nd rev. ed. New York: E.J. Brill.

56 Boerschmann, Ernst 1925. *Chinesischer Architektur*, vol. 2. Berlin: Wasmuth. (Boerschmann was sent to China by the German government for three years in 1906 to study Chinese culture and architecture, and reported on it for the rest of his life. He did not visit the Dong area or comment particularly on bridges, but his books are valuable for photographs and drawings of Chinese monuments, and his texts stress the influence of Daoism).

57 Needham, Joseph 1956. *Science and Civilisation in China, Volume 2, History of Scientific Thought*. Cambridge: Cambridge University Press.

58 The Dong peoples' origins are complex and uncertain, involving probable migrations both from the east and the south-west: see Geary *et al.*: 2003, op. cit.

59 Although regional Chinese bureaucracy could make written records in Mandarin, a language also opens to Daoist priests and intellectuals, and documents and inscriptions could use Mandarin characters, all without recording the local dialect.

60 This brings the danger of suggesting a kind of golden age set vaguely in the past, but such is not the book's intention. My interest lies in how this architecture worked, and it provides a valuable example precisely because of the late reliance on oral discourse.

2 The Cosmology of Separation and Reunion of the Dong

Bridges are taken for granted in the modern world as utilitarian structures and if noticed at all are remarked upon mainly for the elegance of their engineering design, but a mere couple of centuries ago many places in Europe still had chapels in which prayers for a safe crossing could be said. In the Dong areas of south-west China, which remained remote until around two decades ago, the bridges are the principal monuments, elaborately roofed and decorated with shrines to various gods, built with pride and at great local cost. The reasons that I am interested in them begin with the question of why so much trouble has been taken over these bridges, and led on to how they are read by their users and builders, and what they are considered to mean. The consequent excursions into anthropological theory and traditional Chinese ideologies, which reveal a rich and complex network of causes, are fascinating in their multiplicity and interaction. The enquiry is pushed far beyond the bounds of traditional art history, engaging fundamental questions about the significance of architecture as a communicative and ritual medium in traditional oral-based cultures. At a more general level, it also prompts a thought-provoking exploration of the similarities and differences between bridges metaphorical and bridges physical.

Ma'an village of Sanjiang county, located in the northwest of Guangxi province, is a place I have known for over twenty years. In the spring of 2001, for the first time, I carried out a short-term survey of Wind and Rain bridges in Sanjiang county, which enabled me to begin my fieldwork of the Dongs' bridges. Since then, I have maintained a correspondence with the master carpenters and friends. I returned to Sanjiang county to conduct my fieldwork around every three years. I interviewed many Dong experts and master carpenters, my informants including Professor Wu Hao of the College of Nationalities in Liuzhou, and Wu Shihua, who was the director of Sanjiang county museum. In Ma'an village, I interviewed the master craftsman Yang Shanren and his carpentry sons, and a local Fengshui priest Chen Yongqing. Meanwhile, we surveyed and measured the Mapang drum tower and the Yang family house in Bajiang village, and the Mengdong bridge, drum towers and the Meng family house in Longsheng county. I also continued my fieldwork in 2011, 2016 and 2018 respectively, to visit the villages and my informants.

DOI: 10.4324/9781003228837-2

28 *The Cosmology of Separation and Reunion of the Dong*

Each Dong village owns its Wind and Rain bridges. According to the record of Xian, there are over three-hundred bridges built on the rivers or between the fields in Sanjiang and Longsheng counties of Guangxi province, Tongdao county of Hunan province and Congjiang and Liping counties of Guizhou province.[1] In Dudong, Bajiang and Linxi townships of Sanjiang county in particular, over one hundred Wind and Rain bridges have been found. Two notable bridges, the Chengyang bridge and Yanzhai bridge, are built up between Ma'an village with about forty families, its neighbour Yanzhai village with less than seventy households (Figure 2.1). And in Zhongqiao village of Bajiang township with not more than a hundred families, there are four Wind and Rain bridges standing around the villages, located not more than one mile away from the villages (Figure 2.2). Some of the village houses are even adjacent to the bridges. If a gap needs to be filled by a bridge, a simple timber beam bridge or a stone beam bridge can make it. Obviously, the bridges are funded entirely by local people, who attribute to the villagers an importance far beyond the practical business of crossing rivers, sometimes building them in places where there was no great pressure of traffic or where another bridge already existed close by. Why are so many Wind and Rain bridges built in these small Dong villages, and so elaborately?

I still remember the scene that we first met master Yang Shanren and since then, I visited him and his family studio during my fieldworks in Sanjiang to learn to make the Dong models with him (Figure 2.3).[2] It was a sunny afternoon in the summer of 2002, we were around a ten-people group to visit the Chengyang bridge in the Ma'an village. While we were doing a messy job of

Figure 2.1 A Wind and Rain bridge built on the entrance of Ma'an Village, less than two miles from the Chengyang bridge, Sanjiang, 2011.

The Cosmology of Separation and Reunion of the Dong 29

Figure 2.2 The Bajiang bridge in Bajiang village, Sanjiang, 2011.

Figure 2.3 The Dong Master Yang Shanren and myself discussing the Dong architectural models during my fieldwork in his family studio, Sanjiang, 2018 (photo: Weiye Li).

measuring and drawing the bridge, a lean old man, about 70 years old, with a wrinkled face, sitting on the bridge's bench, spatting out his tobacco and watching us quietly. When we sat down for a break, he told us the story of building the bridge. Yang Shanren's father, named Yang Tangfu, was disturbed as he had no offspring. He had been married to his wife for over twenty years and was fifty years old, but still had no child. Yang Tangfu had been wishing for a long time to donate his wealth to charity. While the village heads initiated the idea of building the Chengyang bridge, he decided to take out his money and sponsor the bridge-building work. It took the village twelve years to build up the bridge. While they were building the bridge, his wife became pregnant and just on the day that they finished their work, his first son was born. It is Yang Shanren, who became a master builder of Wind and Rain bridges and drum towers after he grew up. Unfortunately, the Chengyang bridge was first damaged by flood in 1937, and the second-generation carpenter Yang Shanren was mainly responsible for the repair. In 1939, when the repairs to the bridge were completed, his son was born—the third-generation carpenter, Yang Shiping.[3] In Yang's view, the fate of his family is closely connected with the Chengyang bridge, and he told me: "The bridge spirits bring good fortune and bless our family".

The Traditional Cosmology of the Dong People

In the traditional cosmology of many societies, people come from the world of chaos, living in this world, and their souls should return to the dead world after death.[4] In the Dong's view, the cosmos is thought to be tripartite, consisting of the *yang* world (the living world), the *yin* world (the dead world) parallel to the living world and the other world. The question of where their lives are coming from and finally going to is related with the three worlds. The *yin* world and the other world are described as the destinations for souls after death, respectively for the moral souls going to the *yin* world to wait for reincarnation and that of evil souls going to the other underworld never being reborn again.[5] As the Dong Love Song says:

> If we cannot marry in this world, it doesn't matter,
> We would be reborn as two birds sharing the same mountain and forest.
> If we cannot marry in this world, we wouldn't sigh and be so unhappy,
> We would be reborn in good families and work in the same tea garden in the next life.
> If we cannot marry in this world, it doesn't matter,
> We would be reborn as a cock crying every day in your home.
> ......
> If we cannot marry in this world, we wouldn't be so anxious,

The Cosmology of Separation and Reunion of the Dong 31

I would wait for you at the Hun River[6] and cross it after dying.
If we cannot marry in this world, it doesn't matter,
We would live together in the Gaosheng Ya'an village[7] after dying.
Were we married in the living world, we would be happy couples,
How could I meet my lover after I die and become a spirit?
Yan Wang (the king of the dead world) administers the souls of men and women,
Were we registered by him, we would meet again in the *yin* world.[8]

The Dong believe that the dead world (*yin* world) coexists with the living world (*yang* world), the two being separated only by a river.[9] Among these narratives and legends of the Dong, what lies beyond this world is elaborately constructed. In the supernatural world were mountains, rivers, plants and animals, similar to those of the living world. Work of ploughing field and raising livestock are engaged, such as pigs, dogs and other domestic animals. Even singing and dancing festivals are performed just like the communal ceremonies of the living world, although somehow running in different space and time.[10] Similar ideology is found in the ideas of the Daur Mongols of North Asia, where the place named Irmu Khan is the destination for souls after death, and also a source for the reincarnation of souls.[11] The Dong narrative implies some places outside the living world but exactly similar to it. The young couple addresses their uncertain love in the dead world, at a place named Gaosheng Ya'an (高胜牙安村) that is separated by the Hun River from the living world. The lovers wish that they could meet there or be reborn in the *yang* world to sustain their love. But there still exists the third underworld—hell; and if they unfortunately go to hell, they possibly couldn't be reborn and would turn out in some other way. So it is possible that the Dong belief in 'the dead world' not only refers to the hell of the underworld, but also to a hidden nice place, which is separated but exists parallel to the living world.

Although the place associated with the origins and endings of lives is unseen, it is clearly defined as Gaosheng Ya'an village by the Dong. Many Dong legends tell the story that their *yin* world (dead world 阴间) is located in Gaosheng Ya'an village (高胜牙安村).[12] Occupying the valley land surrounded by rivers, in the Dong's language, the remote villages near the source of the river is named 'Gaosheng', and 'Ya'an' means 'wild geese'. The Dong believe that their *yin* world for dead spirits would be a beautiful place in the headstream of a remote river, which is fulfilled with resting wild geese, singing birds, and blooming flowers, and the souls in Gaosheng Ya'an village would live a similar life to that in the *yang* world (the living world 阳间). In the myth, there is a Hualin garden in the *yin* world with flourishing jungles and seasonal blooms. The Hualin temple is set up in the middle of Hualin garden with many spirits living in. The deities called

'Nantang Parents' or 'Hualin God' occupy the south hall of the Hualin temple. The souls of dead people would obtain the permission of the Nantang Parents to wait for reincarnation. The Dong people believe that the souls exist everywhere of trees, bushes, and flowers, and are taken care by the Hualin God. The Hun River meanders through Hualin garden with half clear and half turbid, separating the *yin* world from the *yang* world. The souls to be reborn are delivered by the Hualin God in the forms of flowers to the villages, with a boat traveling along the Hunshui River. It is said that if many girls are born at one time, most of the souls sent by the Hualin spirit in the boat are girls and only with boys rowing for them; and if the opposite, people believe that the boat is especially full of boys and the girls are present only for cooking. Thus, within three days of the birth of a child, the parents would invite the priest to practice the ritual named '*yue nantang*' to appreciate Nantang Parents and the Hualin God.[13]

The traditional cosmology of the Dong has been sophisticated to explain the mystery of life in their myths and legends. The invisible *yin* world would also be a romantic place similar to the *yang* world. A Dong legend recounts how the two young persons, named Jinbi and Xiang*yin,* go to the heaven and search the songs for their ceremonies. When they arrive in the heaven, they saw the young men and fairies are singing and dancing with *lu sheng* music, performing the ceremony of Stepping onto the Singing Stage. Jinbi and Xiang*yin* are so excited, they ask the singers and dancers to teach them, but they are advised to see the headman in the drum tower. After negotiating with the old man, Jinbi and Xiang*yin* are required to contribute three hundred *liangs* of gold (1 *liang*=50 g) for repairing the drum tower before teaching them. After they pay the tuition fee, the old man in the heaven brings them a bundle of songbooks, where Jinbi and Xiangyin carry with a pole on their shoulders down to the *yang* world. Jinbi would be the original ancestor of the Dong people, and Xiang*yin* the Miao people,[14] and that is why the Dong and Miao people would perform 'Stepping and Singing on the Stage' in their festivals.[15]

The Dong's cosmology of the *yin* and *yang* world is also recorded in their *pipa* songs.[16] The *Yin/Yang* Song tells the miserable story of a loving young couple named Longyin and Tuanmei.[17] Longyin gets married with a girl named Tuanmei, and they produce a son and a daughter. Unfortunately, not long after their marriage, Tuanmei passes away and goes to Gaosheng Ya'an, leaving Longyin and the two little kids alone. In sadness, Longyin asks the children's grandmother to look after them, and decides to trace his wife Tuanmei's soul. As the narrative tells the story:

Longyin comes from Hunan Poyang.
Longyin used to be the head of the *lu sheng* consort,
He loves Tuanmei and shares the same hearth with her.

> Tuanmei has made an engagement with her cousin before knowing Longyin,
> However, she and her cousin are unable to settle together like the bird and the eagle.
> So Longyin married Tuanmei,
> After she spends one hundred and twenty *liang* (1 *liang*=50g) of gold to break off the previous engagement.
> She lives with Longyin and has a son and a daughter,
> But she has a short life and goes to the *yin* World, never to return.
> Longyin says: "it is miserable to have lost my wife,
> I am willing to go to the *yin* World to meet with her".
> He asks his mother to take care of his children,
> So that he might leave his hometown and cross mountains.
> Outside the door, he wept,
> He has no idea where Tuanmei's soul goes.
> He searches for her along the road, sighing,
> He arrives at a small town one month later.[18]

He decides to have a break, and tells his story to the owner of the inn:

> Longyin said: "my surname is Qing and I come from Tunbi,
> My heart is broken for my wife's short life, leaving children and me alone.
> I am searching for her and my eyes are almost blind for tears,
> But I have no idea where Gaosheng Ya'an is."
> The inn owner says: "Gaosheng Ya'an is a place for the souls of the dead,
> It is five *li* (1 *li*= 0.5 km) away and separated by a mountain from here.
> My surname is also Qing and we belong to the same Qing family,
> Tonight, we would perform a ritual to become brothers and discuss it.
> Tomorrow I would close the inn,
> And go with you to the place with fog and sunshine.
> You wouldn't believe what I said,
> but you would believe it after you arrive at the Yellow Well with me."

> They arrive at the Yellow Well the next day,
> And see Tuanmei's soul arrive to collect water.
> Longyin is so shocked,
> He catches Tuanmei's arm and wouldn't let her go.
> Longyin says: "you are in 'yin World' and walk fast like wind and lightning,
> Now I catch your arm and please go back with me."
> Tuanmei says: "I am not able to go back though you try to persuade me,
> I hope you forget and forgive me.

> Please go back and take care of our children,
> And hopefully you marry again."
> Longyin is sad: "I can't forget you because we love each other,
> Don't leave us alone."
> Tuanmei said: "we really love each other,
> And that is why I leave you one son and one daughter.
> You please go back and bring them up,
> And I would not worry about them in the *Yin* world."
> Longyin says: "I have trouble to come here and just hope to go home with you,
> I hope you are able to return to life, as smoked garlic grows again in the garden."
> Tuanmei says: "it is different from the onion and garlic in the garden,
> The cooked sticky rice is unable to become grain again.
> Longyin, please don't be so sad and weep,
> Now I must leave and forget me forever please." [19]

These bridges are equally important in transmitting the dead soul into the *yin* world, although much of the life in the *yin* world is imagined as similar to the *yang* world, people at the very end are sadly separated between the two. When an old person is dying, a local priest is invited home to perform the rituals and lead the dead soul to the next world through the bridge. The ceremony named 'send-off the soul' is performed by burning money paper, reciting the send-off words, sending off the dead soul to reunite with their ancestors in the *yin* world in Gaosheng Yanan village, and meanwhile praying for auspiciousness and fertility to the family.[20] As the narrative song sings:

> When a man is 70 years old, he is getting into an unhealthy time and year.
> He has been involved in illness from morning till night, and he wouldn't live with the pain anymore.
> He crosses villages to borrow a duck, and crosses counties for a hen.
> But nobody would like to loan him a duck or a hen.
> The four judges come from the *yin* world (the dead world) and arrives at the bank of the river,
> And his ancestors would not pay for his survival.
> He wouldn't cross the bridge in the *yang* world (the living world) anymore,
> So unavoidably he would walk on the bridge to the *yin* world.
> He would like to stay with the spirits in the *yin* world,
> Because he wouldn't communicate with the people in the *yang* world.
>   (The audience: yes, it is true!)[21]

And then the song goes on how his descendants build the coffin for him:

> So what are his sons and grandsons going to do?
> They go to invite the Golden Lady,
> With locker on her right hand and key on her left hand.
> She opens the box for red quilt and white cloth.
> She dresses the body with nine layers of clothing, and nine pairs of shoes.
> She puts down nine wine cups and nine *liang* (1 *liang* = 0.05kg) of wine.
> Everything is ninety-nine.[22]
> Where are his sons and grandsons going to do it?
> They arrive at Luoshan Mountain and walk to Pukun Mountain to get the wood.
> They wouldn't choose a pine tree or a maple tree.
> What they want is a firm tree in the remote mountain.
> Because, on the fir tree, the baby crows are born in the spring, and the sparrows make their   nests in the winter.
> If the tree falls down to the east, everything sounds auspicious;
> If the tree falls down to the west, everything sounds getting well;
> If the tree falls down to the north, every grain is collected into the granary.
> If the tree falls down to south, the family will flourish.
> If the trunk falls down on the ground, and the hill is fulfilled with branches and leaves.
> It means the family will flourish.
> If the trunk falls down on the ground, with the branches still attached to its trunk,
> It means the descendants would save more money and rice.
> The beams of the coffin are made by the tree trunks,
> And the ropes are made by the vines.
> There is a flat road to the remote mountain,
> And they walk across it with the large trunk carried on their shoulders;
> There is a flat path near the river,
> And they come from there with the heavy trunks carried on their shoulders.
> Carrying the trunks into the yard and dragging the trunks into their house.
> What are put underneath the timbers?
> The timber trestle would be put underneath the trunks.
> What are put on the top?
> Money paper would be put on the top.
> Whom are they going to invite?
> They are going to invite the craftsmen.

> Measured with their rulers, and marking ink on the timber elements.
> The coffin is built with nine pieces of oak and nine-*cun* wide.
> (The audience: Yes! Everything is ninety-nine!)[23]

Finally, the family would select an auspicious date with the help of a Fengshui master, crossing the descendant's personal bridge to bury the dead.[24] Hopefully everything is done perfectly, and after the mourning, it is believed that the dead is transformed into an ancestor spirit, with the capacity of protecting his descendants from evil and bless them with fortune and flourish:

> Fixed the *bazi* (a date selected by Chinese calendar) of his birthday, the dead old man is buried in the dragon mountain and the tiger hill.
> Buried in the mountain, or buried in the hill.
> The family goes to worship it the next day, and hopefully the grave is covered by green leaves;
> And they go to worship it on the second day, and expect that the grass grows one *zhang* (one zhang is about ten-feet) tall;
> They go to the cemetery after a month;
> The graveyard is full of fortune, fertility and big wealth, and it flourishes.
> (The audience: Yes! Yes!)[25]

Here we see a picture of events that happened in the Dong lives, making sense of their particular concern for death, the stage of transformation from awareness to the inanimate world. The destination of every life journey is death, which thus causes anxieties not only to older people but also to younger generations, questioning the future after death. The elders worry about their lives and reincarnation in the unseen world where their souls reside, but their descendants suffer such problems of transformation of the dead souls into spirits, and whether they have paid enough respect to the ancestors so as to obtain their blessing for an auspicious life. In the death ritual, when the coffin is being delivered for burial, the funeral party would pass across the corpse's personal life bridge with the priest leading it, which symbolizes that the soul of the dead is securely led to the road of their ancestors, passing the symbolic bridge on the *Yin/Yang* river, and arriving at the *yin* world to meet with his ancestors.[26] Bridges are thereby understood as a very important metaphor for the resurrection of the dead spirits, playing an essential role of connecting and crossing in the rites of the passage of the Dong's life journey.

The Dong's Bridges as Symbolic Crossing

People from the living world are always supposed to obtain 'the way' to communicate with their parents, husbands, wives, children and friends in the other world, imagining to extend their moving dramas between the edges of two different worlds.[27] The descriptions about 'the way' connecting this world and nether world is found in Eliade's analysis on the symbolic meanings of passage. He notes that bridge and narrow gate are impressive thresholds, particularly in suggesting the idea of a dangerous passage, and for this reason, they frequently occur in initiatory and funerary rituals and mythologies. In Iranian mythology, the Cinvat bridge is traversed by the dead in their journey to the heaven, and under the Cinvat bridge lays the deep hell. The picture of bridge is described by Arabic writers and mystics as 'narrower than a hair', linking the earth to the Paradise.[28]

Among the Dong, bridges are symbolic connections between the living and the dead. In the Dong legends, *Yin/Yang* River (*yin/yang he* 阴阳河) separates the *yang* world and *yin* world, and over the river there is a bridge, which is crossed by both living and dead souls. The dead go through it from the *yang* world to the *yin* world, and the souls waiting to be reborn need to go through the bridge to the *yang* world. Separated by the Hun River, thus the journey to the so-called Gaosheng Ya'an village, could only be completed by crossing the metaphor—the symbolic bridge. Each Dong villager would have his or her personal bridge, which might be a magnificent Wind and Rain bridge, a simple stone or timber beam bridge, a stick tied to an old bridge, or even just a step placed before the family's threshold. The Dong people believe that reincarnation only happens through the mediation of bridge, and bridges are therefore connected with fertility. The infertile family or the family without a son is seriously disturbed, and the father of such a family would place a simple bridge or a link on a humble spot without causing any attention, such as a simple timber beam on a narrow sewer in the village, or to make a wooden complement to the Wind and Rain bridge. They believe that most reincarnations happen by going through the Wind and Rain bridge, and those who cannot get on the large bridge would have to be reborn through the small bridges. The more people step on their small personal bridge, the more fortune it would bring to them. Thus, when a person is born, his fate is connected to his personal bridge, and each person worships his/her bridge on the set ceremony day.[29]

The most famous Wind and Rain bridge in the Dong is the Chenyang bridge in Ma'an village, which was first built by the advice of Yang Shanren's father and several village headmen. The Linxi River meanders through the areas of Manan village, Pingtan village and Yanzhai village. In the record, Yang Tangfu lived in Yanzhai village, who is Yang Shanren's father and an outstanding carpenter in building timber dwellings and drum towers. Once he came back from a neighbouring village, arriving at the bank of Linxi River with another villager named Liang Changzhong. There was no bridge across the river. Under the heavy rain, they were all wet because they had to walk through the river. They suddenly conceived the idea to build a bridge on the river. By their suggestion, the heads of eight neighbouring villages got together, discussing how to build a bridge properly.[30] As the annals record:

> It (Yongji bridge) costs the villagers millions of yuan to build it, and it is the largest bridge in Sanjiang county. Commonly, a Wind and Rain bridge is built at the water—mouth of the watercourse near the Dong village, and a drum tower is built on the central area of the village, with a large square paved with pebbles, for the community meetings and festival ceremonies. The villagers would like to meet in the drum tower in the evening. When a bridge or drum tower is built in a village, each family either donates from ten- yuan to two or three-hundred yuan, or donates materials or labours, no matter they are poor or rich. In the building process, whether men or women, senior or young villagers, all do their best to help it and nobody avoided. Their enthusiasm is admired. Although Yongji Bridge was damaged by a flood in 1937, it was repaired by the villagers in 1940 according to the original one, showing the persistence of their commitment.[31]

According to the texts on the inscription built near the bridge entrance:

> The Dong people believe that building bridges or roads for the public can be credited to personal virtues or merits. Although the river within the areas of Chengyang village is a small branch, and not as large as Yangzi River, it still leaves a crucial gap to cross between villages. There used to be no bridge, and it caused concerns for the people to cross. Particularly in the summer with heavy flood, it was difficult to keep one's footing dry; and in the winter with the icy water, it was scary to cross. At that time, connection between the villages had to be broken, because it was impossible to get a boat past it. The communication between villages was interrupted by the gap. every villager would sigh while faced[facing] this situation. It is upsetting to see the sun rise and sunset, and neighbors separated by the river, just as the earth separated from heaven. So several villages were conscious of their responsibility and met to decide to build a bridge, serving the villagers for crossing the river safely, and they therefore named it Yongji bridge (永济桥), where Yongji means the bridge is to help to cross, also implicates it helps to go through difficulties.[32] Because the bridge construction is very expensive and complicated, it might not be completed by the village alone. So the headman of Chengyang village asked for the support from all the Dong villages. The bridge couldn't have been built without the sponsorship of many kind villagers. They contributed gold and silver to build up their goodness, and timbers and labour to support the fantastic activities. It took them ten years to complete the bridge. The hard job is now finished, and the mountain paths are extended by the bridge with the magnificent pavilions standing up above the river.[33]

Also in the record of Gazetteer of Guangxi:

> While building Chengyang bridge in 1912–24, fifty old men and heads of the bridge organization mortgaged their fields as guarantees, and each family donated whatever they had, including wooden material, money, food and labour, and inviting the best craftsmen and stonemasons to build the bridge. During the construction, the villagers of Chengyang county spent four years cutting stones to construct the piers; another three years cutting timbers and moving them to the building site, preparing the timber elements for the structural columns and beams; and the last five years setting up the structural network and pavilions, covering the roofs with tiles, and finally decorating the bridge. It took the villagers total twelve years and 50,000 yin yuan (silver dollars) to make the bridge.[34] Unfortunately, Chengyang bridge was crushed by the flood in the spring of 1937, and was repaired and fixed up in 1940. Then it was damaged again in 1983. The torrent washed away the east pier of the bridge, and the three pavilions from the middle to the east, fell into the water. Villagers saved the 700m^3 timber beams and columns from the river in five days, and the bridge was reconstructed and completed again in 1985.[35]

The timber structure of Chengyang bridge is over eighty meters long, and about three meters wide, covered with five pavilions (Figure 2.4). Although the lay-out of its plan shows that the structure is symmetrically organized along the long axis of the bridge, the five pavilions in elevation indicate the hierarchy of the space: entering from the entrance, arriving at the particular climax in the middle pavilion, and ending at the way out to Ma'an village. So while people walk on its long passage, they wouldn't miss the altars, shelters, which are celebrated by the pavilions.[36] The middle pavilion is the tallest and raised up to around eight meters, covered with a hexagon pyramid roof; the two beside it rises to seven meters, covered with a quadrilateral pyramid roof; and the other two on both ends of the bridge about six and a half meters tall, covered with a quadrilateral half-gable roof. Each pavilion roof has three tiers of eaves. The pavilions are linked by a covered passage. Under the pavilions, the altars are used to installed, each about 80cm high, 50cm wide and 30cm in length (Figure 2.5).[37] Burning incense tables were set up in front of the altars, serving for the offerings. There are long benches about 40 cm high, constructed in between the columns along both sides of the whole bridge, working as part of the structure to fix columns on the bottom of the bridge.[38] In the Dong ritual calendar, the communal worship rituals for these spirits used to be held at New Year and at the Eating New Festival of the Dong.

Although the bridge is also viewed as an extended passage, continuously moving from this bank to the other, the linear image of the Wind and Rain bridge is celebrated by the sign of the Dong—the multiple-eave pavilions,

40 *The Cosmology of Separation and Reunion of the Dong*

Figure 2.4 The five pavilions of Chengyang bridge, Sanjiang, 2001.

Figure 2.5 The altar under the pavilion of Chengyang bridge, Sanjiang, 2001.

The Cosmology of Separation and Reunion of the Dong

which are arranged and related along the bridge passage, reminding the intensive concern to and from which the passenger is travelling. The typical pavilions identify the Dong with other nationalities, making a familiar journey to the Dong people. The space of the Wind and Rain bridge is occupied by different deities, transferring the message about the relations between the Dong cosmology and the Dong community. In the Dong areas, the typical structure of the Wind and Rain bridges are standardized and shared by the whole society: all the bridges combined with several pavilions, each with multiple eaves and crown with a roof similar to the imperial palaces or houses. Underneath the pavilions are altars for various spirits, all linked with the purpose for rebirth of the dead souls, fortune and security of the living, and the necessity of rising in society. The pavilions are connected by a covered roof passage. The bridge thus becomes a village shrine, constructed around the ritual space of the spirit altars that used to be underneath the bridge pavilions, marking off the bridge space as a sacred space.

Hierarchy of the pavilions are celebrated within the bridge structure to identify the rank of the gods. The five elegant and differently styled pavilions on the Cheng*yang* bridge used to be shelters for five gods. Each was a house of a spirit—Guan Di (King of the War 关帝), Wenchang Xing (God of Scholar 文昌星), Kui Xing (God of Scholar 魁星), Judge God (God of Rebirth 花林神) and the Locality God (God of Locality 土地) respectively (Figure 2.6). The most important shrine of Guan Di was celebrated in the

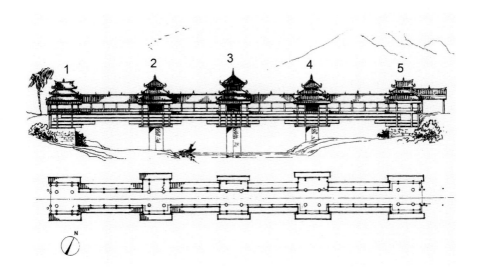

Figure 2.6 The organization of altars for the gods in Chengyang bridge: 1. Judge God (Hualin Spirit); 2. Wenchang Xing (the Literary God 文昌星); 3. Guan Di (花林神 Emperor Guan 关帝); 4. Kui Xing (Literary God 魁星); 5. Locality God (Tudi Gong 土地公) (from Fan *et al.* 1991: 225).

42 *The Cosmology of Separation and Reunion of the Dong*

middle pavilion, who was the God of War and Commerce (Figure 2.7); Wenqu Xing and Kui Xing, the gods of scholarship, were located to left and right of Guan Di; on the pavilion marking the way out to the other village was Judge God, who gives permission to the souls to be reborn; and on the bridge entrance to Ma'an village, the pavilion was owned by Tudi Gong (the Locality God), whose duty was to secure the territory in which it was located. Actually, the Locality God is given most attention by the Dong villagers, because there are many small size temples for the Locality God

Figure 2.7 The altar of Guang Di in Guandong bridge, Sanjiang, 2004.

also built near main roads or drum towers of the villages, just for burning incense inside to worship the Locality God daily.[39]

The middle pavilion is the altar of Guan Di, ranked among the top of the other gods. The story could be traced back to the Romance of Three Kingdoms in the Han Dynasty (206–220 B.C.), in which he is a great warrior and a symbol of honesty and loyalty to his friends. After his death, he is officially celebrated as someone on the highest level of imperial cult as the military god and the god of wealth and loyalty. As the powerful god of war and commerce, he is often worshipped for bringing good fortune in official promotions, getting rid of illnesses, protecting from evil and gaining much prosperity. His statues are usually sheltered in the temples particularly built for him, and his portraits are often posted on domestic entrances, symbolizing power for exorcism. On the Chinese agricultural calendar, he is specifically worshipped on 13th of the first month every year.[40]

On the east side of the Guan Di altar was the pavilion of Kui Xing, the first four stars composing the top of the dipper (Figure 2.8). Because the four stars appear like a crown, they are conceived as the intelligent stars and usually worshipped by scholars. The ritual of worshipping Kui Xing is held on the seventh day of the seventh month in the Chinese calendar. The ritual is usually performed under moonlight in the evening. An image of Kui Xing is prepared, his portrait drawn as an ugly blue-faced ghost, with his right foot

Figure 2.8 The shrines of Kui Xing on Bajiang bridge, Sangjiang, 2011.

standing on the top of a turtle's head and left foot raised to kick the Dipper. His right hand grasps a pen, and the Dipper is held in his left hand to point out the name of a successful scholar. The proverb in Chinese says 'Kui Xing pointing with the Dipper, and the best scholar standing on the top of the turtle's head'. The images of dragon and turtle used to be carved on the stairs of the palace, and in the Tang (618–907) and Song (960–1279) dynasties, the scholars who are ranked at the top in the governmental examination would be qualified to stand on the stairs and be received by the emperor. Only the best scholar is allowed to stand on the top of the turtle head. In the ceremony to worship Kui Xing, offerings include a roasted sheep's head, which must be a ram with a beard and with two horns remaining. Pieces of red paper are wrapped on the horns, and tea and alcohol must be included. They are presented in front of Kui Xing's image with a burning firework. After the ceremony, people would share a communal meal and finally burn Kui Xing's image.[41]

Wenchang Xing (the Literary God 文昌星) was located under the west pavilion to the shrine of Guan Di. A person, who is able to write the best article and is employed by the imperial government as an official, is named Wenchang Xing. *Narrative of the Scholar* tells the story about the God of Scholar. A scholar named Fan Jin is a very poor man. One day he goes crazy because he passes the exam and is selected by the government as an official. His father-in-law Mr. Hu is a butcher and had never respected him before this. Villagers advise him to beat his son-in-law in order to calm him down. After beating, he experiences a slight pain in his hands and gradually lacks the ability to bend it. He realizes his mistake and regrets that he has beaten the person who is Wenchang Xing (the God of Scholars) in the sky. He is so scared that he might be sent to the 18th level of hell and be beaten by Yan Wang (the King of Hell) with one-hundred sticks, never coming back again![42]

The God of Rebirth (Hualin Spirit 花林神) is the judge for the reincarnation of souls, located on the bridge exit to the other village, with the Locality God (Tudi Gong 土地公) pavilion on the village entrance. The Locality God usually sits underneath the local temple or the shrines of its territorial sub-divisions, and its duty is to command these areas (Figure 2.9). Each place is supposed to have its Locality Gong. They are needed as guardians either for a large or for a small area, a neighbourhood or a house. Locality God is particularly paid attention by shopkeepers and businessmen, which are worshipped every day in the small shrine installed on the right side of the door entrance. Every neighbourhood village in the Dong areas has a small shrine for the Locality God, which usually contains the statue of the god and sometimes is accompanied by his wife. Normally, a family pays respect to the God twice a month with incense and offerings presented. In Chinese calendar, the communal rituals for the Locality God are held on the second day of the second month, the fifteenth day of the eighth month, and the ninth day of the ninth month, performed in the local temples.[43]

The Cosmology of Separation and Reunion of the Dong 45

Figure 2.9 The shrines of Locality God built beside the entrance of Yanzhai bridge, Sanjiang, 2011.

Every building site as a territorial unit would have its own cornerstone as territorial guardian, known as the God of the Foundation (*diji zu* 地基祖) (Figure 2.10).[44] Usually, the God of the Foundations would be worshipped for blessing the construction work, while the first breaking of earth on a new site. The beginning of the building work is often marked by presenting the offerings to the god, and a respectful person is invited to break the earth and lay down the cornerstone. A legend tells that the Huian county and Jijiang county in Fujian Province used to be separated by the Luoyang River. The local people could never build a bridge successfully because of torrential flood. One day, an old man was rowing in the middle of the river with a beautiful girl on his boat, and the old man announced that the girl would marry the boy who is able to hit the girl with his coins. The young men tried very hard, however, they all failed and their coins dropped into in the river. After several months, the coins were piled up in the river, forming the cornerstone. Actually, the old man is a manifestation of the Locality God and the young girl a manifestation of Mercy, and they appear to help people build up the bridge. While the coins are gradually piled up and the gap is almost bridged, a young man successfully targets the girl. The young man is invited to a pavilion for the marriage. Taking a seat in the pavilion, he is not able to stand up again. His soul is transformed into a spirit in heaven, and his body remains in the living world as the God of Love, which is set as a moral example of contribution to the communal work, and

Figure 2.10 The collections of God of Foundation found in the middle pier of Chengyang bridge, 2005.

is worshipped by the lovers who pray to marry each other. So the cornerstone, laid down on the new building, is similar to a charm to protect the new building from evil during construction, and to bless the building work completed successfully.[45] In 1985, while the damaged Chengyang bridge was being rebuilt, its cornerstone was found in the middle pier. The cornerstone is a stone container about 60cm long in an ellipse shape, which are now kept in Sanjiang museum. In the container are the golden figures of the Locality God and his wife, three pairs of silver bowls and chopsticks, two pairs of jade and two silver worms as the spirit guardians of the bridge. According to the memory of Yang Shanren, at the auspicious time before starting the bridge construction, the cornerstone was laid by a villager named Yang Tangzhen, which was selected by the village for his flourishing and healthy family. The offerings inside the cornerstone were sponsored by the family of master Yang's father Yang Tangfu. So the cornerstone is called 'the charm of the bridge' (*ding xin wan*定心丸), and believed to be the guardian of the bridge, protecting it securely from evil spirits and damage.

Although voluntary participation of building bridges for the community is one kind of action admired for credited merits and virtues, the Wind and

Rain bridge was mainly contracted and contributed by the Yang's family and the other four villagers. It is interesting that the five pavilions on the Chengyang bridge celebrate the hierarchy not only for the five gods it is sheltering, but also the five occupants it is relying on. In the tradition of China, the hierarchy of Chinese society is identified on different ranks, with particular respect and obedience owed to seniors. Although the bridge seems to be constructed within a natural treatment, the ranks in the social world are clearly encoded in the allocation of pavilion space in the bridge. The form, the number of pavilion eaves and the height of the pavilion roofs further indicate the particularly important space within the bridge. All five pavilions of the Chengyang bridge are square with multiple eaves, but the different feature is marked on the style of the top roof eaves. Under the covered roof, the pavilion spaces house the deities of Hua Lin, Kui Xing, Guan Gong, Wenchang Xing and Tudi Gong according to their different ranks, response to the builders from the four villages and the Yang family—the whole bridge is constructed by an ordered society in which social relations are shown. The heights of pavilions from the bridge entrance to the middle increase gradually, the Yang's family, who is responsible to build the middle pavilion, achieves the most reputation and blessing from the community. With the gods' efficacy manifested in terms of address and space, the social relations between the gods and occupants are built up and manifested, while entering the bridge by the experience or the visual display of physical effort.

The Dong people believe in animism, and in the Dong's view, spirits exist in human being's dairy life. A legend of the Dong tells of mandrills, which are invisible ghosts in the mountains. They look like a monkey with heels in front and toes behind. The mandrill ghosts are not regarded as evil animals in the Dong legends, instead they show human kindness. It is said that a lonely old man lives in the mountain to look after his cows, and has a wok for cooking. The naughty mandrill ghosts often use the wok to cook after he sleeps, and cook some small animals such as frogs and snakes, leaving some in the wok for the old man. The old man feels disgusted by this food, and has an idea. He makes a similar wok with bamboo covered with moss, and hides the real one. One night, the spirits use the bamboo wok to cook and burn it. They feel so sorry. They think the wok is not able to cook on the fire and burnt. The next day they get a new wok and put it back to the old man's cowshed, and never use his wok again.[46] Because the Dong believe in the existence of mandrill ghosts, they would worship these invisible spirits when they are cutting trees or mining in the mountain, in case the spirits are bothered and they get revenged. The children are also advised not to throw stones when they climb in mountains or play in rivers in case they hurt the spirits.

It is interesting that each Wind and Rain bridge seems to have its own guardian spirits, and the bridge spirits are respected by people for their efficacy in transforming the souls. The experience of a dead soul transcending into spirit from this world to another world can be parallel to a trip of adventure. In the Dong cosmology, the other world would be approached by crossing a bridge. However, on conducting this journey, the dead souls might be distracted or taken away by evil spirits. To avoid this, every Dong bridge needs its guardian spirits.[47]

In Dong legends, ghosts are supposed to be haunting around paths, streams and bridges, and at the difficult passage with bandits and accidents, beyond the reach of common people, in which incurs the danger of one's life being taken to become a ghost to replace another. It is said that, when a splendid new Wind and Rain bridge is completed, a stranger leaves his physical body and becomes the guardian ghost of the bridge, and the bridge therefore possesses the efficacy (*ling xing* 灵性) of transformation.[48] Also, the bridge shows its powerful magic to lead the souls to be reborn from the dead world into the living world, and the dying souls from the *yang* world to the *yin* world, waiting for resurrection. In 1978, when the Wind and Rain bridge was built in Bajiang township of Sangjiang county, a young man was believed to have been the victim of the bridge. When the structural frame of the bridge was just set up without roof tiles on, this young man from a neighbouring village came to visit and walked across. He told the craftsmen: "This bridge is so magnificent, and I would come back to visit it after it finishes". Before long, he came back for work and went through the bridge again with his friends. When he stepped on the bridge, he suddenly stumbled and died. He didn't seem to be hurt. According to the old people, because he promised that he would love to come to the bridge, he had become one of the guardian spirits of the bridge.[49]

It thus seems to be unusual among the Dong that some person might die when a bridge is built, because every bridge needs a guardian spirit. So, when people build their bridge, any family with only one son is advised to run far away from the village to avoid the tragedy of becoming the bridge guardian spirit. When the priest has selected a fortunate date for setting up the columns for the bridge, the families with single sons are very concerned. Their sons are told to leave the village three hours before the columns are set up. The further they run, the more security they have. They need to stay in a place where the noise of setting the columns wouldn't be heard, and they are not allowed back home until the bridge has been finished, possibly leaving away the village for some months or even years.[50] But actually, death in the Dong's view doesn't seem so terrible for the hope of reincarnation. In the Dong's cosmology, everyone would go to his last journey of death, but people believe that the soul never dies. After people die, their souls leave their bodies, going through the bridge to the *yin* world and wait for the chance to be reborn through the bridge again, which means that death is not only the end of his first life but also the beginning of a person's next life. Although the Dong concern death, they feel peaceful and hopeful in the promise of reincarnation, being persistent in the passage on the life journey with great enthusiasm.

Rituals on the Dong's Physical Bridges and Symbolic Bridges

The rituals on the Dong's bridges are made up of actions, including communal and personal rituals, although these might be combined variously on different occasions. Typically, the ceremonies include Blocking the Way, Inviting the Spirits, Stepping on the Bridge and the Communal Meal. In contrast, personal ritual is quite private, only including the actions of Worship the Spirit, Crossing the Bridge and Family Meal. These rituals share similar elements in their performance, for instance, constructing a 'path' or setting up an 'obstruction' for invisible energies; burning incense; expelling evil energies by scattering animal blood; repelling or inviting supernatural powers by reciting or shouting auspicious words; making offerings of cooked meat, tea and alcohol, money paper; tying pieces of tree branches or ribbons to the Wind and Rain bridge and eating sacred food. Despite these common elements appear in the different ritual acts, the communal and personal rituals are carried out by the Dong by addressing the general issues of fertility and fortune in life.[51] The communal rituals for the Wind and Rain bridges are usually held every three years within several villages with hundreds of participants. Exceptionally, the communal bridge ceremony is performed after an old bridge is rebuilt, or a new bridge is completed.[52]

The Dong bridge ceremonies include the worship of the physical bridges (yang bridge 阳桥), and the temporary symbolic bridges (yin bridge 阴桥), made with wooden stools and the Dong cloth. The practice of all the rituals involves healing rites, spirit possession and animal sacrifice. They are usually held by the Dong women for fertile delivery, or by the family for their child's healthy and fortune. People believe that the souls of their children would come across bridges to the living world, where the childbirth need the permission of the deities on the bridges, linking the living world and the divine world. As the most splendid bridge, it is believed that the number of souls and reincarnations which come across Chengyang bridge are more than with other Wind and Rain bridges, and the villages near Chengyang bridge are more fertile than in any other place.[53] In order to become pregnant, every woman would go and step on the bridge where many souls gather, and believe their child's soul possession as she walks across the bridge.

After the child is born, rituals are held to pray for the protection of the spirits. Bridges symbolize the hardship that the newborn child must cross in order to achieve the fortune. The 'crossing hardship' and 'adding grain' ceremonies for the newborn baby is held within the first month of his birth in Liping county of Guizhou province. The maternal grandfather invites all his relatives, and lucky money from the guests are expected to present as a gift for this ritual. The money collected for his daughter's family symbolizes the act of receiving health and auspiciousness from others. When girls marry, they do not receive any dowry from their family, and the collected money is also used to pay for the furniture in the daughter's new family. Although participation is voluntary, everyone joins in with enthusiasm because the

'Money Collecting' ceremony continues, which is relevant to every family and might happen some day in each family. On the day of the ceremony, the daughter's husband kills a pig, presented by the maternal family, to serve the guests. 'Worship yin Bridge' is performed as part of the ritual. The participants set up a fortune stool as a *yin* bridge covered with a new Dong cloth, and the cloth is prepared by the maternal grandmother. After the wife's father goes through the fortune stool with the child held in his arm, he passes the child to the maternal relatives, and everyone holds the child and passes through the symbolic stool bridge. At the end, the child is back to the mother or father. Through this ritual, the child is expected to cross every hardship in the future and grow up with fortune.[54]

The Wind and Rain bridges in the Dong play essential roles as ritual space, particularly for the Blocking the Way ceremony (Figure 2.11). On 15th December 1985, when the work of reconstructing Chengyang bridge was completed, a communal ceremony to worship the bridge was held in Ma'an village. There were 30,000 people from the eight villages of Chengyang township participating in the ceremony.[55] The communal ritual is started by the Blocking the Way ceremony, which is usually held within the clans with blood tied through intermarriage, serving the development of existing friendships for the young generation.[56] On the morning of the ceremony, several firecrackers are lit, and their loud bangs

Figure 2.11 Young women and the visitors in the Blocking the Way ceremony, Sanjiang, 2018.

The Cosmology of Separation and Reunion of the Dong 51

announce the beginning of the ceremony. When the visitors from neighbouring villages are on their way, the young women of the host village carry their spinning wheels, weaving looms, bamboo baskets and cages of hen, to block the village entrances, either the entrance of the Wind and Rain bridge or the drum tower or a specially built village gate. The path is blocked by a rope hung across the entrance, and the visitors and the hosts stand on both sides of the blockade. They start the competition by singing Dong songs.

In Ma'an village, the west end of Chengyang bridge serves as the gate of the village. In the ceremony, benches, tree branches and bamboo sticks are symbolic obstacles to block the way, and the Dong villagers are dressed in their traditional costumes, with wine contained in a horn and red eggs in baskets; and they carry the musical instrument *lu sheng* in their hands. After the loud bangs of firecrackers, *lu sheng*s are blown, and groups of people come towards the bridge gate with the music of *lu sheng*. Near the entrance, both groups of the hosts and the guests begin the blocking way ceremony by singing *lan lu ge* (blocking the way songs 拦路歌), which are also named Welcoming Songs and Sending-off Songs:[57]

Host:
Cut a stick of the tree and block the way,
And the fir trees block the entrance of the village,
With many branches of each fir tree,
Which one would you come forward to cut?

Guest:
The sticks can't block the way,
And the fir trees can't be put on the edge of the village,
I wouldn't worry about so many branches on the fir trees,
And would cut the top of the tree by my axe.

Host:
Fir trees block the entrance with their long branches,
And the pear trees block on the gate of village with their long sticks.
We don't know where you come from,
And you would be allowed to get into village if all questions are clear.

Guest:
Fir trees block the entrance with their many branches,
Pear trees block the gate of village with their many sticks.
Trees are cut only for the fences of pigs or sheep,
And it hasn't been seen for blocking a way.

Host:
Not stopping if you would carry on your way,

52 *The Cosmology of Separation and Reunion of the Dong*

And not scared of water if you would cross the river.
You wouldn't mind the long way if you would like to walk along the river,
Although there are many bushes and shrubs in the mountain.
You should change your way because of the way blocked here,
And you should leave here early and walk the other way outside the village.
No regulation of blocking the way can be broken like a strong mountain,
Today why are you coming here?

Guest:
Stepping out of the door, I am wandering,
And climbing on the mountain peaks.
Not scared to meet the tiger halfway,
But only be confused by the wrong way.
We don't mind going a long way by climbing the mountains,
And crossing the river by the boat without oars;
We don't mind the dangers in the journey,
And we come to your village just for our lovers.

Host:
We are firm in blocking the way,
And no stranger can enter without our permission.
The gate of the village is usually closed against thieves,
And troubles caused from enemies.
With many of our villagers,
And our friends and neighbours,
We don't mind your complaints against blocking the way,
And you would go to jail without our consent.

Guest:
Don't block the way please,
Like the guardians blocking the way in front of *yamen*.[58]
We are in a hurry as we have a long way to go,
Don't let us walk halfway in the night please.
Without an oil lamp on another half way,
How can we settle down?
Although we might meet a family house on our way,
But it is difficult to hold so many people.
There is no boiler big enough for tea water,
And no wooden barrel big enough for washing our feet.
We have to walk in the snow without shoes,
Please take pity on us.[59]

After several rounds of songs, the hosts unblock the way. Young girls raise the horns to honour the guests with wine, and present red eggs to their favoured young men, in which way they choose them personally. Symbolically, blocking the way with fir trees is believed to obstruct the evil spirits; wine is pronounced as *jiu* in Chinese, carrying the meaning of eternal love; and the eggs usually symbolize fertility in their future life. Then, the *lu sheng* music from the host and guest groups is mixed, and following the music, they sing the welcome songs to end the Blocking the Way ceremony:

> Host:
> We have been waiting for our guests for a long time, and they have still not come,
> But we feel anxious while they are coming.
> Where can we get the leather of dragon and tiger to serve our guests as seats?
> Where can we find the peaches and apples from fairyland to serve our guests?
>
> Guest:
> We just stepped out of our doors, but you have heard the news for a while,
> You blow your *lu sheng* to welcome us while we arrived at the gate of your village.
> We haven't deserved the honour of sitting on the leather of dragon and tiger,
> We would be appreciated if we could get a straw-made raincoat as our quilt;
> Only the fairies know how sweet the peaches and apples are in the fairyland,
> We are from the living world and not able to tell whether they are sweet or bitter.[60]

The ritual of Blocking the Way seems to have been related to the security of the village, for the fir tree branches are used to block the path against thieves and enemies. However, meanings which may have been attributed to it emerge if the ritual is related to a sacramental tie between the Dong village and their 'eternal' world. The words of the host villagers in the Blocking the Way song exaggerate their worry about the security of the village, yet they also reflect their eagerness for the fortune and prosperity presented by the outside villagers, praying for security by blocking the boundary of the village to protect them from evil spirits. Instead, the guests' words stress the danger of the journey, where they come here just for their lovers and expect hospitality, and in exchange they expect to bring fertility and good fortune to the village. After making this clear, the host villagers express their anxiety about their duty as hosts, being afraid to miss their guests' auspicious blessing and fertility, and especially expecting to keep communication with the guest villagers.

Worshipping and Inviting the Spirits ceremony is also performed near the Chengyang bridge when its renovation is completed (Figure 2.12). In the ceremony, three tables' offerings were sent to the ritual halls, the two temporary wooden roofed structures built on the grain fields near the west end of the bridge. The offerings on the first table were flourishing plants in pottery containers: a bunch of teak on the right, kumquat on the middle and grape on the left (Figure 2.13).[61] Teak is the durable red-brown wood of a South and Southeast Asian tree, which is valued for its timber with a special smell, and is believed to expel the evil spirits; kumquat is a kind of small oval orange fruit, relating to citrus fruits with sweet skin and tart flesh, and symbolizing the fortune and auspiciousness in life; and grape grows with flourishing fruits, implying fertility. On the second table are five cups of alcohol, served for worshipping and inviting the spirits. Generally, three cups of alcohol are used in rituals, which means the three generations of recent ancestors are invited. In this ceremony, five cups of wine meant that many spirits rather than just the previous three generations were involved. In addition, a clean and raw pig was decorated with red colour, put on the third table, with its cleaned windpipes surrounding the top of the body and the head crowned with a bunch of grapes. These tables were carried by the young men selected by the villagers, leading people to the ritual site in a line.[62]

Figure 2.12 The offerings to worship the spirits of the Chengyang bridge sent to the ritual hall, Sanjiang, 1985 (photo: Mei Ling).

The Cosmology of Separation and Reunion of the Dong 55

Figure 2.13 The offerings in Worship the Bridge ceremony organized by the village and ritual heads, 1985 (photo: Mei Ling).

The ritual was conducted and directed by the priest Chen Yongzhang from Ma'an village, accompanied by ritual headmen from the other three villages. Three offering tables were set in front of these ritual actors. Incense was burned, cups of wine raised by the presiding men, with the idea of respecting and inviting spirits with the smoke rising to the heaven. The priest Chen Yongzhang started with the Song of Inviting Spirits (*qing shen ci* 请神词):

'We wouldn't invite mountains,
and we wouldn't invite rivers.
We would like to invite you, Sa Sui, our dear great grandmother,
And invite you, Hualin God (the Judge God).
Please come down with us!'[63]

While cups of wine were spilled to the ground, his rhymed speech announced all their comings and goings to the ancestors, and asked the ancestors of the Dong to accept the people's prayers and the offerings. The ceremony assembly included the elder people of the four villages that supported building the Chengyang bridge, standing in rows behind the ritual heads. After the ritual heads had served offerings of alcohol, other members of the group came forward and participated in the offerings. The spirits inviting ceremony ended with the ritual headmen back alone in front of the tablets. They made a final bow (*kow tow* 叩头), and went up the steps to the entrance of Chengyang bridge, leading the people to step across the bridge, performing the Stepping on the Bridge ceremony.[64] It is accepted that the ancestors act as supernatural forces involved in daily human lives. The ritual of worshipping and inviting the spirits is not just a sacrifice to the original god of the Dong, Sa Sui, but to many other forces of nature, including the heaven gods, the earth gods, the mountain gods and ancestor spirits. People in this ritual pray for village prosperity, male descendants, the elimination of natural disasters and diseases, abundance of the five cereal crops and the flourishing of domestic livestock. After the ritual, the sacrificial items are carried through the bridge with the people participating in the ceremony to another ritual hall near the east end of the bridge. The meat of pigs must be correctly butchered and cooked, and every participant shares the communal feast finally in the ritual hall after the ceremony. The cooked meat is believed to be blessed by the spirits, and the offered deity meat that is shared embodies a symbolic meaning as a material medium for the blessings which are received in return by the participants.[65]

On the stage of Stepping on the Bridge, a piece of Dong cloth, about twelve- *zhang* (1 *zhang*=3.3m) long was prepared by the women from a fertile family, with the colour of red and indigo dyed by the plants. The cloth is covered on the passage of Chengyang bridge, starting from the middle pavilion, and extending to both ends, symbolizing half *yang* world and half *yin* world (Figure 2.14). In the view of the Dong, the Dong cloth symbolizes the *yin* bridge, which leads the reincarnated souls from the dead world to be reborn; yet the souls also need to cross the *yang* bridge—the physical Wind and Rain bridge or personal bridge, to arrive at the living world.[66] The Stepping on the Bridge ceremony was conducted with the priest Chen Yongzhang and other ritual headmen, leading across the bridge passage from the far end starting and arriving at Ma'an village (Figure 2.15). As they stepped on the cloth, the coins were thrown on the bridge passage with some auspicious words announced. The purpose not only leads the reincarnation souls from the *yin* world to this world, but also brings wealth to these villages. Following the ritual heads, 30,000 people form the Dong villages or neighbouring provinces attended the ceremony and crossed the bridge.[67] After the communal ceremony, a communal meal was held to celebrate the festival and to feast the guests from neighbouring villages, relatives and friends. It is conceived that the more guests participate, the more auspiciousness and fertility are presented to the village. The guest villagers were hosted with a communal feast at the ritual halls, sharing the meat, rice and wine of sacrificed items. The guests are expected to stay longer, but if that was impossible, the hosts would politely send them off to the gate of village. At

Figure 2.14 The *fengshui* master crossing the symbolic bridge made of Dong clothing in the bridge worship ceremony, Sanjiang, 1985 (photo: Mei Ling).

the moment of separation, young people sing the Blocking the Way songs again, trying to persuade the guests to stay:

(Host)
Why are you in a hurry to leave,
What are you going for?
You are in a hurry to go back home,
What are you going to do?
Does your wife sew her clothing in the daytime,
And need you to hold the lighting?
Does your wife grind the grains with the stone mill,
And need you to clean the husks of the grains?
Do your pigs in the shed,

58 *The Cosmology of Separation and Reunion of the Dong*

Figure 2.15 The ritual heads leading the Crossing the Bridge ceremony, Sanjiang, 1985 (photo: Mei Ling).

>   Need you to go back to wear hats for them?
>   Do your fishes in the pond,
>   Need you to go back to dress them up?
>   If not for these,
>   Why are you hurrying to get back home?
>
>   (Guest)
>   We are in a hurry to get back home,
>   For the harvest of the grains.
>   The grains planted on the tenth month are still not reaped,
>   Peanut seeds should be planted on the ninth month,

The Cosmology of Separation and Reunion of the Dong 59

Racks haven't been set up for the eighth month pumpkins,
And we haven't decided whether to hang the vines for cucumbers
Lots of farm work are waiting for us,
We might miss the busy spring season if we do not hurry back home for the work.
We would be seen as lazy persons if we miss the busy spring season,
And we would be in bachelordom forever.[68]

The song of Blocking the Way expresses the hosts' reluctant separation from their guests. Through these communal festivals, the villages make communication with each other, and although the guests finally leave, the relationship and network between them are set up.

The Personal and Family Rituals of Worshipping on the Bridges

The personal ritual takes place if serious trouble in the life crisis threatens members of the family, such as pregnancy, birth and illness. These rituals, involving family bridges and personal bridges built individually, are often performed confidentially and are different from the communal rituals. In these ceremonies, women pray specially for getting pregnant and giving birth to male descendants and children pray for health to grow up and the family pray for fertile marriage. Among Dong society, practising shamanism has a long tradition and is still widespread because of their cosmology about the origins of life related with the *yin* world and the *yang* world.[69] The Dong people conceive that it is necessary to communicate with the spirits to forgive their wrongness, and to worship the spirits so as to survive in the world with blessings from them. The agents of spirits are the local priests, who are greatly respected by the Dong. The Dong people believe that the priests are capable of communicating with the spirits who are involved in their work and lives. Through priests and shamanism, people know what happens in the *yin* world through dialogue with the dead, and even by going through into the *yin* world.

The bridges are the medium connecting the celestial world with the living world, through which people hope they can communicate with the spirits. Because the bridges have these special functions in the transformation of life, they are worshipped as spirits in the rites of passage. In the Dong sets of *huan qiao wang yuan* (Worshipping the God of Bridge 还桥王愿) ceremony, including twenty-five ceremony sections, the *he Zhong sheng* (Inviting the Celestial Gods 合众神) and *an qiao* (Setting up Bridge 安桥) ceremonies are relevant to the bridges.[70] In the ceremony of Inviting the Celestial Gods, a symbolic bridge named '*tian qiao*' or *yin* bridge (overpass 天桥) is built to invite the spirits from the celestial world, through which the Dong people plead with the spirits. Similar to the Stepping on the Bridge ceremony, the imaginary bridge is a piece of a Dong cloth, covering the hallway of the house. It extends from the eaves of the main hall, housing the family altar outside the house, and points to the mountains, indicating a connection to the residence of the Hualin God who is responsible for the transformation of reincarnation. The priest steps on the *yin* bridge and recites a prayer to welcome the spirits, inviting all spirits from the celestial world and the Huilin God from Gaosheng Ya'an village through the overpass into the house. The purpose of the ritual is to attract more souls to be reborn in the family.

The ritual of *an qiao* (setting up the bridge 安桥) reaches the climax at the end of the *huan qiao wang yuan* (还桥王愿) ceremony (Figure 2.16). The householders of the family and people from other villages are led by the priest to the spot near the village Fengshui trees or the entrance of the bridge to hold the 'Setting up the Bridge' ceremony.[71] Sometimes the ceremony is held on the square of the drum tower to allow more members of the audience to join in. The priest sets up a temporary bridge with a wooden stool about three or four *chi* (1*chi*=33cm) long, with a piece of Dong cloth covering the stool and extending to the direction of the family's house. When the temporary symbolic bridge is set up, the priest performs the ceremony by dancing with his apprentices. The priest wears a mask of the Qiao Wang (Bridge God), appearing as the bridge spirit, and his apprentices are dressed in the masks appearing the Dong's ancestors Zhang Liang and Zhang Mei. The bridge spirits, Zhang Liang and Zhang Mei dance and imitate sexual activities around the bridge. Then men from neighbouring villages are invited by the priest to walk slowly across the symbolic bridge, up the wooden stool and down on the cloth bridge. When they step on to it, the priest sings songs and expects the wandering souls are attracted to the family anticipating fertility. After all of the male guests have crossed the bridge, the priest steps on to the bench and sings the song while walking across it:

> Today all the spirits come,
> Step on the bridge and bring wealth;
> Guests step first,
> Bless the family with wealth;
> I step second,
> The family become rich and noble,
> The family would have many sons and daughters,
> The family is fertile forever.
> And in my third step,
> Every family is rich and noble.
> The wealth is prosperous on the bridge near the river,
> All men become officeholders;
> Step on the bridge with million fortunes,
> I hope you are rich, noble and fertile forever.
> I come to step on the bridge,
> Wish you a lucky and wealthy, flourished and fertile life![72]

The Cosmology of Separation and Reunion of the Dong 61

Figure 2.16 The *fengshui* master crossing the temporary bridge made of a timber stool in the bridge worship ceremony, Sanjiang, 1985 (photo: Mei Ling).

When the Stepping on the Bridge ceremony is finished, a sow in estrus is carried to the ritual site. The sow's leg is tied with a duck, and the priest and his apprentices poke its genitalia with the sticks and sing the worship genitalia songs. After they finish singing the songs, all the men in the village follow the priest to act on the sow's genitalia with sticks, which symbolize fertilities in the family and also the village.

The Dongs believe that, in order for the dead souls to resurrect in the world, the spirits must cross the symbolic bridges, at last arriving at the

62 *The Cosmology of Separation and Reunion of the Dong*

destination—the living world.[73] In the Dongs' view, every person must have his own bridge, either the Wind and Rain bridge or the personal bridge which ensures his soul across to be reborn. The personal bridge is humble and usually built near a stream after birth of a child by his family, even with a simple plank (Figure 2.17). Its location is selected by a priest depending on the *bazi* (八字 the birthday) of the child, and is oriented to the direction of the family entrance. It must be located in the dragon vein, where it would transmit the vigorous energy of *qi*. The material for these bridges is fir wood, grown by his ancestors, so it is conceived that the ancestors would deliver children's souls to the family. The size of the personal bridge is about one foot and the dimensions are odd numbers, for example, three *cun* (1*cun*= 3.3cm) and three wide, one *chi* (1*chi*=33cm) and three *cun* long. According to the Dong's view, odd numbers act as a symbol of *yang* (male), and even numbers as *yin* (female). The fir trees as bridge material must grow up in a group of three, with the same length and without a broken part, possibly symbolizing a perfect family. When the three firs are cut, the bundle timber are tied up with five-colour yarn where the colours symbolize fertility, and particularly white cotton rope symbolizing that a healthy child is being born in the family. On the first anniversary of its construction, the family would

Figure 2.17 The simple personal or family bridge found in Mapang village, usually built in crossing the narrow gap or channel by individual or family, Sanjiang, 2004.

hold the ceremony to appreciate the bridge spirit. After three years, they would perform the worshipping bridge ritual every year.[74]

Every family holds the Worship Personal Bridge ceremony annually on the 2nd day of the second month in the Chinese calendar. The purpose is to facilitate delivery and to protect mother and child, and this security is extended to the father, relatives, the whole family, or the entire clan. In the early morning of the ceremony day, the family goes to the family member's personal bridge with wine, pork, duck, fish, red eggs, rice, incense, paper money and small wooden statues. After cleaning the bridge, incense and money paper are burned on both sides of the bridge. They recite some words of good fortune, and a cock is killed and its blood is spilled on the bridge. After the ceremony, they bring the offerings back home to share with the whole family.[75] These bridges are also named '*bao ye qiao*' (guardian father bridge 宝爷桥). The personal bridge is built not only for fertility but also for protecting the child from evil spirits. Apart from the annual worship, people also worship bridges on Eat New Festival, the day of newborn child, or anytime when a person in the family falls ill, they look upon the bridges as their children's guardian father, and praying that the bridge spirits to protect them from evil. In the ceremony, people burn the incense and paper money, and the child kowtows to worship the bridge spirit. With a meal near the bridge, the bridge spirit now becomes the guardian father of the child.[76] The offerings for the bridge ceremonies are meat, sour fish and gluten rice, as well as burning incense and money paper (Figure 2.18). Fishes are seen as a presenting a flourishing life and fertility, while the gluten rice is called *zong zi* (planting seeds), connection pregnancy; and roast pork is used to entertain the spirits and absorb the beneficial fortunate *qi* from the ancestors. The burning of incense in the ceremony is of great importance, because image of beneficial link between the prayer and the God resides apparent in the image of the incense stick and its smoke.[77] It is believed that the god sits in meditation on the altar. When the incenses are burnt, his eyes light up and take notice. The smell of the incenses catches the God's attention and the smoke directs him to the person and the matter at hand. While holding the burning incense, the person starts his communication with the names and address given, and an invitation to the god to take the offerings presented. When the incense sticks have been allowed to burn down to half their length in the incense burner, a generalized plea for protection is believed to have been accepted by the god.[78]

As an agricultural society, the Dongs are rich in rice. According to the record in the local gazetteer of Sanjiang county,[79] gluten rice is their primary food. The gluten rice would be steamed with a bamboo bowl. The Dong people just cook it once a day in the morning, and eat it for the whole day with pork meat, sour fishes and vegetables. The Dong worship fishes because they stand for prosperous fertility in the Dong culture. When a child is born, his family starts to make a piece of *suan yu* (sour salted fish 酸鱼) in the jar, and add one piece for him each year until he leaves the living

64 *The Cosmology of Separation and Reunion of the Dong*

Figure 2.18 The festival food with pork, sour fishes and ducks and colourful gluten rice, symbolizing fortune and fertility, Sanjiang, 1985 (photo: Mei Ling).

world (Figure 2.19). The sour fishes are specially made with fresh fish in a jar with clean rice-washed water.[80]

A cock is killed and its blood is spilled on the bridge in the Worship Bridge Spirits ceremony. People possibly believe that the bridge is the popular place, around which any kinds of ghosts would like to haunt, good or evil spirits. In the case of being bothered by evil ghosts in the ceremony, the blood of a cock would effectively protect people from *sha qi* (evil power 煞气), and the meat of the cock is made as an offering to worship the spirits. It is believed that the transmission of fortune would be accomplished through a chicken or pig sacrificed in the sacrificial ritual held at the bridge. These chicken or pigs are the propitious agency, through which the spirit *qi* is imbued in the bridge and made available to the family. The sacrificial meat of the roasted offerings is thought to have been exposed in some way to the spirits of the bridge, absorbing the essence and blessings from the bridge gods. The family believes they achieve the blessing when the offerings are shared among the family or by the community after the ceremony.[81]

Apart from the personal bridge, a family bridge needs to be set up by each family. While the reincarnated souls might not cross the Wind and Rain bridge to be reborn in the family, they might be channeled through the family bridge, which is named the *di qiao* (earth bridge 地桥). These small family bridges are similar to the personal bridge, the dimensions of which are about one foot and three *cun* by three wide, or one *foot* and three *cun* long. They are built in front of the threshold of the main hall, reluctantly

Figure 2.19 Sour fish-making and its container, Longsheng, 2004.

arresting the attention of visitors.[82] The earth under the family bridge is taken from the mountain of dragon vein, wrapped in a red cloth, and buried under the entrance bridge over one *chi* in depth. Alternatively, the earth is wrapped in a five-colour yarn (cyan, blue, red, yellow and white) and put in the bottom of the family's shrine cabinet. Coloured stickers of red, yellow, white and green are also used on the bridges, which are symbols of children's souls.[83] In Kaili of Guizhou province, yellow bamboo represents boys and green bamboo girls. When they worship *di qiao*, they burn the paper money and put three incense burners on the altar along with offerings of wine, meat and eggs.[84]

In the Dong area of Guizhou, people hold the ceremonies of Welcome the Dragon and Warming the Bridge, such ceremonies are related with the family bridges in order to ensure the blessing of fortune and fertility. The family people bring the sacrifice with them, such as wine, meat, eggs, fish and glutinous rice, in order to worship the land spirits near the bridges and to have a meal together thereafter. In Sandu, Dushan and Dujiang of Guizhou, those families which are desperate for a son would hold a *nuan qiao* (暖桥 Warm the Bridge) ceremony on New Year's Day or a selected fortune day, requesting descendants. People believe that the dead world on the other side of the bridge is cool, and that this ceremony delivers warmth from the living side to the opposite side via the structure of the bridge. In return, the

66 *The Cosmology of Separation and Reunion of the Dong*

families may receive the rebirth of souls from the *yin* world. Before they hold the ceremony, incense, candles, paper money, chicken, pork, wine, and rice would be presented. Then, the priest performs a *guo yin* (the crossing into the *yin* 过阴) ceremony in order to communicate with the nether world of *yin*. The reason that child's soul has not been delivered to the family might be that there is a river or barrier separating the family's home from the *yin* world.[85] So, the family master would build a family bridge on a fortunate day with the master's *bazi* (birthday in Chinese calendar). A straw is covered on his offerings to the built bridge. After the ceremony, the family shares a meal with relatives. The leaf of *zong zi* (the leaves of sticky rice cake) and the shell of eggs are left on the bridge, indicating that the bridge spirits have accepted their worship. At the end, the straw mat is burnt on the bridge entrance to the village side, indicates the warming the bridge. People use straw mat in the ceremony because traditionally when a child is born, he is placed on a straw mat. After the ceremony, the family master brings home coloured paper attached to the bamboo sticks taken from the bridge. On his way home, he would continue to recite: "good boy/girl, back home with

Figure 2.20 The bride crossing the symbolic threshold in front of the groom's house, 1985 (photo: Mei Ling).

me!" It is believed that the soul to be reborn follows the colour paper on the bamboo sticks that is brought home by the family master.[86]

The Stepping on the Wind and Rain bridge and Crossing the Family Bridge are also ceremonies which are held as part of Dong marriages (Figure 2.20). In Sanjiang county, the Stealing Marriage ceremony is held when the couples marry. On the wedding night, the groom and his groomsman would 'steal' the bride from her family at 10pm in the night, and arrive at the groom's family not later than three o'clock in the next morning. Between these hours, they are invisible and hidden from the public. They walk across the Wind and Rain bridge outside the village without causing any attention.[87] The reason that the Stealing Marriage ritual takes place at midnight is that, in the Dong's view, the resurrection of souls happens at that time, and the noise, made by the couple when they step on the bridge, would attract the attention of the guardian bridge ghosts, causing the spirits haunting on the bridge to hurry home with them. The couples envisage the soul possession of the bride through this ritual so that she becomes pregnant and the groom's family will gain a son immediately. When the 'stolen' bride arrives at the groom's family, she needs to cross a symbolic family bridge made by a shoulder in front of the family entrance. After she crosses this shoulder bridge, she becomes a member of the groom's family, the souls destined resurrection being thus infused to the family.[88]

Conclusion

As the boundaries of Dong villages, Wind and Rain bridges are especially associated with the processes of separation and reunion in the communication between the villages. Both personal and communal ceremonies on the bridges are reciprocal rituals. In the agricultural society, the existence of a village depends on an enlarged clan, and each member of the lineage has the duty of providing descendants. However, the social life and sophisticated cosmology of the Dong assumes two clearly opposed forms: separation and reunion occur in both the living and the dead worlds, and symbolic transitions may take place either on their elaborate Wind and Rain bridges or on temporary bridges of wood and cloth. The bridges are thus built as the thresholds on the rites of the passage rather than a simple physical crossing, between two different worlds. As Stafford argues, doors and gates thus constitute an 'open' borderline or threshold between the inside (nei 内) and the outside (wai 外), and thus they serve as a mediating space between members of any 'inside' group and those in the 'outside' world.[89]

The meaning of the gap built up by the bridge between the two different places in the material world extends to that of imaginary world, as much inside as outside. The twofold meanings of real and imaginary identify them with their physical function as normal bridges, and the social culture is directly related with their special building types. The Wind and Rain bridges, which became absolutely integral part of this, are therefore essential to the culture of the Dong. Furthermore, the construction and meanings of Wind and Rain bridges are elaborately organized by the Dong people, not only as types of construction but also as systems of relationship, mediating between the social culture and physical form. Although built for particular ceremonies, which are significantly related to the social culture, the construction and the typology of initiatory Wind and Rain bridges must be considered key part of architectural activity. Indeed, they are the integral works of the Dong legend and myth, as well representing the own cosmology in terms of 'wind and rain'. As the representation of the efficiency of gods, these bridges constitute a valid means for identifying the significance of the Dong buildings in a cultural rather than geographical landscape.

Yet the journey of crossing the river through the bridge from this world to that world is always considered a dangerous and challenged adventure for both living and deceased souls. The bridges thus are built not only as practical crossings but also as temples. They house altars for various gods and are decorated with carved mythical beasts, rendering them visible and memorable for a predominantly oral culture, promising security both for the people and the dead souls crossing the river. Serving as the ritual centre, the bridge's many connections with birth, marriage and death, are fulfilled in rituals and supported by references to myth, linking the eternal flow of the life-giving river with the cycle of returning souls undergoing reincarnation. Accordingly, there is an underlying continuous movement of spirits. Since the dead continue to move, the bridges must be elaborately built in order to support the complicated and necessary rituals, associated with the greeting and sending-off of powerful or 'effective' spirits, the dead souls crossing between the two worlds, while impending the passage of dangerous and evil ghosts. Thus, Wind and Rain bridges exert their prominent symbolic roles as the threshold between inside and outside within the Dong communities.

All such bridges are categorized into different types, that is real vs symbolic, permanent vs temporary, large vs small, communal vs personal bridges by the Dong, leading to the fact that the bridge is always a threshold symbolic of transition in a culture acutely sensitive to questions of time and space, and threshold and boundary. In fact, thresholds involving doors or gates are also read as symbolic manifestations of families and their internal and external relations.[90] The thresholds, which must be crossed by the living and the dead when arriving and departing, become the focus of attention and concern. As Bray says, 'the Chinese house was designed as a magical shelter from wind and evil influences, a site that could channel cosmic energies *qi* for the benefit of its occupants'.[91] That means that the good and bad spirits, or welcome and unwelcome guests, may be brought into the village or family with the flow of *qi* through any threshold. In this regard, Wind and Rain bridges, which serve as barriers and entryways for exit and entry, may be capable against the undesirable movements caused by inauspicious spirits and forces in their uncommon movements. Not only human beings but also spirits cross the threshold, and thus it is associated with the common ideas how they are built and orientated.

Notes

1 Xian, Guangwei 1995. *Dongzu Tonglan* 侗族通览 (A General Survey of the Dong Nationality). Nanning: Guangxi Minzu Press.
2 Yang Shanren is one of the most famous craftsmen in the Dong areas, who attempted to organize the repairs to Chengyang bridge in 1937 and 1985.
3 Yang Shiping was good at making building models, who once helped me to make a small model of Chengyang bridge.
4 The belief in rebirth is elaborately explained by Eliade, linking with the phases of the moon in its appearance, increase, wane, disappearance, followed by reappearance after three nights of darkness, which plays 'an immense part in the elaboration of cyclical concepts' (1954: 87–8). In his view, the moon is the first of creatures to die and also the first to live again, which is similar to birth and rebirth of life. He stresses:

> This means that the lunar rhythm not only reveals short intervals (week, month) but also serves as the archetype for extended durations; in fact, the 'birth' of a humanity, its growth, decrepitude (wear), and disappearance are assimilated to the lunar circle. And this assimilation is important not only because it shows us the 'lunar' structure of universal becoming but also because of its optimistic consequences: for, just as the disappearance of the moon is never final, since it is necessarily followed by a new moon, the disappearance of man is not final either; in particular, even the disappearance of an entire humanity is never total, for a new humanity is born form a pair of survivors.
>
> (Eliade, 1954: 87–8)

5 See Humphrey, Caroline with Onon, Urgunge 1996. *Shamans and Elders: Experience, Knowledge, and Power among the Daur Mongols*. Oxford: Clarendon Press, p. 119.
6 It is a river separated the people in the *yang* world from the *yin* world in the Dong myths.
7 In the Dong legend, it represents the *yin* world.
8 See Wu, Hao 1989. *Sanjiang Gezu Minge* 三江各族民歌 (The Folk Ballads of Sanjiang), in Zhongguo Geyao Jicheng, Guangxi Fenjuan: Sanjiang Dongzhu Zhizixian Zhiliaoji (3). Sanjiang: Sanjiang County Office Press, pp. 12–13, my translation. The song is popular in the townships of Bajiang, Linxi and Dudong.
9 Zhe, Jun and Nian, Haoxi (eds.) 1994. *Dongzu Minjian Wenhua Shenmeilun* 侗族民间文化审美论 (Aesthetics of the Dong Folk Custom). Nanning: Guanxi Renmen Press, p. 4.
10 Ibid. p. 5.
11 Humphrey, Caroline with Onon, Urgunge 1996. *Shamans and Elders: Experience, Knowledge, and Power among the Daur Mongols*. Oxford: Clarendon Press, p. 119.
12 I am very grateful to Wu Shihua to bring this fascinating idea to my attention in the summer of 2004. About the legend of Dong yin world also see Zhe, Jun and Nian, Haoxi (eds.) 1994. *Dongzu Minjian Wenhua Shenmeilun* 侗族民间文化审美论 (Aesthetics of the Dong Folk Custom). Nanning: Guanxi Renmen Press; and Yang, Tongshan *et al*. (eds.) 1987. *Dongzu Pipage* 侗族琵琶歌 (Collection of Chinese Nationality Folk Ballads: Dong Pipa Songs). Sanjiang: Sanjiang County Office Press.

13 The whole story sees Zhe, Jun and Nian, Haoxi (eds.) 1994. *Dongzu Minjian Wenhua Shenmeilun*侗族民间文化审美论 (Aesthetics of the Dong Folk Custom). Nanning: Guanxi Renmen Press, pp. 4–5.
14 Miao is one of 56 nationalities in southern China.
15 Zhe and Nian (eds.) 1994: 5.
16 The *pipa* songs are one kind of Dong song, which are accompanied by the *pipa*, a wooden mandolin-like instrument, which is especially ideal for sad songs, love songs and narrative songs.
17 See Wu, Hao (eds.) 1987. *Dongzu Kuanchi, Yege, Jiuge* 侗族款词, 耶歌, 酒歌 (Collection of Chinese Folk Ballads, Volume from Sanjiang). Sanjiang: Sanjiang County Office Press, pp. 486–7, the author's translation. The song was oral record by Hao Wu with Liang Tongyun, who was a 50-year-old peasant of Mapang Village in Bajiang Township, and a *pipa* singer. *Yin/yang* Song (*yin/yang ge*) is a popular narrative *pipa* song among the Dong. It tells six stories about people in the *yang* world communicating with the people in the *yin* world, all related to the idea of dead people going to Gaosheng Ya'an village.
18 *Ibid.* p. 486.
19 *Ibid.* p. 487.
20 The whole story sees the record of Wu, Hao (eds.) 1987. *Dongzu Kuanchi, Yege, Jiuge* 侗族款词, 耶歌, 酒歌 (Collection of Chinese Folk Ballads, Volume from Sanjiang). Sanjiang: Sanjiang County Office Press. The whole story is told by the following narrative song, which is Hao Wu's oral record with Wu Changren who was a 68 years old peasant of the Dong, the author's translation.
21 *Ibid.* p. 149.
22 The reason that all the numbers are related with nine is possibly that nine is heaven and the *yang* number in Fengshui and also an auspicious number in traditional numerology, see 5.5.
23 Wu 1987: 150. The author's translation.
24 Interviewed with Hao Wu in the summer of 2004.
25 Wu 1987: 153. The author's translation.
26 Wu, Hao 2001. '*Qiaoqu*' 桥趣 (The Legends and Custom of the Bridge), in Zhang Zhezhong (ed.), *Dongzu Fengyuqiao* 侗族风雨桥 (The Wind and Rain Bridge of the Dong). Guizhou: Huaxia Wenhua Press, p. 46.
27 About the rituals and shamans as the vehicle bridging the living and nether world see Humphrey, Caroline with Onon, Urgunge 1996. *Shamans and Elders: Experience, Knowledge, and Power among the Daur Mongols*. Oxford: Clarendon Press.
28 Eliade, Mircea 1959. *The Sacred and the Profane: the Nature of Religion*, translated from French by Willard R. Trask. San Diego, New York, London: Harcourt Brace & Company, pp. 180–3.
29 Wu, Hao 2001. '*Qiaoqu*' 桥趣 (The Legends and Custom of the Bridge), in Zhang Zhezhong (ed.), *Dongzu Fengyuqiao*侗族风雨桥 (The Wind and Rain Bridge of the Dong). Guizhou: Huaxia Wenhua Press, p. 45.
30 Interview with Yang Shanren by the author on the August of 2004. The idea of building Chengyang bridge was initiated in the summer of 1911 by several Dong leaders: Chen Dongliang, Chen Dongcai, Yang Jinhua, Yang Jinbang, Yang Tangfu, Liang Changzhong, Chen Wenming and Chen Yangming.
31 See Compilation Group of Annals of the Nationalities in Sanjiang County 2002 (first published 1946), *Sanjiangxian Minzuzhi* 三江县民族志 (Annals of the Nationalities in Sanjiang County). Nanning: Guangxi Minzu Press, p. 200. The author's translation. According Yang Shanren, although the building of the bridge was organized by the heads of eight villages, it was finally built by four: Ma'an village, Pingtan Village, Yanzhai Village and Pingzhai Village, each

village taking responsibility for one pier. Yang Tangfu was one of the heads and richest men in Pingtan Village, and he was seriously bothered by the problem of having made no offering in his fifties. He hoped to sponsor building the bridge, expecting to benefit from it. So the middle pavilion was sponsored by the family of Yang Tangfu.

32 The original name of Chengyang bridge which means to provide help to people.
33 In 1925, the inscription was written by Dongliang Chen, who is one of village leaders from Ma'an village of Chengyang county, suggesting building Chengyang bridge. The original plaque used to be set up on the entrance of the bridge, unfortunately, it was lost. This copy was made in 1985, according to the copy of Shibing Wu in Pingzhai Village. The author's translation of the Chinese inscription.
34 Compilation Group of Local Gazette of Guangxi Province 1996. *Guangxi Tongzhi Jiaotongzhi* 广西通志:交通志 (General Gazette of Guangxi Province: Traffic Section). Nanning: Guangxi Renmin Press, p. 16.
35 Interviewed with Wu Shihua in the summer of 2004. Also see Compilation Group of Annals of the Nationalities in Sanjiang County 2002 (first published 1946), *Sanjiangxian Minzuzhi* 三江县民族志 (Annals of the Nationalities in Sanjiang County). Nanning: Guangxi Minzu Press, p. 200.
36 Cf. Li 1990; and Fan, C. *et al.* 1991.
37 The dimensions of the god tablet are usually selected elaborately. It is often 12 *cun* in height representing the 12 months, 4 *cun* in width for four seasons, and 1 *cun* and a half in thickness, standing for the 12 hours. It is usually composed of three pieces of wood, one being a pedestal and the other two upright pieces. The top is usually curved representing heaven, whereas the bottom is square implying the earth (Chao 1983: 115).
38 Li, Changjie (ed.) 1990. *Guibei Minjian Jianzhu* 桂北民间建筑(Vernacular Architecture in Northern Guangxi). Beijing: Zhongguo Jianzhu Press, pp. 239–49; and Fan, C. *et al.* 1991. *Guangxi Minzu Chuantong Jianzhu Shilu* 广西民族传统建筑实录 (The Record of Vernacular Architecture in Guangxi). Nanning: Guanxi Kexue Jishu Press, pp. 223–5.
39 See the record in Compilation Group of Local Gazette of Guangxi Province 1992. *Guangxi Tongzhi Minsuzhi*, 广西通志: 民俗志 (General Gazette of Guangxi Province: Custom Section). Nanning: Guangxi Renmin Press, p. 364.
40 Feuchtwang, Stephan 2001. *Popular Religion in China: The Imperial Metaphor*. Richmond, Surrey: Curzon Press, p. 199.
41 Yang, C. K. 1967. *Religion in Chinese Society: A Study of Contemporary Social Functions of Religion and Some of their Historical Factors*. Berkeley and Los Angeles: University of California Press, p. 270.
42 *Ibid.* p. 271. Also see *Narrative of the Scholar* (儒林外史) was written by Wu Jingzhi (1710–54) in Qing dynasty (1636–1911AD).
43 Feuchtwang 2001: 97.
44 See Feuchtwang 2001: 98–100. He notes that 'A household is ritually defined as a unit in several ways: as a house, as a family, as part of a Tudi Gong and of a local festival area'.
45 http://www.china.com.cn/culture/txt/2007-02/01/content_7747033_5.htm.
46 Zhe, Jun and Nian, Haoxi (eds.) 1994. *Dongzu Minjian Wenhua Shenmeilun* 侗族民间文化审美论 (Aesthetics of the Dong Folk Custom). Nanning: Guanxi Renmen Press, pp. 112–3.
47 I would like to thank Wu Hao to draw my attention on these stories in the summer of 2004.
48 The bridge as the threshold separates and indicates the distance between two modes of being, the profane and the sacred. As Eliade discovers, 'the threshold

has its guardians—gods and spirits who forbid entrance both to human enemies and to demons and the powers of pestilence' (1959: 25). The guardian divinities are worshipped on the threshold, and hence it is an additional ritual of efficacy to be symbols and vehicles of passage, transforming beings from the one world to the other.

49 Wu, Hao 2001. 'Qiaoqu' 桥趣 (The Legends and Custom of the Bridge), in Zhang Zhezhong (ed.), *Dongzu Fengyuqiao* 侗族风雨桥 (The Wind and Rain Bridge of the Dong). Guizhou: Huaxia Wenhua Press, pp. 47–8.
50 Interview with Wu Hao in 2004.
51 See Compilation Group of Local Gazette of Guangxi Province 1996. *Guangxi Tongzhi Jiaotongzhi* 广西通志:交通志 (General Gazette of Guangxi Province: Traffic Section). Nanning: Guangxi Renmin Press, pp. 308–53.
52 Interviewed with Wu Hao and Yang Shanren in the summer of 2004.
53 Wind and Rain bridges used to be the place for lovers. Young women would often weave there, and young men would like to go to chat with them or sing and play with *lu sheng*. But today, young men and young women all go out of the mountains to make their living. On the day in 2004 when I went to Chengyang bridge, the only persons I met on the bridge were middle-aged women, who were weaving and selling their artificial textiles made of Dong cloth to the visitors, and they told me many interesting rites about bridges.
54 Zhou, Xing 1998. *Jingjie Yu Xiangzheng*: 'Qiao He Minsu' 境界与象征：桥和民俗 (Boundary and Symbol: Bridge and Folk Custom). Shanghai: Shanghai Wenyi Press, p. 48.
55 Interviewed with Wu Shihuaon in the August of 2004.
56 Geary, D. Norman 2003. *The Kam People of China: Turning Nineteen*. London: RoutledgeCurzon, p. 204.
57 The descriptions of blocking the way ceremony see cf. Yang, Tongshan et al. 1983. *Dongxiang Fengqinglu* 侗乡风情录 (The customs of Dong). Chengdu: Shichuan Minzhu Press, pp. 253–6; Wu 1995: 148–51; Yu, Dazhong 2001. *Dongzu Minju* 侗族民居 (The Dwellings of the Dong). Guiyang: Huaxia Wenhua Yishu Press, pp. 149–52; and Geary, D. Norman 2003. *The Kam People of China: Turning Nineteen*. London: RoutledgeCurzon, pp. 205–6.
58 Residence of imperial Chinese official.
59 Yu, Dazhong 2001. *Dongzu Minju* 侗族民居 (The Dwellings of the Dong). Guiyang: Huaxia Wenhua Yishu Press, pp. 149–52, my translation.
60 Wu, Hao and Zhang, Zhezhong 1991. *Dongzu Geyao Yanjiu* 侗族歌谣研究 (Research on the Dong Songs). Nanning: Guangxi Renmin Press, pp. 58–9, my translation.
61 Oral record with Wu Hao in 2005, who attended the bridge ceremony as one of the organizers.
62 Oral record with Wu Shihua and Yang Shanren in 2005, who attended the bridge ceremony as the organizers.
63 Oral record with Wu Hao in 2005.
64 Oral record with Wu Hao and Wu Shihua in 2005.
65 Oral record with Wu Hao and Wu Shihua in 2005.
66 The whole story was told by oral record with Wu Hao in 2005.
67 Oral record with Wu Hao in 2005.
68 Yu, Dazhong 2001. *Dongzu Minju* 侗族民居 (The Dwellings of the Dong). Guiyang: Huaxia Wenhua Yishu Press, pp. 163–4, the author's translation.
69 See Compilation Group of Local Gazette of Guangxi Province 1992. *Guangxi Tongzhi Minsuzhi*, 广西通志：民俗志 (General Gazette of Guangxi Province: Custom Section). Nanning: Guangxi Renmin Press, pp. 360–84.
70 The whole story sees Wu, Hao 2001. 'Qiaoqu' 桥趣 (The Legends and Custom of the Bridge), in Zhang Zhezhong (ed.), *Dongzu Fengyuqiao* 侗族风雨桥 (The Wind and Rain Bridge of the Dong), Guizhou: Huaxia Wenhua Press.

71 *Ibid.* p. 50.
72 *Ibid.* pp. 51–2.
73 *Ibid.* pp. 51–2.
74 Cf. Zhou, Xing 1998. *Jingjie Yu Xiangzheng: Qiao He Minsu* 境界与象征: 桥和民俗 (Boundary and Symbol: Bridge and Folk Custom). Shanghai: Shanghai Wenyi Press, p. 15; and Wu 2001: 45.
75 Cf. Zhou 1998: 23; and Wu 2001: 45–6.
76 Zhou 1998: 63–4.
77 As Feuchtwang discovers, it is polite and respectful to present an invitation to the God while opening communication like handing out an invitation card or like offering a cigarette or a cup of tea. See Feuchtwang, Stephan 2001. *Popular Religion in China: The Imperial Metaphor*. Surrey: Curzon Press, p. 135.
78 The function of burning incense in rituals to entertain the spirits sees Feuchtwang 2001: 40.
79 Compilation Group of Annals of the Nationalities in Sanjiang County 2002 (first published 1946), *Sanjiangxian Minzuzhi* 三江县民族志 (Annals of the Nationalities in Sanjiang County). Nanning: Guangxi Minzu Press, p. 50.
80 Compilation Group of Local Gazette of Guangxi Province 1992. *Guangxi Tongzhi Minsuzhi*, 广西通志: 民俗志 (General Gazette of Guangxi Province: Custom Section). Nanning: Guangxi Renmin Press, p. 83.
81 Personal communication with Wu Hao in the summer of 2004.
82 Zhou, Xing 1998. *Jingjie Yu Xiangzheng: 'Qiao He Minsu'* 境界与象征: 桥和民俗 (Boundary and Symbol: Bridge and Folk Custom). Shanghai: Shanghai Wenyi Press, pp. 27–8.
83 *Ibid.* p. 27.
84 *Ibid.* p. 28.
85 *Ibid.* pp. 25–7.
86 *Ibid.* p. 24.
87 Oral record with Wu Hao and Wu Shihua in 2005.
88 Cf. Compilation Group of Local Gazette of Guangxi Province 1992. *Guangxi Tongzhi Minsuzhi*, 广西通志: 民俗志 (General Gazette of Guangxi Province: Custom Section). Nanning: Guangxi Renmin Press, p. 248; Zhou, Xing 1998. *Jingjie Yu Xiangzheng: 'Qiao He Minsu'* 境界与象征: 桥和民俗 (Boundary and Symbol: Bridge and Folk Custom). Shanghai: Shanghai Wenyi Press, p. 129; Wu, Hao 2001. *'Qiaoqu'* 桥趣 (The Legends and Custom of the Bridge), in Zhang Zhezhong (ed.), *Dongzu Fengyuqiao* 侗族风雨桥 (The Wind and Rain Bridge of the Dong). Guizhou: Huaxia Wenhua Press, pp. 52–3.
89 Stafford, Charles 2000. *Separation and Reunion in Modern China*. Cambridge: Cambridge University Press, pp. 87–8.
90 Cf. Bray, Francesca 1997. *Technology and Gender: Fabrics of Power in Late Imperia China*. Berkeley, Los Angeles, London: University of California Press; Stafford, Charles 2000. *Separation and Reunion in Modern China*. Cambridge: Cambridge University Press; and Feuchtwang, Stephan 2001. *Popular Religion in China: the Imperial Metaphor*. Richmond, Surrey: Curzon Press.
91 Bray 1997: 60.

3 The Drum Towers as the Cosmological Centre of Separation and Reunion

The Dong drum tower works as the communal centre of people with one surname in the village. As the monument of the Dong, the drum tower occupies the village centre with its square, providing space not only for communal assembly but also for the ceremonies of Blocking the Way and worshipping the gods. According to Yang Shanren, who is the master for bridges and drum towers, the forms and structure of the raised pavilions on the bridges are very similar to the roofs of the drum towers. So both the Wind and Rain bridges and drum towers display a common feature— the pavilion roofs combined with multiple eaves. Because the Dong has a long preliterate history, we might only guess at the past through their customs, myths, legends and songs. In the book 'The Kingdom without King: Research on Dong Laws' (*Mei You Guo Wang De Wang Guo: Dong kuan Yan jiu*没有国王的王国: 侗款研究), Wu Hao explores the origins of the drum towers as the authority of the Dong by tracing the communal regulations or named *kuan* alliance which are established and enforced through the assemblies and ceremonies happened around the drum towers;[1] also, in his book Research on the Dong Songs *(Dongzu Ge Yao Yan Jiu* 侗族歌谣研究), he records the narrative songs of *kuan* laws, which are recited in the communal assemblies and rituals to educate the group of people and worship their gods.[2] In The Customs of the Dong (*Dong Xiang Feng Qing Lu* 侗乡风情录), Yang Tongshan reveals various customs of the Dong, particularly the process of various communal rituals performed on the square of the drum towers.[3] Geary's *The Kam People* provides a sketch of the Dong society, including the politics, customs and daily life of the Dong.[4]

In my fieldwork on the Dong, I particularly draw on the origins of the Mapang drum tower in Mapang village, by investigating not only the village environment, architectural form and structure of the drum tower, but also the myths and legends of the Dong. The literary sources I consulted as well as my fieldwork reveal the background of the drum tower. Compared to the Wind and Rain bridge, the drum tower is the centre of the village and in contrast, the bridge is the boundary; the drum tower is the sacred space, which is built both for the Dong gods and is also a place for the Dong people to entertain the gods, and the bridge is the sacred passage to greet and

The Drum Towers as the Cosmological Centre of Separation and Reunion 75

send off the gods. Thus, in both architectures, the pavilions as a desirable sign, which are identified with the gods of the Dong culture and the Dong communities, are employed repeatedly in the Wind and Rain bridges and drum towers.

Mapang village is one of the eleven villages in the Mapang township, located in the north of Sanjiang County (Figure 3.1).[5] It is a typical Dong village settled in the basin area of the mountain, with Wuluo river[6] meandering through from south to north (Figure 3.2). The village extends from north to south and Mapang drum tower is located in the heart of the village square as the symbol of Mapang village. Mapang drum tower is a monument in the Dong area, which was built in 1928 (Figure 3.3).[7] According to the inscription of the plaques inside the drum tower, it used to be the highest and largest drum tower in the Dong. In 1943, the drum tower was rebuilt, following the suggestion of the village headman Wu Changhong, Wu Changyuan, Wu Shilu and Wu Shilin. The drum tower was repaired in 1993 again, where it can hold the ceremonies for large *kuan* assemblies with over two-hundred families.[8] The particular meeting spot for a *kuan* assembly is the drum tower and the square in front of the drum tower, which is named *gu lou ping* (鼓楼坪 drum tower square); it is built with a performance stage opposite to the drum tower (Figure 3.4). In the event, each clan would meet at their clan drum tower or the whole village would meet at the village drum tower. But for the assembly of large *kuan*, they would meet at a large open spot called *Kuan Ping* (款坪 the square for *kuan* assembly) on the outskirts of the villages.[9]

Figure 3.1 Mapang village viewed from the east bank of the Wuluo river, Sanjiang, 2004.

76 *The Drum Towers as the Cosmological Centre of Separation and Reunion*

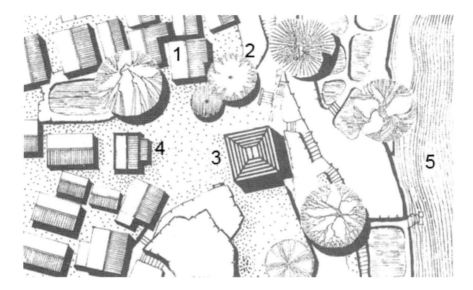

Figure 3.2 Mapang village plan: 1. The large village house; 2. *fengshui* tree; 3. Mapang drum tower; 4. The village performance stage; 5. The Wuluo river, Sanjiang, 2004 (reconstructed after Li 1990: 111).

Figure 3.3 The Mapang drum, Sanjang, 2004.

The Drum Towers as the Cosmological Centre of Separation and Reunion 77

Figure 3.4 The performance stage opposite the drum tower, Sanjiang, 2004.

Following the path running from north to south, which is the main entrance leading to the drum tower, a large family house is erected. The axis starts there, and then meets under a century-old Fengshui tree, with its huge and flourishing branches projecting out (Figure 3.5). In the Dong's view, it is the symbol of Sa Sui of sunshine, good fortune and fertility to the Dong. Under the Fengshui tree is a *tu di gong* (Locality God) altar worshipped by the villagers daily. This is an area where the whole village believes they are secure under the protection of the Locality Spirit. On the west side of the drum tower is the village performance stage, which is located on the east–west axis of the plan in relation to the drum tower as well as to the square. The north–south axis ends with another large Sa Sui altar. Small family houses are scattered around, orientating the desirable southeast direction instead of conforming to the four cardinal directions occupied by the God and sacred buildings and spots, such as the drum tower, Fengshui tree and communal altars.

The *Tang Wa* (堂瓦) and *Tang Sa* (堂萨)

In the Dong communities, a drum tower is also named *tang wa* (堂瓦), which is built along with a Sa Sui altar inside (*tang sa* 堂萨) (Figure 3.6). But sometimes, a Sa Sui altar is built near the village houses (Figure 3.7). The drum

78　*The Drum Towers as the Cosmological Centre of Separation and Reunion*

Figure 3.5 The *fengshui* tree and the altar of the Locality God under it, Mapang village, Sanjiang, 2004.

tower is the tallest building in the village, surrounded by the village houses and clearly distinguishing the village from the others. The drum towers provide the spaces for worshipping the general Gods in communal meetings and village communication ceremonies.[10] As Xian argues, the original name and function of the drum tower might be related with the patriarchal society, symbolizing the power of men. And the drum tower was originally named *tang wa*, which means 'community house'. The earliest drum tower was built like the shape of a fir tree, which is similar to a bird's nest on a tree; then it was named *bai*, indicating that this kind of building was made of timber, and possibly as the habitation for the head of the clan. Only recently was it named drum tower.[11] In the earliest record of *Chi Ya* in Ming dynasty (1368–1644), it is named *luo han lou* (men's building 罗汉楼), which was

The Drum Towers as the Cosmological Centre of Separation and Reunion 79

Figure 3.6 The Sa Sui altar inside the Mapang drum tower with the offerings on the top, Sanjiang, 2004.

Figure 3.7 The Sa Sui altar built in Bajiang village, Sanjiang, 2011.

supported by a single wooden column buried in the ground, was about hundreds of metres high, and covered with coloured tiles that looked like fish scales. After dancing and drinking in the festivals, the men slept inside.[12]

As perhistorical record, the Dong villages had been administered under their *kuan* till the end of Qing Dynasty (1636–1911).[13] The term *kuan* refers not only to alliances and political assembly, but also to the Dong's covenants. According to the Annals of the Nationalities in Sanjiang County:

> Ji kuan (集款) means to execute the covenants of kuan to administer the Dong areas. It is said that the earliest twenty-one regulations (kuan) were established by two persons from Zunzhou, and have been passed down till today. While the Dong assemble sometimes, they are named qi kuan (起款executing kuan). Since then, any covenant made by the kuan alliance must be obeyed, and every person must obey the head of the kuan alliance. Occasionally in times of emergency, feathers of cock and charcoal are booked on a wooden board, marking the very urgent condition, and sent to the villages under the kuan alliance without any delay. The number of villagers in an assembly is usually over 10,000 people. Therefore, the tradition of kuan alliance can be traced back a long history ago of the Dong.[14]

The *kuan* alliance is built with special rituals, to reinforce its power and authority in the society. Literally, *kuan* in Dong language means making a solemn pledge. In a record of the thirteenth century:

> The leaders of each clan meet together, smearing blood of a sacrifice on their mouths as a way of making a solemn pledge to help one another in the circumstance of emergency or difficulty: this meeting to make an alliance is called a kuan. The Dong kuan thus is originally an alliance of promise for mutual protection and well-being.[15]

Kuan might possibly also originate from marriage alliances in a patriarchal society.[16] The Dong social structure is based on a single family, which is named *lan* or *yan* in Dong language and is dominated by men. Clan is also named *bu la*, meaning the relation between father and son in a family, and is composed of several families extended with the same patriarchal lineage. Kinship is named *dou*. It is composed of several *bu la* or over ten families developed by the patriarchal clan. Over ten kinships construct the *kuan* alliance. Large *kuan (da kuan* 大款) is composed by several *kuan*, and extra-large *kuan (te da kuan* 特大款) by several large *kuan*. The traditional custom of Dong marriage is intermarriage between cousins, which is called 'back to uncle's door'.[17] When a Dong girl is born, she is bound to her uncle's family (her mother's brother). According to the custom, a woman was married and separated from her brother, but her daughter needed to marry her brother's son, bringing back the female lineage to the family. As a result, the lost

The Drum Towers as the Cosmological Centre of Separation and Reunion 81

female lineage was kept in the family, and thus the matriarchal power was passed down by the descendants. This marriage custom preserved the simple surname in the village and the two families linked by marriage became much closer. But with the development of the clan, this marriage style is no longer sustainable.[18] The only way to solve the problem is to 'split the surname'.[19] So, having more than one surname is allowed to live in the village or within the clan, which meant that more than one drum tower would be built so that each surname can occupy its own.[20]

Combined with over ten kinships named dou, *kuan* and *dou* take their responsibilities and duties respectively. *Dou* membership originates from the same ancestor, sharing the same rituals and ceremonies. They have their communal meeting place in the drum tower and village *lu sheng* teams with chores, and sometimes even organize their own *kuan* team. The kinship has a village or clan head, dominating the right of admission for other clans into the *dou*; and they organize the events and ceremonies in the village, the others must get their permission to join the kinship. They punish illegal deeds in the *dou* and share the same mountains and burial fields. Similarly, as the features of *kuan* have been exhibited in the Dong *kuan* alliance since the Tang dynasty (618–907), a *kuan* is constituted by setting up a stone stele, symbolizing the firm solemn pledge and *kuan* laws unchangeable like the stone. *Dou*, village and *kuan* each would have its drum tower, although the social structure of *kuan* is basically constituted by *dou* or villages. Each *kuan* has its head, and the head of a *kuan* is decided by the heads from several *dou*. The head of a large *kuan* is elected by several small *kuan*, and the head of an extra-large *kuan* by several large *kuan*. The duty of *kuan* includes setting down the laws, revising the laws, educating the clans to understand the laws, organizing an assembly of *kuan* for punishments and defending the *kuan* by fighting off intruders and offenders. *Kuan* keeps its army, constituted of the young men in the villages, who work there except when fighting.[21] Large and super-large *kuan* were assembled occasionally in particularly urgent periods. In the Tang dynasty (618–907), the super-large *kuan* was assembled by the Dong people of Langxi, Fenshan, Nanshi and Sanlao, including almost all from Guizhou, Hunan and Guangxi provinces, to defend against the intruders of Chu King of Han Chinese. Another super-large *kuan* was assembled in the Ming dynasty (1368–1644), led by Wu Main to fight with the armies of the Ming empire, who mistreated the Dong people.[22]

Kuan (款) and *Kuan* Alliance (款组织)

The creation of the drum tower is closely related to the Dong regulation (*kuan* 款) and its executive organization (*kuan* alliance 款组织), where it is the place for the Dong villagers to be educated and to perform the judgement with the leaders of *kuan* alliance. *Kuan* was the authority law of the Dong before 1949, dealing with the issues or problems between the villages or families and individual activities. The *kuan* alliance includes the head of the village and senior villagers with high reputation. These *kuan* heads were often the wise and intelligent senior people in the village, who usually obtained great respect from the villagers and would help the villagers to go through any difficulties in their lives. Particularly, since each family obtained its independent property and social status, the disputes about land and property within the families, the villagers or with other villages had to be resolved. *kuan* and the *kuan* heads played a central role in judgements about individual deeds while also ordering the whole community. It is interesting that when two villagers or families had troubles, the *kuan* heads were invited to mediate between them to solve the knots made by coarse grass. In order to judge the problem, both the sides were asked to sit down with some knots of couch grass, and the number of knots depended on how many problems they had. Then the *kuan* heads discussed these two troubled sides according to the *kuan* laws. When one of them won part of the argument, one of his knots was released, and the one with more knots left at the end was defeated. The troubles between the two sides were resolved, and they had to submit to the decision made by the *kuan* heads.[23] *Kuan*, as one kind of covenants through pledge, was submitted by each clan of the Dong.[24] As the Dong narrative song says:

(Song leader)

> Originally, when the villagers have no rules and regulations to obey, and the communities have no constitution to reign,
> Good deeds are not rewarded with any praise and bad deeds are not repaid by any punishment;
> There is no ability to solve internal disturbances, and no strength to withstand external aggression.
> The activities of some people are despicable: they would steal vegetables and melons from other people's gardens, and grope for hens and ducks in the bird cages.
> Malicious intent would swell in their hearts.
> They would commit physical assault by day, grasping knives in their hands, and they would rustle cattle and steal horses by night.
> They would strive to cause trouble and create confusion, and would get involved in fierce fighting, killing good people, causing calamity, robbing villages of their peace and tranquillity, until the whole social order became threatened.
> Every villager is yearning for regulations on such disorder; every community is demanding punishment for the wrongdoers.
> Yes, yes! (audients together)
> Then the kuan leader calls the village elders together, and the kuan secretary summones the people to a meeting.
> Everyone assembles at the meeting place and together agree on village regulations,

Killing a buffalo and taking an oath of allegiance to join the kuan and collectively to formulate rules.[25]

The Contents of *Kuan* Laws

In the preliterate Dong society, the *kuan* laws, which are a set of guidelines for the people's behaviour in the form of covenants and prohibitions, only come down by oral recitation. In the Dong areas such as Sanjiang County in Guangxi Province and Tongdao in Hunan Province, the assemblies of educating *kuan*, led and recited by the village heads, the *kuan* heads or the distinguished *kuan* teachers, are usually accompanied by rituals to invite the Sa Spirit, Flying Mountain Spirit and general spirits, symbolizing authority and sacred. The *kuan* assemblies used to be held in spring and autumn every year. The assembly in spring is held at the start of March in the Chinese calendar, named 'Guidelines of Green' (*yue qing* 约青). It means that, while spring is arriving, the plants are getting green and people are very busy, the *kuan* assemblies remind the village about the security of working in the mountains and in the village. The assembly in autumn used to be held at the start of September, also called 'Guidelines of Yellow' (*yue huang* 约黄), where the *kuan* assemblies at this time draw the people's attention to the gathering of the harvest, watching out for thieves. After the harvest in autumn, the ceremonies are followed and held within the villages to worship the ancestors.[26]

The *kuan* law is divided into three sections, including Six Sections of *Yin* (*liu mian Yin gui* 六面阴规), Six Sections of *Yang* (*liu mian Yang gui* 六面阳规) and Six Sections of Authority (*liu mian Wei gui* 六面威规), indicating the domination by God of the six directions: east, west, south, north, above, and below, and implying that the society is involved with all these directions.[27] On one hand, this is a reflection of the inherited Taoist classification system and shows its all-permeating nature; on the other, it strongly suggests that the law needs and possesses spatial directions, creating automatic symbolic associations. The three kinds of *kuan* law associated with both major and minor crimes often generally involve damaging mountains and jungles, a tomb or a wall, the fields or the ponds; stealing money, grain, fish, plants, hens or geese, timber or water from others; cheating, stealing, arson and murder; and breaking with customs or traditions. The *kuan* laws of *Liu Mian Yin Gui* are usually associated with very serious crimes, involving punishment by death. The laws of *Liu Mian Yang Gui* are associated with crimes that are serious but do not deserve death penalty, and the major penalty is expulsion from the village for the criminal deeds. One frequent form of compensation for an offender is to kill a pig, to cook it and to share its meat among all households in the community, making sense of educating everyone to learn from the errors of others and to avoid such behaviour in future. A lesser penalty related to the law of *Liu Mian Wei Gui* involves respecting and being polite to each other.[28]

The order of the Dong society is maintained by the punishment rules. One special feature of punishment in the traditional Dong *kuan* system is that punishment must be conducted by the family of the offender, where the purpose is to draw attention not only to the family of the offender but also to the whole society, celebrating the seriousness of the crime, though it was more difficult for the families of the offenders to execute a relative. Not far from Gaoding village, for instance, there is a lonely grave on the Sanxing Hill with a moss lawn, in which a young Dong man named Wu Hongmiao was buried. In 1933, Wu Hongmiao occasionally stole from villager's houses, and was punished with execution in the village drum tower. He was a good Dong singer, and it was his first act of theft. Although the village head and all the villagers believed that Wu should be forgiven by a light punishment with a fine of 40 *liang* in silver, Wu Hongmiao himself insisted that he had offended the *kuan* law of stealing in villages, and asked for the punishment of death. His only request was to sing a Dong song before the death execution. According to *kuan* law, he was buried alive by his clan in the mountain. Although he is dead, his lonely grave and his songs still remind quietly the Dong people of the power of *kuan* law in the Dong society.[29]

The plan and orientation of the drum tower are generally conceived to be associated with the legend of the Dongs' original spirit Sa Sui. Sa Sui is the most important deity treated with the most serious respect, which are figured in many songs, myths and legends. As the narrative song *Sa Sui Ye* (admiration Sa Spirit songs 萨岁耶)[30] sings:

> Originally who gives birth to Sa Sui?
> Who gives birth to Sa Yang?[31]
> Who gives birth to Tai Yi in the heaven?
> Who gives birth to Zhang Liang[32] in the world?
>
> Originally Lao Gong gives birth to Sa Sui,
> Tong Luo[33] kisses the ground and gives birth to Sa Yang,
> Tai Bai gives birth to Tai Yi in the heaven,
> And Song En[34] gives birth to Jiang Liang in the world.
> Who attempts to make trouble in the heaven?
> Who attempts to make trouble in mountains and rivers?
> Who attempts to make chaos in the court and made trouble in the mountain ranges?
> Who leads Sa Sui here from the upper world? Where do they arrive at here marked with three rocks?
> Who kisses the ground and beats it with three hammers?
> What is presented to Sa Sui with twelve folds?
> Are you sure that you are able to sing the Sa Sui Song?
>
> The Heaven God creates trouble in the heaven,
> Tiger creates trouble in mountains and dragon in rivers,

The Drum Towers as the Cosmological Centre of Separation and Reunion 85

The emperor makes chaos the court and cock makes trouble on mountain ranges,
Sa Sui is led by the Dipper in the northern sky,
Arriving at the river marked with three rocks,
Tong Luo kisses the ground and beats it with three hammers,
The fan with twelve folds is presented to Sa Sui,
What I begin to sing is the Sa Sui Song.

Originally where is the Sa Sui altar from?
Where is she going to from the upper world about 7000 miles away?
Who is invited to build the house temple?
Who is invited to build the foundation?
Who invites Sa Sui to stay?
Where to stay when she arrives at our village?

Originally the Sa Sui altar is constructed in Shang Tang,[35]
Sa Sui comes down from the upper world over 7000 miles away,
Kuan Gong[36] is invited to build the temple house,
Wang Shu[37] is invited to make the foundation,
The Dipper stars are invited to persuade Sa Sui to stay,
She is led to the village and stands on the zi (子) place.[38]

Originally who rides on the horse across the south sea?
Who falls down from the dragon?
Who dresses in special?
Who dresses well and stands at the centre of the village?

Originally Sa Sui rides on horse across the south sea,
Sa Sui comes down from the dragon with her umbrella,
Sa Sui dresses in special,
She dresses well and stands in the centre of the village.

Who is the most powerful spirit in the villages of six countries?
Who dresses in special?
Who dresses well and shines thousands of miles away?
Who meets her and witnesses her presence?

Sa Sui is the most powerful spirit in the villages of six countries?
Sa Sui dresses in special,
Sa Sui dresses well and shining thousands of miles away,
I am sure that I see her.[39]

The origins of Sa Spirit and creation of the drum tower are described in the *ye song* (耶歌). According to Wu, the song tells the birth of Sa Sui associated with the sun, for she comes from the sky, and she is directed to the living

86 *The Drum Towers as the Cosmological Centre of Separation and Reunion*

world by the seven stars. The sun is believed to hide at night in the north by the ancient people. When the sun comes, the moon leaves, but the temple house built by the moon spirit remains for the sun. Sa Sui would cross the south sea in *chou* (丑) direction[40] by riding on a dragon horse, which is similar to the ancient record of the origins of the sun spirit. In the *yin* (寅) direction[41] are two objects marked by Sa Sui: the fan with twelve folds and the umbrella, creating the shape of sunshine, and is believed by the Dong to imply the sunshine of the spirit. In the *mao* (卯) direction[42] Sa Sui is dressed specially, her brilliance reaching thousands of miles away, symbolizing the sunshine.[43] All the myths indicate that Sa Sui is possibly one of the spirits from the heaven similar to the sun spirit, coming to the Dong village by the route of sun movement, and thus she becomes one of the most powerful spirits in Dong society, bringing fortune and flourish to the Dong villages.[44]

The Mapang Drum Tower as the Ritual Space

It is possible that the lay-out of Mapang drum tower is elaborately planned by the legend in the narrative song of *Sa Sui Ye*. It follows the path to Mapang village and goes on the stone staircase up to twenty steps to the Mapang drum tower (Figure 3.8). The drum tower has seats on the four cardinal directions, with the entrance façade on the west. However, the gate of the drum tower, also serving as the entrance of Mapang village, is offset from the axis of the communal building, oriented to the northwest. The village gate is simply set

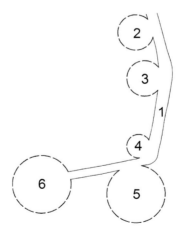

Figure 3.8 The ritual routine of Mapang villagers (drawn by author):
1. the path access to the village;
2. the large house;
3. *fengshui* tree;
4. the gate of Mapang drum tower;
5. Mapang drum tower;
6. the square of drum tower.

The Drum Towers as the Cosmological Centre of Separation and Reunion 87

Figure 3.9 The stairs accessing to the Mapang drum tower gate, Sanjiang, 2004.

up with eight columns and covered by a gable roof. The gate is opened to the visitors, with two wooden door panels fixed by two columns on both sides, leaving the middle space as the aisle, exhibiting a gesture of welcoming the visitors (Figure 3.9). Crossing the threshold of the entrance gate, one reaches the northern façade of the drum tower. The door of Mapang drum tower opens on the west, adjacent to the drum tower square.

According to the Dong narrative songs, the plan and orientation of the Mapang drum tower is conceived to associate with the Fengshui principles of *Yin/Yang* and the Five-element. In the Fengshui practice with the compass, the quarter of the northeast is believed to be the most dangerous orientation (Figure 3.10). On the compass, the four cardinal orientations are marked by the heavenly stems and the earthly branches,[45] with *zi* 子 designated to north, *wu* 午 to south, *mao* 卯 to east and *you* 酉 to west. In between the four cardinal points, *chou* 丑 and *yin* 寅 are designated to northeast, *chen* 辰 and *si* 巳 to southeast, *wei* 未 and *shen* 申 to southwest, and *xun* 巽 and *hai* 亥 to northwest, dominating the other four quarters. According to the

Fengshui Compass School, the quarter of northwest (*qian* 乾) is the heaven gate, southeast (*xun* 巽) the earth gate, southwest (*kun* 坤) the human gate and northeast (*gen* 艮) the hell gate, which is marked by *chou* 丑 and *yin* 寅, and between *zi* 子 and *mao* 卯. In the view of five-elements, *zi* 子 represents water, locates in the north, and relates with the colour of black, the season of winter, November and night, which symbolizes *yin*. *Mao* 卯 represents wood, locates in the east, its colour belonging to cyan, season to spring, and the month is February and morning, which belongs to *yang*. Accordingly, in the quarter of northeast, located between *zi* 子 and *mao* 卯, is essential, which means transfer from 'north *yin*' to 'east *yang*'. Furthermore, *zi* 子 means birth and increase, and belongs to *ren* 壬 and *gui* 癸. While belonging to *zi* 子 direction, it carries the meanings of pregnancy and encompassing, and accordingly, *zi* 子 refers to pregnancy. *Jia* 甲 and *yi* 乙, which belong to *mao* 卯, refer to the hard shell broken by the seed, stretching and extending, and so *mao* 卯 possibly means birth and the initiation of everything. Thus, the quarter of northeast, crossing from *zi* 子 to *mao* 卯 and occupying the space from North to East on the compass, is believed to be the abnormal boundary of *yin* and *yang* for birth. It is conceived as the hell gate not only in orientations but also in time and seasons, meaning that if crossing it successfully, spring arrives and birth is initiated.[46] Thus, the gate of the Mapang village and drum tower is located to the northwest possibly carrying the symbolic meanings as the threshold, separating the *yin* and *yang*, the heaven and the earth, the living world and the dead world, inside and outside and providing a space for human transformation in between.

Identified with the drum tower, the Sa Sui altar is the place of worshipping the Dong Goodness, quite modest and simply built inside or beside the drum tower. With several round stones and wooden sticks inside symbolizing hatching eggs, the Dong believe they come from the turtle's eggs. The Sa Sui altar and drum tower are typical representations of matriarchal and patriarchal society that the Dong has been through in the primitive period.[47] *Tang sa* is the place for the Dong to worship the Sa Sui spirit, which is the original ancestor of the Dong and is respected by the Dong people. In the legends of the Dong, the matriarchal society was ruled by Sa Sui. Grandmother is pronounced as 'Sa' in the Dong Language, and it is the name for all the Dong goddesses. Among all the spirits worshipped by the Dong, Sa is ranked at the top of the spirits in the hierarchy, and also called 'Sa Sui', 'Sa Ma' or 'Sa Ma Qing Sui'. Apart from the Sa Sui spirit, there are other Sa spirits associated with the Dong life. Sa Yang is also the original spirit of the village, and is the spirit of the harvest of grain and wine; Sa Mian is the original ancestor of the Dong, incubating the turtle's eggs when the first Dong were born; Shi Sa Hualin is in charge of fertility, which is responsible for delivering the flowers to the living world from the dead world, where the flowers symbolize the reincarnation of souls; Sa Jingmei is the ancestor spirit who saved the Dong society from a flood disaster, and she is also the spirit of marriage among the Dong people; Sa Yi is responsible for wind, rain and thunder; Sa Gaoqiao is the guardian spirit for the souls

The Drum Towers as the Cosmological Centre of Separation and Reunion   89

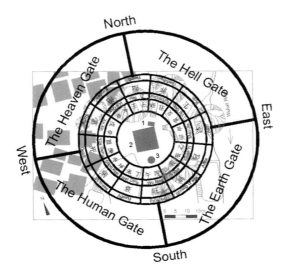

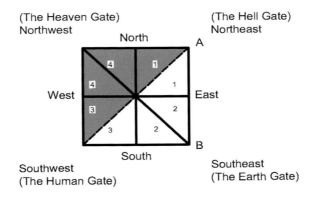

Figure 3.10 (top) The orientation of the Mapang drum tower and its gate oriented by the *fengshui* compass. (bottom) The auspicious and inauspicious orientation on the *fengshui* compass (drawn by author).

passing through the bridge, worshipped on the entrance of Wind and Rain bridges; and Sa Tudui is the locality spirit, in charge of the security of the mountains, forests and fields.[48]

The gates of Mapang village and drum tower are also shelters of the Sa Sui altar. The Sa Shui altar under the village gate roof is similar to the other one built on the open space to the south of the drum tower. Both altars are constructed with a square base and are open on top; the structure provides shelter to Sa spirit worshipped by the Dong people. The cube-like base on the ground, with sides 1.0m long, 0.73m wide and height 0.9m, forms a foundation composed of piled-up stones, on which the upper altar, constructed of bricks, rest. The upper altar serves as a container to keep the offerings by the villagers, including burning incense, wine, tea and roasted pork or chicken. The offerings such as a half-open umbrella and cobblestones from the river are placed on the top of the altar, symbolizing the Sa Sui spirit of the life-giving Goddess.

Setting up the Sa Sui altar involves a series of ceremonies, and the offerings would be placed properly in their special directions with the symbolic meanings.[49] In Chinese legends, a day is divided into twelve hours, responding to the activities of the twelve animals in Chinese zodiac. On the top of the altar, north side *zi* (子) belongs to eleven to one o'clock in the morning, occupied by five cobblestones of the Sa altar. The white stones are burned on the altar in the ceremony, and then buried under the Sa altar. The white stones are similar to the sun, and create fire when they are in friction with each other, inspiring the Dong to make fire. Because the Fire Spirit comes from the sun, the cobblestone possibly has the symbolic meanings to representing the Sun Spirit. On the northeast corner (*chou* 丑) is the sacrifice of cock with three feet, by inserting one more cock leg into one of the two legs to identify with the common cock. The three legged-cock might symbolize the distinguished Bird Spirit as the messenger, which is capable of communicating with the gods in the sky for the people on the earth. According to the *San Hai Jing*, the sun is also named as a *yang* bird with three feet, because the sun rises by the back of three feet birds. In Chinese legends, the sun is a kind of bird, which has the capacity to fly with its wings. Once ten suns in the sky kept shining on the earth and people almost melted down. A hero called Hou Yi (后羿) appeared and shot down the nine suns, leaving one of them hurt, and hid in the forest. However, people on the earth needed the sun to survive. The phoenix came out and discovered the sun. She healed the sun, and carries him, rising from the east and down in the west every day before he recovers. One day, the sun got stronger and ready to rise by himself, the phoenix pushed him hard to the sky, and is burnt down by the sun. *you* (酉) time on the compass refers to five to six o'clock in the afternoon, and the cock in Chinese twelve zodiac belongs to you (酉). A man born in *you* (酉) year *you* (酉) month and *you* (酉) time symbolizes the phoenix and is also associated with the appearance of the sun bird, and so he is a desirable person to light up the first light of the altar fire.[50]

The northeast corner of the altar is *yin* (寅) direction, occupying three to five o'clock in the morning on the compass, and is occupied by a white goat, representing the Sa Shui spirit of the Dong. In some places such as Sangjiang and Dudong County, while setting up the Sa altar, a white goat is fed and taken care of by the whole village, respected like a senior and named Sa. The coat of the goat should be white like snow without any other colour; holes are made in both sides of its ears and tied with five-colour threads, symbolizing the Sa Sui Spirit which brings fertility and fortune to the village. In the east direction *mao* (卯) from five to seven o'clock in the morning is owned by an umbrella usually put on the top of the altar, half opened and a boxwood tree is planted beside it. It represents sunrise and sunshine appearing with Goddess Sa, shining on the Dong villages forever. In many communal communications, it is believed that if the headman brings a leaf from a boxwood tree and carries an open umbrella with him, he is able to get rid of evil and harvest good fortune for the village. On the southeast corner *chen* (辰), from nine to eleven o'clock in the morning, where a round stick, rice cakes and carp fish are offered. All the offerings carry the symbolic meanings of good fortune and fertility. People who take care of these altars would be the descendants from the lineage of the village or are chosen by divining. Each family in the village would contribute 1.5 kg rice each month to the villagers who look after the drum tower and the Sa altars.[51]

Many rituals are involved in building or repairing a Sa Sui altar. In the Dong areas of Lipin County and Congjiang County in Guizhou Province, if a new village is to be built, or if a village has been built without setting up a Sa altar, or while the altar has to be rebuilt, a ceremony named *jie huo zhong* (welcome the kindling 接火种) would be performed by the whole village. Three days before the ceremony is held, the village gate is closed to neighbouring villages, and entertainment is not allowed in the village. Before setting up the altar, fires in the village are not allowed to light up for three days, and the whole village lives under darkness during these days. No family is allowed to cook, and all they could eat is instant food, such as sticky rice cakes (*zong zi* 粽子), acid fish and meat, which used to be offerings to worship the Sa Sui Spirit. A similar Welcome Kindling ceremony is also held in the Longsheng County in Guangxi province.[52] The fire from Sa Sui also has a significant symbolic meaning of flourishing life, which symbolizes that the Dong society will continue forever. Sa Sui not only belongs to one surname or kinship group, but is the guardian spirit to the whole village. Every family comes to the altar to worship the Sa Sui spirit, and to invite the kindling to light their homes up, which means that they are all the descendants of Sa Sui, because they sustain the fire of the Sa Sui spirit for the family lineage.[53] People believe that if they obtain the first kindling from Sa Sui to their homes, the Sa Sui spirit would bless every generation to be fertile and continue their *xiang huo* (incense and fire 香火). On the day of the ceremony, senior people over 60 years old are invited to sit around the altar to sing about the origins of the Dong. Senior women on the stage wear silver earrings, bracelets and necklaces. On the last ceremony day, a young man is chosen to climb up to the tallest Fengshui tree in the village to collect bird's nests, which is piled up on fir sticks, and kindling for the altar. At the midnight of this day, a man whose birthday is exactly the same as the ceremony day, named 'being born with the sky and earth', would kindle the fire with the original method, by rubbing a metal hook on the stone. He makes a light at first, and then the fire is burned in the Sa Sui altar.

The Ceremonies around the Drum Tower

The *yue ye* (月也) Ceremony is held every Chinese New Year, the first day of the first month of the Chinese calendar. The communal ceremony is hosted by a village to welcome visitors from guest villages. In the Dong language, '*yue*' means visiting between villages, and '*ye*' means friends. On the ceremony day, the *lu sheng* group of guest village performs the 'assembly song' on the square in front of the drum tower, and the visiting villagers assemble quickly in a queue on the square. They appear in similar costumes: men dress in the traditional blue Dong costume of white trousers with a gun hung on the shoulder and a calabash on the back; women dress in blue clothes made and dyed by themselves, wearing silver necklaces decorated with five colour-headdress to manifest auspicious and fertile expectation. The Dong cloth is wrapped around the head as a hat, which is decorated with a feather from a cock's tail, called 'cock tail guest'. The event involves everyone in the village, either young or senior, male or female. The number of the visitors depends on the size of the village, and usually, there are about a hundred participants in a large village; but sometimes there are only about twenty to thirty in a small village. The leaders of the visitor are well- appearing specially: the principal leader of the team wears a red cape, holds a red umbrella in his hand, and carries a Fengshui compass in front; the associate leader of the team is a young man, but he would appear like a woman and also wear a colourful cape, representative of the Sa Sui Spirit; and the other three leaders would have swords with them, and show them when they arrive at the host village. The leaders are followed by the *lu sheng* group and other participants. Before they leave for the ceremony, they need to worship the Sa Sui altar in their own village. On the way to the guest village, the Attending Song and Leading Song are played by their *lu sheng* team. Arriving at the host village, they take positions to hold the Stepping on the Singing Stage ceremony on the square of the drum tower.[54]

It is interesting that the Blocking the Way ceremony would be held in the host village boundary, either in the entrance of Wind and Rain bridge or the gate of village or drum tower, before being allowed to get into the host village (Figure 3.11). Performance of the Blocking the Way ceremony announces the start of the Dong's communal ceremony to who would like to attend, not only to the villagers but also to the spirits. The guests sing the song with auspicious words, expressing their desire to get permission into the village to communicate with the host villagers. Once again it celebrates the special relation between the bridge or the village gate and the drum tower—as the boundary and the village centre.

Walking near the gate of the host village, the leader of visiting group picks up a bunch of reeds, distributes them to each villager, and each one inserts it on his hat to identify them with the host villagers. The *lu sheng* group starts the Informing Song, sending the message that the visitors have come a long way to arrive at the village. They expect to meet the *lu sheng* group of the host village, because they would cooperate in the next few days of ceremony. Then a Picking up the Vegetable Song is played to make sure they are welcome while they are staying in the village. The villagers of the host village stand on both sides of the path from the drum tower to the village gate to welcome their friends, with the *lu sheng* team led by their leader. While they

Figure 3.11 Young men in the Blocking the Way ceremony carrying with a calabash and a gun, the symbols of manhood, Sanjiang, 1985 (photo: Mei Ling).

are meeting the visitors at the village gate, they play Welcome Song and Mushroom Song, which means that the visitors are very welcome, and the guests are served with the Dong rice wine in the assembly, and mushroom in dinner, a vegetable that grows abundantly in the mountainous villages of the Dong (Figure 3.12).

Joining the cluster of the host villagers, all the people then go to the drum tower. Led by their leaders, the guest villagers first walk around the drum tower square three times to show their respect, and the leader needs to decide the location for singing and dancing with his Fengshui compass. When he arrives at the proper directions of *zi* 子(north) and *wu* 午(south) on the compass, he stops, seating on the south and facing north, and spinning the umbrella in his hand. The teams of dancers from the host village and guest village parade into the square from the drum tower gate in the north under his guidance, with *lu sheng*'s blowing the Stepping into the Stage Song. With the *lu sheng* music, all the people in the group step into the square in a single row, preparing to perform the most notable ceremony to worship the Sa Sui Spirit.[55]

The most striking stage of the ceremony is called *cai ge tang* (stepping on the singing stage 踩歌堂) or named *duo ye ji sa* (singing and dancing ceremony for worshipping Sa Sui 多耶), which is an important public

Figure 3.12 Young women welcoming the guests in the Blocking the Way ceremony wearing with colourful decoration on their heads, implying the fertility of the female, Sanjiang, 1985 (photo: Mei Ling).

communication among the Dong villages. '*duo*' has the meaning of singing and dancing, and '*ye*' is one kind of Dong song. The *cai ge tang* ceremony is on one hand to worship their ancestor Sa spirit, and on the other hand, is a festival for all the young people together to communicate with each other and finally lead to a courtship or a marriage. The ceremony could be held sometimes between two villages or two kinships in the same village. Sometimes it is also held by a group of men going out to visit other villages to sing and dance, leaving women in their village to welcome people from other neighbouring villages.[56] This is a really exciting moment for the whole village, for each surname, kinship, family and even for each person who really expect to attend the ceremony enthusiastically, to distinguish them from other nationalities and show their responsibility for their nationality, villages and kinships. In various rituals, dancing is often the essential action in the reciprocal rituals, which offers entertainment and respect to the spirits and pray for blessing and protection by them. With *lu sheng* music, the *cai ge tang* ceremony begins. The priest of the host village sings to start the Welcoming Song to invite the Sa Spirit to the ceremony:

> Coming to sing on the stage,
> Stepping on the outdoor singing stage with hand in hand.

> With first step on the left and second on the right,
> You sing with my answer in happiness.
> Before stepping on the stage, we need our original grandmother's leading,
> With her leading, everyone would be happy.
> Like the carp fishes travelling outside their nest,
> Wandering in the clear pond;
> Like the thrush birds flying out of the forest,
> Singing the songs as much as they want.
>
> Singing on the stage needs the leading of our grandmother,
> With her leading, we obtain the support like a rock;
> She would let us step in order,
> And hundreds of *ye* songs sung from our hearts.
> People's hearts are connected by hand in hand,
> Like thousands of pieces of palm tied into a string.
>
> We worship *Sa* every year although we don't know where she is,
> It is said that she is in an auspicious place;
> Invite her to come to bless the whole village,
> Bless us with fertility and fortune.
> White stone bricks construct the grandmother's altar,
> With our grandmother, we are fortunate.
> Grandmother! The world is in chaos everywhere,
> And you would not go to the other place,
> Please be staying here forever,
> You would live with us together.
>
> If Grandmother settles down in our village,
> The evil spirits would leave us.
> With our grandmother,
> Every family would have good fortune.[57]

Then the narrative songs about her life are answered by both the host and guest villages. Turning around the Stage song follows the Stepping into the Stage song for young men and young women. Sometimes the leader sings with others as a chorus, and sometimes there is just a chorus. Many famous Dong songs are initiated in this ceremony:

> I come to the singing stage with my lover in the New Year's Day,
> A moment of good fortune is coming with the songs.
> With smile put on their faces,
> People whether old or young, male or female all come to see us stepping on the stage.
> Your questions with my answers,

My heart is just like sweet rice wine mixed with honey;
Everyone would be happy in the blessing of our goddess,
The great harvest makes people feel much joyfulness.
Today people sing *Duo Ye* songs, which give people much energy to work.
The hard-working family would lack nothing, instead fulfilled with more songs and much harvest.

I come to the singing stage with my lover in the New Year's Day,
And we have a good time while singing and dancing;
Grandmother's spirit would accompany us joyfully,
People of the whole village would celebrate and rejoice.
The society would be blessed with peace and abundance of food and clothing.
The field would not be barren with everybody working hard.
Seeds are planted in the spring,
Harvest would be in autumn.
Grandmother would feel joyful for us,
And she brings good fortune to us.[58]

Following the start of greeting songs, the next performance is dancing on the stage. While the dance scene is taking place on the square, three circular tracks are created by the dancers (Figure 3.13). Young men take the outside, which symbolizes *yang*, the heaven and the sun; young women occupy the middle circle, representing *yin*, the earth and the moon; and the seniors sit in the middle. Offerings are placed in the centre. Corresponding to the rhythms of the Dong songs, young men and young women move shoulder to shoulder and hand in hand. The two circles move in opposite directions, surrounding senior people in the centre, and imitating the movement of the sun's daily course from east to the west, and the moon from the west to the east.[59] The dancing route is called *chai shui e* (踩岁俄), and it is believed that, if people step exactly on the *zi* (子) and *wu* (午) positions, they are blessed by the Sa spirit. The performance route of the Dong in their ceremony is possibly the imitation of the running route of the sun, and the circle movement dance represents the sun, manifesting lighting, and bringing energy and good fortune to the village.[60] Within their songs, the communication between the general spirits, their ancestors, their kin, and the natural world are processing. Their ceremony is combined with a united ethnic group, which hold a collective belief of being descendants under blessing of the Sa Sui spirit. They appreciate their life-giving spirit Sa Sui, and with her blessing, the incense and fire of their kin and villages would be renewed with fertile descendants.

At the end of the *Duo Ye* ceremony, people are reluctant to leave. So the song leader has to sing the *shan tang ye* (dismissing singing stage songs 散堂耶)[61] to announce the ending. As he sings:

The Drum Towers as the Cosmological Centre of Separation and Reunion 97

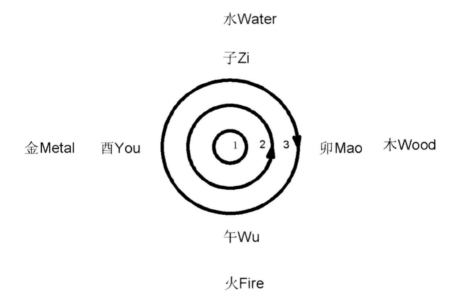

Figure 3.13 (top) The villagers dancing in the *duoye* ceremony, Sanjiang, 1985 (photo: Mei Ling). (bottom) the routine of dancing people (drawn by author): (1) The center for the senior villagers; (2) Middle circle for the young women; (3) The young men dancing in the outside circle.

> Finishing Ye Ge (ceremony songs), people are going to be dismissed,
> Not like the baby pigs out of the shed.
> Baby pigs leave for their food,
> although they have heads, no mind and wouldn't miss each other.
> We are still keeping close touch although set part,
> How do we not weep?
>
> Today we sing a sending off song,
> Not like baby geese leaving on the river.
> Although baby geese grow up on the river,
> they separate to build up their own family.
> We are still friends although have to be separated,
> How do we not weep?
>
> Young men and women have to be separated after the singing in the night,
> Like the seeds that are planted in the fourth month and transplanted
>   in the fifth month.
> Like the sun rising in the east and setting in the west,
> Brothers come back at home and are separated from sisters in the
>   daybreak.
> Young girls still sitting here please leave for home,
> Young boys living far from here please say goodbye to girls.
> Like the cloud floating in the sky,
> Brothers would love to talk with sisters with endless speeches.
> We would make a date later after separating,
> If possible, we would like to make a date tomorrow night.[62]

These narrative songs reflect the close relationship that has been built up between these villages. Although they temporarily separate, they would reunite in the feature. As an animism belief society, the song leaders never ignore the spirits which have attended the performance, and they also need to sing dismissive songs to show respect and send off the spirits. It is believed that, in the singing ceremony, every spirit would manifest to listen to them. The moving narrative songs not only attract the birds of forest to come, but also spirits from the *yin* world, who would meet behind people. If the song leader forgets to sing the songs to send off every spirit to return to its place and birds to their forest, or being rude while dismissing them, they would not only stay at the singing stage to make trouble, cheer or weep, but also lead to a result of hurting the village. As the song leader sings:

> Please leave the singing stage,
> People go home and birds to forests;
> It is full of frost and dew,
> Spirits please leave for their belongings;
> Please leave, please,
> Animals and spirits please go back to your places.[63]

The Drum Towers as the Cosmological Centre of Separation and Reunion 99

When the ceremony is completed, the guests remain in the village to sleep over for one night. Firecrackers are set off again to announce the ending of the ceremony, and people from the families of host village come to the square to welcome the guests to stay in their homes. The colourful sticky rice cakes are put in new bamboo baskets by young women and presented to young men. The guest villagers are surrounded by the young men and young women hosts who try to grab the feather or couch grass from their guests' hats, which is called 'robbing a guest'. Every person is proud to have a guest to stay in his or her home for the night, and a big meal of sour fish, pork meat, gluten rice with rice alcohol would be served. In the night after dinner, the village is getting noisy again. Standing on the balcony of the house, you would see some young boys and girls wandering on the path of the village and singing love songs with their *niu tui qing* (the Dong music instrument like a calf leg 牛腿琴).[64] The lovers have had dates with each other. With the fire burning in the drum tower, the famous Dong narrative songs just begin in the balconies of the timber-suspended house.[65]

The Communal Meals and the Carrying the Official (*tai guan ren* 抬官人) Ceremony

The *Yue Ye* festival ends with an exciting ceremony named *tai guan ren* (抬官人 carrying the official), performed by the guest villagers (Figure 3.14).[66] A communal meal on the day is served on the drum tower square, contributed by the host villagers with traditional Dong food such as pickled

Figure 3.14 The *tai guan ren* Ceremony, Sanjiang, 1985 (photo: Mei Ling).

sour fishes, gluten rice cakes and rice alcohol (Figure 3.15). Before the meal, there is a singing competition of Dong *Kuan*. Usually, the young girls of the host village sing in opposition to the young men from the guest village, and the young men of the hosts to the young girls of the guests, offering them an opportunity to meet and hopefully leading to their courtship. The competition is carried on throughout the meal. A young man is selected on behalf of the guest village to recite *kuan*, the contents including the origins of the heaven and the earth, the Dong ancestors, the musical instrument *lu sheng*, the history of 'splitting up the surname in marriage', the present *kuan* laws and to express their appreciation of the hospitality. While drinking the rice alcohol, the girls of the host village initiate the singing stage to challenge the guests, and the guests would answer their questions in songs, appreciating the hostility of the village, the songs involving almost

Figure 3.15 A communal meal served to the guests in the drum tower square after the ceremony, Sanjiang, 2018 (photo: Weiye Li).

everything such as the bowls of food, chopsticks, rice alcohol and meats. Whoever is not able to respond and carry on the songs would be 'punished' with a cup of wine.[67]

In the *tai guan ren* ceremony, a young man appears as an official dressed up in a grey costume, sitting on a bamboo chair which is carried by four people, and arriving at the host village crowded with a cluster of young people. When they arrive at the host village gate, five young men are first sent to inform the leader of the host village with a red paper note: "I am glad to hear that you are celebrating your New Year festival. I am coming to congratulate you with my fellows. May God bless you!" On obtaining this message, the villagers led by their head go to the village gate to welcome them. After letting off of three fireworks, the group of people including the 'official', his 'wife' and several young men with guns and swords in their hands are welcomed and led to the drum tower. The people following the 'official' are dressed in the appearance of ancestors, ghosts, soldiers and beggars. Some of the men dress like women, some appear with black faces with the images of tiger and lion decorated on their bodies, and some dress up with skirts made with grass and leaves. When the official group arrives at the drum tower, they would show their respect by walking around the drum tower three times. Meanwhile, the *lu sheng* team blow their *lu sheng*, burn the fireworks and serve them with tea and water. After the 'official' has finished his cup of tea, he would appreciate being served with lucky money in red envelopes. While they are ready to leave, some people appear as 'robbers' and block the way again. Then, 'beggars' appear to ask for lucky money, the villagers would dismiss the lucky money to them. They are stopped on their way by the young girls who sing and dance in the *duo ye* ceremony with their songs:

> Where did the 'official' come from?
> You are really a handsome gentleman.
> Your ears look like two auspicious fans,
> And your wide face looks like a bright bronze mirror.
> You should distribute all your money to people,
> Because I have never heard of any 'official' who wouldn't try to help their people.[68]

Various young girls continue to sing to block their way, until the 'official' distributes all his money. Then the people who are following the 'official' act in a comic way. They dance around the leader in chao, imitating hunting, collecting and fishing activities from primitive times. While they are dancing, they walk towards the drum tower square. People usually play tricks on the leader, who is still carried on their shoulders; sometimes they speed up, and sometime slow down and sometimes turn to the left, but sometimes to the right. The people appeared in ancestors still dance around him without stopping. When they arrive at the pond near a grain field, they throw the official into the pond. As if the spirit has fallen down to the pond, where the villagers believe that good fortune would stay and bless their village. After the 'official' begs and makes promises, people drag him out and respect him again. Then people dance around the grain field, and sing:

> Stepping into the square,
> I sing this paragraph and you would continue the next.
> The torrential river is running down,
> But bamboo would grow up.
>
> Oil tea would be renewed for such a long time,
> Water in a jar would be changed lest it grow sour tasting.
> We are bored with the songs while stepping onto the dance ground,
> for we have sung them too long,
> Now we turn to sing the spring songs.
>
> In the first month of New Year,
> Tobacco shouldn't be planted on the field,
> Because the earth would be used for growing the grain,
> On which people would depend.
>
> In the second month,
> Cabbage shouldn't be planted in the field,
> And sesame replaces cotton,
> Because food and clothing both are not neglected.
>
> In the third month,
> The sun is rising in the sky,
> With its sunshine,
> Shining on the roof of the house.
> It pushes us to go to work,
> preparing the fertilizer for the seeding.
> People expect for harvest,
> They are only able to sing after they harvest an abundance of food.
>
> In the fourth month,
> The sun hangs in the west, shining on the hemp sticks.
> The white hemps grow up every day,
> The green waves of seeding turn over the field,
> With the spring sunshine pushing us young people,
> working hard rather than just at play.
> Young persons would work with their loves on the growing up grain,
> And marriage depends on food and clothing.[69]

The Drum Towers as the Cosmological Centre of Separation and Reunion

After singing, the 'official' and his fellows walk around the field with the crowd of people. The 'official' group also includes many young girls with traditional Dong dress, decorated with silver and cock feathers on their hats. These girls hold umbrellas in their right hands and a basket in their left hands with gluten rice cakes in it. During the ceremony, they are responsible for distributing the foods to the village heads and the dancing young men, which is called 'distortable flowers of fairies' (*xian nv san hua* 仙女散花). After they have run out of food, the 'official' group is sent off to the village gate by the *lu sheng* team of the host village, and the *tai guan ren* ceremony is ended. The guests pick up their *lu sheng* and baskets and prepare to leave the village. Yet before they leave, they would sing three songs to appreciate the hosts. The hosts send off the guests at the village gate, with both groups singing the Blocking the Way and Unblocking the Way songs to express reluctance to the guests. It is interesting that the hosts would present the guests a gift of pig's head with a meaning: if the pig's head is not adjacent to a tail, in Chinese it means 'good start and perfect ending'(*you tou you wei* 有头有尾), and their relationship would continue, where the guests would be invited for the next ceremony; but if the pig's head is adjacent to a tail, it means 'good start but no ending' (*you tou mei wei* 有头没尾) and their relationships are perhaps ended.[70]

The Dong people commemorate the work of daily life through the special Carrying the Official ceremony to request blessings from the sprits for harvest. The journey of the ceremony demonstrates a sacred action. The people in the display become the representation of a series of spirit beings, and they present their journey on this world from another world just in order to bring fortune and wealth to the village. They are particularly welcome, and people are constantly excited by their appearance, movement and dramatic appeals. The routine of their journey involves the village entrance to the ritual centre—drum tower, and then around the grain fields, and their footprints are left everywhere in the village. With the ritual experience, what is important is that the village and the participants perceive that they all receive the blessings of the gods while the ritual happens.

It is very interesting that the Blocking the Way ceremony is repeatedly performed on the occasion of the event, reflecting the strong wishes of the Dong people for abundance and fertility. Thus, the primitives pursue their saviours to acquire effectiveness for sustainable good fortune. For an agricultural society, growing and hunting for the food all depend on the uncertain natural world, and circumstance of difficulties and illnesses depend on ceremonies ended with the expectation of restoration. The Dong narrative songs linked to the myth of the Creation of the World would always concern fertility, childbirth, illness cures, agricultural activities and so on. These ceremonies and rituals actually constitute the rites of passage in the critical moment of Dong's life, and lead to the origins and construction of the Dong drum towers.

Conclusion

As the village centre of the Dong, the drum tower plays an essential role in the communal rituals, to worship the gods of their traditional cosmology and keep the order in the Dong's life. Architecture is often carried with it spiritual and emotional loads, and set up as a ritual space of influence by giving particular meanings to sites in terms of the cultural context, making an ethnic domain visible. The ethnic group is defined by Barth as a "largely biologically self-perpetuating" group, which shares fundamental cultural values that are realized in overt unity in cultural forms, making up a field of communication and interaction, and identifying himself and being identified by others with their particular membership.[71] According to Fredrik Barth, the cultural contents of ethnic distinctions include two aspects, which are "overt signals or signs", referring to the diacritical features such as dress, language, house form or general style of life, which people look for to show identity; and "basic value orientations", referring to the standards of morality and excellence by which performance is judged.[72] Of these characteristics, the most important to the culture-bearing units is sharing of a common culture. So people belonging to an ethnic category would share unchanged values and ideas, even when they are spread over a territory with various ecological environments, and faced with different opportunities. The features that are considered are not only ecological variations, but also those cultural traits that are regarded as most significant. Rapoport compares the built environment of two different cultures of ethnic groups in southwestern United States, the Pueblo Indians and the Navajo, although sharing the similar topography, climate and the constraints of materials and technology, their buildings are identified within the context of their distinguished culture. As Rapoport argues, for any given physical forces, the determination of the form of dwellings is socio-cultural forces.[73]

The drum tower provides ritual space for the Dong community, and the gate of drum tower is particularly built as the boundary for the 'Blocking the Way' ceremony. Boundary serves to indicate the borders or limits of anything, whether material or immaterial. These may be the official lines separating one area from another, or the limit defining the difference or similarities collected in categories.[74] A territory is occupied when it supports a historically and geographically determined group, with the natural or artificial boundary carrying special symbolic meanings. According to Van Gennep, the natural boundary might be a sacred rock, tree, river, or lake, which is set up in the particular spot with rites of consecration that cannot be crossed or passed "without the risk of supernatural sanctions".[75] When milestones or boundary signs are placed by a defined ethnic group on a delimited area, the group possesses the area in such a way that its inhabitants and their neighbours know quite well whose rights and privileges extend within the boundary.[76] These very simple signs are often loaded with important symbolic meanings to indicate the boundary and define the

The Drum Towers as the Cosmological Centre of Separation and Reunion 105

territory. However, as Van Gennep argues, it is clear that the prohibition against entering an ethnic group territory is not the boundary itself, because the signs of boundary are not always placed along the entire boundary line, where it is because the power of significant meaning is comprised by the signs of boundary.[77]

Thus, the meaning of boundary-making in the Dong's social-cultural dictionary is more complex than its frequent bounding function for defence. Boundaries are erected as barriers to separate the site with explicit categories of inner/outer, purity/pollution, living/dead, and so on, and a fundamental boundary is drawn to form a 'sacred space', with the separating ritual to mark a boundary in between: between the known or unknowable, the controlled and uncontrolled and order and disorder. The purpose to draw a boundary with a visibly expressive form and symbolic meanings is fundamental to make the permissible sites of transgression.[78]

Notes

1 Deng, Minwen and Wu, Hao 1995. *Meiyou Guowang De Wangguo: Dongkuan Yanjiu* 没有国王的王国: 侗款研究 (The Kingdom without King: Research on Dong Kuan). Beijing: Zhongguo Sehui Kexue Press.
2 Wu, Hao and Zhang, Zhezhong 1991. *Dongzu Geyao Yanjiu* 侗族歌谣研究 (Research on the Dong Songs). Nanning: Guangxi Renmin Press.
3 Yang, Tongshan, *et al.* 1983. *Dongxiang Fengqinglu* 侗乡风情录 (The Customs of Dong). Chengdu: Shichuan Minzhu Press.
4 Geary, D. Norman, *et al.* 2003. *The Kam people of China: Turning Nineteen.* London: RoutledgeCurzon.
5 See Compilation Group of Annals of the Nationalities in Sanjiang County 2002 (first published 1946), *Sanjiangxian Minzuzhi* 三江县民族志 (Annals of the Nationalities in Sanjiang County). Nanning: Guangxi Minzu Press, p. 104. The 11 villages in Mapang township include Mapang, Yanzhai, Shanyan, Shanwang, Pingbu, Guizhuo, Qinjiang, guipei, Qima, Jima and Gaotan villages.
6 According to the Annals of the Nationalities in Sanjiang County (2002: 18), the source of Wu Luo river is in the mountain of Gaotan village northwest of Mapang village, going through Badou and Guanghui villages, exiting from Liuhe village and joining the Linxi river, later forming a branch of the Xun river.
7 See Xian 1995: 154.
8 See the inscription of plaques inside the Mapang drum tower. The author's translation.
9 *Kuanping* (款坪) is the place particular for speaking *kuan*, punishing the criminals, and calling on villagers to resist intruders. The largest *kuan ping* has responsibility for a territory with a circumference of hundreds of miles, and smaller *kuanping* dominates an area with a circumference of only 40 or 50 miles.
10 See Zhang, Shishan and Yang, Changsi 1992. *Dongzu Wenhua Gailun* 侗族文化概论 (A Survey of Dong Culture). Guiyang: Guizhou Renmin Press, p. 87. The earliest written text from the period 550–77 A.D. relates to the drum towers to be built for sounding the alarm against intruders. Also see Zhang, Min (ed.) 1985. *Dongzu Jianshi* 侗族简史 (A Concise History of the Dong Nationality). Guiyang: Guizhou Renmin Press, p. 138. By the fifteenth century, drum towers were scattered throughout the Dong areas such as Congjiang, Liping, and

Rongjiang counties in Guizhou province, Sanjiang and Longsheng counties in Guangxi province, and Tondao County in Hunan province.
11 See Xian 1995: 81–2. The drum tower provides the community space for the Dong men, and women are only allowed to enter for the rituals of ancestor worship, community meeting, and village's communication. Until the 1940s, the custom that women dressed in skirts were not allowed into the drum tower was still passed down in most of the southern Dong areas. Most old drum towers were built with the threshold over 1m in height, indicating admission for men only, for it was hard for women to cross with skirts. In the stepping on the stage ceremony, women singers usually occupy the location near *tangsa*, but men sit near the drum tower.
12 Quoted from Compilation Group of Annals of the Nationalities in Sanjiang County 2002 (first published 1946), *Sanjiangxian Minzuzhi* 三江县民族志 (Annals of the Nationalities in Sanjiang County). Nanning: Guangxi Minzu Press, p. 64. Kuang Lu, *Chiya* (Records of minority nationality customs in Guangxi and Guizhou during the Ming dynasty), 1604–50.
13 Cf. Xian 1995; and Geary 2003.
14 The quotation from Compilation Group of Annals of the Nationalities in Sanjiang County 2002 (first published 1946), *Sanjiangxian Minzuzhi* 三江县民族志 (Annals of the Nationalities in Sanjiang County). Nanning: Guangxi Minzu Press, p. 61, translated by the author.
15 See *Ximan Congxiao* 溪蛮丛笑 (Collected Ridicule of the Stream Barbarians), which was written in A.D. 1245–79 by Zhu Fu, translated by Geary (2003: 62–3).
16 Cf. Xian 1995: 85; and Deng, Minwen and Wu, Hao 1995. *Meiyou Guowang De Wangguo: Dongkuan Yanjiu* 没有国王的王国: 侗款研究 (The Kingdom without King: Research on Dong Kuan). Beijing: Zhongguo Sehui Kexue Press.
17 See Compilation Group of Local Gazette of Guangxi Province 1992. *Guangxi Tongzhi Minsuzhi* 广西通志: 民俗志 (General Gazette of Guangxi Province: Custom Section). Nanning: Guangxi Renmin Press, pp. 210–4. This marriage custom was conducted before Qin and Han dynasty (221–220 B.C.), and partly changed to marry other surname after the Han culture woven in the Dong areas in Qin and Han dynasty. However, it was existence until 1949.
18 See Xian 1995: 81–3; and Compilation Group of Local Gazette of Guangxi Province 1992. *Guangxi Tongzhi Minsuzhi* 广西通志: 民俗志 (General Gazette of Guangxi Province: Custom Section). Nanning: Guangxi Renmin Press, p. 210.
19 See Geary 2003: 89–90. The Dong people often had to travel a great distance to find a marriage partner. To address the problem, the Dong 'Conference of the ninety-nine elders', convened in Yuezhai sometime between 1723 and 1736, ruled that Dong villages should 'split the surnames and intermarry'. Thus villages which had formerly had only one surname 'split' their surnames according to the original clans. After this was done, several surnames arose in the same village and folk from the same village could intermarry, and a drum towers was built for each surname.
20 Cf. Xian 1995: 82; and Geary 2003: 64.
21 See Xian 1995: 83–6.
22 See Deng, Minwen and Wu, Hao 1995. *Meiyou Guowang De Wangguo: Dongkuan Yanjiu* 没有国王的王国: 侗款研究 (The Kingdom without King: Research on Dong Kuan). Beijing: Zhongguo Sehui Kexue Press, pp. 31–3; and Geary 2003: 64.
23 See Yang, Tongshan, *et al.* 1983. *Dongxiang Fengqinglu* 侗乡风情录 (The Customs of Dong). Chengdu: Shichuan Minzhu Press, pp. 239–43.
24 See Geary 2003: 62.
25 *Ibid.* pp. 63–4.
26 See Deng and Wu 1995: 67.

The Drum Towers as the Cosmological Centre of Separation and Reunion 107

27 Cf. Deng and Wu 1995: 69–79; and Geary 2003: 66.
28 Deng and Wu 1995: 79–80.
29 Interviewed with Wu Hao and Wu Shihua in 2005.
30 See Wu, Hao and Zhang, Zhezhong 1991. *Dongzu Geyao Yanjiu* 侗族歌谣研究 (Research on the Dong Songs). Nanning: Guangxi Renmin Press, pp. 19–21. Sa Sui *ye* (萨岁耶) is also named *shengmu ye* (圣母耶), in the Dongs' rituals, people usually sing these songs to admire the virtues and merits of the Sa spirit. But before they sing these songs, they need to worship Sa spirit in the Sa altar, and basically, in the stepping into singing stage, the singing competition is usually begun with *shengmu ye*. The spirits' names in the song were oral recorded with Wu Hao in 2006.
31 Another name of Sa Sui spirit.
32 The ancestor of the Dong.
33 It symbolizes the sun, implying the Sun Spirit down to the world from the heaven.
34 One of the ancestors of the Dong.
35 It indicates that the Sa Sui place was in the heaven.
36 See Deng, Minwen and Wu, Hao 1995. *Meiyou Guowang De Wangguo: Dongkuan Yanjiu* 没有国王的王国: 侗款研究 (The Kingdom without King: Research on Dong Kuan). Beijing: Zhongguo Sehui Kexue Press, pp. 92–4. In the Dong legend, *Kuan* Gong is a wise head of a *kuan* organization, which builds up the communication between villages for their intermarriage, and so establishes the groups of *kuan* organization.
37 She is a moon spirit, who helped to build the drum tower for Sa Sui.
38 It refers to north on the Fengshui compass.
39 See Wu, Hao, *et al.* (eds.) 1987. *Dongzu Kuan*ci, *Yege, and Jiuge* 侗族款词, 耶歌, 酒歌 (The *Kuan, Ye* Songs, and Drinking Wine Songs of the Dong). Sanjiang: Sanjiang Dongzu Zhizixian Santao Jicheng Bangongshi Press, pp. 216–9, the author's translation.
40 It locates on the northeast on the compass, and refers to 2am.
41 It locates on the northeast on the compass, and refers to 4am.
42 It locates on the east on the compass, and refers to 6am.
43 See the explanation in Wu and Zhang 1991: 108.
44 Personal communication with Wu Hao in 2004.
45 *Jia* 甲, *yi* 乙, *bing* 丙, *ding* 丁, *wu* 戊, *ji* 己, *geng* 庚, *xin* 辛 and *gui* 癸 are ten heavenly stems, and *zi* 子, *chou* 丑, *yin* 寅, *mao* 卯, *chen* 辰, *si* 巳, *wu* 戊, *wei* 未, *shen* 申, *you* 酉, *shu* 戌, and *hai* 亥 are twelve earthly branches, which mark space and time on the compass.
46 See Wang, Xiuwen, 'The Supernatural Force of Gate of Hell and Peach and the Worship of Sun', in Yasuda Yoshinori (ed.) 2002, *Myths and Rituals of the Yangtze River Civilization*. Beijing: Wenwu Press, pp. 134–44.
47 Cf. Xian, Guangwei 1995. *Dongzu Tonglan* 侗族通览 (A General Survey of the *Kam* Nationality). Nanning: Guangxi Minzhu Press, pp. 79–82; and Geary, D. Norman, *et al.* 2003. *The Kam people of China: Turning Nineteen*. London: RoutledgeCurzon, pp. 88–9.
48 See Xian 1995: 79.
49 The building ritual of Sa Sui altar sees Wu, Hao and Zhang, Zhezhong 1991. *Dongzu Geyao Yanjiu* 侗族歌谣研究 (Research on the Dong Songs). Nanning: Guangxi Renmin Press.
50 *Ibid*. pp. 108–9.
51 *Ibid*. p. 109.
52 *Ibid*. p. 143.
53 See Yu, Dazhong 2001. *Dongzu Minju* 侗族民居 (The Dwellings of the Dong). Guiyang: Huaxia Wenhua Yishu Press, pp. 142–3.

54 See Yang, Tongshan (ed.) 1983. *Dongxiang Fengqing Lu* 侗乡风情录 (The customs of the Dong). Chengdu: Shichuan Minzu Press, pp. 253–9.
55 *Ibid.* pp. 267–9. Also see Wu, Hao and Zhang, Zhezhong 1991. *Dongzu Geyao Yanjiu* 侗族歌谣研究 (Research on the Dong Songs). Nanning: Guangxi Renmin Press, pp. 109–10; and Yu, Dazhong 2001. *Dongzu Minju* 侗族民居 (The Dwellings of the Dong). Guiyang: Huaxia Wenhua Yishu Press, pp. 152–6.
56 Yang, Tongshan (ed.) 1983. *Dongxiang Fengqing Lu* 侗乡风情录 (The Customs of the Dong). Chengdu: Shichuan Minzu Press, p. 269.
57 See Yu, Dazhong 2001. *Dongzu Minju* 侗族民居 (The Dwellings of the Dong). Guiyang: Huaxia Wenhua Yishu Press, pp. 152–4, author's translation.
58 *Ibid.* pp. 154–5, author's translation.
59 See Wu, Hao and Zhang, Zhezhong 1991. *Dongzu Geyao Yanjiu* 侗族歌谣研究 (Research on the Dong Songs). Nanning: Guangxi Renmin Press, pp. 109–10.
60 Personal communication with Wu Hao in the summer of 2004.
61 See Wu 1991: 19–21. *shan tang ye* （散堂耶） refers to the dismissing songs. When the singing stage reaches its end, in order to express the sense of being reluctant to leave, and to be appreciated or to apologize to the audience, they sing *shan tang ye*.
62 See Yang, Tongshan and Wu, Hao 1987. *Dongzu Pipa Ge* 侗族琵琶歌 (The *Pipa* Songs of the Dong), Sanjiang: Sanjiang Dongzu Zizhixian Guji Zhengli Bangongshi Press, pp. 612–3. The translation of the author.
63 *Ibid.* p. 617. The translation of the author.
64 A kind of Dong music equipment like lute, with a plucked string instrument with a fretted fingerboard, is usually made of a whole large timber.
65 Personal communication with Wu Hao and Wu Shihua in the summer of 2004.
66 The descriptions about the ceremony see Yu 2001: 158–9.
67 See Yang, Tongshan (ed.) 1983. *Dongxiang Fengqing Lu* 侗乡风情录 (The customs of the Dong). Chengdu: Shichuan Minzu Press, pp. 257–9.
68 Yang, Tongshan (ed.) 1983. *Dongxiang Fengqing Lu* 侗乡风情录 (The Customs of the Dong). Chengdu: Shichuan Minzu Press, p. 261. The translation of the author.
69 See Yu, Dazhong 2001. *Dongzu Minju* 侗族民居 (The Dwellings of the Dong). Guiyang: Huaxia Wenhua Yishu Press, pp. 159–60, the translation of the author.
70 Yang, Tongshan (ed.) 1983. *Dongxiang Fengqing Lu* 侗乡风情录 (The Customs of the Dong). Chengdu: Shichuan Minzu Press, p. 259.
71 Barth, Fredrik 1969. *Ethnic Groups and Boundaries: the Social Organization Culture Difference*. Bergen-oslo: Universitetsforlaget, pp. 10–11.
72 Barth, Fredrik 1969. *Ethnic Groups and Boundaries: the Social Organization Culture Difference*. Bergen-oslo: Universitetsforlaget, pp. 11–12.
73 Rapoport, Amos 1969. 'The Pueblo and The Hogan', in Paul Oliver (ed.), *Shelter & Society*. London: Barrie & Jenkins, p. 66.
74 Hay, John (ed.) 1994. *Boundaries in China*. London: Reaktion Books, p. 2.
75 Gennep, Arnold Van 1960. *The Rites of Passage*, Monika B. Vizedom and Gabrielle L. Caffee (trans.). Chicago: The University of Chicago Press.
76 *Ibid.* p 15.
77 Gennep, Arnold Van 1960. *The Rites of Passage*, Monika B. Vizedom and Gabrielle L. Caffee (trans.). Chicago: The University of Chicago Press, p. 17.
78 Hay, John (ed.) 1994. *Boundaries in China*. London: Reaktion Books. p. 17.

4 Wind and Water (*fengshui* 风水) in Shaping the Dong Villages

> The qi of *yin* and *yang* flows out and thus becomes wind; it ascends and thus becomes cloud; it descends and thus becomes rain; and it moves through the ground and thus becomes the generative qi. The five qi move within the ground, and develop, thus generate the ten thousand things. The Book says, when qi rides with the wind, it disperses; when it reaches water, it ends. The ancients were able to conserve the qi and keep it from dispersion, to move it and to make it cease. Therefore, they called it Fengshui.
>
> Guo Pu

Each Dong village is organized in a typical hierarchical plan with the drum tower built as a community centre, the village houses constructed around the drum tower, and a Wind and Rain bridge that sits on the periphery as the threshold in the village (Figure 4.1). Although the Dong have settled their villages in river basins, in order to rely on the mountains for protection and to take advantage of water for irrigation, their timber dwellings are concentrated rather than dispersed along the banks of a river or on the top of a mountain (Figure 4.2). Both the Pingzhai and Yanzhai villages are typical Dong villages, and are adjacent neighbourhoods, settled on the north bank of the Linxi river about two miles west of Sanjiang county (Figure 4.3). Each village houses about two hundred and thirty families. The Yanzhai drum tower and the Pingzhai drum tower are built as community centres for the Yanzhai and Pingzhai villages, with the Helong bridge and Pingzhai bridge as the crossings, linking these two villages to other villages. However, it is important to note that, although both the Yanzhai and Pingzhai villages share similar topography, the houses of each village have a unique orientation differentiating the villages from each other. A similar situation happens in many Dong villages, such as the Shangzhai and Xiazhai villages, which are located five miles southeast of Sanjiang county.

110 *Wind and Water in Shaping the Dong Villages*

Figure 4.1 Ma'an village and the Chengyang bridge in Sanjiang county, 2004.

Figure 4.2 A typical pattern of Dong village plan, Bajiang village, 2011.

Wind and Water in Shaping the Dong Villages 111

Figure 4.3 A perspective of Pinzhai village, Yanzhai village and Helong bridge, each village owning an individual drum tower, and the houses belonging to different villages oriented in the identifiable directions, Sanjiang, 2011.

In the summer of 2011, I carried out fieldwork in the Dong villages of Longsheng county and Sanjiang county again. In a hot and humid sunset, after a whole day's survey work, I was sitting on the Helong bridge in Yan Zhai village, enjoying the scene of meandering river beneath and the villages hidden in the jungle. There were several villagers relaxing on the bridge, who greeted to me (Figure 4.4). After I offered them cigarettes, they talked to me about the story of the bridge. In the communication, they kept comparing their Wind and Rain bridge to their neighbouring bridge, as a monument of pride in the village to other such bridges in the vicinity and I realize that the villagers are very sensitive about their bridges. Thus the questions occurred to me: what have been the Dong's environmental ideals? How do the Dong perceive, manipulate and integrate these ideals into the constructions of their physical environment? Moreover, why do the bridges carry more expectations on part of the villagers than the other village bridges? Are they relevant to organize the Dong villages? And how do these factors influence the siting of their villages, specifically, illustrated by the example of four differently oriented villages? By looking at the way these towns developed, one comes closer to understanding how this system produced different solutions.

Figure 4.4 The Helong bridge in Yanzhai village, Sanjiang, 2011.

The Chinese Cosmology of Vital Energy *Qi*

In their attempt to make sense of their environment, human manipulate the natural environment in relation to their overall world view or cosmology. The cultural geographer Yi-Fu Tuan writes that, "landscapes serve as background for commonplace human activities when they no longer harbour the spirits of the earth".[1] He believes that nature is rich in symbols and these can be interpreted on several levels, thereby affording a range of emotional responses. Applying the sacred cosmology meaning to places and landscapes involves metaphorical thinking. It should be understood that the Dong certainly 'harbour the spirit of the earth' and as such are immersed in the landscape and do not view it simply as background as Western scholars may suggest, but rather as something which is integral to their belief system. As an example, the concepts of 'mountain' and 'valley' are 'types in a topographical category,' they also however embody meaning such as 'high and low'.[2] Natural elements such as "sky, earth, water, rock, and vegetation are interpreted in similar ways by different peoples" and also in the case of the Dong their own translation of *qi*.[3] A fundamental concept of sacredness of place reflecting a community representation of 'centre' and their efforts to 'create order out of disorder'.[4] This act of creation, and/or transformation of the landscape testifies to the sacredness of their social cosmology.

It is not clear when a written text of *fengshui* was introduced from the Han because the Dong lacked written descriptions before 1958. However, it is evident that the Dong village sites, drum towers, bridges and dwellings were built with the practice of Wind and Water (*fengshui*, or *yin/yang*).[5] According to the record of the Gazette of Sanjiang county, each Dong village must have its drum tower and Wind and Rain bridge which are primarily concerned with *fengshui*. Particularly, the Wind and Rain bridges are believed by the Dong to provide an atmosphere of prosperity, wealth and fertility, as well as ensure their security.[6] The strong bridge consciousness is highlighted and raised by the Dong's cosmology which plays a central part in the separation and reunion of Dong life by exercising power over its occupants. According to the record in the gazette of Sanjiang county states that the Wind and Rain bridges in the Dong area are mainly concerned with *fengshui* (wind and water 风水), which is surely related to superstition.[7] The gazette also says that Wind and Rain bridges of the Dong are concerned with the flourishing or declining of a village, assuring the wealth and fertility of a villager, as well as its security. From the day the bridge is built, it is viewed as an effective spirit, carrying supernatural power to sustain in villages and bring them wealth and fertility.[8]

Although the Dong traditionally did not name their belief system as *fengshui*, their practices are consistent with those chronicled by the Han culture who formalized and recorded its practice. From the records of their narrative songs, the Dong are believers of animism and practice divination in their daily life. The philosophy of the Dong is humble, emerging from their perception of the natural world. It may be compared to that of Taoism, which shares common roots in that they listen to the voice of nature, and recognize that human beings flourish only through harmony with the rhythms of the universe.[9] This comparison was confirmed by the *fengshui* master of the Yanzhai village while showing his *fengshui* encyclopaedia to the bridge building master Yang Shanren in the company of the author. Both *fengshui* and bridge masters were interviewed by the author in the summer of 2011.[10]

In the traditional cosmology of China, *qi* is an abstract concept, and the purpose of *fengshui* is to deal with the phenomena *qi*. In order to understand the practice of *fengshui*, it is necessary to trace back the traditional cosmology of vital energy (qi 气) in China. It is not the perceptible, natural movement of air in the form of currents blowing from a particular direction. Instead, *qi* is the origin of the world, combined with *yin* and *yang* in one body, where the concept of *qi* is defined in *Zang Jing* (The Book of Burial) by Guo Pu, *fengshui* is regarded as 'geomancy' in the West, where the term has particular meaning in Chinese as the art of differentiating between the residences of the living and the tombs of the dead, so as to cooperate and harmonize with the local currents of the cosmic breath.[11] However, the wind does not mean just the flowing air of everyday life, but rather the abstract concept of vital energy named *qi*, circulating through the veins and vessels of the earth, and affecting the fortune or misfortune of the houses and families of the living, as well as the descendants of those who lie in the tombs. Similarly water in visible streams and rivers is capable of removing impurities, but also of carrying the vital energy *qi*. Rooted in Chinese traditional culture, the practice of *fengshui* mainly concerns the topographical features of any locality, the forms of the hills, the directions and windings of the streams and the orientation and dimensions of buildings. The central purpose is to protect a site from harmful influences through the achievement of a balance of proper (*yang* 阳) and evil (*yin* 阴) forces.[12]

There are few societies in the world with a concept similar to the Chinese idea *qi*, which is associated with almost every aspect of life. In the traditional Chinese cosmology, the flow of *qi* is the origin and causes everything in the world. According to the *Huang di Nei jing* of 200 B.C. (the Yellow Emperor's Classic of Internal Medicine 黄帝内经), the Chinese *qi* would be subdivided into the proper qi (*zheng qi* 正气) and evil qi (*xie qi* 邪气). The diseases, suffered by human bodies, which are classified in terms of different seasons and climates, are caused by various evil *qi* intruding into human bodies.[13] The vital energy *qi* in *Huangdi Neijing* is related with the theory of the Five-phases and Six-*qi* (*wu yun liu qi* 五运六气).[14] According to this theory, the interaction of the proper *qi* (yang qi 阳气) and the evil *qi* (yin qi 阴气) accounts for the creation of spring, summer, long summer, autumn and winter as five seasons in a year, which are response to the materials of metal, wood, water, fire and earth (*jin, mu, shui, huo* and *tu* 金, 木, 水, 火, 土) in the Five-phase system, the five organs of human body, five tastes and five motions, and even connected with five directions and five seasons (Table 4.1).

A site with negative winds is undesirable, because negative winds initiate negative *qi* (*xie qi* 邪气) within the human body, and thus may cause seasonal

Table 4.1 The features of nature and human matched with the Five-phase

Five-phases	Five-directions	Five-seasons	Five-qi	Five-tastes	Five-organs	Five-motions
Wood	East	Spring	Wind	Sour	Liver	Angry
Fire	South	Summer	Hotness	Bitter	Heart	Happy
Earth	Centre	Long Summer	Dampness	Sweet	Spleen	Anxiousness
Metal	West	Autumn	Dryness	Spicy	Lung	Sadness
Water	North	Winter	Coolness	Salty	Kidney	Scariness

disease in human beings. In terms of *Huang di nei jing* (the Yellow Emperor's Classic of Internal Medicine, 1983), the negative winds originating from different directions may cause various *qi* to permeate human bodies. These are the six negative *qi,* defined as wind (*feng* 风), coolness (*han* 寒), dryness (*zao* 燥), dampness (*shi* 湿), fieriness (*huo* 火) and hotness (*re* 热). These diseases occur in a seasonal cycle and can be predicted. For instance, spring belongs to wood and within the range of the Five-phase, wood corresponds to the evil *qi* that coming from unexpected directions attacks the liver in human beings. Thus, in the season of spring, the liver *qi* suffers from the change induced by spring wind and liver disease is often caused. The fire in the Five-phase response to summer causes hotness in the natural world and in the heart of the human body, thus heart disease often occurs in the season of summer. The period between summer and autumn belongs to the earth, and earth refers to dampness in nature and the spleen of the body. Thus, abdominal diseases occur frequently during this time. Autumn belongs to metal, which represents dryness in the natural world and in the lungs of the human body, thus resulting in lung disease. Winter belongs to water, responding to coolness and to the kidney in human body, and kidney disease is induced in winter.[15] Thus, in Chinese tradition, a human's health is identified with the proper and improper qualities associated with *qi*. If the vitality of *qi* is positive, it is believed to be lucky, and in contrast, if the vitality of *qi* is negative it is seen as unlucky. Good health is only obtained by maintaining the persistence of proper *qi* (*zheng qi* 正气) in the human body and rejecting the intrusion of negative *qi* caused by unexpected winds.

The manipulation of *qi* is responsible for the quality of production, the flourishing plants and the fertility of animals, evident in the places with proper vital energy *qi*. In the Chinese technical tradition, according to *Kaogong Ji*,[16] good quality production depends on timing (*tian shi* 天时), the earth energy (*di qi* 地气), fine materials and intelligent techniques. The produce will be made imperfectly, if it lacks earth energy and fails to obey the exact time of heaven, even though made with fine materials and intelligent techniques. *Tian shi* (天时) and *di qi* (地气) indicate the aspects related with the natural world. As *Kao gong ji* points out, sometimes the climate helps plants to grow, but sometimes it makes them die; trees and grasses sometimes flourish, but sometimes decline; stone sometimes breaks following its texture; water sometimes transforms into ice, and sometimes it becomes the rain. These are related to the climate through the unchanging law of the natural world. In *Kao Gong Ji*, the production of artefacts is connected to the nature of the place, and for instance, Zheng State is famous for knife-production, Song State for axes, Lu State for paper-knives and the Wu State for swords, and these things are not thought to be well-made in other places, for each follows the local earth energy.[17] Similarly, particular species of plants and animals belong to specific places. Often green trees and grasses flourish, and at other times they decline although growing in the same spot. Oranges *ju*, originally grown in the south of China, would become another species, osage oranges *ji*, and taste differently if they are relocated to the north of Huai river. A *qu yu* (mynah bird) is not able to survive on the inappropriate side of the Ji river. A raccoon dog would die if it is taken to the area across the Wen river. The properties of a material are also influenced by the local earth *qi*.[18] A specific product is not properly 'well-made' when it is produced in another place. This is because it is not able to receive the local earth *qi* when generated in an improper environment. So appropriate timing and the earth energy *qi* are responsible for forming a harmonious environment and assuring the quality of products.[19]

The Origins of *Fengshui* Compass Linking the Time with the Space

Fengshui practice played a major part in determining the locations and orientations of Chinese cities, buildings and tombs. *Qi* is a crucial philosophical conception in the Chinese view of cosmology, which is involved in everything of Chinese daily life, including traditional perceptions of environment and space. The discipline about finding the right place to build for both the living and the dead is deeply concerned with manipulation of *qi*, wherin the practice to identify the proper *qi* in various times and locations are manipulated by the tool so called *fengshui* compass. Basically, there are two kind of theories in the practice of *fengshui*: one is named *Fang Wei* School (the School of the *fengshui* compass 方位), which depends on the *fengshui* compass. Another branch is named *Xing Shi* School (the School of Form and Attitude 形势), which follows the theory of the book *Zang Jing* (The Canon of Burials 葬经) to judge the attitudes of a spot of the environment. In *fengshui* practice, the compass is originally named *luo-jing* (罗经). It literally is not only able to display directions for the heaven and the earth, but also to predict every phenomenon and occasion in the world. The *fengshui* compass evidently originates from *sin an* (司南), the earliest tool for orientation. The *fengshui* compass is created when it is combined with the *liu ren shi pan* (liu ren compass 六壬盘) for divination; the *fengshui* compass is created.[20] Divided up into the system of the eight trigrams, the Heavenly Stems and Earthly Branches, and the 28 *siu* (Lunar mansions), *luo jing* is the key principle in *fengshui* practice. The oldest form of compass developed by the Chinese in the practice of *fengshui*, as Needham argues, from its original discovery in the divination practices of imperial magicians in an agrarian-terrestrial, rather than in a primarily maritime civilization. For centuries it was limited to a specific form of Chinese Taoist geomancy.[21]

Before the creation of the *fengshui* compass, orientation was identified in ancient China by employment of a sundial by in relation to the movement of the sun. A sundial is also known by the name *kuei piao*, and the character *kuei* combines the sun radical with an old word *jiu*, meaning correcting the fault in Chinese. In the record of *Kao Gong Ji*, the builders set up a vertical post on the ground, distinguishing the east and west directions by the post's shadow under the sunshine (Figure 4.5).[22] According to Needham, the most ancient astronomical instrument in China was the simple vertical pole-gnomon from the Shang dynasty (1600-1046 B.C.), which could measure the length of the sun's shadow by day to determine the solstices, and observe the sidereal year, depending on the transits of stars at night. A pole is set up in the ground, points to the north in relation to the sun, and displays the long shadow of the low sun at the winter solstice, the moment which is taken as the beginning of the year in Chinese calendar. The earliest literary reference to solstice observations is found in the passage of *Zhuo Zhuan* in the Spring and Autumn period (654 B.C.):

> In the fifth year of Duke His, in spring, in the first month (December), on a hsin-hai day, the first of the month, the sun (reached its) furthest south point. The duke (of Lu), having caused the new moon to be

Figure 4.5 Identifying the south and north directions with a post under the sunshine (redrawn by Jie Zhou after Dai 2003: 61).

118   *Wind and Water in Shaping the Dong Villages*

> announced in the ancestral temple, ascended to the observation tower (kuan thai) in order to view (the shadow), and (the astronomers) noted down (its length) according to custom. At every equinox and every solstice, whether at the beginning (chhi) of spring or summer, or at the beginning (pi) of autumn or winter, it is necessary to note the appearance of the cloud and vapours, for (prognostication and) preparations against coming events.[23]

An early reference is found in the *Qian Han Shu* (前汉书), a book connected with the assembly of calendar in 104 B.C. In the record puts:

> (The experts) determined the true east and west points, set up sundials and gnomons, and contrived water clocks (li kuei i hsia lou kho). With such means they marked out the twenty-eight hsiu according to their position at various points in the four quarters, fixing the first and the last days of each month, the equinoxes and solstices, the movements and relative positions of the heavenly bodies and the phases of the moon.[24]

In *Zhou Li* (164), a record can be found about a standard jade tablet, named the Gnomon Shadow Template, which was applied in determining the centre of the earth by the shadow:

> The Ta Ssu Thu (a high official) [says the Chou Li], using the gnomon shadow template, determines the distance of the earth below the sun, fixes the exact (length of the) sun's shadow, and thus finds the centre of the earth ... the centre of the earth is (that place where) the sun's shadow at the summer solstice is 1 ft. 5 in.[25]

The sundial thus is created as the connection between time and space. Working with the template, the shadow of the gnomon, marked on the template with its length and orientation, not only shows the direction (east, south, west and north), but also relates it with proper time (spring, summer, autumn and winter). The template therefore is endowed with meanings, with the divisions and lines of shadow marked on it. The template of the sundial contains the divination symbols and since then have been applied in order to detect auspicious and inauspicious time and place for the Chinese.[26]

The appearance of magnetic needle makes a big step of progress in the creation of *fengshui* compass, which no longer relies on sun shadow and the post of sundial to identify the directions. In the Warring Stage period (475-221 B.C.), the magnetic compass, also named *shi nan* (司南) in Chinese, was created with the discovery of magnetism (Figure 4.6).[27] According to the record of *Han Fei Zi*, *shi nan* was first used by the emperor to decide the orientation of his seat;[28] and also in *Gui Gu Zi*, the Zhen people seek jade in mountains with *shi nan* in order to determine their direction and to avoid losing their way.[29] The earliest *shi nan* is simply combined with *shao*

Wind and Water in Shaping the Dong Villages 119

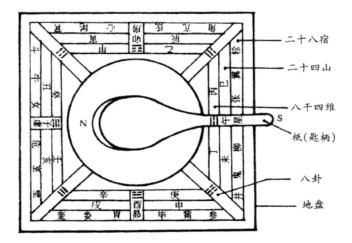

Figure 4.6 The *sinan* model (from Chen 1999: 2).

(spoon 杓) and *shi* (plate 拭). *Shi* is a square plate, made of the material of bronze or wood. The spoon is made of magnetic iron, and its handle always swings to south on the smooth plate. The square plate is divided and marked with 24 sections, including the eight Heavenly Stems, the 24 Earthly Branches, Eight-trigrams (*ba gua* 八卦), and 28 *siu* (constellations 宿), identifying the 24 directions on the compass.[30]

The first mention of a magnetic compass dates back to roughly 1040, which is a bowl of water floating a south-pointing 'fish', then followed by the use of suspended 'turtle' whose head always points to south. Till today, the Chinese term for compass means a 'south pointing needle' (指南针). According to Needham, the fish is possibly always related with water while turtles crawl on the land, and both shapes of animals are simple and easy to balance, the wooden fish containing a lodestone was usually described as a wet magnetic compass, and the wooden turtle shape as a dry one.[31] The description in *Shi Lin Guang Ji* (Guide through the Forest of Affairs, 1100 to 1250) reports that:

> The (magicians) also cut a piece of wood into the shape of a turtle, and arranged it in the same way as before, only that the needle is fixed at the tail end. A bamboo pin about as thick as the end of a chopstick is set up on a small board, and sustains the turtle by the concave under-surface of its body, where there is a small hole. Then when the turtle is rotated, it will always point to the north, which must be due to the needle at the tail.[32]

This is of great interest, as Needham notes, both types of magnetic compass, fish and turtle shapes were adopted instead of the spoon shape on the diviner's compass.[33] It is arguable that fishes and turtles are auspicious traditional symbols in China, where fishes represent flourishing offerings with their strong fertility, and turtles symbolize longevity. In Chinese proverb, it says 'to be fortunate as the immensity of the Eastern Sea, and to live as long as the Sothern mountain'. The magnetic compass was thus endowed with the significance of fortune and time became the diviners' tool in traditional China.

The invention of the magnetic needle is also described by Shen Kuo in about 1088 in the *Meng Xi Bi Tan*. The magicians rub the point of a needle with the lodestones, and then it is able to point to the south. The making of floating needle compass is described in *Wu Jing Zhong Yao* in 1044 of the Song Dynasty

> When troops encountered gloomy weather or dark nights, and the directions of space could not be distinguished, they let an old horse go on before to lead them, or else they made use of the south-pointing carriage, or the south-pointing fish (chih nan yu 指南鱼) to identify the directions. Now the carriage method has not been handed down, but in the fish method a thin leaf of iron is cut into the shape of a fish two inches long and half an inch broad, having a pointing head and tail. This is then heated in a charcoal fire, and when it has become thoroughly red-hot, it is taken out by the head with iron tongs and placed so that its tail points to north (in the Tzu direction). In this position it is quenched (chan shu) with water in a basin, so that its tail is submerged for several tenths of an inch. It is then kept in a tightly closed box. To use it, a small bowl filled with water is set up in a windless place, and the fish is laid as flat as possible upon the water-surface so that it floats, whereupon its head will point south.[34]

Another divine tool related with the origins of *fengshui* compass is the TLV-board, also named *Liu Ren Shi Pan* (六壬盘). In Chinese archaeology, 'TLV-mirror' of the Han dynasty (206 B.C.-220 A.D.) was possibly a divination instrument, named *shih* (diviner's plate 拭) (Figure 4.7).[35] A 'TLV-mirror' is made of bronze, the front of the mirror is finely polished so that it reflects the user's face. The back is often decorated with symbols, and various motifs and images, notably the phoenix, with other beasts, flowers, leaves and lattice. Some also have inscriptions. In the myths and legends of ancient China, mirrors have magic to see through the evil spirits because of the nature of reflection. They are usually hung on the lintels of main door and windows, in order to dispel the evils and keep the houses safe from the evil spirits, criminals and misfortune, and for this reason, they are also a favorite burial accessory. The earliest of such mirrors is datable to about 250 B.C., where a picture from the Wu Liang tomb shrines (147) depicts the scene of magical operations. In the picture, a TLV-board is carefully drawn on a small table which may be identified as the diviner's plate or *shi*, the square table representing earth surmounted by a rotating disc representing heaven. It is

Figure 4.7 The TLV board for the diviners in the Han dynasty (206 B.C.-220) (redrawn by Jie Zhou after Nreedham 1959: 303–4).

extremely striking that the existing Han sundials bear both the graduated instrument and TLV markings, as Needham discovers, The sundial board thus has been related to the diviner's board (*shi*) and the magnetic compass, since the Han dynasty (206 B.C. -220A.D.).[36] On the 'cosmic mirrors', the compass indications are given on the diviner's board with the various compass points, names of divinities, trigrams, the cyclical characters, and so on. Each side of the square is divided into three by the eight radiating divisions that separate the twenty-four azimuth points into groups of three, and then nine squares (*jiu gong* 九宮) are formed. On the background of the mirror the five sacred mountains (*wu yue* 五岳) are sometimes represented.[37]

A bronze mirror of the Tang period (620–900), from the collection of the American Museum of National History, shows constellation diagrams of the twenty-eight *siu* (second circle from the outside), the eight trigrams (next circle), the twelve animals of the animal cycle (next innermost circle), and the four symbolic animals of the Celestial Palaces (innermost disc) (Figure 4.8).[38] The outer circle is inscribed with a poem beginning at the floret on the right:

> (This mirror) has the virtue of Chhang-keng (the Evening Star, Hesperus, Venus)
> And the essence of the White Tiger (symbol of the Western Palace),
> The Mutual endowments of Yin and Yang (are present in it),
> The mysterious spirituality of Mountains and Rivers (is fulfilled in it).
> With due observance of the regularities of the Heavens,
> And due regard to the tranquility of Earth,
> The Eight Trigrams are exhibited upon it,
> And the Five-phases disposed in order on it.

Figure 4.8 The brazen mirror with 28 mansions (*siu*) and the eight trigrams (*bagua* 八卦) (from Chen 1999: 3).

Let none of the hundred spiritual beings hide their face from it;
Let none of the myriad things withhold their reflection from it.
Whoever possesses this mirror and treasures it,
Will meet with good fortune and achieve exalted rank.[39]

The discovery of Chinese lunar mansions must be contributed to the calendrical needs of the agricultural society. Space and time are relevant while the 28 constellations marked on the compass, identifying fortunate or unfortunate directions with the lunar mansions. The numbers of the constellations are divided into 28 Lunar mansions possibly because of the moon, the greatest nightly luminary. According to Needham, while the moon takes 29.53 days to complete its physic cycle from full to full or new to new (the lunation month), it takes only 27.33 days to return the same place among the stars (the sidereal month). These periods are always out of step but 28 was a very convenient average.[40]

In another record of *Shu Jing* (800-500 B.C.), the ancient Chinese have familiarly divided the four seasons and calculated the days of the whole year by identifying the position of stars:

> The day of medium length and the (culmination of the) star Niao (serve to) adjust the middle of spring ... the day of greatest length and the (culmination of the) star Huo (serve to) fix the middle of the summer ... the night of medium length and the (culmination of the) star Hsu (serve to) adjust the middle of autumn ... the night of greatest length and the (culmination of the) star Mao (serve to) fix the middle of the winter ... the year has 366 days. The four seasons are regulated by means of intercalary months (jun yueh).[41]

The diviner's board is usually composed of two level of boards or plates, the lower one being square to symbolize the earth, named *di pan* (the earthly plate 地盘); and the upper one being round to symbolize the heaven, named *tian pan* (the heavenly plate 天盘). The *dipan* revolved on a central pivot and engraved upon it are 24 compass-points, composed of cyclical characters of Eight-trigrams, the Heavenly-stems and Earthly-branches. Moreover, it carries the eight chief trigrams, arranged according to the *hou tian* system with *qian* occupied the north-west and *kun* the south-east.[42] The Earthly Plate is marked all about its edge with the names of the 28 constellations, and the 24 directions are repeated along its inner gradations. Late in the Tang dynasty (618–907), the divine compass with a magnetic needle, was invented and used in *fengshui* practice (Figure 4.9).[43] The compass is combined with a magnetic needle compass in the centre to identify south and north, and marked with symbols and characters representing the seasons and times, where not only possible to decide the dates and calendar for marriage, work, building, ritual and burial are decided, but wealth, rank of officials and illnesses are also predicted.

In the *Huang Di Zai Jing* of the Tang dynasty, this *fengshui* compass was used to select an auspicious orientation for building. The typical *fengshui* compass is designed with 24 on the plate, which are defined as 24 mountains, marked by the eight Heavenly Stems, twelve Earthly Branches, and combined with the four *gua* - *qian, gen, kun* and *xun*.[44] Basically, the compass with 20 scales is popularly used in modern *fengshui* practice, and divisions of the scales mainly concern heaven, human beings and earth, which are named Heaven Plate (*tian pan* 天盘), Human Plate (*ren pan* 人盘) and Earth Plate (*di pan* 地盘). The meanings of typical scales are as follows (the meanings of the 20 significant scales see Appendix):[45]

124 *Wind and Water in Shaping the Dong Villages*

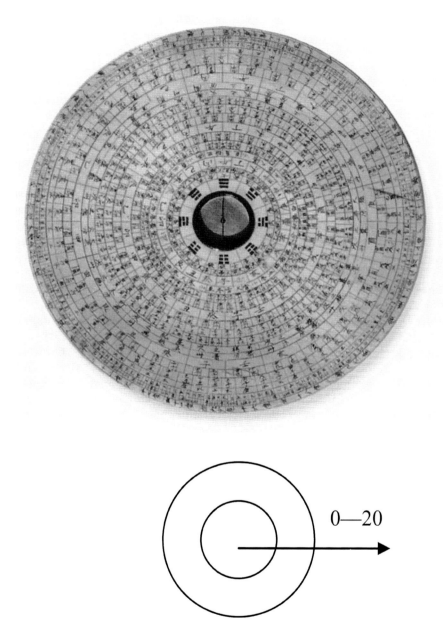

Figure 4.9 A *fengshui* compass marked by the rings with meanings (drawn by author).

The centre of the magnetic compass is named the Heaven Pool (*tian chi* or *tai ji* 天池). The magnetic needle is located at the centre, with red side pointing to south and black to north. The first scale shows the cycle of the 'Former Eight Trigrams'. The fourth scale on the compass is the 'Earth Plate Correct Needle 24-mountain scale' (地盘正针 24 山圈), divided into 24 directions named as 24 mountains. The 24 sections are defined by the cyclical characters of the Heavenly Stems and Earthly Branches (天干地支).[46] The cardinal directions are identified with the system of *gua* (trigram 卦). In *fengshui* practice, the 24 directions are usually used to identify the orientations of mountain and water, and search for *qi* is based on the 24 solar terms marked on the compass. The sixth scale is the 'Earth Plate Correct Needle Penetrating mountain 72-dragon scale' (*chuanshan 72 long* 地盘正针穿山 72 龙). Fortune and misfortune are identified by the Penetrating mountain 72-dragon to distinguish the Heavenly Stems or Earthly Branches of the mountain vein. The eighth scale is 'Human Plate Central Needle 24 Mountains' (人盘中针 24 山), and its *zi* 子 and *wu* 午 mountain point to the middle of *ren zi* 壬子 and *bing wu* 丙午 of the Earthly Plate, which is half *gua* forward to the Earthly Plate and points to the north pole. The fourteenth is the 'Heaven Plate Seam Needle 24-Mountain scale' (天盘缝针 24 山). The nineteenth scale is Five-phase characters in each degree of 28 mansions. Generally, the Earthly Plate is mostly used in distinguishing the dragon vein (龙脉) and searching for *qi*, identifying the watercourse mouth and avoiding the evil shape of a hill, so locating the auspicious site; and the Human Plate scale and the Heavenly Plate scale only provide the complement to the Earthly Plate.

Although the name of *fengshui* replaced the popular words *yin/yang* by the Tang (618–907) dynasty,[47] the earliest use of the words *yin/yang* has been found in the Gong Liu chapter of the Odes (*Shi Jing*), which tells the story of Duke Liu in the Western Chou period (1046-771 B.C.). He was the ancestor of the Zhou tribe, who moved to a basin area with his tribe and was going to build a new city. After he climbed the mountains to investigate the topography, he finally settled on a proper site with the mountains and rivers surrounding it. In the narrative poetry, Duke Liu arrived at the spot and "surveyed the people, they were numerous and flourishing"; then he was "either high up in the hills or down in the plains"; he "reached the Hundred Springs and gazed at the wide plain"; and he "noted the shadows and the height of the hills, which parts were in the shade (*yin*) and which in the sun (*yang*), and viewed the streams and the springs".[48] The survey of Duke Liu aimed to choose a place conserved with auspicious *qi*. Through inspection of the topography, he distinguished that the *qi* was fortunate or unfortunate for the area, where he finally obtained a desirable site to settle down in.

Apart from *Fang Wei* School (the School of the *fengshui* compass 方位), another branch in *fengshui* performance is *Xing Shi* School (the School of Form and Attitude 形势), which follows the theory of the book *Zang Jing* (The Canon of Burials 葬经) (Figure 4.10). The earliest conception of *fengshui*

126 *Wind and Water in Shaping the Dong Villages*

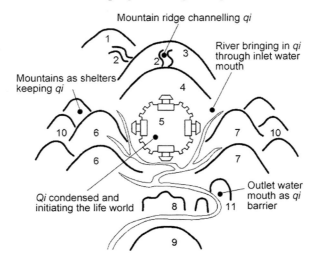

Figure 4.10 The ideal resident site in *fengshui* practice (redrawn by author after Shang 1992:27):
1. great grandparents mountain;
2. the *longmai* (dragon vein);
3. grandparents mountain;
4. the dark tortoise mountain;
5. the building site;
6. the white tiger mountain;
7. the azure dragon mountain;
8. the table-mountain;
9. the vermilion bird mountain;
10. the guardian mountain;
11. the mountains of the watercourse mouth.

is defined in the book of *Zang Jing*, which was written by Guo Pu in the *Ji* Dynasty (265–316), and was obtained by Yang Yunsong and brought back to Ganzhou of Jiangxi province in the Tang dynasty (618–907).[49] Following the *Zang Jing* about the significant principle of searching *qi*, Yang Yunsong built a practical theory in *fengshui* with his classics *Qing Nang Ao Yu*, which led to the division of the geomancers from the Tang onwards into two schools.[50] In the record of Needham, the School of Ganzhou of Jiangxi followed Yang Yunsong of that province, mainly concerned with the shapes of mountains and the course of rivers; and the School of Fujian on the other hand followed Wang Ji of that maritime region, regarding the compass as the significant vehicle for determining the indications of the topography with the use of the *gua* (卦) of *Yi Jing* (Book of Changes 易经), and the astrological elements were more prominent in their ideas. Yang Yunsong's chief work, the *Han Long Jing* (Manual of the Moving Dragon) certainly contains some astrology, but nothing about the use of the compass.[51]

In the theory of *Xing Shi* (the School of Form and Attitude), five factors of the environment are most concerned in *fengshui* practice: dragon vein, hill, watercourse, dragon den and orientation, also named the 'five geomantic elements'.[52] According to *Qing Nang Hai Jiao Jing*, mountain and watercourse carry the vital energy *qi*. Practising on the 'five geomantic elements' would mean searching the most important mountain or hill, named dragon's vein, rested by the habitation (*long mai* 龙脉); surveying the mountains or hills around the site (*sha* 砂); and the river through the spot (*shui* 水). So the location of the habitation (*long xue* 龙穴 dragon den) and orientation of the building (*xiang* 向) would be decided.[53]

Dragon Vein (*long mai* 龙脉) and Hill (*sha* 砂)

In the view of *fengshui*, a mountain ridge, on which the habitation relies, is defined as dragon's vein (*long mai* 龙脉). As *Guan Shi Di Li Meng* notes, the appearance of the mountain rises up and down just like the movement of a dragon, and thus are exactly described by the metaphor of the dragon's body; and *Di Li Ren Zi Xu Zhi* defines the attitude and tendency of mountain ridge movement as the veins in a human body, around which the blood and vital energy *qi* flow and move, and similar to a tree, the dragon vein has a main body and many branches, long and short. In Chinese idioms, *lai long qu mai* (dragon in and vein out 来龙去脉) names the starting of a mountain as 'dragon in' and the ending as 'vein out'; it is now an analogy for reason or origin of people or event. And *xun long wang shi* (searching dragon and inspecting attitude 寻龙望势) means to trace the origins of mountain ranges, and inspect the attitude and form of mountains. In *fengshui* practice, mountain ranges are usually an analogy for a family, the main body of the dragon vein or the original mountain being ranked on the top as 'Grandparents' mountain', and the search for the auspicious location would trace back to the grandparents' mountains.[54]

The image of the dragon is the most significant totem among China's sacred animals, because Chinese people always considered themselves as the descendants of dragons. The sacred dragon is portrayed as an original shape or body that is composed by the bodily parts of many other species in the animal kingdom, such as bird, crocodile and fish, and its habitat and forms of movement are more powerful and magical than any animal species. The virtue of the dragon is admired by Confucius, and he puts it in the following manner:

> The several disciples asked, saying: "the Changes often mentions dragon; what is the virtue of the dragon like?" Confucius said: "the dragon is great indeed. The dragon's form shifts. When it approaches the Lord in audience, it manifests the virtue of a spiritual sage … into the deep currents, the fishes and reptiles surround it and of those beings of the watery currents there is none that does not follow it; perched up high, the god of thunder nourishes it, the wind and rain avoid facing it, and the birds and beasts do not disturb it". (He said): "The dragon is great indeed. While the dragon is able to change into a cloud, it is also able to change into a reptile and also able to change into a fish, a flying

bird or a slithery reptile. No matter how it wants to transform, that it does not lose its basic form (ben xing) is because it is the epitome of spiritual ability (shen neng)".[55]

The idea of greatness in the dragon is possibly related with its physical changes, which evoke the powerful capability of many other animals on the earth, under the water and in the air. The expression 'to transform like a dragon' (*longbian* 龙变) also shows the authority and virtue for sagehood. As the Guanzi says:

> The dragon lives in water and, covered in the five colors, it roams about. Therefore, it is daemonic (shen). If it wants to become small, then it transforms like a silkworm or caterpillar. If it wants to become big, then it conceals all under heaven. If it wants to ascend, then it rises with the cloudy vapors. If it wants to descend, then it enters into the deep springs. There is no (fixed) day for its transformations and no (fixed) season for its ascending and descending. Thus it is called daemonic.[56]

Thus, the dragon is respected by the Chinese for the assumption of unexplained powers in the natural world, and it also represents all animals in one without losing its solid 'original shape' even within changes. The image of the mountain range is linked to the dragon possibly because of the changeable features in its form. The body of the mountain range sometimes enlarges and ascends to the sky, but sometimes shrinks and descends to the water, analogous to the daemonic dragon embodying the power of transformation. In addition, mountains also provide the seedbed for the initiation of plants, animals and human beings. Thus they are conceived to be authoritative, and always compared with the moral sage.

Particularly, in the view of *fengshui*, mountain ranges are the containers of *qi*, and their attitude and form are invented and based on the *qi*, flowing and moving within the body of the dragon's vein. As the *Huang Di Zai Jing* says, the earth is an analogy for the dragon's flesh, the rocks are for its bones, and the grasses are for its hairs.[57] *Qi* is defined in two categories in *fengshui*, which are external *qi* (*wai qi* 外气), running out of the ground with the water; and internal *qi* (*nei qi* 内气), hidden underneath the ground.[58] As the *Zang Jing* also says, internal *qi* is conserved by external *qi*, because the emerging dragon mountain is stopped by surrounding water.[59] While *qi* moves through the ground, its movement follows the course of the earth; and when external *qi* is blocked, it thus creates the attitude and form of mountain range and generates life.[60] Although *qi* moves underground invisibly, its origin and movement are known because of the topography changing on the earth, and the location of its conservation is known because of the creation of the mountain ranges. Therefore, it means that *qi* exists in the earth, and with the movement of *qi* within it, everything is generated by the condensation of *qi*. It further explains the principle of using water as the obstacle to the mountain, obtaining interior *qi* as the predominating concern of *fengshui* practice.

The attribution of sacredness to places lies in its symbolic interpretation and metaphorical thinking. When the Dong people locate a desirable site with the life breath of *qi*, it is important to identify the shape of the mountain, trace the quality of the earth and plants and understand the context of the mountains. The evergreen trees near the Dong village are believed to bless the community. The Dong tradition relates that 'The village is blessed by the ageing trees and supervised by the seniors. These trees are spiritual and are named the '*fengshui* tree', 'nourishing tree' and 'blessing tree'. It is remarked that when the Dong villagers settle with these flourishing aged trees, the village believes it would be forever abundant and fertile with the bliss of the tree spirits.[61]

Investigating the mountains surrounding the proper building site is called *cha sha* (investigating the attitudes and flourishing plants of the hills or mountains around 查砂), including the identification of the hierarchy of the mountains around the auspicious site.[62] *Qing Nang Hai Jiao Jing* distinguishes the dragon mountains and *sha* mountains, as the dragon mountain with a higher rank is analogous to the sovereign, and *sha* mountains obey it; and the sovereign comes from a highest place, and the *sha* mountains bow down in front of it, showing loyalty. Viewed from a distance, the environment of the resident site appears elegant, splendid and lucky with the arrangement, and protection is given by them against the evil wind from eight directions.[63]

It is striking that the movement tendency and shape of the mountain and the characteristics of mountains around the location, such as the mountain's *shi* (attitude 势) and *xing* (form 形) would be identified and considered in the determination of an auspicious site in *fengshui* practice. The origins of the terms 'attitude' (*shi*) and form (*xing*) are found in the *Zang Jing*. The *Zang Jing* says that view from a length of a thousand feet is defined as 'attitude', and a hundred feet is 'form'. However, this is just an idea about general scale: the terms are not actually the meanings of an exact or specific measurement. As defined in the *Zang Jing*, 'form' usually describes the physical shape, feature or outline of mountains viewed close up, while 'attitude' is more dynamic and abstract concerning the appearance of a mountain viewed from a distance, showing the tendency of a mountain course to be viewed as constantly moving dragons.[64] It is conceived to be auspicious that, according to the *Zang Jing*, the favourite shapes for mountains seem like dragons lying on the ground and landing from heaven; hidden among peaceful water and plains, like waves in water; appearing like the galloping of horses; like the plumpness of bellows or a filled container, which means an abundance of *qi* or condensing of *qi*; like the prancing and circling dragon and phoenix, full of energy; or like birds lying and beasts crouching, being served by thousands of chariots. The dragon and tiger mountains embrace and guard the favourite site, showing the tendency of greeting not only to hosts and guests but also to the seas and arching towards the stars (Figure 4.11).[65]

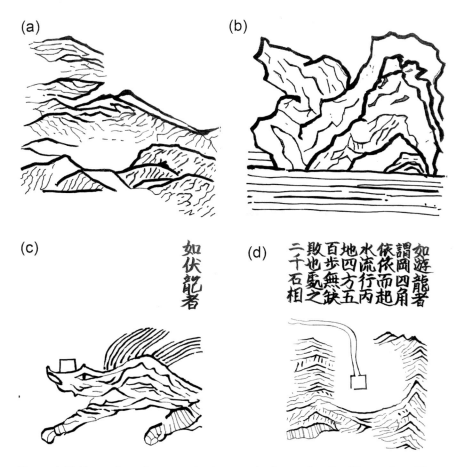

Figure 4.11 Examples of mountain images (redrawn by Jie Zhou after Zhang 2004:171):
(a) flying dragon—the waist is good for dukes;
(b) dragon at riverside—causing admiration;
(c) crouching tiger in the northwest—this type of hill-producing generals;
(d) meandering dragon hill-producing officials.

According to the *Zang Jing*, the auspicious site must be surrounded by mountains in the four cardinal orientations, which are the dark-blue dragon on the left (east), white tiger on the right (west), vermilion bird in the front (south) and dark tortoise at the back (north). These are conceived to correspond with the twenty-eight constellations moving across the sky in accordance with the four seasons.[66] The tortoise mountain rises with wings extending openly beautiful and bright, as if offering a respectful bow, and showing human sentiments, like the vermilion bird dancing with open wings.[67] The vermilion bird mountain with the residents resting on it must not be too high, but appears to lower its head and gradually come down from the main dragon vein as if being ready to accept the location. Three kinds of mountain with the characteristics of pointed, round and square are favourite. The mountain on the east appears alive, gentle, wide open, like the controlled and undulating dark-blue dragon; and the white tiger on the west is abasing itself, showing gentleness and obedience, like tamely obedient domesticated cattle.[68] While people identify constellations in the sky by joining the dots and seeing figures, it is possible to 'read' mountain shapes, especially within a vocabulary of classification with which to express it: the association of the shape with a name allows people to identify and discuss a phenomenon, but it also creates symbolic connections between different classes of phenomena.

In the Dong's cosmology, fog and wind (also called *qi*) are the origins of the world. They believe that the world was originally covered with fog, and the heavens were not separate from the earth until the coming of the God of Wind. Consequently, everything in the world was initiated when the fog was blown away by the God of Wind. The narrative songs of origin in the Dong's epic relate that,

> In the beginning, the God of Wind lived in the heaven, and the God of Earth went up to the heaven and invited Him down. And then the four seasons—Spring, Summer, Autumn and Winter were elaborately formed when the God of Wind came down to the earth. The God of Wind is powerful, his head is sharp like a cattle's horn; when He exhales the life breath qi in the spring, the weather is warm; when he exhales the qi in the summer, it rains; when He exhales the qi in the autumn, it frosts; and He exhales in the winter, it snows.[69]

In the Dong tradition, a site would be considered desirable, and secured with the life breath *qi* when it is sheltered by the surrounding mountains. The mountains running through the Dong regions are believed to have spiritual divinity, which is called 'the pulse of earth and the spirit of dragon' (*di mai long shen* 地脉龙神) or '*long mai*' (dragon vein 龙脉). The mountains are given different names that correspond to their shapes to remind this community of their spiritual qualities. The Dong villagers must burn incense to worship the Dragon Spirits as they harvest the timber.[70] A mountain ridge that resembles the image of a dragon, and the merit of its dynamic context, indicates a source of eternal life breath *qi*. The shape of a sacred dragon is composed of many other species in the animal kingdom. So a mountain ridge, within its remote context, implies the vein of a powerful dragon. Identified with these dynamic dragon characteristics, the mountain ridge filled with desirable vital energy *qi* is named by the term *long xue* (dragon lair 龙穴) and defined as an ideal spot for a settlement. In the Dong's view, the Dragon Spirits of the mountain must not be disturbed by allowing the dead to be buried there. Otherwise the villagers and the livestock become ill, the dogs bark, the cocks crow and the pigs become mad in their sty. To return to the normalcy of life, a *fengshui* master must be invited to perform ritual offerings while the tomb is removed.

The Dong villages enjoy the valley basin surrounded by the mountains. Apart from acting as a channel to transport vital energy *qi*, these mountain ridges are also viewed as shelters that protect the vital *qi* from being blown away by the unexpected direction of evil winds. According to the leaders of the Dong community, this is a desirable location because it is surrounded by the mountains or hills comprising the four cardinal directions.[71] The mountains surrounding a typical auspicious site are particularly celebrated and given the names of four animals: the dark blue dragon on the left (east), white tiger on the right (west), vermilion bird in the front (south) and dark tortoise at the back (north). The favourite orientation for the Dong villages ranges from southeast to southwest. In their view, it is auspicious to face *yang* and be sited in *yin* with harmonious *qi*. The south orientation, related with fire in the five-element system and representing summer, is warm and *yang;* and north, related with water and representing winter, is cool and *yin*. East is conceived as *yang* and associated with the vitality of wood and the initiation of spring, and thus buildings oriented to the range from the east to the south are thought to be auspicious. The western direction is believed to relate to *yin* and is associated with gold and autumn, so cemeteries are placed to the west of the villages. However, the four cardinal directions are only occupied by the sacred temple that contains sages and spirits, and thus, the drum towers are oriented precisely to the four cardinal directions to evoke these eternal beings to connect the earth and heavens. Conversely, the villagers' dwellings seldom face directly to the four cardinal directions so that they would not receive the *evil qi* (*sha qi* 煞气) emanating from the exact cardinal directions.[72] The components of the natural landscape are reflected in the Dong's cosmos and beliefs, where at the same time they are interpreted with the corresponding context.

Water (*shui* 水), Watercourse Mouth (*shui kou* 水口) and Dragon Den (*long xue* 龙穴)

In every culture and religion, water has been regarded as a source of life and a symbol of life in spiritual metaphor. In the first chapter of the Bible, Genesis, it is written that "The earth was formless and empty, and darkness covered the deep waters. And the Spirit of God was hovering over the surface of the waters".[73] Another reference to the importance of water includes, "Let the waters swarm with swarms of living animals ... great sea creatures and every living animal that moves, with which the waters swarmed, according to their kind ... Be fruitful and multiply, and fill the waters in the seas...".[74] Water was the source of life even before light, sun or moon, earth, plants, or living creatures were created. John 4:14 further explains that "Everyone who drinks of this water will be thirsty again. The water that I will give will become in them a spring of water gushing up to eternal life".[75] As a result, the ritual of baptism symbolically cleanses human beings from their impurities, while the pure, colourless, transparent, odourless, tasteless water flows through a human's being. This ritual separates them from the world of the dead and brings them to the living world through rebirth. As a symbol of chastity, water epitomizes the power of spiritual regeneration and promises an eternal salvation through this baptismal ceremony.[76]

In the Dong's view, water is not only the source of life but also partakes in the definition of divinity. They believe in the God of Water and perform rituals to worship this god. They must burn incense the first time when they collect water from a river or well in the Chinese New Year. Showing the importance of water in the Dong culture, often a small altar is built near a well with woodcut status inside that symbolizes the God of Water. In December, the New Year's Day, and at the beginning of spring in the Chinese calendar, they burn incense in the altar when collecting their water. In some villages, during the spring festival of Chinese New Year, a woman from each family prepares the meat and drink offered to the wells. They then burn incense to worship the God of Water and subsequently share the meal with the family. After the meal, they dance and sing the Dong narrative songs around the wells. This is intended to praise the God of Water that would supply them pure water during the four seasons—the eternal source of life.[77]

The miracle of flowing water carries moral connotations in traditional Chinese philosophy with such concepts as purity, flexibility, shaping, offering, peacefulness and agreeability. As Guan Zi writes,

> Water is the blood and breath of the earth, flowing and communicating within its body as if in sinews and veins. Therefore we say that water is the preparatory raw material of all things ... Water is yielding, weak and clean, and likes to wash away the evils of man – this may be called its benevolence ... When you measure it you cannot force it to level off, for when the vessel is full it does that by itself – this may be called its rectitude ... There is no space into which it will not flow, and when it is level it stops – this may be called its fairness.[78]

Thus, people admired for their morals, as Dao de Jing writes, must occupy the characters of water. It survives the beings in the world but never contend, and it is modest and always dwells on the lower place that most of the people do not admire. So it acts with the criteria of Taoism. A person with high morality should take the seven images of water: dwelling depending on the topography; with a heart which is peaceful and profound; in a kind relationship which never expects any return; with words which are credible; with an organization in governing the states; with a proper ability in the work; and with an action relying on the time. In conclusion, people with high morality never worry about making mistakes, because they never contend and offend others.[79]

The Dong view spiritual water as a source of wealth and life breath qi in addition to being an agent of moral admiration. Abundant water is a symbol of fertility. The tame river with its clear and fresh water runs through the landscape suggesting health and energy. Because the movement of water originates in the action of generative qi, the speed, the sound and

134 *Wind and Water in Shaping the Dong Villages*

the collection of the movement are most concerned. According to the Zang Jing, rivers, creeks and streams, running in a route of winding or zigzagging are admired, but they are not auspicious if running fast like an arrow or with turbulented.[80] Turbulent water is taboo, which is refered to 'sobbing in sorrow'.[81] Also in mountain areas, when a river reaches a bend, it forms a pool. According to *Zang Jing*, the water pools at a bend and then disperses, conserved before flowing away, implying emotions and a sentimental reluctance with abundant and gentle draining, as if reluctant to leave is related to the view of conservation of *qi* and fortune in the located site (Figure 4.11). In *fengshui* practice, when the clear, crystal and clean water is collected in front of the site and forms a pond, lake, or deep pool, the site is most favourable. Therefore, in order to obtain good fortune, the favourable image of the river is expected to be meandering around the foot of mountain, where it makes the sense of flowing away invisibly.[82]

According to the *Zang Jing*, the site is auspicious if surrounded by clear and meandering water of distant origin; but if the river is rushing out of the building site taking the *qi* with it, the location is unfortunate (Figure 4.12).[83] So apart from identifying the mouth of watercourse, it is necessary to distinguish the shapes of the hills (*shui kou sha* 水口砂) on either side of the watercourse mouth, whose function is believed to be an obstacle to the water, i.e. serving to restrict its way out. The watercourse mouth, with mountains standing on both sides and projecting out to form the shape of gnashing teeth, is named 'gnashing teeth watercourse mouth' (*jiao ya shui kou* 交牙水口). A watercourse mouth, with gnashing teeth mountains on both sides, as it flows away, is preferable, because it is conceived that these mountains would 'lock' the watercourse in to prevent the water from flowing away too fast. The Dong's perception of moving water as that which brings purities or removes impurities indicates the moral aspects of water as the carrier of life breath *qi*. This creates the balance between the closed 'watercourse mouth' and the visible flowing out of the water.

Human beings tend to order their worlds within a limited domain that is rooted in their unique world view, and this reflects the rules that guide nearly every facet of the communal and physical setting of a society. The most significant difference between the Dong and Han traditions is that the Dong construct their Wind and Rain bridges over watercourses so as to reconcile the visual conflict between the inward and outward flow of the river flow. Before a Dong village is settled in a valley, two features of the river, also called 'watercourse mouths' (*shui kou* 水口), must be investigated and identified, and they are the 'inlet mouth' and 'outlet mouth.' These two 'mouths' are bound by a serpentine valley between mountains that form the bend of the river adjacent to the village. The 'inlet watercourse mouth' symbolizes the emergence of the river, which suggests its origin, or beginning, as the source of life. Conversely, 'the outlet watercourse mouth' represents the retreating fresh river, which is seen as a symbol of death considered in the imagination as the departure and 'hoped-for' return.[84] According to the Dong bridge master Yang Shanren, the site of a Wind and Rain bridge

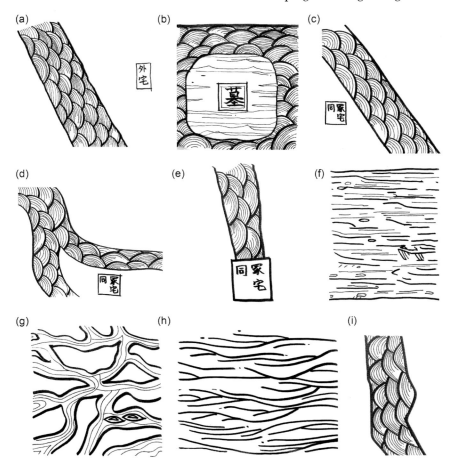

Figure 4.12 Nine types of auspicious and inauspicious water images (redrawn by Jie Zhou after Zhang 2004: 190):
a. running water—it is auspicious to be sixty steps beyond on the east side of houses but misfortunate within sixty steps;
b. still pond water—causing heart diseases when surrounding graves;
c. sword blade water—causing robbery and injury when crossing the house and grave;
d. struggling water—causing descendants to fight to death when passing by the house and grave;
e. arrow water—eliminating descendants when going towards the house and grave;
f. clear blood water—causing descendants to hate each other;
g. disorderly water—causing descendants to be evil and harmful to the mother;
h. guest water—causing descendants to die away from home or be defeated;
i. counter-current water—causing descendants not to be filial without virtues, or harmed by servants.

must be carefully determined and built on the 'exit' of the river, the 'outlet mouth of watercourse'. Thus, the Wind and Rain bridge is located on the periphery of the village, not only as the place to define the threshold of the village with the 'blocking' ceremony but also as the celebration of the life-bringing *qi* of the river.

An inhabitable place sought as the ideal *fengshui* site is called *long xue* (龙穴), which means the den of the dragon in Chinese. The auspicious site is usually obtained by searching the area with the maximum concentration of life-giving breath *qi* (*sheng qi* 生气), which is supposed to be haunting around the dragon vein of the mountains. And since the life-giving breath *qi* should be collected rather than dispersed water and especially calm pooled water, is desirable to obtain the beneficial influence of the *qi*. It is preferred that the water comes from an unknown source and goes to a place unseen, from which the mountains emerge and the water returns, while people settled on the site would not only be occurred with long life but also wealth.[85] So the house backed by the mountains and the bridges on the watercourse mouth of the river are remarkable. It is a typical picture of an auspicious village plan.[86]

According to *Zang Jing*, the selection of the village site on the opening basin valley (*ming tang* 明堂) is named *dian xue* (locating the dragon den 点穴), and it is necessary to locate the appropriate spot by tracing the dragon mountain (dragon vein 龙脉) to prove that it is the right place by investigating the hills surrounding it. Normally, starting from the location of the village, and following the mountains backing the rear of the site, both the nearest mountain—the Grandfather mountain and the farther one—the Great Grandfather mountain must come from a prosperous direction, and be located in the same direction on the compass with the village site and its watercourse mouth. For instance, the 'Metal Dragon Grandfather mountain' pattern would come from southeast or southwest; Water Dragon pattern from southwest or northwest; Wood Dragon pattern from northeast or northwest; and Fire Dragon pattern from northeast or southeast. Generally, the chosen mountain needs to show several changes of direction as a dancing dragon, symbolizing life and energy, which will arrive at the building site. But the most auspicious site would have the changes following the same direction. For instance, starting with the Metal Dragon and the backing mountain ending also with the Metal Dragon, or else the backing mountain must share the same *gua* with the watercourse mouth, which is named after the same pattern (*he ju* 合局). The site is named *long zhen xue* (real dragon den 龙真穴), only if the backing mountain shares the same *Gua* with the watercourse mouth, or else it is called *jia xue* (fake dragon den 假穴) or *jia long* (fake dragon 假龙). If the mountain is located in the Metal Pattern when arriving at the site, but the watercourse mouth is not of the Metal Pattern, the site is named *jia xue*. In practice, by turning the compass and making its pointing south needle matched with the red line of Heaven Pool, the *fengshui* masters would find out what is the dragon of the backing mountain by reading the direction of the peak of the mountain with the compass.[87] For example, the orientation of Ma'an village points to *qian* and *dui* in the diagram of Former Heaven Eight-trigrams, so it belongs to Fire Pattern; and the rear mountain and watercourse mouth also belong to Fire Pattern, which share the same *gua* and thus the site location is auspicious. However, if they do not share the same *gua*, the location needs to be changed until it shares the same *gua* with the watercourse mouth.

Fengshui Practice on the Arrangement of Ma'an Village

Before the building site of Chengyang bridge was decided, according to the *fengshui* Master Chen Yongqing of Ma'an village, the topography around the drum tower and the village would be first considered (Figure 4.13). According to the School of Form and Attitude of *fengshui*, the auspicious village settlement would be surrounded by favourable mountains and watercourse mouth 'locked' by the Wind and Rain bridge, and the site of the watercourse mouth depends on the location of the village centre—the drum tower (Figure 4.14). The plan arrangement of Ma'an village is typical of the Dong areas, with the Linxi river meandering in the south of the village. Following the rules in *fengshui* practice, the village is located on the mountain basin surrounded by four desirable mountains—the dragon mountain Qilin to the north, the Long mountain to the east, the Chanlan mountain

Figure 4.13 The *fengshui* master Chen Yongqing explaining *fengshui* practice on the Chengyang bridge with author and master Yang Shanren, Sanjiang, 2004 (photo: Li LIn).

138   *Wind and Water in Shaping the Dong Villages*

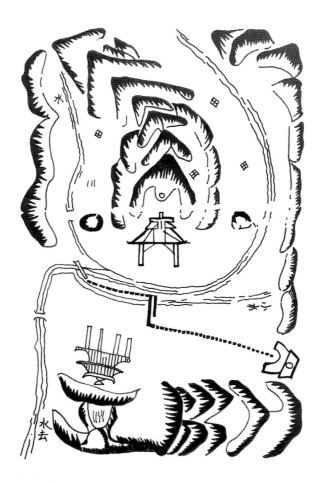

Figure 4.14 The desirable location of a resident site related to the mountains and watercourse mouth (redrawn by Jie Zhou after Needham 1962: 240).

to the west and the Chengsha mountain to the south. This is a typical picture of a preferred place for the inhabitants, a respond to the images of four animals—the dragon, the tiger, the vermilion bird and the tortoise, to collect the vital energy *qi* in this place and protect it from the evil wind (Figure 4.15). Dwellings are built following the different contours of Qilin mountain around Ma'an drum tower, which is the centre of the village. Both the Chengyang bridge and Pingyan bridge on the northwest and northeast of the village, are major links connecting the gaps between the villages. The bridge orientation is also influenced by the shape and distance of the mountains around it. According to the Dong *fengshui* master Chen Yongqing and the craftsman Yang Shanren, the bridge was built on the place connecting two dragon veins, named '*er long xi zhu*' (two dragons entertaining with a ball 二龙戏珠), symbolizing the favourable scene. The view from the bridge wouldn't be stuck by the mountains around it, otherwise it would influence the wealth and flourishing of the village. And the whole thing must be exactly conducted by the *fengshui* practice of both the School of Form and Attitude and the School of Compass, by investigating the village environment and examining the bridge site with the compass.[88] Thus the action of building the Wind and Rain bridge in Ma'an village involves these stages: first, investigating the environment of Ma'an village, particularly involving the dragon mountain and the hills surrounding the village; second, locating the village site and drum tower in the basin areas; thirdly, searching the position of the watercourse mouth of the village, and locating the bridge building site; and finally, adjusting the orientation of the village houses.

The watercourse mouths, which are responsible for keeping the wealthy *qi*, must be determined before the settlement and the orientation of the residences. The outlet mouth for a bridge must be selected to provide an auspicious layout for the village. For example, to identify the watercourse mouths of the village, a compass was supported horizontally on the location of drum tower—the village centre. In *fengshui* practice, when the compass is used to decide the fortune or misfortune of the location, it is usually lian on a rice bag, and kept horizontal and still. As the main agricultural product, rice is evidently a primary symbol of fertility and abundance. The orientation of main façade of the building is often defined as the facing mountain (*xiang shan* 向山), and the opposite façade is named seating mountain (*zuo shan* 坐山) (Figure 4.16). The compass stops turning until its needle of the heaven pool points to the south and north poles, and then fortune or misfortune of the building site is identified by reading the scales in relation to the main building facade.[89] The compass is turned so that the needle aligned with the south–north axis acts as a way to find the inauspicious palace (*gong wei* 宫位) (the Tomb Palace) on the compass as the 'outlet watercourse mouth'.[90]

In the *fengshui* Practise, the dragon mountain (*long mai* 龙脉), inhabitant's site (*xue chang* 穴场) and watercourse mouth (*shui kou* 水口), are related to each other while selecting a favourable location. According to the School of Form and Attitude, while investigating the river through the habitant's site and hills around it, the most important thing is to inspect the watercourse mouth, the place where the river flows out the enclosed site. The watercourse mouth is properly identified by the *fengshui* compass, following Master Yang Yunsong's theory of the School of Compass. In addition, the characters of surrounding mountains (形 *xing*) by the Five-element would influence the direction of the bridge, and then the bridge direction would be adjusted with the *fengshui* compass. In the *Qin Nang Ao Yu*,[91] Master Yang Yunsong concludes that 'golden dragon, a longitude and a latitude' (*jing long, yi jing, yi wei*, 金龙, 一经, 一纬) are the secret of manipulating *qi* as the principles of *fengshui* practice in locating the proper site and deciding the

140 *Wind and Water in Shaping the Dong Villages*

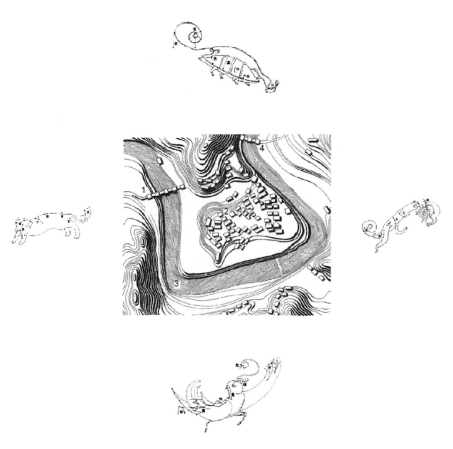

Figure 4.15 The layout of Ma'an village surrounded by the mountains represented by four animal images in the view of *fengshui* (reconstructed as an image):
1. Chengyang bridge;
2. Ma'an village and drum tower;
3. Linxi river;
4. Yanzhai bridge.

building's auspicious orientation. Golden dragon refers to four patterns of watercourse mouths; a longitude means the 'reversal 72-dragon', and latitude refers to the '24-mountain orientation'. This means that the mountains around the site, the selected location and the watercourse mouth must all share the same *gua* (卦). A *xue chang* (building site 穴 场) is not ideal without water, and thus the identification of watercourse mouth and the forms of hills around the location are crucial in the selection of *xue chang*. The selection of watercourse mouth for the auspicious building site depends on the orientation of the residential location. Watercourse mouth (*shui kou* 水口) is defined as the position, through which the water surrounding the village named *ming tang* (明堂) goes to exit. Manipulating the vital energy *qi* of *ming tang* means mingling the interior *qi* from the mountain with the exterior *qi* coming with the river. In *fengshui* practice, the four cardinal directions belong to the four trigrams, *kan* 坎, *li* 离, *zhen* 震 and *dui* 兑, which are related to Water, Fire, Wood and Metal of the Five-element, and according to the *Di Li Shu* by Yang Yunsong, which are involved in four patterns by 'two-mountain and life 12-palace' on the Heaven Plate scale by the principles of Five-element and Three-harmony.[92] Five refers to the elements of Wood, Fire, Earth, Metal and Water, and harmony to the conflict between them in generating the circle of birth and death. The four patterns of watercourse mouth are Metal Pattern (*jin ju* 金局), Water Pattern (*shui ju* 水局), Wood Pattern (*mu ju* 木局), and Fire Pattern (*huo ju* 火局), and three palaces of Tomb Palace (*mu gong* 墓宫), Repose Palace (*jue gong* 绝宫), and Womb Palace (*tai gong* 胎宫) serve for the watercourse mouth (Figure 4.17).

On the Eight-trigram system, the four *gua* of *kan* 坎, *li* 离, *zhen* 震 and *dui* 兑 dominate the *yang* patterns (阳局); another four *gua* of *xun* 巽, *gen* 艮, *kun* 坤 and *qian* 乾 control the *yin* patterns; and the other directions can be deduced by the clockwise rotation with respect the organization of

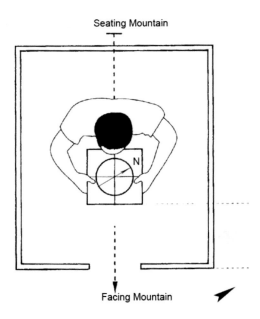

Figure 4.16 Application of a *fengshui* compass in orientating the building (reconstructed by author after Chen 1999: 19)

mountains on the compass for the *gua* of *yang* patterns and anti-clockwise for the *gua* of *yin* patterns (阴局).⁹³ For instance, in the *yang* pattern, the east direction is *zhen* 震 *gua*, related to wood in the Five-element and seating in *jia* 甲 of 24-mountain, named *jia mu qi* (甲木气 *jia* and wood pattern). According to the Three-harmony diagram, for Wood Pattern's watercourse mouth, Tomb Palace is *ding* 丁 and *wei* 未, Repose Palace is *kun* 坤 and *shen* 申, and Womb Palace is *geng* 庚 and *you* 酉, and the 12 fortunate and unfortunate directions are thus identified by the river flowing out of the watercourse mouth on the spots of the *ding* 丁 and *wei* 未 of the Tomb Palace.

The south direction belongs to *li gua*, related to *fire* and seating on *bin* thus named *bing huo qi* (*bing* and fire pattern 丙火气). For Fire Pattern's watercourse mouth, Tomb Palace is *xin* 辛 and *xu* 戌, Repose Palace is *qian* 乾 and *hai* 亥, and Womb Palace is *ren* 壬 and *zi* 子. The 12 fortunate and unfortunate directions can be identified by the river flowing out in the watercourse mouth of the *xin* 辛 and *xu* 戌 of Tomb Palace. The west direction is *dui gua* belonging to metal, seating on *gen* mountain and named *gen jin qi* (*gen* and metal pattern 艮金气). For Metal Pattern watercourse mouth, Tomb Palace is *gui* 癸 and *chou* 丑, for Repose Palace it is *geng* 庚 and *yin* 寅, and for Womb Palace it is *jia* 甲 and *mao* 卯, and the 12 fortunate and unfortunate directions can be identified by the river flowing out in watercourse mouth of the *gui* 癸 and *chou* 丑 directions of the Tomb Palace. The north is *kan gua* related with water and seating on *ren* direction named *ren shui qi* (*ren* and water pattern 壬水气). For Water Pattern's watercourse mouth, Tomb Palace is *yi* 乙 and *chen* 辰, Repose Palace is *xun* 巽 and *si* 巳, and Womb Palace is *bing* 丙 and *wu* 午, and the 12 fortunate and unfortunate directions can be identified by the river flowing out of the watercourse mouth of the *yi* 乙 and *chen* 辰 directions of the Tomb Palace.⁹⁴

According to the above theory, the watercourse mouth of the Chengyang bridge would be exactly organized, assuming an auspicious lay-out for Ma'an village. The Chengyang bridge is built to the northwest of Ma'an village on the Linxi river, with its northeast end connecting with the Qilin mountain and Ma'an village, and northwest entrance connecting with the Chanlan mountain and Pingtan village. To locate the watercourse mouth of Ma'an village, a compass is supported horizontally on the site location (*xue chang* 穴场) of Ma'an drum tower—the village centre, turning it so that the south–north direction needle matches with the red line of the heaven pool; and then checking out the palace (*gong wei* 宫位) on the Heaven Plate scale of compass, which is also the pattern of the watercourse mouth. Reading the compass, the drum tower seats north and faces south, matching the *li gua* of the Eight-trigram sequence, which belongs to *Bing Fire Qi* of *yang* pattern, so according to the Five-element and Three-harmony Principle, the Birth Palace is located on *yin* 寅 and *gen* 艮, the Prosperity Palace is *bing* 丙 and *wu* 午, and Tomb Palace is *xin* 辛 and *xu* 戌. From the pattern on the compass, within the Ma'an village, the arrangement is auspicious while

Wind and Water in Shaping the Dong Villages 143

the river flows out of the village in the *xin* 辛 and *xu* 戌 direction of the Tomb Palace. The village site is believed to be favourable if the watercourse mouth is identified with Tomb Palace, because, for the village, water could always be seen to be flowing in instead of out (Figure 4.18). However, if the watercourse flows away in the *xun* direction, for instance, and the building sits on *ren* mountain and faces *bing* mountain, the direction indicating the watercourse mouth is named Eighth Evil Spirit of Hell Scale (*ba sha huang quan pan* 八煞黄泉盘), and the orientation of the building is considered inauspicious (Figure 4.19).[95]

Similar to the Han culture, if the river flows out of the village in the direction of the Tomb Palace on the compass, it is considered unfortunate.

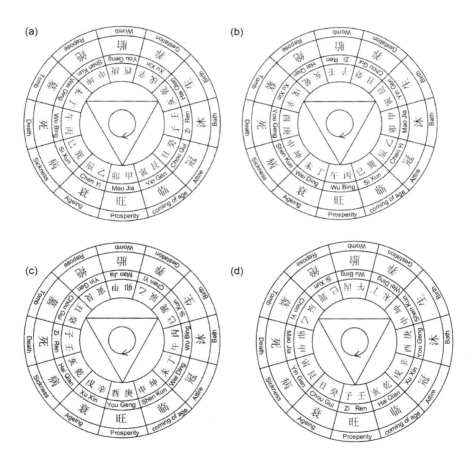

Figure 4.17 Four patterns of Tomb Palace (redrawn by author after Chen 1999: 94):
(a) The Wood Pattern and its watercourse mouth on *wei* and *ding* of Tomb Palace;
(b) The Fire Pattern and its watercourse mouth on *xu* and *xin* of Tomb Palace;
(c) The Metal Pattern and its watercourse mouth on *chou* and *gui* of Tomb Palace;
(d) The Water Pattern and its watercourse mouth on *chen* and *yi* of Tomb Palace.

144 *Wind and Water in Shaping the Dong Villages*

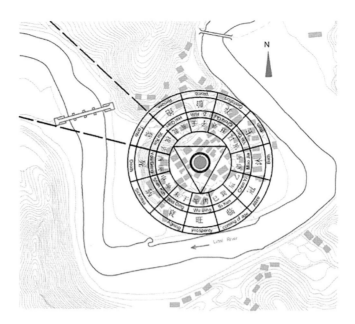

Figure 4.18 Locating the watercourse mouth of Ma'an village by Bing-fire Pattern on *fengshui* compass (drawn by author).

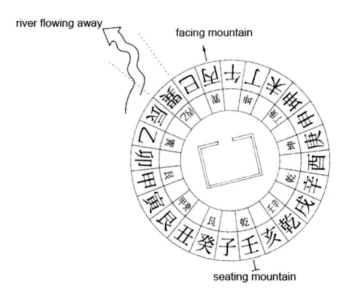

Figure 4.19 An example of watercourse mouth of the Eighth Evil Spirit of Hell scale (drawn by author after Chen 1999: 117).

However, different from the Han, the Dong rectify this situation by building a Wind and Rain bridge in the place where the water is always seen to arrive in the village rather than to leave it away. Thus, most of the village houses are oriented towards the southeast, with the Wind and Rain bridge as the symbol of retaining the wealthy *qi*. For orienting the village houses, south and southeast orientations are favourable selections for the Dong people. In the Chinese view, the vital energy qi comes from East (紫气东来), and on the compass this is the direction related with Spring, which is the beginning season of the year; and related with Wood, symbolizing life in the Five-elements. While selecting the sitting and facing mountains of the building, it is important to judge where the *qi*, the vitality energy comes from, and normally, the direction from which the *qi* comes is the favourable direction for the building. As Lao Zi says, it is auspicious to face *yang* and be sited in *yin* with harmonious *qi*. According to the Eight-trigrams system, moving clockwise from *dui gua* to *kan gua*, the sun rises from the east, through the south and down in the west; and from *gen gua* to *li gua*, the night comes forward with the sunset. The sun rises from the east, which is conceived as *yang*, associated with the vitality of wood and the initiation of spring in terms of Five-elements, and thus building orientations associated with *yang* are thought to be auspicious. The west is believed to relate to *yin*, associated with gold and autumn, so areas with orientation related to *yin* such as the cemetery would usually be organized to the west and north of the village. With this movement of the compass, the fortunate directions and time transform to unfortunate directions gradually. While directions are related with time on the compass, south is warm and *yang*, and north is cool and *yin*, as the season changes from summer to winter. The traditional plan of an architectural complex exhibits the arrangement of balance with *yin and yang*, opposition and reunion.

Although both the Pingzhai and Yanzhai villages are settled on the north bank of the Linxi river and enjoy southeast orientation, the dwellings of each village are, however, built with a unique orientation. This situation also happens with the villages of Shangzhai and Xiazhai (Figure 4.20). The houses of Pingzhai village are oriented to the south, and the Helong bridge of this village is built to the west of the village and to the south of Yanzhai village. This orientation symbolizes a 'good' keeping of vital energy *qi* for the Pingzhai village. However, it may cause problems and be considered as an 'evil' blocker of *qi* for its neighbouring Yanzhai village. To obtain an auspicious view and avoid seeing a neighbour's Wind and Rain bridge as a *qi* barrier, the orientation of the houses in the Yanzhai village are adjusted to the southwestern direction. Similarly, located on the opposite banks of the Linxi river, the Shangzhai village and the Xiazhai village, respectively, occupy the favourable basin region near the bend of the river and thus can view the water flowing inward. The houses of Shangzhai village face nearly south, and its bridge is built on the west side of the village. To avoid seeing the bridge of the Shangzhai village, the houses of the Xiazhai village are arranged so that they face southwest, still enjoying the bend of river 'flowing in.' This leads to the lay-out of these two typical Dong villages. They have

146 *Wind and Water in Shaping the Dong Villages*

identifiable differences especially in the orientation of the houses, although they share similar topography and southeast is their favourable orientation. Settled on the site surrounded by mountains and rivers, and guarded by the Wind and Rain bridges, the Dong villagers from both towns believe that they have secured a desirable arrangement.

As threshold entrances to the Dong villages, the Wind and Rain bridges are not solely concerned with being a ritual centre but also dramatizing a

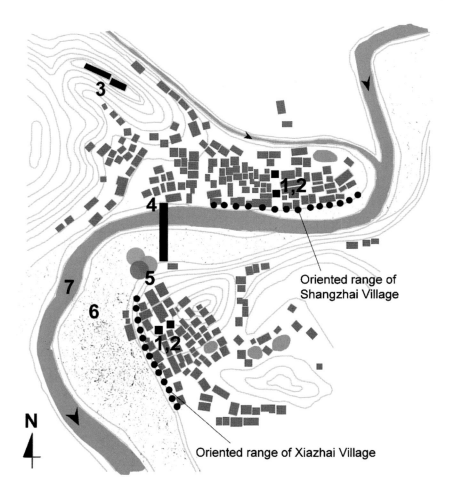

Figure 4.20 The layout of Shangzhai village, the Wind and Rain bridges and Xiazhai village in Linxi county (drawn by author):
1 & 2. The drum towers and performance stages of Shangzhai village on the south bank and Xiazhai village on the north bank;
3. The school of Shangzhai village;
4. Shangzhai Wind and Rain bridge;
5. *fengshui* trees;
6. The fields for cultivation;
7. Linxi river.

transition, providing a ritual space and marking the crossing of the route in and out of the village. The progress of the river, along with its *qi* and its 'returning souls,' provides the value of this demarcation. The thresholds, which may be crossed by the living and the dead while arriving and departing, became a focus of attention and concern. As not only 'persons' but also 'spirits' cross the threshold, the bridges are associated with common ideas of how they were built and oriented. So Wind and Rain bridges, which serve as barriers and entryways for both exiting and entry, embody the desire to resist the undesirable movements caused by inauspicious spirits and forces.

Conclusion

Although various buildings are constructed in different ways by various societies, they usually contain both physical and mental aspects that are often related with people who use them.[96] Chinese vernacular architecture has developed in connection with traditional cosmology, which is exhibited through the performance of *fengshui* with a series of rules to recognize an environment favourable to human beings. The space and each element constructing the space are thus arranged with regard to the rituals that are carried out within them and thus subject to special symbolic meanings. The traditional perception of space in China concerns the place that can hold and maintain *qi*. This is initially set up as the boundary to separate the profane taboo between interior and exterior space.[97] In a rural culture where most people never strayed more than a few miles from home and there are few visitors from outside, a general belief in an unknown 'beyond' is more easily sustained, as is the more general connection with life-sustaining *qi* been all of which was reinforced the sense of the bridge as an appropriate place for the return of souls. A bridge is doubly a crossing: on one side, it is a meeting of a road and a river, so if you stand on the middle of it you encounter the arriving water, which from the Dong viewpoint presumably allows a privileged proximity to the arriving *qi*; on the other side, the bridge also offers a transition between two banks as a potential link between two worlds. Bridges have often acted as frontiers, since rivers are invariably natural barriers, and in the Dong case a bridge usually marks the entrance to a village, a significant threshold. For these customs to take place at all there needed to be clearly defined thresholds to each group's territory, and a bridge, if it linked two villages, provided an ideal marker as a village entrance, a threshold that is always known and acknowledged.

A traditional cosmology strongly influences peoples' awareness of their natural environment and of the places upon which they base their spaces. As Edward Relph defines them, places 'are constructed in our memories and affections through repeated encounters and complex associations.'[98] Place experiences are necessarily time-dependent and memory qualified. Cosmology is the human systematic attempt to answer the question of concerning place of human beings in nature, finding an order and a harmonious relationship between nature and society. As Tuan points out, a symbolic cosmology is promoted and tied to a place through peoples' experience in "the practice of structuring the world into substances, colours, directions, animals, and human traits", which recalls a succession of interrelated phenomena, both analogically and metaphorically.[99] Tuan also argues, myths function both as a conceptual extension given by direct and familiar experience as a component in a world view or cosmology in the time of an absence of precise knowledge. Myths are pursued by human beings in an attempt to seek a proper guide for their practical activities, to avoid offending the gods or spirits of nature in a coherent world system.[100]

Being rooted in a social and physical setting, cosmology is related to a culture where the detailed ordering of the components varies greatly from culture to culture, and from individual to individual. As Rapoport argues, for instance, choice of site is important, and the selection may be either influenced by supernatural aspects or depend on social viewpoint. The land would be carefully orchestrated so as to fit the myth or legends of a place, because a building is set up on it, as the case in the Gilbert and Ellice Islands where the houses are oriented towards the forces of the universe rather than following the topography. The impact of the site selection is impressive in cultural rather than physical terms, since the desirability of the site depends on "the goals, ideals, and values of a people or a period, and the choice of the 'good' site— whether lake, river, mountain, or coast-depends on this cultural definition".[101] As Chinese used a spatial frame based on cardinal points to organize the components of nature, it is typical of the Dong to search for a fortunate place having the collective life breath *qi*. Thus, the local culture sustains the conventional contexts of architecture, beliefs construct the essential and meaningful parts of a structure and human experience makes people open to understanding metaphor, therefore finding rules to guide the construction of their environment. Just as George Lakeoff and Mark Johnson point out, metaphor is capable of highlighting and making coherent certain aspects of our experience, and thus may create social realities for people, but also be a guide for their future action.[102]

Notes

1 Tuan, Y.-f. 1974. *Topophilia: A Study of Environmental Perception, Attitudes, and Values*. Engle Wood Cliffs, NJ: Prentice-Hall Inc., p. 141.
2 *Ibid.* p. 141.
3 *Ibid.* p. 145.
4 *Ibid.* p. 146.
5 Based on an interview with Wu Hao and Yang Shanren, Sanjiang county, July 22, 2004.
6 Compilation Group of Annals of the Nationalities in Sanjiang county (2002) (first published 1946). *Sanjiangxian Minzuzhi* [Annals of the Nationalities in Sanjiang County 三江县民族志]. Nanning: Guangxi Minzhu Press, p. 200.

7 See Li, Xi 2001. *Fengshui Qiao* 风水桥 (Fengshui bridge), in Zhang Zhezhong (ed.) 2001. *Dongzu Fengyuqiao* 侗族风雨桥 (The Wind and Rain Bridge of the Dong). Guiyang: Huaxia Press, pp. 26–8.

8 In the record of gazette of Sanjiang county 2002 (first published 1935): 200. These bridges are not called Wind and Rain bridges in the Dong areas, and the Dong usually names them by the names of the village. For the name 'Fengshui bridge' making the sense of superstition, after the poet Guo Moruo wrote poetry for it and named it Wind and Rain bridge, and since then the name of Wind and Rain bridge was spread.

9 Xian, G. 1995. *Dongzu Tonglan* [A General Survey of the Dong Nationality 侗族通览]. Nanning: Guangxi Minzhu Press. Zhang, J. (2004).

10 Interviewed with Master Yang Shanren and Fengshui Master Yang Yongqing in 2011, Sanjiang county.

11 Needham, Joseph 1962. *Science and Civilisation in China*, Vol. 4: Physics and Physical Technology. Cambridge: Cambridge University Press, p. 239.

12 *Ibid.* p. 240.

13 *Huangdi Neijing* is mainly composed by two sections, including Basic Questions (*su wen*) and Divine Pivot (*ling shu*), which is considered to have been written during in the middle of Han dynasty (206 B.C.-220). The classic canon is presented with the form of interview between the Yellow Emperor and his vassals Qi Bo, Bo Gao, Gui Yuqu, Shao Shi, Shao Yu and Lei Gong, which also concerns the knowledge of philosophy, chronometer, climate, calendar, geography and biology, apart from focusing on the traditional Chinese medical theory.

14 The Five Movement and Six *Qi* theory, which is one of the most important parts about the transmissions of *qi* in the traditional Chinese medical classic *Huangdi Neijing*, mainly concerns the influence of changeable season and climate on the health of human body. Based on the variety of season and climate in the natural world and respect response to the changes in human body, the theory ties the vital phenomena with the natural climate phenomena within the frame of Five-element theory, relates the human disorder with the variety of natural climate, and therefore predicts the human diseases within the regular change of the natural world. The theory reflects the view of harmony between human and natural world (*tianren heyi* 天人合一) in traditional Chinese medical system. Also see Wang, Qiheng (ed.) 1992. *Fengshui Lilun Yanjiu* 风水理论研究 (Research on the Theory of Fengshui School). Tianjin: Tianjin University Press.

15 See Chen 2000: 8–16.

16 See *Kaogong Ji,* which was written by the scholars of Qi people between Spring and Autumn period and Warring stage. This passage is quoted from *Zhouguan Xinyi* (周官新义) by Wang Anshi (1021–86). Shanghai: Shangwu Yinshuguan Press 1937, p. 241, the translation of the author; and Dai, Wusan (ed.) 2003. *Kaogong Ji Tushuo* 考工记图说 (The Illumination of *Kaogong Ji*). Jinan: Shandong Huabao Press, pp. 97–8.

17 *Ibid.* pp. 97–8.

18 Dai, Wusan (ed.). 2003. *Kaogong Ji Tushuo* [The Illumination of Kaogong Ji 考工记图说]. Jinan: Shandong Huabao Press, pp. 97–8.

19 See Dai 2003: 20–1. Huai river originates in Henan province, flowing east through Henan, Anhui and Jiangsu provinces, and finally runs into the Yangzi river. Ji river refers to the south and north branches of Huang He. Wen river is located in the south of Shandong province.

20 Chen 1999: 1–3.

21 See Needham, Joseph 1962. *Science and Civilisation in China*, Vol. 4: Physics and Physical Technology. Cambridge: Cambridge University Press, p. 239.

22 *Kao gong ji*: 255; and Dai 2003: 59–61.

23 Quoted from Needham, Joseph 1959. *Science and Civilisation in China*, Vol. 3: Mathematics and the Sciences of the Heavens and the Earth. Cambridge: Cambridge University press, p. 284.
24 *Ibid.* p. 302.
25 *Ibid.* p. 286.
26 *Ibid.*
27 Gao 1995: 208.
28 *Ibid.*
29 *Ibid.*
30 Gao 1995: 209–10.
31 *Ibid.*
32 *Ibid.* p. 255.
33 *Ibid.*
34 *Ibid.* p. 252.
35 Needham, Joseph 1959. *Science and Civilisation in China*, Vol. 3: Mathematics and the Sciences of the Heavens and the Earth. Cambridge: Cambridge University press, pp. 303–4.
36 *Ibid.* p. 305.
37 The eastern mountain in China is Tai Mountain in Shandong Taian, the western mountain is Hua Mountain in Shanxi 陕西, the south is Hen Mountain in Hunan, the north is Heng Mountain in Shanxi 山西, and the middle is Shong Mountain.
38 Needham, Joseph 1959. *Science and Civilisation in China*, Vol. 3: Mathematics and the Sciences of the Heavens and the Earth. Cambridge: at the University press, p. 248.
39 *Ibid.*
40 *Ibid.* p. 239.
41 *Ibid.* p. 245.
42 See Needham 1962, Vol. 4: 296. In Han times two alternative azimuthal arrangements of the eight trigrams were used on the *fengshui* compass. Both of these are in the *I Jing*, and they are named after the legendary sage Fu Xi, with *qian* in the south, called *Xian Tian* (prior to Heaven 先天八卦) system, and corresponded with the *He Tu* diagram. The allegedly later system, named after the Wen Wang, with the *qian* in the north-west, was called *Hou Tian* system (后天八卦), and corresponded with the *Luo Shu* magic square. The *shi* followed the latter system. The difference was only in symbolism, which the Fu Xi system allocated the *gua* cosmically; the Wen Wang system did so according to the march of the seasons of the year, starting at the south and going round clockwise.
43 Needham, Joseph 1962. *Science and Civilisation in China*, Vol. 4: Physics and Physical Technology. Cambridge: Cambridge University Press, pp. 273–9.
44 *Ibid.* and also see Chen 1999: 24.
45 See Li 1997, Chen 1999, and Gao 1995. Most compasses are produced in the cities of southern China, such as Yanzhou city of Fujian province and Xingning city of Guangdong province; or in the mainland China, such as Shuzhou of Jiangshu province and Xiuning of Anhui province.
46 See Neddham 1959, Vol. 3: 397. The most ancient day-count in Chinese culture did not depend on the sun and the moon, but the sexagesimal cyclical system, with a series of twelve characters (called 'branches', *zhi*) being combined alternately with a series of ten (called 'trunks' or 'stems'; *gan*) so as to make sixty combinations at the end of which the cycle started all over again. These characters are found on the oracle-bones of the mid-2nd millennium, and since the Shang period (1600–1046 B.C.) they have been used as a day-count till modern times.

47 See Shi 1992: 11–25. Fengshui is also named *kanyu* 堪輿, *dili* 地理, *qingnang* 青囊 and *qingwu* 青乌.
48 Quoted from Wheatley, Paul 1971. *The Pivot of the Four Quarters*. Edinburgh: Edinburgh University Press, pp. 244—6.
49 See Li, Dingxin 1990. *Ganzhou Yang Jiupin Fengshui Shu Rumeng* 赣州杨救贫风水术入门 (Introduction to the Fendshui School by Yang Jiuping). Hongkong: Tianma Tushu Youxian Gongshi Press, p. 5; and Chen 1999: 8.
50 See Li 1990: 5; and Chen 1992: 8.
51 See Needham 1962 Vol.4: 242. The marks of this division are still evident in the Ming and *Qi*ng literature. In the *Di Li Zhuo Yu Fu* (Precious Tools of Geomancy), written by Xu Zhimo about 1570 AD and by Zhang Jiuyi and others in 1716 AD, the authors follow the Jiangxi school, saying much of mountains and watercourses and relatively little of the compass. Another source is the *Yin Yang Er Zhai Quanshu* (Complete Treatise on Siting in relation to the Two Geodic Currents) in 1744 AD, which emphasizes pure topography and includes an interesting variety of contour-mapping in a style which goes back to the Tang delineations of the five sacred mountains. But the *Di Li Wu Jue* (Five Transmitted Teachings in Geomancy), written by Zhao Jiufeng in 1786 AD, is also full of details about the use of the compass in selecting the most auspicious sites for tombs and buildings.
52 Gao, Shouxian 1995. Xingxiang, Fengshui, He Yundao 星象, 风水和运道 (Horoscopy, Fengshui, and Divination). Nanning: Guangxi Jiaoyu Press, p. 220.
53 *Ibid.*
54 See Qi, Heng and Fan, Wei 1992. '*Gucheng Langzhong Fengshui Geju: Qianshi Fengshui Geju yu Gucheng Huanjing Yixiang*' 古城阆中风水格局: 浅释风水理论与古城环境意象 (The Fengshui Pattern of Langzhong City), in Wang, Qiheng (ed.), *Fengshui Lilun Yanjiu* 风水理论研究 (Research on the Theory of Fengshui School). Tianjin: Tianjin University Press, p. 48.
55 Quoted from Sterckx, Roel 2002. *The Animal and the Daemon in Early China*. Albany: State University of New York, pp. 179–80.
56 *Ibid.*
57 See Song and Yi 1992: 70.
58 See Zhang 2004: 63–4.
59 *Ibid.*
60 *Ibid.* pp. 67–8.
61 Xian, G. 1995. *Dongzu Tonglan* [A General Survey of the Dong Nationality 侗族通览]. Nanning: Guangxi Minzhu Press. Zhang, J. (2004). p. 200.
62 Qi and Fan 1992: 50–5.
63 *Ibid.*
64 *Ibid.* p. 70. During the Qin (220 B.C.-206 B.C.) and the Han (206 B.C. -220A.D.) periods, one *chi* (foot) was about 0.333m, or about 1.094 feet.
65 *Ibid.* pp. 91–5.
66 See Zhang 2004: 121–6.
67 See *Zang Jing*. The translation by zhang 2004: 123. *zhuque* is described as a bird similar to a peacock, but with a long neck, as seen in the above drawings from the Han dynasty.
68 *Ibid.*
69 Xian, G. 1995. *Dongzu Tonglan* [A General survey of the Dong Nationality 侗族通览]. Nanning: Guangxi Minzhu Press. Zhang, J. (2004). p. 183.
70 Xian, G. 1995. *Dongzu Tonglan* [A general survey of the Dong nationality 侗族通览]. Nanning: Guangxi Minzhu Press. Zhang, J. (2004) p. 199.
71 Interviewed with Wu Hao and Yang Shanren, Sanjiang county, July 2004.

72 Chen, J. 1991. *Zhongguo Gudai Jianzhu Yu Zhouyi Zhexue* [Chinese Primitive Architecture and Zhou Yi Philosophy 中国古 代建筑与周易哲学]. Changchun: Jilin Jiaoyu Press,p. 254.
73 Full Recover Version Bible, Genesis 1:2.
74 Full Recover Version Bible, Genesis 1:20–23.
75 *Ibid.* John 4:14.
76 *Ibid.* Ezekiel 36:25.
77 Xian, G. 1995. *Dongzu Tonglan* [A General Survey of the Dong Nationality 侗族通览]. Nanning: Guangxi Minzhu Press. Zhang, J. (2004), p. 199
78 Quoted from Needham 1956, vol. 2: 42.
79 Chen, G. 1984. *Lao Zi Zhu Yi Ji Ping Jia* [The Comments and Explanation of Lao Zi 老子注译及评价]. Beijing: Zhonghua Shuju Press,p. 89.
80 See Zhang 2004: 129.
81 *Ibid.*
82 *Ibid.* pp. 135–6.
83 *Ibid.*; also see Qi and Fan 1992: 55–7.
84 Interview with Wu Hao and Yang Shanren, Sanjiang county, July 2004.
85 See *Zang Jing*, the translation of Zhang 2004: 134–5.
86 Needham 1962, vol. 4: 240.
87 See Qi and Fan 1992: 48–9; Li 1995: 55.
88 Interviewed with Yongqing Chen and Shanren Yang in the summer of 2004.
89 Chen 1999: 19–20.
90 See Li, D., & 李定信 (1990). *Ganzhou Yang Jiupin Fengshui Shu Rumeng* [Introduction to the Fendshui School of Yang Jiuping 赣 州杨救贫风水术入门]. Hongkong: Tianma Tushu Youxian Gongshi Press; and Chen, J., & Shun, S. (1992). *Fengshuii Yu Jianzhu* [风水与建筑 Fengshui and Architecture]. Nanchang: Jiangxi Kexue Jishu Press.
91 About the book *Qinnang Aoyu* which was written by Yang Yunsong in Tang dynasty (618-907AD) see Chen 1992: 8.
92 See Li 1995: 53–4; and Chen 1999: 92–7.
93 *Ibid.*
94 Chen 1999: 93–7.
95 See Chen, Jianjun 1999. *Zhongguo Fengshui Luopan* 中国风水罗盘 (Chinese *Fengshui* Compass). Nanchang: Jiangxi Kexue Press, p. 117.
96 See Blundell Jones, Peter 1987. 'The Social Construction of Space' in *Space & Society*, No. 40: 62–71.
97 See Hay, John (ed.) 1994. *Boundaries in China*. London: Reaktion Books Ltd, pp. 125–70; and Li, Xiaodong 2002. 'The Aesthetic of the Absent: The Chinese Conception of Space' in *Journal of Architecture*, Volume 7, Spring 2002, pp. 10–20.
98 Relph, E. 1985. *Place and Placelessness*. London: Pion Limited [1976], pp. 26–7.
99 Tuan, Y.-f. 1977. *Space and Place: The Perspective of Experience*. Minneapolis: The University of Minnesota, p. 23.
100 Tuan, Y.-f. 1977. *Space and Place: The Perspective of Experience*. Minneapolis: The University of Minnesota. pp. 85–8.
101 Rapoport, Amos 1960. *House Form and Culture*. Englewood Cliffs, NJ: Prentice-Hall. pp. 29–30.
102 Lakoff, G., & Johnson, M. 2003. *Metaphors We Live by*. Chicago: University of Chicago Press, p. 156.

5 The Traditional Building Techniques of the Dong

The human body has long been an analogy for architecture and a source for measurement in both East and West. For early humans, measure was a way to engage the world that was physical and also suggested conceptual thinking. Measurement was a concept that grew from observation and evoked questions relating to the study of the universe and cosmology, indicating the environment had a spiritual dimension.[1] Babylonian and Egyptian architects employed units of measurement extracted from the length of arms, hands and fingers. They passed these traditions on to the Greeks and Romans , establishing units of measure such as the cubit. Vitruvius, in his treatise *The Ten Books on Architecture*, writes that the proportions initially adopted for temples and columns were based on the human body, as an accepted model of strength and beauty. In his view, proportion is a correspondence between the measures of the members of an entire work and of the whole, to a certain part selected as standard.[2] In like manner, measurement in the West traditionally referenced the human body.[3]

Inspired by mathematical proportions and the golden ratio, found in the human body and in nature, modern architects attempted to relate the proportion of the human body to architectural design.[4] Le Corbusier's modular, the image of a man with an upraised arm, establishes "a range of harmonious measurements to suit the human scale". It provides a series of golden section units based on human segments, rather than abstract dimensions, to guide the measure of the building. As Le Corbusier described, it is "universally applicable to architecture and to mechanical things".[5] In originating his modular, Le Corbusier combined the metric system with human scale, a system that is rational and the other having a dimension of nature that may be considered mystical or spiritual.[6] Le Corbusier was not necessarily religious but felt an affinity for the natural laws and harmonies evident in nature and the human body. The modular was not composed of abstractions but revealed an attempt to explore hidden truths. The golden section, with its long history, is derived from geometry and proportion, and for Le Corbusier it was imbued with latent meaning. He used golden section proportions to formulate the height of his ideal modular man and as a scale, but also employed its geometries to organize facades with regulating lines.

DOI: 10.4324/9781003228837-5

In the Dong community, a measurement-ruler system, which is called *zhanggan* (wooden or bamboo rule) – based both on the human body and geometric proportions, is applied by the Dong carpenters in their construction.[7] Shaped by this measurement system, the Dong architecture has obtained a meaning relating to their lives. Although not identical to the proportional segments of the Vitruvian Man, Le Corbusier's Modular Man or the golden section, and possibly not quite a 'module' in the same sense, the Dong ruler is a comparable set of units that divide the lucky and unlucky (favourable and unfavourable units)—and may be viewed in terms of the human body.[8] These units may not represent scale or abstract geometries, but the units emphasize more critical aspects of the human body such as the head, feet or joints. As a measurement system derived from the human body, the Dong ruler may not be a projection of an 'ideal' human, as in Le Corbusier's modular, but instead relates to the proportions of the 'master craftsman'. This ruler, also echoing the historic Lu Ban measurement, is reflective of the Dong's cultural tradition and construction methods, related to human dimensions. On a construction site the human body serves to convey scale and measurement and for the Dong 'master craftsmen' this ruler holds the human proportion for sacred buildings, specifically drum towers and Wind and Rain bridges.

Ying Zao Fa Shi (营造法式), Major Carpentry (*da mu zuo* 大木作), Minor Carpentry (*xiao mu zuo* 小木作) and Material Modular System (*Cai-fen zhi* 材分制)

Although the Dong community lacks any form of written record on their building skills, the traditional Chinese structural techniques have been recorded in the building manual named *Ying Zao Fa Shi* that dating back over 1000 years ago is notable for exhibiting the great achievements of Chinese traditional structural technique as a visible expression. This book concentrates on units of measurement, design standards and construction principles with structural patterns and building elements illustrated in drawings. The last part contains drawn illustrations aimed at practical details for carpentry and joinery, such as the jointing of elements, structural forms of structures and patterns of decoration.[9] Most importantly in *Ying Zao Fa Shi* divides the traditional Chinese structural systems into Major Carpentry (大木作) and Minor Carpentry (小木作), within it the material system of the *Cai-fen* Modular System (材分制) is recorded for the first time.[10]

Ying Zao Fa Shi, which is described by Joseph Needham as the "Treatise on Architectural Methods", has been the best-known as the earliest comprehensive work on architecture published in China.[11] It has been referred to as the building manual for most of the traditional timber buildings since the Song dynasty (960–1276), including palaces, temples and houses, which were constructed following its rules.

Ying Zao Fa Shi first appeared as the result of the 'Wang Anshi Reform' (1069–74).[12] Under the Song dynasty, public works projects such as canal maintenance, road construction and the erection of state buildings were carried out mainly by labourers, and there wasn't a standard to assess their work and calculate the payment. Furthermore, the court was also concerned about rising construction budgets without an effective evaluation of building costs, materials and labours. By this means, following Wang's urging for a standard of building construction manual, the old *Ying Zao Fa Shi* was established between 1070 and 1091. As an official book of building technology, *Ying Zao Fa Shi* for the first time provided a standard unit or module for timber structures, creating a building manual to standardize building procedure, which was part of the Song government's policy of trying to control the whole nation.[13] However, the old version only specified forms and positions of building elements but did not clarify their size variations; and it did not give exact estimates of labours and materials. As a result, it could not be productively enforced.

Based on the previous edition, Li Jie (1065–110) received the commission from Emperor Zhe Zhong to compile a new version of *Ying Zao Fa Shi* in 1097. Li Jie was one of the few great figures known from ancient times in the field of building science and technology.[14] Working as a superintendent for State Buildings in the Ministry of Works, he carried out many building projects that gave him first-hand experience at the time when he was commissioned to compile the state building standards in the *Ying Zao Fa Shi*. However, as Li Jie says in his preface, the hard work *Ying Zao Fa Shi* would not be complete without research on classics, history and many other books, and the practices and orally transmitted rules of the master-carpenters and other responsible craftsmen who explain almost everything in construction.[15] For the sake of easily memorizing and understanding, this carpentry knowledge and experience usually appeared in verse. Such verse relied upon oral transmission and was accompanied by working drawings and building models, some of which have been preserved to the present day though not all of them are understood, and thus the crafts were successfully handed down from generation to generation.

The archetypal structural system of traditional Chinese architecture is based on a framework of beams and columns (Figure 5.1). The typical rectangular plan is the favourite choice in Chinese traditional architecture, where the length of the plan is named *kuan* (span 宽), and the width is named *jin shen* (depth of bay dimension 进深). *Jian* (bay 间) is the fundamental element of the structure, where it is combined by two frameworks and crossing beams. Thus the width of bay is called *mian kuan* (the span of bay dimension 面宽) or *mian kuo* (the length of bay dimension 面阔). Number of the bay shows the hierarchy of the building, because of the numerology and symbolism according to the system of five-phrase and Yin/Yang cosmology. In *fengshui* practice, odd numbers are yang which are fortunate and desirable;

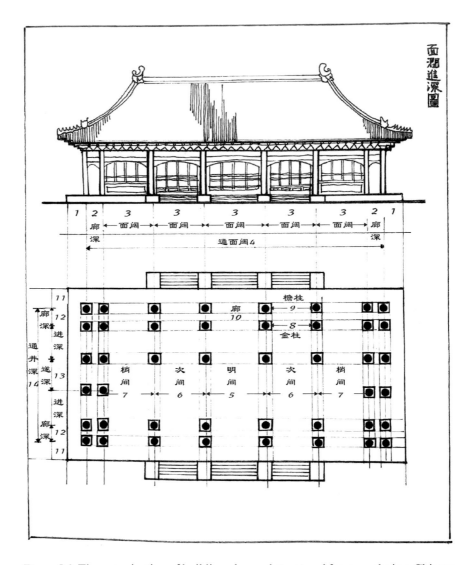

Figure 5.1 The organization of building plan and structural frameworks in a Chinese traditional building (redrawn by Jie Zhou after Ying Zao Fa Shi):
1. lower projected eave;
2. veranda length;
3. *mian kuan* (bay dimension in length);
4. general *mian kuan*;
5. principal room;
6. less important room;
7. least important room;
8. principal column;
9. eave column;
10. veranda;
11. width of lower projection;
12. width of veranda;
13. *jin shen* (bay dimension in width);
14. general *jin shen*.

and even numbers are yin and unfortunate. The biggest yang number is nine, and so the number of bays would be nine, seven, five and three, in a high-profile building with a big number of bays. However, the bay numbers for the houses of the Dong people are usually five or three. The total dimension in length of a bay for each room establishes the overall in length of a building. The main hall located on the central axis of the house is the most important in the whole building, and its bay dimension in length would be first decided, and then referred to when selecting dimensions for the other less important rooms beside it.[16]

According to the *Ying Zao Fa Shi*, traditional Chinese buildings are categorized under several structural types such as *dian tang* (palace 殿堂), *ting tang* (mansion 厅堂), *yu wu* (dwelling 宇屋) and *ting xie* (pavilion 亭榭). Construction of timber structure is defined as *da mu zuo* (Major Carpentry 大木作), which is divided into two types, *da mu da shi* (大木大式) construction with brackets for building palaces, official buildings, imperial houses and gardens; and *da mu xiao shi* (大木小式) construction without brackets. *da mu da shi* is usually employed in imperial and monumental buildings, and the module of scale and size is decided by the *cai-fen* system. Construction of *da mu xiao shi* is used in low profile buildings, identified by humble building scale, types of compound, structural material and decoration.[17]

Normally, a traditional timber structure consists of three sections: the platform in front, the major structural network of beams and columns, and the curved roof on the top. Each transverse framework would be respectively constructed before being assembled to form a stable structure. A typical fan of the structural framework includes a network of columns mainly carrying the vertical loads, connected with tied-beams. Through these single frameworks, connected by crossing-beams, a stable structure extended in the longitudinal direction is achieved. Only monumental buildings are constructed with brackets, as the transverse jointing between columns and beams. Transverse frameworks would be built in a variety of forms and details, flexibly serving different functions of the building. Unlike western building practice, there is no reliance on diagonal bracing, stiffness being provided instead by the interlocking joints. The timber partition walls only serve to separate the internal space from the external without carrying any load.

The columns, located in different positions as the main load-bearers and serving various purposes, are classified under several types depending on their positions, functions and special names.[18] *Yan zhu* (external principal column 檐柱) refers to the external post of timber-building, which mainly carries the loads of the eaves. *Jin zhu* (principal column 金柱) is the major column which carries the loads from roof to floor, and this kind of column is also catalogued into *wai jin zhu* (external principal column 外檐柱), which is located near external principal column beneath eaves, and *nei jin zhu* (internal principal column 内檐柱), which is located inside external principal column. The principal column, extending to upstairs and supporting

158 *The Traditional Building Techniques of the Dong*

the loads of upper eaves, is named *chong yan jin zhu* (the principal column of multiple eaves 重檐金柱), which is usually present in buildings with multiple eaves. *Zhong zhu* (centre column 中柱) is the name of the post located on the central axis. *Shan zhu* (gable column 山柱) refers to the column located in the middle of both gable frames. *Tong zhu* (queen column 童柱) rests on other beams, which are usually used to support the cantilever eaves in buildings with multiple eaves. *Lei gong zhu* (king post 雷公柱) is hung on and rests on the middle of the *tai ping liang* (golden beam 金梁), supporting the raised roof on the top. *Jiao zhu* (corner column 脚柱) is located on the corner of the structure, carrying the loads of columns from different angles.

The size of the timber for columns, the diameter (D) and the length (H) of the columns, depends on the bay number of the building. According to *Ying Zao Fa Shi*, the *Cai-fen* Modular System (材分制) is particularly important because it introduces a standard of sectional dimension for timber elements, which are based on from the dimensions of naturally growing tree-trunks of certain sizes (Figure 5.2). The traditional modular system includes the *cai-fen* modular system—*fen*, *cai* and the metrological system—*fen* (分), *cun* (寸), *chi* (尺), *zhang* (丈),[19] for different structural circumstances. *Cai* (材) means timber material in Chinese, and *fen* (分) means timber grades. *Cai* has been categorized into eight grades to response to various scales of buildings, and each timber element is graded by size.[20] In building practice, a standard *cai* of a rectangular timber section means that the ratio of width and the thickness of the standard section is 3:2.[21]

So the eight-grade system enables the use of timber section sizes from very small to large, corresponding to the size of structure, and this creates

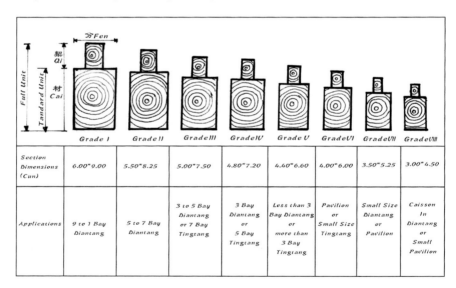

Figure 5.2 The *cai-fen* system of Ying Zao Fa Shi (redrawn by Jie Zhou afrer Guo 1995: 37).

the proper size of the building. For instance, when a small grade *cai* is used, the entire structure is correspondingly small, whereas for large-grade *cai*, the entire building is large. An investigation of existing buildings shows that Grade I to VI are employed for special load-bearing elements and the Grade III to V are the most often used in construction.[22] Traditional Chinese architecture is based on a standardized structural system established through experimentation and practice over thousands of years, and traditional construction was achieved through by prefabricated, standard components. As a result, this led to a typology of structural patterns accompanied by the specification of the construction methods, and thus it also easily provided a rough estimate of the building budget once the size of the structure and the material grade of *cai* are decided.

According to the Qing architectural regulation— *Qing Shi Ying Zao Ze Li*, the dimension and scale of buildings, such as the dimensions of bays, columns, *shou fen* (收分)[23] and *ce jiao* (侧脚),[24] upper projecting and lower projecting frames, the height of platform and the construction of the gable roof or pavilion roof, are related to the dimensions of structural elements. The bay dimensions are specially selected to serve for various functions of the building. The bay length in a less important rooms is 8/10 of main hall, and the bay width, according to the Qing building manual, would encompass not more than five purlins and four steps. If necessary, it would be sorted out by adding corridors on both sides of the front or the rear of the main structure. If a house is equipped with seven or six purlins, the scale of the main hall *mian kuan* (the bay dimension in length 面宽) to the height of column is 10/8, which means the height of a column is 8 *chi* (1 *chi*=33cm) while the bay dimension in length of main room is 1 *zhang* (1 *zhang*=330cm), and the ratio of height to diameter of column is 11/1. If a house is set up with 5 or 4 purlins, the ratio of bay dimension to the height of column is 10/7. The column diameter (D) is usually used as the basic module for a small-scale building, and the structural dimensions of the building depends on it (Table 5.1). For instance, in a small-scale house, the diameter of an external column section D is 7 *cun* (1 *cun* =3.3cm), the height of the column is 11 D (about 250cm), the bay dimension is 13.5 D (about 300cm) and the column rafter is 1/3D (about 8cm). Therefore, the dimensions of bay and height of columns are decided by the diameter of external column section.[25]

Table 5.1 The relation between the dimensions of column and bay

External column diameter	D
The height of external column	H = 11D
The dimensions of bay	L = 10/8 H (building with 7 or 6 purlins)
	L = 10/7 H (building with 5 or 4 purlins)
Less important room	L' = 8/10 L

The curved roof is remarkable in traditional Chinese timber structure, which is made by specific ratio of raised eave ridges, named by *ju* (raised height) (Figure 5.3). According to *Qing Shi Ying Zao Ze Li*, the distance between the centres of two purlin sections is named *bu jia* (step distance 步架), which is classified as *yan bu* (eave step 檐步), *jin bu* (principal step 金步), *ji bu* (ridge step 脊步). Usually, in the same building, except *yan bu* (eave step 檐步), the span between two purlins would be the same. For instance, in a small-scale house, the distance between two purlins is 4D~5D (D-external column diameter). *Ju jia* (the ratio of raised height 举架) refers to the value compared by the vertical distance with the horizontal distance from the centre of two purlins. In the Qing dynasty, five *ju*, six and half *ju*, seven and half *ju*, nine *ju* are often used, equating to 0.5, 0.65, 0.75, and 0.9,

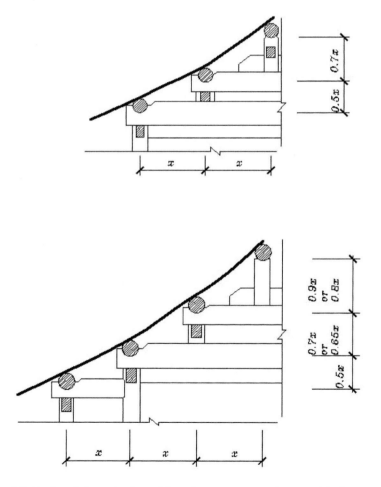

Figure 5.3 Ratio of the raised roof in minor carpentry house with five or seven purlins (reconstructed by author after Ma 1991: 7).

which decide the curve ratio of roof. However, the value is not more than 0.85 in small scale house, and 10 in the large-scale house. In a house with 5 purlins, the span of *yan bu* is 5 *ju*, and *ji bu* is 7 *ju*; in house with 7 purlins, the span from the external purlin is five *ju*, six and half *ju*, and eight and half *ju*.[26] This differentiation in raised height creates various shapes of curved roofs.

In traditional Chinese architecture, it is necessary to protect the timber structure from the damage caused by rain. According to the Qing building manual, the roof eaves would usually be built to project outside the building (Figure 5.4). In a house, the distance between the centre of an external purlin and the edge of the external rafter is defined as the dimension of

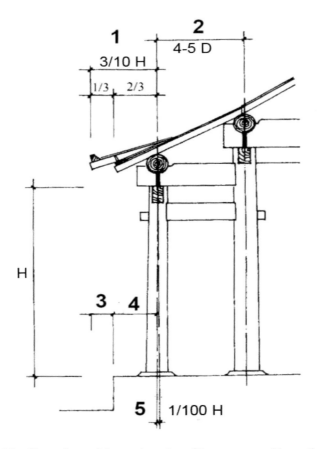

Figure 5.4 The dimensions of the projected roof (reconstructed by author after Ma 1991:6):
1. projected top eave;
2. *bu jia* (distance between principal column and eave column);
3. *hui shui* (further projecting eave);
4. *xia chu* (lower projection);
5. *che jiao* (sloping column) (D-external column diameter, H-height of external column).

projecting eave, which is also named *shang yan chu* (projecting upper eave 上檐出). Because the rain water is led down by the roof eave, it is also named *chu shui* (water flowing out 出水). The eave of a house without brackets is usually projected 3/10 of the height of the external column. For instance, if the height of the external column is 300cm, the eave projecting dimension is 90cm. If the cantilever dimension is divided into three sections, the rafter on the external purlin is projected 2/3 of total cantilever dimension, and the rafter overlapping the external purlin eave projects by 1/3. The flying eave is projected outside the upper eave, with the purpose of protecting the platform from the rainwater when it falls to the ground, protecting the bottom of the columns and the body of the timber wall from the damage by rain.

Joinery of tenons and mortises in the *Ying Zao Fa Shi* is defined as Minor Carpentry, non-structural carpentry (*xiao mu zuo* 小木作), to be distinguished from Major Structural Carpentry (*da mu zuo* 大木作) (Figure 5.5). According to the structural manual, joinery involves in the connection of every timber elements, not only in the columns and beams of the structure, but also the delicate carpentry, such as fixed, movable or removable partitions, screens, doors and windows, decorative or ornamental ceilings, floors and staircases, as well as pavilions or huts, entrance gates, fences and balustrades and gigantic furniture.[27] The forms, shapes and dimensions of mortises or tenons depend on their positions on the timbers, the angles they connect, the installation procedure and structural methods. They usually work as joinery connecting vertical elements with horizontal, such as the connection of frameworks with crossing-beams, and columns in a framework with tie-beams. According to the Qing building manual, the biggest dimension of the mortise on the column section would be less than 3/10 of the column diameter.

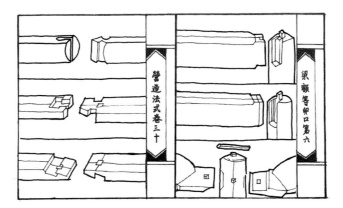

Figure 5.5 The mortises and tenons recorded in Ying Zao Fa Shi (redrawn by Jie Zhou after Ma 1991: 119).

A large-scale palace usually involves thousands of timber elements, and a small-scale building needs hundreds of timbers as well. Because each timber element would be fixed and connected with others by mortises and tenons, many types of joints are created.[28] These joints aim to tie up timber elements, thereby forming an entire frame estabilised by the overall weight of the building.[29] Under the Tang (618–907) and Song (960–1279) dynasties, this technique was further developed. The book *Ying Zao Fa Shi* remains a detailed record of how to make mortise and tenon joints with diagrams, and provides suggestions about the dimensions of each kind of mortise and tenon. Although in the Ming (1368–644) and Qing (1636–911) dynasties the structure of a building tended to be simplified compared with that of Tang and Song dynasties, mortise and tenon joints are still used up to the present, and their functions remained the same. Most timber structures built since then have survived hundreds of years, and are seldom damaged by the external forces or by the internal loads on them, which provides surely evidence of a certain security and skill.

Lu Ban Chi (鲁班尺) and *Zhanggan* (匠杆 the Carpenter's Rule) of the Dong

Complementing the texts of *Ying Zao Fa Shi*, *Lu Ban Jing Jiang Jia Jing* (Official Classic of Lu Ban and Artisans Mirror for Carpenters and Carvers) is another important building manual of carpentry for craftsmen. It was written by Wu Rong in the Ming dynasty (1368–644), which includes four chapters—three of text and one of carpentry diagrams.[30] The contents concern the rules, institutions and rituals associated with carpentry and building procedure and also how to select an auspicious day while constructing. Particularly, in one chapter it introduces the application of *Lu Ban chi*, which integrates carpentry techniques into fruitful rituals affecting the dimensions of each building section.

In the preface of *Lu Ban Jing* is the legend of carpenter master Lu Ban. It says that he came from Dongping village in Xian sheng Road in Lu (475-221 B.C.), and was also called by his family name Gong Shu or his courtesy name Yi Zhi. Master Lu Ban was born at the noon on the seventh day of the fifth month of the year Jiaxu, the third year of the reign of Duke of Lu Ding. According to the record, on the day he was born, white cranes flocked together around his house, which was filled with a distinct aromatic smell for a month, and everybody in the village was amazed. His parents were quite worried about him, because he wouldn't try to learn at the age of seven. However, at the age of fifteen, he seemed to be aware of the problem, and started following Duan Mu Qi, a well-known craftsman. Within a few months he fully understood the subtlest aspects of the work. He was dissatisfied with the feudal lords, who arrogated to themselves the title of king, and therefore he travelled through provinces, trying to persuade people to respect Emperor Zhou. After he failed in this, he retired and lived as a recluse inside Xiaohe Hill in the south of Mount Tai. Thirteen years later, he returned to his carpentry skill and followed another famous craftsman, drawing attention to carving and cutting, engraving and painting, for the purpose of making Chinese buildings more splendid and creative. He usually argued that neither the round shape is original from the compass nor the rectangle from a ruler, but they originated as the natural images of Heaven and Earth. He kept arguing that it actually came from human being's sense that a round shape would be created by compass and a rectangular shape by ruler.[31]

Many legends tell the story about which Lu Ban would reveal to craftsmen when they encountered the difficulty in their building work. One story tells that, in the Yongle period of the Ming dynasty (1368–644), an imperial palace had to be erected in Beijing, but it had not been completed on time even with millions of craftsmen at work. The builders were full of awe, but with the guidance of Master Lu Ban they finally succeeded in completing the work. Thus a temple is built to worship him as a carpentry spirit on the entrance, which is called the Gate of Lu Ban, to worship the master in the seasons of Spring and Autumn. Since then, during the construction procedure, he never fails to respond to the craftsmen who pray for help from him, and his image that is worshipped forever by the craftsmen.[32]

Lu Ban chi carries the measuring system of the *Lu Ban Jing*, which is created from the Eight-trigrams, the Five-phases, *na jia* (纳甲) combined with crafts ruler, and also the application of *I Jing* in Chinese traditional architecture.[33] The length of one *Lu Ban chi* is about 46cm, corresponding to the official foot, which can be subdivided into eight equal units, with corresponding favourable and unfavourable symbolic meanings, including Wealth (*cai* 财), Illness (*bing* 病), Separation (*li* 离), Justice (*yi* 义), Office (*guan* 官), Plunder (*jie* 劫), Harm (*hai* 害) and Luck (*ji* 吉), where the meanings on the ruler are linked with the nine-star cluster of the Big Dipper (Figure 5.6).[34] One of the two arcane stars are customarily added to the series, including Greedy Wolf (*tan lang* 贪狼), Broken Army (*po jun* 破军), Military Twist (*wu qu* 武曲), Great Gate (*ju men* 巨门), Civil Twist (*wen qu* 文曲), Honest and Steadfast (*lian zhen* 廉贞), Job Keeper (*lu cun* 禄存) and Left Assistant (*zuo fu* 左辅). Furthermore, the auspicious and inauspicious dimensions on each scale of the ruler are also linked with different colours, such as one to white (*bai* 白), two to black (*hei* 黑), three to green (*lu* 绿), four to blue (*bi* 碧), five to yellow (*huang* 黄), six to white (*bai* 白), seven to red (*chi* 赤), eight to white (*bai* 白) and nine to purple (*zi* 紫), with a recurrance on the next dimension. In order to conduct easily, the dimension units of one, six and eight, which are matched with the white colour, are preferred to be used in building dimensions, and the *Lu Ban chi* is also named *ya bai* foot (压白尺).[35]

The *ya bai* foot involves the large size dimensions of *chi* and small size dimension of *cun*. *Ya bai chi* (压白尺) is classified into *chi bai* (尺白), which decides the *chi* unit in dimensions, and *cun bai* (寸白) for the *cun* unit. The

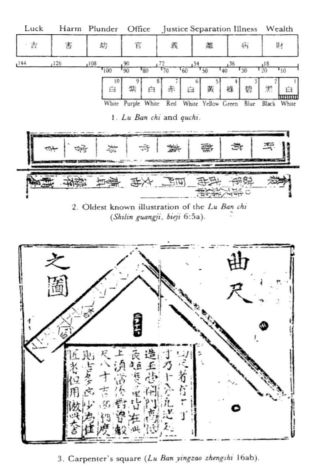

Figure 5.6 Luban *chi* and the symbolic meanings on each foot scale (from Ruitenbeek 1996: 77).

favourable dimensions decided by *chi bai* (尺白) or *cun bai* (寸白) depends on the five-phase characters of the building, which means the auspicious dimensions are affected by the orientation of the building, and different orientations have different *chi bai* (尺白) or *cun bai* (寸白).[36] The dimensions matched with the auspicious and inauspicious units of both *chi bai* (尺白) and *cun bai* are obtained from the proverbs of the Heaven Father *Gua* (天父卦) and the Earth Mother *Gua* (地母卦), associated with the traditional cosmology of the heaven father and the earth mother. Therefore, *chi bai* (尺白) or *cun bai* (寸白) of *tian fu gua* (*qian gua*, heaven father trigram 天父卦) charges for the dimensions of the vertical dimensions of the building; and the *ch ibai* (尺白) or *cun bai* (寸白) of *di mu gua* (*kun gua*, earth mother trigram 地母卦) is usually used in horizontal plan dimensions such as the length and width of the bay. However, not every dimension of building is decided by the dimensions from *ya bai chi*, and it mainly dominates the dimensions of the column network in plan and the height in elevation. These dimensions include the heights from ground floor to the roof ridge, and from ground floor to lower of eave rafter or flying-eave. The overall length of building, and particularly the length of the main hall, would fit the auspicious dimensions matched with *ya bai chi* (压白尺).[37] If the dimensions of other less important rooms cannot be matched to auspicious units because of difficulties of topography or building materials, the horizontal distances form the centre of *yan zhu* (external principal column 檐柱) to the boundary of the projecting eave rafter or stair on the ground would fit the favoured units of *ya bai chi* (压白尺).[38] Generally, large communal buildings use the dimensions matched with both *chi bai* (尺白) and *cun bai* (寸白), but dwellings only involve *cun bai* (寸白).

Lu Ban chi thus provides the auspicious references for the structure, possibly also promising a secured and fortunate shelter for the users in psychology. Building as human's shelter is relevant to their daily life. Either in the ancient agricultural societies or in the modern scientific societies, it is impossible to remove the puzzling anxiousness fate and being attacked by the evil. Given to the complicated future and changeability of life, the human instinct is to turn to divination, in an attempt to oversee their future, to obtain good fortune and avoid evil through the supernatural power. In this regarding, there is no difference between ancient and modern people who are equally eager to foresee their future life.

The Structure and Meanings of the Dong Measurement System

The Dong measurement system is based on three types of carpenters' rules: the master's Lu Ban foot rule 鲁班尺 (ranging from 30 to 32 cm); *Zhanggan* (the measurement rule 杖杆), about 3 m long for each rule rod); and bamboo strip rule (each piece about 33 cm) (Figure 5.7).[39] A carpenter's manual, the *Lu Ban Jing*—named after the fifth-century Chinese craftsman Lu Ban, consisted of information on the technical aspects of construction and also sections concerning ritual meaning.[40] The master's Lu Ban foot rule was passed down to the craftsman who used ink to mark structural members. Referencing the Lu Ban foot rule, the detail dimensions of mortises and tenons involve the use of bamboo strip rules which are marked with ink and applied on the measurement of mortises and tenons. Apart from these specific rules, the first act of construction is to build scale models. Besides their function as a measuring instrument, it is interesting that the carpenter's rules are associated with the fate of the building's owner. The master's Lu Ban foot rule is not only divided into proper sections, but also marked with colours or texts, indicating the desirable (lucky) and undesirable (unlucky)

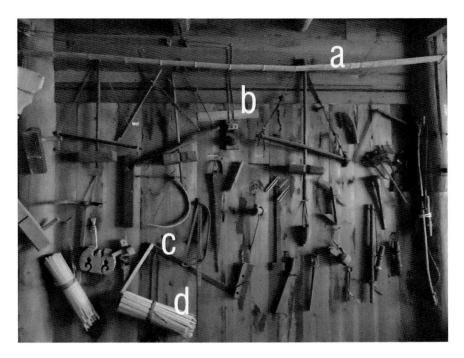

Figure 5.7 The carpenter's rules of Master Yang Shanren, Sanjiang county, 2011.
(a) *Zhanggan* (the measurement rule)
(b) Yang's Lu Ban foot rule
(c) Carpenter's square
(d) Bamboo strip rulers for mortise and tenon.

units of measure. Following the rules of the master's Lu Ban rule, the measurement rules *zhanggan* dominate all the dimensions of the building-height of the architecture, requested by the building owners for the purpose of promotion, wealth and fertility.[41] The building dimensions—such as the length and width of a bay and the height of the door—are also desirable if they are matched with the favourable units on the *zhanggan*. Before setting up the construction, the columns, cross beams, projected eaves and mortises and tenons, must have been marked in ink with the measurement rules on a carpentry trestle.

Local builders each adapt various Lu Ban rules to their individual communities—and according to Klaas Ruitenbeek (translator of the *Lu Ban Jing*)—over twenty master rulers have been found in China.[42] However, among the four carpentry groups which are responsible for the five pavilions of the new Longsheng bridge, each owns their master's Lu Ban rule respectively, although they compelled forced to use the notable Dong master builder Yang Shanren's foot rule as a standard on this new bridge.[43] In spite of that, these Lu Ban rules are striking in that they have common characters

168 *The Traditional Building Techniques of the Dong*

for their structural arrangement and distribution, which are endowed with symbolic meanings.

In the Dong community, each master is proud to have his own Lu Ban rule. On the wall of Yang's main hall hangs his master Lu Ban rule (Figure 5.8). It is about 30.9 cm long according to the official foot, which was divided into eight equal lengths, and each unit represents 1 cun (similar to 1 inch), about 3.85 cm. The two sides of the rule are separated into eight units, and marked with different meanings. If the main side of the rule is defined as *yang* or *sun,* the other side is named *yin* or *moon*. So on the *yang* side of Yang's ruler, from left to right, each cun is named: Heaven's noble (*tian gui* 天贵), Heaven's grief (*tian ku* 天哭), Heaven's disaster (*tian huo* 天祸), Heaven's talent (*tian cai* 天才), Heaven's wealth (*tian lu* 天禄), Loneliness (*gu du* 孤独), Heaven's decline (*tian bai* 天败), and First minister (*zai xiang* 宰相). The first, fourth, fifth and the last cun are marked with red ink texts, indicating favourable meanings and desirable dimensions; and the rest of these cun units are marked with blue ink, symbolizing unfavourable meanings and dimensions.

The Lu Ban rule of Wu Hao (a Dong scholar from Sanjiang county) is identified with Yang's, as its length and texts determine the units on the foot rule (Figure 5.9).[44] Wu's foot rule is also divided into eight cun units, but with a different length, about 32 cm long, compared with the official ruler. It

Figure 5.8 Master Yang Shanren's Lu ban foot rule, Sanjiang, 2011.

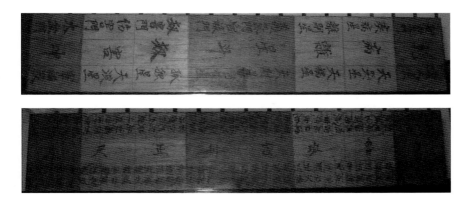

Figure 5.9 The *yang* side (top) and *yin* side (bottom) of Wu Hao's Lu ban foot rule, Sanjiang, 2011.

was marked with different texts on both sides of the ruler. On the *yang* side, the cun units from left to right are described as: Heaven (*qian* 乾), Illness (*bing* 病), Separation (*li* 离), Civil Stars (*xing* 星), Wealth (*dou* 斗), Plunder (*jie* 劫), Harm (*hai* 害), and the Earth (*kun* 坤). On the *yin* side from left to right are: Sun (*ri* 日), Lu (鲁), Ban (班), Luck (*ji* 吉), Benefit (*li* 利), Righteous (*zheng* 正), Foot (*chi* 尺), Moon (*yue* 月). In a similar way, the lucky cun units are marked with purple ink, where all other units remain the original colour.

By contrast, the modern steel Lu Ban tape is divided by each foot unit, about 39 cm long, corresponding to the official foot (Figure 5.10). It is also subdivided into eight equal cun units. The favourable and unfavourable symbolic meanings described on the ruler from left to right are: Luck (*ji*吉), Harm (*hai* 害), Plunder (*jie* 劫), Office (*guan* 官), Justice (*yi* 义), Separation (*li* 离), Illness (*bing* 病) and Wealth (*cai* 财). According to the *Lu Ban Jing*, the fortunate and unfortunate meanings on the foot rule are linked and defined by the names of stars that cluster on the Big Dipper.[45] One of the two arcane stars is, customarily, added to that series, including: Greedy Wolf (*tan lang* 贪狼), Broken Army (*po jun* 破军), Military Twist (*wu qu* 武曲), Great Gate (*ju men* 巨门), Civil Twist (*wen qu* 文曲), Honest and Steadfast (*lian zhen* 廉贞), Job Keeper (*lu cun* 禄存) and Left Assistant (*zuo fu* 左辅).[46] Thus, as a fundamental foot rule in Dong carpentry, the master's Lu Ban rules were shaped into different lengths, divided into different unit numbers, and marked with different meanings, all subject to the master who created this foot rule.

The reason that different kinds of Lu Ban rulers, which were passed down by the masters, have traditionally existed, is not because of man-made errors, but considering the masters' body size.[47] In the record of Chinese Language Etymology in the Han Dynasty (100–21), cun (寸) was equal to 10

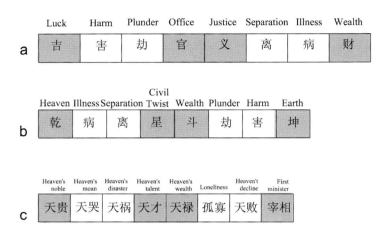

a. The modern Lu Ban rule
b. Wu's Lu Ban rule
c. Yang's Lu Ban rule

Figure 5.10 The carpenters' Lu ban foot rules with different lengths (drawn by author).

fen and was defined by cun kou (寸口), which is the width of three fingers, in Chinese medicine, locating the radial artery of the wrist. Chi (尺) was equal to 10 cun. In the Zhou Dynasty (1066–221BC), 1 chi was equal to 8 cun, and 10 chi was equal to 1 zhang (丈). A human male is almost 8 chi high, and so 'husband' is also called 'zhang fu' (丈夫), a man within 8 chi of his wife. So in the Zhou Dynasty, chi was created and recognized individually by the owner as a measure, defined by referencing the human body.[48] According to Yang and Wu, the Dong masters measure the building site with through span of their horizontally extended arms, which is about to their height (Figure 5.11). They used the span of their opened hand and stretched fingers, from the tip of the thumb to the tip of the middle finger, as the half foot (一拃半尺). Compared with a master's cubit, which is about 30–40 cm long, the master's Lu Ban rule was almost equal to the length of the forearm from the tip of the middle finger to the elbow. Most masters' Lu Ban rules were divided into eight cun units, but rules of various lengths have also been found.[49] Yang's Lu Ban rule was divided into eight cun lengths—each cun about 4 cm, almost the length of his thumb.

As a comparison, the Lu Ban foot rule actually reflects the Chinese view of beautiful proportion or ratio that is inspired by the organization and divisions of the human body (Figure 5.12). The Lu Ban rule is symmetrical in design, and is divided into even units. Thus, read from left to right or from right to left, the lucky units always occupy the first, the middle and the final sections, similar to the human body which is designed by nature with the principles of

The Traditional Building Techniques of the Dong 171

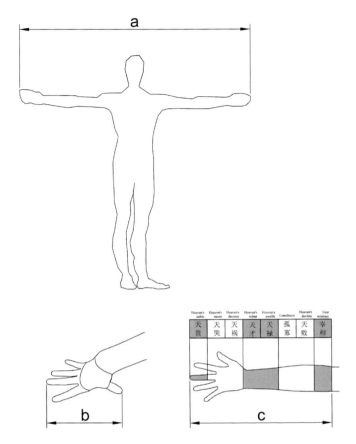

Figure 5.11 Human body as measures in the Dong (drawn by author):
(a) The length of the body used by the Dong carpenters for measuring the building site;
(b) The length of half foot by the hand;
(c) The units on the foot rule and human forearm.

symmetry. However, considering the segments of the human body, the head from the chin to the crown is an eighth of the whole height; and for the open hand, the length of the thumb is also an eighth of a forearm, from the elbow to the tip of the middle finger. So the lucky cun units on the Lu Ban rule are always located on the essential parts of the body—the head, the navel, the human foot and three critical points on the forearm.[50] Consequently, the foot rule also provides a range of proportion and a series of ratios in architectural design—the beauty of symmetry—and, although not identical to Le Corbusier's Modular, it reflects a beauty comparable to the golden ratio.

It is striking that the cun units and proportions are celebrated by colours or texts which invite human attention—rather than by abstract numbers. In order to work easily with the Lu Ban rule, the auspicious and inauspicious

172　*The Traditional Building Techniques of the Dong*

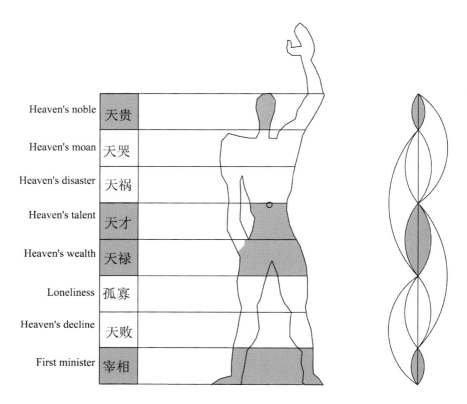

Figure 5.12 The Lu ban foot rule matched with the proportion of human body (drawn by author).

cun units of each rule are identified through writing (the texts) and marked with coloured ink. In particular, the foot rule is constructed by the lay-out of descriptive texts, following the sequence of the unchanging life cycle of humans. From left to right, the rulers tell the same story about the passages of life that every person must experience. These narratives are marked with various stages of life including a mark of the 'noble'; by using this term the texts speak of allegorical aspirations for a better life. These narratives relay that when noble children are born, they meet the hardness of illness or separation during the time of their maturation. However, after they cross a difficult threshold they become intelligent and wealthy people. In their middle age, they may be required to deal with difficult situations that may harm them or cause their decline. But in the end, they will become successful after overcoming numerous obstacles. Thus, the masters' Lu Ban rulers act as the carpentry scales, which are endowed with meaning and convey more than just a measuring device.

Making the *Zhanggan* (*pai zhang gan* 排杖杆)

The measurement rule *zhanggan* is derived from the master's Lu Ban foot rule, and provides the measure for the large dimensions of the building (Figure 5.13). According to the Dong craftsmen, all the timbers for columns and crossing beams would be marked with ink on the trestle before they are placed as part of a structural frame. The measurement rules are portable, making it easy to measure and fabricate the wooden elements when laid out on the horizontal surface of a trestle. Although originated in a period prior to the common use of drawing, this act of marking performs a similar role to building construction drawings.

Making the measurement rule is called *pai zhanggan* (rule making 排杖杆) (Figure 5.14). The measurement rule is made of the hard and inflexible wood of the fir tree or bamboo, and its length depends on the height of the building. Usually, for easy operation, a *zhanggan* is pieced together from several timber rods. One piece of the measurement rule is made about 3 metres long, and divided by the master's Lu Ban rule into foot units. It could be extended with the other pieces of rod to comprise the height of the entire building. The rough surface of a measurement rule is marked with symbols which are

Figure 5.13 Master Yang Shanren compared the modern steel tape of Lu Ban rule with his measurement rule, Sanjiang county, 2011.

174 *The Traditional Building Techniques of the Dong*

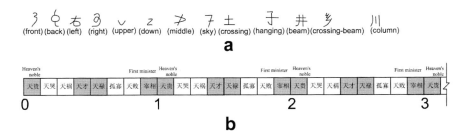

Figure 5.14 a. Symbols marked on the measurement rule by the Dong carpenters (drawn by author); b. The measurement rule divided by the Lu Ban foot rule units (drawn by author).

only recognized by the ink marking craftsman. The symbols used by the Dong craftsmen are equal to the meanings respectively: front (前), back (后), left (左), right (右), upper (上), down (下), middle (中), sky (天), crossing (穿), hanging (挂), beam (梁), crossing-beam (枋), column (柱).[51]

The measurement rules are catalogued into two types: the first principal rule and the second principal rule (Figure 5.15).[52] The first principal rule is responsible for the length of columns, and the second principal rule is marked with the length of crossing beams, corresponding with the bay length and width. The front side of the first principal rule is marked with the important dimensions for principal columns and external columns, and the height of the projected eaves and the locations of mortises for the tie-beams are marked on the rear side. Thus, the two types of carpentry rules decide the general plan and height of building. Based on the master's Lu Ban rule, the Dong *zhanggan* receives meaning as it is extended with the marked—favourable and unfavourable—cun units.[53] Although not every dimension of the building must fit the desirable units on the measurement rule, the column height of each floor must occupy the fortunate cun units that reflect the desires of the householders. For Dong architecture—including the communal buildings such as Wind and Rain bridges, drum towers and individual houses—the dimension of each height would reside on a lucky section.[54]

Thus, the Dong *zhanggan* not only offers the measurement for the building but also defines the function of the building. For the drum towers and bridges, which are constructed for the community, the column height of about 2.96–2.98 metres is used. It is recognized as the fortunate meaning of 'Heaven Talent', named for the intelligent descendants of the community. However, for an individual house, there is more than one choice for the house owner. The measurement of the height ranges from 2.26 to 2.28 metres, involving the desirable cun units defined with Heaven's noble (*tian gui* 天贵) for fertility, Heaven's talent (*tian cai* 天才) for intelligent

The Traditional Building Techniques of the Dong 175

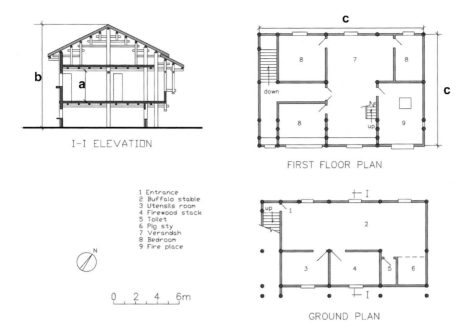

Figure 5.15 The measurement rules made for a Dong building (drawn by author):
(a) The height must fit desirable *cun* unit, which dominates the size of the whole building (头不碰黑);
(b) The length of first principal measurement rule;
(c) The length of second principal measurement rule.

descendants, Heaven's wealth (*tian lu* 天禄) for a good business and First minister (*zai xiang* 宰相) for a high ranked officer.[55] The phrase, a "Human's head should not touch the dark colour on the rule" (*tou bu peng hei* 头不碰黑) is an essential law for Dong building practices (Figure 5.16). This means that the height of a column, from the floor to the bottom of crossing-beam on the ceiling, must be described in favorable *cun* units. Thus, after the height of building elevation has been decided, the width of the building can be developed. Depending on the construction site, the plan of the building is extended in length by increasing the number of frameworks, and in width with additional external columns (Figure 5.17). The roof with multiple eaves is supported by cantilever pillars resting on the cross beam.[56] If the dimensions of less important rooms cannot fit into auspicious *cun* units because of the difficulties of topography or building materials, then the horizontal distances from the centre of the *yanzhu* (external principal column 檐柱) to the edge of a projecting eave rafter or stair on the ground would fit the favoured units of the carpentry ruler.[57]

176 *The Traditional Building Techniques of the Dong*

Figure 5.16 Master Yang Shanren showing the most important height of the principal column to the author, Sanjiang, 2011.

Apart from the measurement rules that are used for the dimensions of beams and columns, short bamboo strip rules are made for the mortises and tenons (Figure 5.18). The bamboo is sliced into strips about 1 cm by 33 cm by the craftsman, and symbols are marked on the rough surface of the bamboo strips. When the ink-marking craftsman works on the mortises (which have been previously completed on the columns and crossing beams), in order to shape the tenons, he inserts his carpenter's square to measure the length, width and the depth of mortise, and transfers the dimensions by marking ink on the bamboo rules. He then labels the mortise with the bamboo strip rule as a reference to the work on the corresponding tenon.[58] Thus, each mortise owns its one ink-marked bamboo rule.

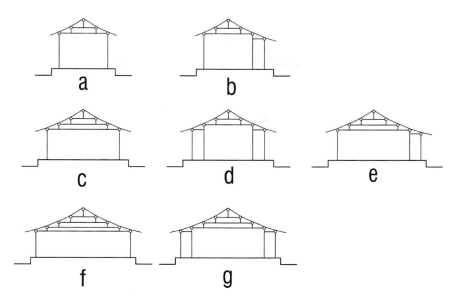

Figure 5.17 Developing the width of the building with purlin added (drawn by author):
(a) Five-purlin beams without porch (五架无檐);
(b) Six-purlin beams with front porch (六架前廊檐);
(c) Seven-purlin beams (七架无檐);
(d) Seven-purlin beams with both front and rear porches (七架前后廊);
(e) Eight-purlin beams with front porch (八架前檐廊);
(f) Nine-purlin beams without porch (九架无廊);
(g) Nine-purlin beams with both front and rear porches (九架前后廊).

Since the Dong craftsmen work with hundreds or thousands of timber elements, all of these elements are created referring to the simple building model, which records the number of storeys, bays and their collaboration that forms the plan. The columns and cross beams, which have been marked in ink through a complex operation, are piled in their groups respectively until the structural frame is installed.[59] In Dong carpentry work, the construction of a building model is particularly important as it allows the ability to organize timber elements in construction, and it reveals a role as a modular scale and element reference in the productive work (Figure 5.19). Similar to the master's Lu Ban rule, building models are passed from generation to generation by the carpentry master.[60] These building models are always present on a building site. As an essential architectural representation, they are the only reference that the craftsmen and carpenters rely on to mark and operate the wooden elements. The building models show the typical wooden structure of the Dong, which has been evident for thousands of years, although the height of the building, the form of the pavilions and the number of cantilever eaves have been modified for every design.

178 The Traditional Building Techniques of the Dong

Figure 5.18 The carpenter's square and bamboo strip rules used in measuring the mortises for making tenons, Sanjiang, 2011.

Figure 5.19 The Dong structural models and carpenters' rules at the building site of the new Longsheng bridge, Sanjiang county, 2011.

Constructing the Wind and Rain bridges with the Traditional Techniques

The structure of the Wind and Rain bridge is often combined with three parts: the stone piers, the spanning structure of timber logs as foundation and the upper timber frameworks (Figure 5.20). Standing in the centre of a torrential river, the bridge piers are usually built of cut stone filled with rubble. Each pier is about 2m high, hexagonal in plan, and forming two 30° sharp angle stone piers in the middle to reduce the force load of flowing water pushing on the pier. Large timber logs, spanned to support the upper bridge structure crossing the river, are piled up and rest on the piers. Structurally, a cantilever system is often used to fill the gap between two piers, with two layers of short large logs placed directly on the pier. These are named *tuo jia liang* (foundational beam 托架梁), which consist of about 6–7 beams, the diameter of each section about 40–50cm, connected by thick planks through mortises on both ends of the logs. The bottom beams project beyond both ends of the piers by 1.5–2m, and the upper beams project the same amount beyond the ends of the bottom beams. The upper foundational beams receive another two layers of long logs. They fill the gaps between piers, connecting them all, and form the whole platform of the bridge. Through the support of the two bottom layers of projecting beams, the cantilever distance of the upper long log is reduced, producing a rational structure, which allows a considerable span to be achieved with short timbers.

The long logs are also connected by a thick cross-beam with mortises at both ends of the logs. Because of the varying sizes of the logs, small planks

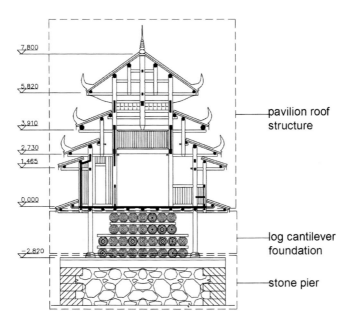

Figure 5.20 The typical structure of a pavilion of Wind and Rain bridge (drawn by author).

are usually added as spacers between two layers of logs, producing a horizontal plate, and allowing ventilation against rot. The use of whole logs keeps the fibres intact and requires less work preparing the timber, for there is a need to keep a stable structure not only after it is built but also during construction which was done traditionally without cranes. With a pavilion crowning each pier, loads from above are predominantly taken on the timber log foundation and stone piers, and these load the upper foundational beams on both ends to prevent any movement, while aiming at the same time to reduce the vertical distance in the middle of the long logs, thereby protecting them from being overstressed, and stabilizing the stable structure. As the major load-bearers, the stone piers express their advanced character as compression elements in order to support the vertical loads imposed on them. This cantilever technique following the mechanical characteristics of stone and timber elements and thereby create an elaborate rational structure for the Dong buildings.[61]

The Dong's drum towers, Wind and Rain bridges, and timber houses share the common structural column-beam network as the main body of the structure. The structural typology is named *chuandou shi* (cross-beam structure 穿斗式) frameworks, which is also the basis of the *ganlan* structure of the Dong building.[62] The structure of a Dong building consists a framework of beams and columns, which is named a *shan* (framework 扇), supporting the multiple eaves of the roof and forming the passage and pavilions through the bridge. Two frameworks form a bay (jian 间), and the scale and size of the structure depend on the size of the timber materials (see the material grades in *Ying Zao Fa Shi*) (Figure 5.21). According to the modular system of *Ying Zao Fa Shi*, while selecting the timber elements in a building without brackets, the dimension of one bay of the plan is 13.5 D, and the height of the eaves column is 11D (D-diameter of the eave's column). In the case of Chengyang bridge, the bay is 2.8m, the height of the eave column is 2.2m with the diameter of 20cm of timber, and in this way the scale of the entiry structure is determined. As the main load-bearing elements, the principal columns often run from the ground to the rooftop, providing a support to the short tie-beams and struts as well as for the eave columns (Figure 5.22). The lower eaves are supported by the *tiaoshou fang* (projecting tie-beam 挑手枋), crossing through both internal and external eaves columns and projecting outside the external eaves column; the middle layer of eaves is raised by the *yi yanfang* (first eave tie-beam 一檐枋), connected between the internal eave column and principal column, with the top end resting on the purlin supported by the *zhubi* (pig nose 猪鼻) projecting from the upper melon strut; and the upper eave is supported by the *er yanfang* (second eave tie-beam 二檐枋), crossing through either principal or melon columns and projecting from the melon column, with the top end resting on the *zhubi* (pig nose 猪鼻) from the principle column.[63] The top roof structure of the hexagon pavilion is built on six melon struts (*gua zhu* 瓜柱) sitting on the four tie-beams raised up with the support of four short struts, named *cha gua* (inserted melon column 插瓜). These rest on the second large tie-beams, and

The Traditional Building Techniques of the Dong 181

a *leigong zhu* (king post 雷公柱) supported in the middle and resting on the *san dafang* (third large tie-beam 三大枋), which is the most important golden beam in the roof structure, associated with the *shangliang* (raising the beam 上梁) ceremony, and it is constructed between two *cha gua* (inserted melon column 插瓜).

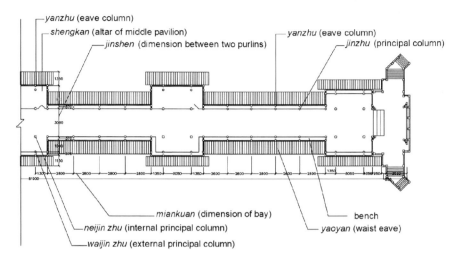

Figure 5.21 The arrangement of the structural frameworks combined with columns and crossing-beams of the Chengyang bridge (drawn by author).

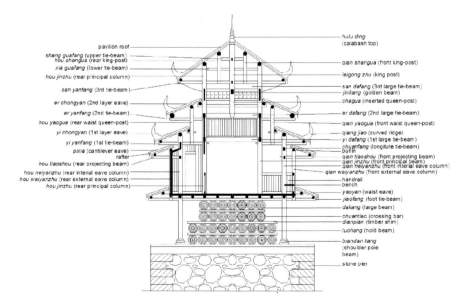

Figure 5.22 The section of the framework of columns and crossing-beams of the Chengyang bridge (drawn by author).

182 *The Traditional Building Techniques of the Dong*

Supported by the timber foundation, the principal and eave columns of the upper bridge structure are tied by a *jiao fang* (foot of tie-beam 脚枋) at the bottom, projecting outside the eave columns on both sides, supporting two eaves to provide protection for the timber foundation and bridge floor, and running through the whole bridge. About 40cm above the bridge floor, the principal and eave columns on both sides of the bridge are tied again by two long timber benches, extended throughout the whole bridge. The tops of these columns are connected by the beam named *tailu* (raising beam 抬卢), which not only ties these columns together to form a stable network, but also provides the support for the upper struts resting on it, which in turn support the roof (Figure 5.23). Underneath the raising beam are two *tiaoshou*[64] (projecting hand 挑手) or *baotou liang* (beam holding the head

Figure 5.23 The eave rest on the cantilever structure *tiaoshou fang* (the projected beam) and the principal column and eave column connected by the foot tie-beam in the corner, Sanjiang, 2001.

Figure 5.24 The side pavilion roof supported by the *tailu* (projected curve-beam), Sanjiang, 2004.

抱头梁), which are used to support the roof end (Figure 5.24). On the *tailu* (raising beam 抬卢) rest two short struts (queen post) connected by a *xiagua fang* (lower tie-beam 下瓜枋), and a *leigong zhu* (king post 雷公柱), with the purlins resting on top of each group of columns and beams, forming a complicated and stable timber structure to support the roof.[65]

The Wind and Rain bridge is particularly celebrated for its raised pavilion roofs, and techniques to construct the pavilion roofs are analogous in the same architectural language to the drum tower and the timber houses. The regular structural frameworks of the bridge passage are only broken by adding the corner columns for the sake of forming a special square for the pavilion with multiple eaves. Basically, each pavilion is raised with the support of two frameworks, connected by the crossing beams. In the middle

184 *The Traditional Building Techniques of the Dong*

hexagon pavilion roof of Chengyang bridge, on the top of the four melon columns are six pieces of colourful window screens, crowned with the hexagonal pavilion roof, which is raised and supported by the golden beam (Figure 5.25). This treatment makes the multiple rising eaves have a break, with a rhythm of rise and stop. The multiple square eaves topped with a distinguished roof suggest a crucial innovation of the Dong. Structurally, these tiled eaves of the pavilion roof with a sloping angle of about 30° produce a natural ventilation system.[66] Apart from these roof eaves, a *yaoyan* (waist eave) is usually built and located underneath the roof eaves but above the timber log foundation. With these multiple projecting eaves produces an elaborated protective system, keeping the beams and columns free from damage by rain in the humid weather of the Dong areas (Figure 5.26).

The Dong technique to construct the corner eaves is particularly striking (Figure 5.27). The five pavilions of Chengyang bridge are set up symmetrically with rectangular plans, and each pavilion is crowned with a top roof and two tiers of eaves underneath. The roof plan is antithetical to a round plan with the even number of edges, but it is rectangular. While constructing the pavilion roof, on the plan version, three corner columns are added on the corner of each principal column, enlarging the width of the bridge, and forming a square column support system with four columns on each corner. Thus, the multiple eaves of the square pavilion roof are supported

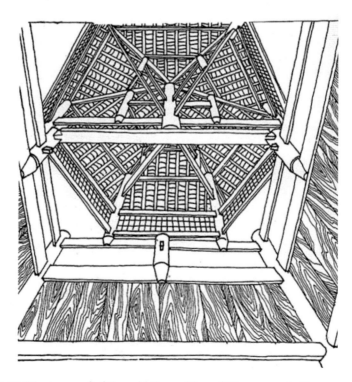

Figure 5.25 The top roof of the middle pavilion of Chengyang bridge supported by the golden beam (from Li 1990: 248).

Figure 5.26 The *yaoyan* (waist eave) of Batuan bridge protecting the foundation structure from the damage of rain, Sanjiang, 2011.

by 16 columns, with four internal principal columns and 12 external eaves columns. The four internal principal columns extend from the ground to the top layer of the roof, acting as the main load-bearing elements for the beams crossing through and projecting from them as the support for the short struts and tie-beams of the upper eaves.

The curved ridges on its multiple eaves and roofs are impressive, producing the sense of a flying roof (Figure 5.28). According to the *Ying Zao Fa Shi* and *Qing Shi Ying Zao Ze Li*, this structure is named *qiang jiao* (curved ridge 戗角), constructed by the corner rafter structure, supporting the loads of the eaves and forms part of the roof ridge, to produce an elegant roof curve featured in the traditional Chinese buildings.[67] There are two types of curved ridge in the buildings of southern China according to the materials in constructing it, including wooden and clay, and with the differentia of construction, the curved ridges are catalogued into the wooden ridge covered with tiles, which is often used in half-gabled roof buildings, and usually constructed with *jiao fei chuan* (flying eave-rafters 角飞椽); and the roof curve is created by clay with cantilever eave-rafter or flying eave-rafter added on the large rafter.[68] Distinguished from them, the curved ridge in the Dong bridge is created by adding a timber element with one end fixed on the middle of the lowest eave purlin and another end on the eave corner beam, while the purlins are covered with eave rafters and tiles, producing a slightly raised elegant curve on the eave instead of a flat roof, the purpose being to gain more ventilation, and providing shades for the building in hot and humid weather.

Figure 5.27 The structure of the drum tower with the curve eaves, Sanjiang, 2001.

Auspicious forms of decoration, such as birds and plants, are mostly applied and usually decorated in the motif of the raised roof ridge (Figure 5.29). A calabash is fixed on the top of the pavilion roof of bridge, or storks are decorated on the bottom ridges of each eave, indicating the fortune and symbolizing fertility. The calabash and stork are always worshipped by the Dong. In the Dong legend, the disaster of flood damaged everything in the world except Zhang Liang and his sister Zhang Mei, who hid inside a calabash and avoided the disaster. In order to sustain the society, a stork suggested them to marry and make the descendants.[69] According to the myth, the society originated from the calabash, and it would retain fertility and secure abundance.

In Chinese ideology, the heaven is round and the earth square (*tian yuan di fang* 天圆地方), correspondingly odd number named yang or heavenly number, and even number named yin or Earthly number. In phenomenology, on the one hand, the sky seems like a vault rounded overhead, and visible

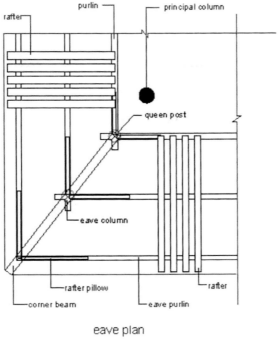

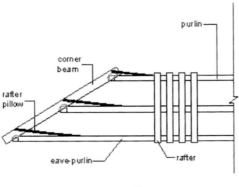

Figure 5.28 (Top) The plan of the corner structure of roof eave (drawn by author); (bottom) the elevation of the structure of eave corner (drawn by author).

heavenly bodies are all round, while the whole cosmic system appears to rotate. On the other hand the earth looks flat and water seems to lie flat, and the same flatness seems to go on from one place to the next, creating a sense of a flat earth. The passage of the heavenly bodies makes the visible

Figure 5.29 The decoration on the roof of Bajiang bridge, Sanjiang, 2011.

difference between north/south and east/west, and the right angle. Added to this, is the inevitable production of rectangles in ploughing and in weaving as well as in building with linear elements like timber.

In traditional Chinese architecture, roof is curved and symbolizes the round heaven, and the structural plan under the roof is rectangle, implying the square earth. Heavenly numbers are applied on the dimensions of facade, and earthly numbers on the plans (Figure 5.30). The dimensions of the plan and elevation in a Wind and Rain bridge or drum tower would obey the rules of *yin* number and *yang* number corresponding to round heaven and square earth. The pavilion numbers of the Wind and Rain bridges are odd, where three, five and seven pavilions are applied, each pavilion usually covered with three-layer eaves. The Chengyang bridge consists of five pavilions, each with three-layer eaves, which are connected by 19-bay bridge galleries. On the bridge plan, the length of the bridge is 24 *zhang* (1 *zhang*=3.3 meters), and its width is 1 *zhang* 2 *chi* (1 *chi*=33cm), which are all even numbers. But heavenly numbers dominate the elevation, with a total height of 1 *zhang* 7 *chi*. The height of the tallest pavilion is linked to heaven number of 3 *zhang* 3 *chi,* and the plan of central pavilion is 1 *zhang* 6 *chi* by 2 *zhang*, belonging to earthly number. The pavilion structure shares the common architectural language in the bridges and the drum towers. The roof of the bridges and the drum tower is supported by four principal columns, and the

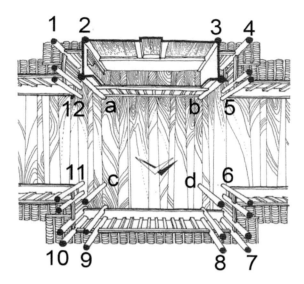

Figure 5.30 The organization of columns in the middle pavilion of Chengyang Bridge: (a)-(d) columns symbolizing the four seasons; and (1)-(12) columns of 12 months of the year (reconstructed by author after LI: 1990:250).

multiple eaves are created by the cantilever structure supported by these columns and beams. The four principal columns at the centre of each pavilion, from the ground to the top of the roof, are conceived to be linked with the four seasons in a year, the 12 columns around them symbolizing the months of the year.[70] The way the projecting eaves are made to turn the corner, end the structure of eave's purlins and rafters into a curved ridge. The golden beam in the middle pavilion, which supports the structure of the top roof, is decorated with an image of Eight-trigrams on its bottom, symbolizing the origins of the world.

Conclusion

The most portable measuring instrument applied in the Dong architecture reflects how the Dong master views the world, or a specific habitation, in proportion to his perception of space around him. Because his body dictates the basis for the measuring sticks, the ruler's or master's body is reflected in the measuring device that determines the physical environment—becoming the 'ruler'. Although the measure for a building is consistent within that building, each master closely guards the origins of the ruler. Similar to medieval guilds, these units of measure are secret and also unique to a community, which have been passed down for generations and based in the myths and secrets perpetuated by a master builder. In this way, the unit of measure is not a western 'inch', the Lu Ban foot rule (and every rule made by a master builder) is flexible and changing. As the auspicious units of the rule reflect a life cycle, the mathematical harmony has roots in human spirituality. D'Arcy Wentworth Thompson writes that "...for the harmony of the world is made manifest in Form and Number, and the heart and soul and all the poetry of Natural Philosophy are embodied in the concept of mathematical beauty".[71] The Dong building master uses his body to find the measure of the building and the spirituality of the units represents the auspicious and inauspicious units of life. The sticks that compare to the Lu Ban foot rules, also present the units of a human body in the dimension from wrist to fingertip, for example, of the human limb—wrist, hand—member, joint.

There is little difference between Western and Eastern peoples in their eagerness to discover a facilitative measuring system that is capable of ordering architectural proportion and dimension. The words compared to the inches on the Lu Ban foot rule mark dimensions to establish the relationship between a human being and the human body—unlike the abstract numbers used on modern rulers, the characters take the form of movements of human's life cycle—inverting, transferring, uniting and separating, and linking them with the essential portions of the human body—to celebrate proportion and dimension through the crucial encounters of human life. This is the reason why the Lu Ban rule has existed for over 1000 years—it brings order.

Notes

1 Iain Morley and Colin Renfrew (eds.) 2010. *The Archaeology of Measurement: Comprehending Heaven, Earth and Time in Ancient Societies.* Cambridge: Cambridge University Press, 2010.
2 Vitruvius 1914. *The Ten Books on Architecture*, trans. by Morris Hicky Morgan. Cambridge, MA: Harvard University Press.
3 Interestingly, the English language uses the word 'foot' to mean humans' lowest appendage and, also, as a unit of measurement in the United States. Other Western languages have converted to the metric system and no longer use these terms, although prior to 1789 in France a unit of measure *pied du roi* can be translated as 'the King's foot'. Le Corbusier's modulor was an attempt to reinstate a connection to the human body.
4 See: Claude Bragdon 1922 [2010]. *The Beautiful Necessity*, 2nd edn. New York: Alfred A. Knopf; Le Corbusier 1955. *Modulor 2 (Continuation of The Modulor of 1948).* Cambridge, MA: Harvard University Press, 1955; and Joseph Rykwert. *The Dancing Column: On Order in Architecture* (Cambridge, MA: MIT Press, 1996).
5 Le Corbusier, *Modulor 2*.
6 See: Richard A. Moore 1979. *Le Corbusier and the Mecanique Spirituelle: An Investigation into Le Corbusier's Architectural Symbolism and its Background in Beaux-Arts Dessin.* College Park: University of Maryland, University Microfilms International; Tim Benton 2007. *The Villas of Le Corbusier and Pierre Jeanneret 1920–1930.* Birkhäuser and Editions de La Villette, 2007; and Kenneth Frampton 2001 *Le Corbusier.* London: Thames and Hudson, 2001.

The Traditional Building Techniques of the Dong 191

7 In July 2011, there was a research trip to a Yanzhai village at Sanjiang County to interview Yang Shanren in his house. Mr. Yang is a notable builder of the Dong, who has been a designer and ink-marking craftsman for many drum towers, 'Wind and Rain' bridges and village dwellings. On the wall of his main hall (*tang wu*), he displays all of his carpentry instruments and the building models that he has used.
8 The comparison between Dong measuring systems and Le Corbusier's modular has been discussed by Klaas Ruitenbeek in his book 1996. *Carpentry and Building in Late Imperial China: A Study of the Fifteenth-Century Carpenter's Manual Lu Ban Jing*. Leiden, New York, Cologne: E. J. Brill.
9 See *Ying Zao Fa Shi* (营造法式), which is written by Li Jie in Song dynasty (960–1279), in *Si Ku Quan Shu* (四库全书) 1987, Vol. 673. Shanghai: Shanghai Guji Press; and see Liang, Shicheng 1981. It gives full references in a glossary of forty-eight building technicalities, mathematical formulae, building proportions and information on construction, such as foundations, roofs, and site topography and orientation. It prescribes the standards and regulations for building design, methods of construction, working procedures and the manufacture of bricks, clay tiles and glazed tiles for the purpose of standardization, organization and technical specification. It provides standard estimates for the costs for hiring different labours, based on each day's work and materials used in particular seasons; summarizes the material quotas and mixture proportioning of mortars, colour pigments and glazes.
10 See *Ying Zao Fa Shi* (营造法式), which is written by Li Jie in Song dynasty (960–1279), in *Si Ku Quan Shu* (四库全书) 1987, Vol. 673. Shanghai: Shanghai Guji Press; and see Liang, Shicheng 1981. p. 407; Guo, Qinghua 1995. *The Structure of Chinese Timber Architecture: Twelfth Century Design Standards and Construction Principles*. Sweden: Chalmers University Press. pp. 36–8; and Ruitenbeek, Klaas 1996. *Carpentry and Building in Late Imperial China: A Study of the Fifteenth-Century Carpenter's Manual Lu Ban Jing*. Leiden, New York, Koln: E. J. Brill, p. 27.
11 Cf. Needham, Joseph 1971. *Science and Civilization in China*, Vol. 4, Physics and Physical Technology, Part 3: Engineering and Nautics. Cambridge: Cambridge University Press, p. 84; Guo 1995 and 1998.
12 See Guo, Qinghua 1995. *The Structure of Chinese Timber Architecture: Twelfth Century Design Standards and Construction Principles*. Sweden: Chalmers University Press, pp. 29–30. Wang Anshi (1021–86) was a shrewd statesman, poet and scholar who served as premier at the court for many years. He introduced specialized studies on economy, taxation, book-keeping, law and administration into the state examination system. He insisted that officials should understand every aspect of their specialized professions. However, the unification of China had been conducted by the Qin emperor since founding of the first centralized empire in 221 B.C. The Qin emperor had built up a universal standardization in the administration to extend his domination to every geographical boundary, and unified the internal communication system by standardizing the dimensions of roads and vehicles, systems of weights and measures, monetary forms, as well as written characters. This universal standardization made it possible to create a cohesive state out of initially separate societies.
13 *Ibid.* pp. 29–30.
14 *Ibid.* p. 30. Even before moving to the Directorate of Buildings and Construction in 1092, he showed an outstanding talent as an architect. Apart from his role as writer, he was a distinguished practicing architect and supervisor of construction, erecting administrative offices, palace apartments, gates and gate-towers, and temples of the Song dynasty. Li Jie was also an intellectual, painter, and author of books on geography, history and philology.

15 *Ibid.* p. 31.
16 Liu, Dunzhen 1980. *Zhongguo Gudai Jianzhu Shi* 中国古代建筑史 (The History of Chinese Traditional Architecture). Beijing: Zhingguo Jianzhu Gongye Press. p. 2.
17 Cf. Liu, Dunzhen 1980. *Zhongguo Gudai Jianzhu Shi* 中国古代建筑史 (The History of Chinese Traditional Architecture). Beijing: Zhingguo Jianzhu Gongye Press; Ma, Binjian 1991. *Zhongguo Gujianzu Muzuo Yingzao Jishu* 中国古建筑木作营造技术 (The Techniques of Timber Structure in Chinese Traditional Architecture). Beijing: Kexue Press; and Zhang, Yuhuan, *et al.* (eds.) 2000. *Zhongguo Gudai Jianzhu Jishushi* 中国古代建筑技术史 (The Techniques of Chinese Traditional Architecture). Beijing: Kexue Press.
18 Cf. Liang1981: 26–7; and Ma 1991: 16–17.
19 1 *fen*=0.33cm , 1*cun*=3.3cm , 1 *chi*=33cm , 1 *zhang*=3.3m.
20 *Ying Zao Fa Shi* (营造法式) is written by Li Jie in Song dynasty (960–1279), in *Siku Quanshu* (四库全书) 1987, Vol. 673. Shanghai: Shanghai Guji Press; and Liang, Shicheng 1981, p. 428; and Guo 1995: 36–7.
21 See Guo 1995: 36–7. The dimensions of length either for the whole building or individual timber element are given in *fen, cai* and *zu cai*. 1 *cai* =15 *fen*, and 1 *zu cai*=21 *fen*; and the dimensions of each cross-section of timber element is single standard unit (*dan cai*), 15×10 *fen*, and full standard unit (*zu cai*), 21×10 *fen*.
22 See Guo, Qinghua 1995. *The Structure of Chinese Timber Architecture: Twelfth Century Design Standards and Construction Principles*. Sweden: Chalmers University Press, pp. 5–6.
23 See Ma, Binjian 1991. *Zhongguo Gujianzu Muzuo Yingzao Jishu* 中国古建筑木作营造技术 (The Techniques of Timber Structure in Chinese Traditional Architecture). Beijing: Kexue Press, p. 4. In Chinese traditional buildings, apart from the short struts like king post or queen post, the diameters on both end of each column are different, and the bottom diameter is larger than the top of the column, which is called *shou fen* 收分.
24 *Ibid.* The bottom of external column usually offset outside and the top slopes slightly inside, producing a stable structure, which is named *ce jiao* 侧脚.
25 Cf. Liang, Shicheng 1981. *Qingshi Yingzao Zeli* 清式营造则例 (The Architectural Manual of Qing dynasty). Beijing: Zhongguo Jianzhu Press, pp. 148–9; and Ma, Binjian 1991. *Zhongguo Gujianzu Muzuo Yingzao Jishu* 中国古建筑木作营造技术 (The Techniques of Timber Structure in Chinese Traditional Architecture). Beijing: Kexue Press, pp. 8–14.
26 See Ma 1991: 6–7.
27 Guo, Qinghua 1999. 'The Architecture of Joinery: the Form and Construction of Rotating Sutra-Case Cabinets', in *Architectural History* 42: 96–109.
28 Cf. *Ying zao Fa shi* 营造法式, which is written by Li Jie in Song dynasty (960-1279), in *Siku Quanshu* 四库全书 1987, Vol. 673. Shanghai: Shanghai Guji Press, pp. 644–5; Liang, Shicheng 1981. *Qingshi Yingzao Zeli* 清式营造则例 (The Architectural Manual of Qing dynasty). Beijing: Zhongguo Jianzhu Press, pp. 88–9; and Ma, Binjian 1991. *Zhongguo Gujianzu Muzuo Yingzao Jishu* 中国古建筑木作营造技术 (The Techniques of Timber Structure in Chinese Traditional Architecture). Beijing: Kexue Press, pp. 119–20.
29 See Zhang, Yuhuan, *et al.* (eds.) 2000. *Zhongguo Gudai Jianzhu Jishushi* 中国古代建筑技术史 (The Techniques of Chinese Traditional Architecture). Beijing: Kexue Press, p. 9. From the excavated evidence, timber houses built with mortises and tenons can be traced back to about four thousand years ago.
30 See the facsimile of the *Lu Ban Jing*, in Ruitenbeek 1996: 313–465.
31 *Ibid.* pp. 152–3.
32 *Ibid.* pp. 153–4.

33 See Chen 1992.
34 Cf. Chen, Jianjun and Shun, Shangpu 1992. *fengshui Yu Jianzhu* 风水与建筑 (*fengshui* and Architecture). Nanchang: Jiangxi Kexue Jishu Press, pp. 128–9; Ruitenbeek 1996: 90; and Li 2003: 49. Big Dippers is combined by 7 stars similar to a spoon, with which is named *Tian Shu* on the first place, *Tian Xuan* on the second, *Tian Ji* on the third, *Tian Quan* on the fourth, forming a infundibular shape; and the fifth is *Yu Hen*, the sixth *Kai Yang*, the seventh *Yao Guang*, which the three stars form the handle of the spoon. On beside *Kai Yang* star and *Yao Guang* Star are *Zhuo Fu* and *You Bi*.
35 *Ibid.*
36 See Chen 1991: 246–7 and 1992: 128–31.
37 *Ibid.*
38 See Chen 1992: 132–3.
39 Interview with Yang Shanren and Wu Hao in Sanjiang County, 22 July 2011. See Klaas Ruitenbeek, *Carpentry and Building in Late Imperial China*.
40 Klaas Ruitenbeek, *Carpentry and Building in Late Imperial China*, pp. 1–2.
41 Interview with Yang Shanren and Wu Hao in Sanjiang County, July 2011.
42 See Jianjun Chen and Shangpu Shun, *fengshui Yu Jianzhu* 风水与建筑 *(fengshui and Architecture)* (Nanchang: Jiangxi Kexue Jishu Press, 1992), p. 127; and Ruitenbeek, *Carpentry and Building in Late Imperial China*, p. 91.
43 Interview with Yang Shiyu and Yang Qiaoshui at the Longsheng bridge building site, 21 July 2011. To celebrate the 60th birthday of Longsheng County in 2010, the county government decided to support this project at Longsheng County. The new Wind and Rain bridge is 326 metres long and 5 metres wide, sponsored by the government, firms and individuals. The bridge is planned to cost 12 million Chinese Yuan. Over 5 million has been committed by the government of Longsheng County, and over 3 million raised from individuals to this date. After the bridge is completed, it will be the longest Wind and Rain bridge in Guangxi province.
44 Interview with Wu Hao in Sanjiang County, 22 July 2011. His Lu Ban ruler was passed down by his Master Lai Quantai in the 1990s. He is one of the executives responsible for the project in the downtown of Sanjiang County, including the new drum tower and Wind and Rain bridge. The new downtown bridge building event was organized by a committee, comprised of 22 persons from the government of Sanjiang county, the Transport department, the Forest and Park Department, and the Civil Affairs Bureau. The Dong expert, Professor Wu Hao, the bridge building Master Yang Shanren and his son Yang Shiyu were participants.
45 Cf. Chen and Shun, *fengshui Yu Jianzhu*, pp. 128–9; Ruitenbeek, *Carpentry and Building in Late Imperial China*, p. 90. The Big Dipper consists of seven stars in a shape like a spoon: the star named Tian Shu occupies the first place, Tian Xuan the second, Tian Ji the third, Tian Quan the fourth, which form an infundibular shape. The fifth is Yu Hen, the sixth Kai Yang, the seventh Yao Guang, and these three stars form the handle of the spoon. Beside Kai Yang star and Yao Guang Star are Zhuo Fu and You Bi.
46 *Ibid.* Among them, Greedy Wolf (tanlang 贪狼), Military Twist (wuqu 武曲), Great Gate (jumen 巨门), and Left Assistant (zuofu 左辅) are associated with good fortune, and the other stars, Civil Twist (wenqu 文曲), Honest and Steadfast (lianzhen 廉贞), Job Keeper (lucun 禄存), and Broken Army (pojun 破军) are related to evil fortune. Thus, the *Lu Ban chi* was originally named yabai foot (压白尺), for the unfavourable inches, that are distinguished with dark colour, and the favourable inches are left with the original wooden colour.
47 Interview with Wu Hao and Yang Shanren on 22 July 2011.

194 The Traditional Building Techniques of the Dong

48 Teng Hua Xie Cang Ban (藤花榭藏 版) 1929. *Chinese Language Etymology (Shuo wen jie zi* 说文解字*)*, first published in the Han dynasty (100–21).
49 Ruitenbeek, *Carpentry and Building in Late Imperial China*, p. 91.
50 In the view of Chinese medicine of meridian (*jing luo* 经络), there are three critical acupuncture points in the forearm: Laogong point, Neiguan point, and Quchi point. Respectively, they are responsible for many causes of disease, and action on them may calm and release those symptoms. So a critical section of the human's forearm and hand are identified by these important points.
51 See *Compilation Group of Local Gazette of Guangxi Province, Guangxi Tongzhi Minsuzhi,* 广西通志: 民俗志 (General Gazette of Guangxi Province: Custom Section) (Nanning: Guangxi Renmin Press, 1992), p. 70.
52 Interview with Wu Hao and Yang Shanren in July 2011.
53 Interview with Yang Shanren, Yang Shiyu and Yang Qiaoshuion in July 2011, Sanjiang County.
54 Interview with Yang Shanren in July 2011, Sanjiang County.
55 Interview with Yang Shanren in July 2011, Sanjiang County.
56 Interview with Yang Shanren, 22 July 2011. See Liang Shicheng, Qingshi Yingzuo Zeli 清式营造则例 (The Architectural Manual of Qing Dynasty, 1981), p.114; also see: Ma Binjian, *Zhongguo Gujianzu Muzuo Yingzao Jishu* 中国古建筑木作营造技术 *(The Techniques of Traditional Timber Structure in China)* (Beijing: Kexue Press, 1991), pp. 15–19.
57 Interview with Yang Shanren, 22 July 2011. Also, see Chen, *fengshui and Architecture*, pp. 132–3.
58 Interview with Yang Shiyu and Yang Qiaoshui in July 2011, at the Longsheng bridge building site.
59 See Gombrich, E. H. 1984. *The Story of Art.* Englewood Cliffs, NJ: Prentice-Hall, 1984, p. 20. At this point it might be useful to consider a Western view of the meaning of model. This is the view that a model is considered typically a small object usually built to scale, that represents another, often larger, object. Models are seen as a preliminary pattern, serving as a plan, from which an item not yet constructed will be produced. It is the view that typically a model also can offer a tentative description of a theory or system that accounts for all its known properties. This broader view of model can also be seen through the connection between architectural scale models and the completed building, measure and the relationship to a culture's understanding of their universe. It is important to note the close similarity between the Dong and the Western use of scale architectural models. Both use architectural scale models to create their future buildings and define their culture's cosmos. Also, see: Lethaby, W. R. 1974. *Architecture, Mysticism and Myth.* London: Architectural Press, 1974, p. 1.
60 Interview with Yang Shanren, 22 July 2011.
61 From my fieldwork to the Wind and Rain bridges in Sanjiang and Longsheng counties.
62 *Tailiang* and *chuandou* were two types of timber structural system used in traditional Chinese architecture. The tailiang system was used in buildings and houses in northern China. A tailiang beam-column network is defined by the width of the building; the main beam is supported by the principal column, and short pillars rest on the main beam, forming the frame that supports the big roof. In a chuandou structure, the columns are set along the wide sides of the building, and roof purlins rest on the tops of columns directly. The columns are connected by crossbeams, forming a beam-column framework, and each frame is connected by crossbeams. Compared with tailiang structure, chuang-dou structure is lighter and uses materials more economically. The diameter of a chuandou structural column is usually 20 to 30 cm, and that of cross-beam is 6

by 12 cm, or 10 by 20 cm. Cf. Dunzhen Liu, Zhongguo Gudai Jianzhu Shi 中国古代建筑史†(The History of Chinese Traditional Architecture). Beijing: Zhingguo Jianzhu Gongye Press, 1980; Binjian Ma, Zhongguo Gujianzu Muzuo Yingzao Jishu 1991. 中国古建筑木作营造技术† (The Techniques of Timber Structure in Chinese Traditional Architecture). Beijing: Kexue Press, 1991; and Yuhuan Zhang *et al.* (eds.) Zhongguo Gudai Jianzhu Jishushi 2000. 中国古代建筑技术史† (The Techniques of Chinese Traditional Architecture). Beijing: Kexue Press.
63 Interviewed with Yang Shanren in the summer of 2004.
64 See Li 1990; and Fan, C. *et al.* 1991. *Guangxi Minzhu Chuantong Jianzhu Shilu* 广西民族传统建筑实录 (The Record of Vernacular Architecture in Guangxi). Nanning: Guanxi Kexue Jishu Press, p. 256. *Tiaoshou* (projecting beam) is typical Dong carpentry techniques used construct the woodwork and provide support to eaves and roof, and the styles are involved in the catalogues including single purlin, double purlins, three purlins and four purlins with single *taioshou*, double *tiaoshou* and three *tiaoshou*. Two purlins with single *tiaoshou* are usually used while supporting single eaves in a Dong bridge, and purlins are often rest on *tiaoshou* directly. The treatment of eaves is focused on the edge of the eaves-rafter, which is usually decorated with elaborated motif of dragon, bird or vane plant, composed a series of elegant eaves cover on pavilion.
65 Personal communication with my informant Yang Shanren in the summer of 2004.
66 Cf. Li, Changjie (ed.) 1990. *Guibei Minjian Jianzhu* 桂北民间建筑 (Vernacular Architecture in Northern Guangxi). Beijing: Zhongguo Jianzhu Press, p. 229; and Fan, C. *et al.* 1991. *Guangxi Minzu Chuantong Jianzhu Shilu* 广西民族传统建筑实录 (The Record of Vernacular Architecture in Guangxi). Nanning, Guanxi Kexue Jishu Press, p. 223.
67 See Guo, Hanquan 2004. *Gu jian zhu Mu gong* 古建筑木工 (The Carpentry Techniques in Traditional Buildings), Beijing: Zhongguo Jianzhu Press, p. 122. It was widely used in building the palaces of northern China, the garden buildings in the regions near the Yangzi river, and the traditional dwellings of southern China, and although they vary in style, form and structural technology in different areas, the basic skills derive from the context of traditional building skills recorded in the *Ying Zao Fa Shi*.
68 *Ibid.*, pp. 123–4. The roof curve in traditional buildings of northern China is raised slightly with a small cantilever and a rather flat curve, and the roofs are usually covered with glazed tiles, demonstrating the important and splendid features of these buildings. However, the curved ridge on the garden buildings in the areas of Yangzi river is quite different. The cantilever dimension and raised angle of the roof ridge are much larger than that of northern China, exhibiting the romantic and elegant characters in the garden buildings, and the roofs are often covered with grey roof tiles, the same as the roofs in the dwellings of southern China.
69 Zhang, Boru 2004. *Dong zu Jian zhu Yi shu* 侗族建筑艺术 (The Art of the Dong Architecture). Changsha: Hunan Meishu Press,p. 21.
70 Personal communication with Yang Shanren in the summer of 2004.
71 Richard Padovan 1999. *Proportion: Science, Philosophy, Architecture*. London; New York: E & FN Spon, 1999, p. 5.

6 The Rituals which Accompany the Construction of Dong Houses

All cultures attempt to find meaning in their buildings to relate with the world. The *gan lan* structure of Dong people appears to be related to the *chuan dou* structural system which is constructed with through-jointed (穿斗结构) columns and beams and is popular in south China, distinguished from the *tailiang* structure (抬梁结构) popular in the temples of north China, which is constructed with beams on top of columns (Figure 6.1).[1] As Western cultures have utilized magic numbers, body metaphors and blessing ceremonies in making architecture, in the Dong community, constructing a *gan lan* is far more than simple carpentry. A charm "开工大吉" (starting with auspicious carpentry) on the entrance door indicates the lucky beginning of the carpenters' work.[2] This auspicious date or time is usually celebrated with special rituals, called *li*, which have their origins in both secular and sacred behavior and human communication.[3]

Dong rituals are performed throughout the entire process of construction: while preparing materials, setting up the structure, and during the final stage of raising the golden beam. These rituals occupy an important place in the lives of the people—both craftsmen and villagers. They play a critical role at every stage, expressing the awareness of time and space that defines the Dong sensibility of creating a building. Beyond preserving the traditional visual characteristics of their vernacular buildings and communities, these rituals may also ensure structural soundness, avoiding dangerous, untested construction. The rituals also explicitly and repeatedly celebrate the themes of sacredness and good fortune, which they impart to the "newborn" structure.[4]

Emulating proven dimensioning of beams and bay-spacing truly assures an auspicious and safe building. The Dong craftsmen and community members also perform ceremonies and make gifts to solidify the spiritual dimension of their architecture. Thanks to replicable rituals, their distinctive vernacular architecture and technology have been passed down through generations. Although ancient, many of these rituals, such as Stealing the Golden Beam to ensure the success of construction, are still practiced in the twenty-first century. Their origins may no longer be known, but they continue because of the persistence of belief in their power, telling a story whose original meaning has been partially lost.

DOI: 10.4324/9781003228837-6

Figure 6.1 The *ganlan* structure of the Dong and the new building constructed with through-joined columns and beams, Sanjiang, 2011, (photo: Weiye Li).

The Rituals accompanying the Construction of Timber Houses of the Dong

In the Dong society, construction is one of the remarkably important events in a village, a family and even in one's life. Whether it is a dwelling, the drum tower or the Wind and Rain bridge, it carries expectation of security, fortune and fertility for the peasants. To the Dong, building is not an easy job to be finished within a few days, but is also viewed as a great work, and sometimes needs several years to finish, even one generation or several generations. As believers in animism, the Dongs perform rites both in their lives and in their constructions, which reflect the order of things as they understand it.[5] In Dong cosmology, the world is created and ruled by various gods: the upper world with cloud, fog, the sun, the moon, stars, thunder and lightening, created and ruled by the Heaven God; the earth world with mountain, forest, rivers and lakes, controlled by the Earth God; and the living world with millions of men and women, who are administered by the king. Every spirit involved in these three worlds must be respected and worshipped. Their cosmology of the world is described in the following song Origins of the World:

The ancestor Zhang,
The ancestor Pan Gu,
Opened the sky and the earth, and they created the world.
The Heaven God was born,
The Earth God was born,
And the king of the living world was born.
The Heaven God had twelve brothers,
Who created clouds to cover the sky,
And created fog to cover the earth;
Who created the sun and around in the sky,
And created the moon to lighten the world;
He also created a Thunder God,
Who lived in the heaven.
He killed the evil spirits for us in the daytime,
And searched for them in the night;
In the drought day, he created the rain for us,
In the wet day, he created the sunshine.
Among the twelve brothers in the sky,
The most powerful is Thunder God.
The Earth God has twelve brothers,
They set up thousands of hillsides,
And millions of mountains.
They set up five famous mountains,
And they are named
Tai Mountain in the east,
Hua Mountain in the west,
Hen Mountain in the south,
Huan Mountain in the north,
And the Shong Mountain is in the middle.
This is why five columns are used to support the sky,
Which are between the high sky and remote earth.
They also created rivers, lakes, and seas,
With riptide and dangerous shoal.
They let the Dragon King live in a deep pond,
And fishes and prawns live in the shallows.
Therefore each living being had its own location,
And the sky was separated from the earth by the movement.
When we talk about the nine brothers of the King of the living world,
They arrived on the earth.
They created thousands of men and women,
And millions of women and men.
The living beings had nothing to eat,
And nothing to dress in.
They hunted goats and found wild fruits,
To make food for men and women.

Leaves wrapped their heads,
And with leather they were dressed,
These protected people from mosquitoes in spring and summer,
And kept them warm in winter.[6]

Various ceremonies are needed to perform in constructing their buildings to worship different spirits related with the construction. The Dong construction thus would be inevitably constituted in the same way as other sorts of life procedure, worshipping the spirits in order to obtain blessings and sharing a common purpose: creating the building with a new life of sedulity and fortune.

The Fortunate Location, Orientation and Organization of Dong Houses

The Dong house usually has three-floor supported on the frameworks combined with columns and beams, and each floor is arranged according to its function (Figure 6.2). When the Dongs decide to build a timber house, they prepare carefully for the building, and the first important thing is to select a head carpenter who is able to design the house. A good foreman of carpenters should be both skillful and honest, and is needed for the general design of the house. Therefore, the style of the building, the quality of the house and the materials used in the structure all depend on him. The selected headman is invited formally to the houseowner's home for a meal, accompanied by all of the owner's relatives, to discuss building affairs. After surveying the topography of the building site, and listening to the particular requests of the whole family, he should know it all in his heart.[7]

The favourable forms and measurements of the building are recorded in the classic building manual of *Lu Ban Jing* (Figure 6.3).[8] The square and rectangle plans are auspicious for a house, but the house would follow the shape of the available platform. According to *Lu Ban Jing*, if the back of the house is wide and the front is narrow, then this is named a Crab's Lair, which is believed to retain *qi* and to cause wealth to arrive by itself; if the front is the wider side, then this is named a Barred Mouth, which makes a sense of instability, and the householder is poor and dies soon; the house with rectangular plan is auspicious, even if the rear edge is longer or shorter than that of the front; however, the house with an irregular plan is unfortunate. According to *Lu Ban Jing*, when a new house is erected beside an old house, its height of ridge must not equal or exceed the old one, because the proverb says: "when the new roof competes between the old ridges, the householders will die together soon". The new house must not be parallel to the old house with the new entrance opposite to the old one, which is called heart-piercing houses, and is unfavourable.[9]

The size and scale of the dwellings depend on the number of householders in the house. In general, according to *Lu Ban Jing*, the favourable number of

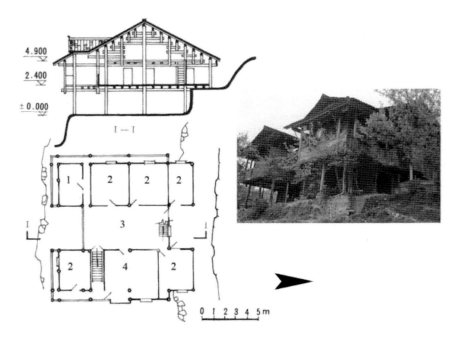

Figure 6.2 Yang's house in Longsheng county, with the support of frameworks similar to the structure of the drum towers and the bridges (from Fan *et al.* 1991: 66):
1. granary;
2. bedroom;
3. main hall (*tang wu*);
4. hearth room.

bays in building a house is an odd number, such as one, three, five, seven and nine; and even numbers are unfavourable, such as two, four, six and eight.[10] Normally, in the Dong areas, south and southeast are the favourable orientations. Houses are usually rectangular or square with 3 bays, the dimension of each bay being about 3 metres. Three bays with five columns per frame is the popular selection plan style by most of the Dong, though this could be enlarged depending on their needs. These favourable measurements are decided by the *zhanggan* (the Dong ruler), and are also found in the Dong proverbs: "everything goes through well, if the measurement of height ends with eight", "both the family and the master get wealthy, if the measurement of width ends with eight", "grain is shouldered upstairs, if the measurement of stair ends with six", "fire will warm the house thousands of years, if the measurement of hearth ends with six", "ghosts are obstructed from getting into the house, if the measurement of a window frame ends with six".[11]

Before construction, another important thing is the orientation of the house. It is most important for the houseowner to select an auspicious

The Rituals which Accompany the Construction of Dong Houses 201

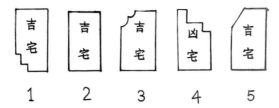

Figure 6.3 The auspicious and inauspicious types of house plan: (redrawn by Jie Zhou after Li (ed.) 1990: 609)
1. Fortune. This type of house produces intelligent people, and the normal people living inside won't be poor. The descendants are promoted as officials, and the family lineage would be proud of them.
2. Fortune. Although this type of house lack of *chen* and *si*, the family would be auspicious and wealthy. The whole family would benefit from it, and the descendants and livestock are all fertile.
3. Fortune. In the past, this type of house is preferred by Zhou God, it lacks of chou and yin but conserves wealth. The family would obtain longevity and wealth, and they won't know about it without the guild of the God.
4. This type of house with its left dimension longer than its right side wouldn't be lived in, because the family would be from poor and infertile. The descendants would be unintelligent without anything remained from the ancestors.
5. This type of house with its right dimension longer than its left side, is very auspicious for the family. The family would be very rich.

direction for the house depending on the *ba zi* (八字) of the master. It is believed to relate closely with the family's future, whose life, also named *xiang huo* (incense and fire 香火), is expected to extend from this generation to future ones in the house. Especially to an agricultural society like the Dong, it is an unchangeable fact that the house carries their own strong desire for fertility, and particularly, the hearth in each house symbolizes the lives and unbroken 'incense and fire' in their family, indicating that their lives would continue forever.

Among these basic architectural elements arranged within the interior space, the main hall concerns the craftsman the most, because it is located in the centre of the house, and houses the family altar. The *fengshui* master needs to decide the fortunate position for the main hall first, because the orientation of the house depends on it. Before doing this, a ceremony is held, which aims to remove evil spirits from the building area with sacred water, and is performed by the *fengshui* master. In this rite, a small table is set up on the site of the building, and pork, five cups of alcohol and a cup of rice are put on it, with three sticks of incense inserted into the rice. 1 *yuan* and 2 *jiao* (1 *yuan* =10 *jiao*) are packed in a red paper, which is the gift to the *fengshui* master, and it means the houseowner would be rich for twelve months every year.¹² Having prepared these, the *fengshui* master burns the incense and speaks loudly:

With a bunch of golden incense, a bunch of silver incense and within the rise of the incense smoke, please bless everything to go through well and bring fertility. It gained the supernatural power from the ancestor spirits, so year, month, date, and time are all controlled in my hand; all of the mountains and dragon veins are ruled by me, and twenty-four hours are decided by me. I am not only able to decide which year, month, day and times are favourable, but also what is the unfavourable direction according to the heaven, the earth, the date and the time. Pigs, horses, cows and sheep walk on the wide range of the plain; cocks and hens, dogs, geese and ducks run in the town with rich grain; however, the evil spirits are banished from heaven and earth. After everything is finished, each spirit is invited to be back to its location.¹³

Finishing his speech, he takes out the bunch of incense with a cup of wine held in his hand, scattering the cup of wine on the place, on which the house is to be built, and the ceremony is finished. Then, a square bench is set up on the centre of the site for the main hall with some red rice packed into a red cloth placed on it, and a compass is located on the red rice package by the *fengshui* master. The compass is believed to operate exactly with the help of the rice. The orientation of the main hall would first be decided, which dominates the direction of the whole building. According to the favourable mountain shapes in *fengshui* practice, the house is fortunate with several favourable shapes of mountains or hills in front of it (Figure 6.4).

In the Dongs' view, the direction towards the cliff mountain is unfortunate, and towards the valley is favourable, indicating the communication between the inside and outside world which would bridge the wealth and fertility to the houseowner. However, a house view blocked by a mountain or facing a river vein is unfavourable and such veins need to be avoided. Another unfortunate direction is towards the conjoining of two mountains like an intersection of scissors, named *jian dao jia* (剪刀架), as it is believed that the house will collapse and people living inside will die if the house faces towards this conjoining. The *fengshui* master puts a thread aligned with the favourable direction on the compass, and then two short timber columns are set up, according to the direction decided by the string, on both ends of the compass. This is the axis of the house, which is called *zhong mai* (middle axis 中脉) of the house. The craftsman decides the site of the house and begins work by the middle axis with precision.¹⁴ It is interesting that each stage of the construction would be accompanied with the rituals, from the timber materials prepared to the whole structure set up, and with the rituals, the newborn ordinary structure would be marvelous. Dong villages are usually developed by familial communities, where a village belongs to people of the same surname, usually comprising fifty to sixty families, but sometimes more than a hundred. The whole villagers would contribute to the construction, and participate the rituals with great enthusiasm. The sustained tradition of Dong building crafts, passed down by craft masters or

The Rituals which Accompany the Construction of Dong Houses   203

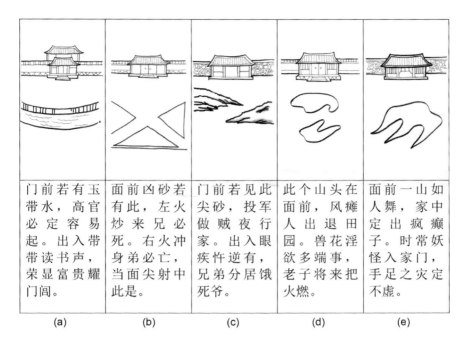

Figure 6.4 The fortunate and unfortunate landscape in front of the house: (a) is preferred with the river around it, and (b), (c), (d) and (e) are unfortunate with the undesirable mountain shapes around them (redrawn by Jie Zhou from Li *et al.* (eds.) 1991: 620–30).

parents, has ensured the continued predominance of their distinctive elevated timber buildings.[15]

The main floor of the Dong house is raised a story above the ground level (*jia kong ceng* 架空层), which serves mainly as a shelter for livestock, a storeroom and a workshop (Figure 6.5). The main floor accommodates a veranda, main hall, hearth and bedroom. The veranda is an open communal area and work place, which usually occupies two to three bays. The main hall (*tang wu* 堂屋) in the Dong house may be connected with the veranda, forming an undivided space, or separated, providing a location for the family shrine. The hearth room (*huo tang jian* 火塘间) holds the hearth and functions as a communal place. Because of the strong sunshine and abundant rain, projecting eaves (*chu yan* 出檐) provide a shade and protect the wooden elements from rain damage, and also create a visually changeable façade. Most of the Dongs' houses have small houses named *pi xia* (披厦) attached to them, providing working areas for the people. Almost every Dong house has an attic (*ge lou* 阁楼) underneath a sloping roof, providing storage for grain and promoting ventilation. A Veranda (廊 *lang*) is a main concern of the Dong at the centre of the house, and is always present in their houses as a opened communal areas and working place and usually occupies two

204 *The Rituals which Accompany the Construction of Dong Houses*

to three bays. The verandas, which are also used as passages, are naturally connected with the main hall, and conceived as the extension of it. The front veranda provides the areas not only for sunshine and ventilation, but also as the transition between internal and external space to import the outdoor natural landscape, making the sense of penetration from outside, where the Dong enjoys views of their beautiful landscape (Figure 6.6).

Dong houses share common structural characteristics with landmark Dong drum towers and the Wind and Rain bridges (Figure 6.7). Each framework comprises three or five columns of various types, with about three

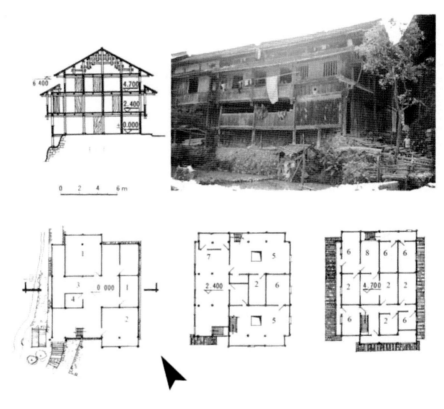

Figure 6.5 Yang's house in Sanjiang county with a front veranda in Longsheng county, arranged with different functions (from Fan *et al.* 1991: 69):
1. pig sty;
2. storage;
3. firewood stack;
4. toilet;
5. hearth room;
6. bedroom;
7. main hall (*tang wu*);
8. living room.

The Rituals which Accompany the Construction of Dong Houses 205

Figure 6.6 The veranda connecting the living rooms with the kitchen in Yang's house, Sanjiang, 2011.

Figure 6.7 The structural frameworks of Helong bridge, Sanjiang, 2011.

meters between them. The load of the whole roof is supported by a structural network with beams resting on main columns that transfer the load to the foundations. In through-jointed structure, the crossbeams are mortised into the columns, and roof purlins rest directly on the top of columns. All timber elements are connected by tenons and mortises. The columns are connected by crossbeams, together forming a rigid transversal frame. In the Dong building structure, the bay is the basic element. The desired number of frameworks are connected by longitudinal beams, and the interval of two to four meters between two frames defines the "bay" (*jian* 间). An odd number of bays (one, three, five, seven or nine) is favored, and various bay numbers respond to the demand for buildings of particular heights and widths. Purlins rest on principal columns (*jin zhu* 金柱), on eave columns (*yan zhu* 檐柱), and on melon columns (*gua zhu* 瓜柱), which are connected by crossbeams (*chuan fang* 穿枋) supporting the cantilevered projecting eaves. Interior partitions are movable, only to enclose and divide the space. The column number of each frame is usually odd, such as three-column style, five-column style. Gable roofs exhibit their lightness and elegance. Decorations of these houses are quite simple, and tend to concentrate on treatment of the envelope of eaves, the cantilever structure, and the handrails. Meanwhile, a projecting eave is built on the top of the handrail for protection from the rain, and a wooden bench is set up on the lower section of the handrail. These handrails are usually decorated with the motif of flower and grass, creating a sense of fortune and fertility.

Cantilever structures are the Dongs' favourite choice in constructing their houses because of the flexibility character of timber elements. Connected by mortise and tenon joints, a cantilever structure is commonly used to make the richest styles in their facades. The cantilever is usually projected from the first floor, or from every floor, on two or four façades of the house (Figure 6.8), which projects 0.6~1.2m, and makes the house a 'hanging dwelling' on the first floor. The cantilever structure of the Dong house is supported by the crossing beams projecting outside the main column, or connecting between internal and external eave columns. Particularly, the curve and decoration on the end of the projecting columns show their roughness, simplicity, lightness and the nature of wood. The Dongs are good at using simple timber elements to construct their vital space. Viewed from outside, the exposed timbers form a rhythmic division on the façade. The appearance of waist eaves is impressive in the Dong building. In the Dong areas, owing to the abundant rain, the overlapping projecting eaves are necessary and are projected from the crossing beam and covered by terracotta tiles, outside the main column 1.0~1.5m and the angle is 26~30°. These protect the ends of columns, beams, joints and floor panels from damage by the rain, or protect the house from sunshine and keep it cool in summer. *Chu tiao* (projecting structure 出挑) and *diao gui* (projecting cabinet 吊柜) are used to obtain more space without occupying the ground areas, and they are a popular treatment in almost every *gan lan* structure (Figure 6.9).

The Rituals which Accompany the Construction of Dong Houses   207

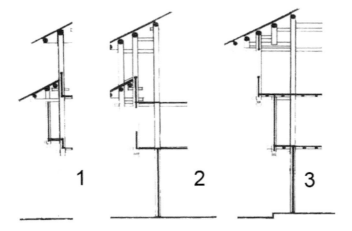

Figure 6.8 The cantilever structures of a Dong house (from Li 1990: 395).

Figure 6.9 The cantilever structure in the rear of Yang's house in Sanjiang county, 2004.

The height of different floors in the Dong house depends on their function. For instance, the height of ground floor, used for livestock and storage, is normally 2.2~2.4m; and the living room and bedroom are usually organized on first and second floors, which are commonly about 2.6m. The attic, which is arranged for storage or as a granary, is only 1.6~2m.[16]

208 *The Rituals which Accompany the Construction of Dong Houses*

For the rational arrangement of different heights, the three-floor house space is productively organized. The internal space of the house is separated flexibly by wooden walls. In the Dong dwelling, the space is divided according to its functions, providing relatively private space. In various seasons and festivals, the wooden walls are removed temporarily to gain more space. The living floor is also separated into noisy and quiet areas. Customs such as *zuo ye* (lovers talking and drinking oil tea overnight 坐夜), *mai liang dui* (the team for adding grain to the host for longevity 买粮队) and *zuo mei* (young people playing and singing with *pipa*, weaving and drinking oil tea 坐妹), need larger space, so the larger hearth room is designed as a crowded place with a hearth for cooking (Figure 6.10).[17] In addition, there is usually a private hearth room for communication between young people. The hearth is most important in the Dongs' house. Apart from cooking and drying the meat suspended from the ceiling, the hearth room is also used for meeting or communication at the times of their festivals within the four seasons during the year. Similar to the hearth in the drum tower, the house hearth is necessary to the Dong for their worship of fire. The drum tower is the public temple for regular meeting and communication in festivals, so the hearth room is relatively simple in the Dong house. The hearth room breaks away from the standard house plan of the Han Chinese, which is arranged strictly around a central axis according to the hierarchy of old, young, important

Figure 6.10 The hearth in the Yang's house, Sanjiang, 2004.

and less important. A family altar is usually set up in the main hall, which provides the space for the family rituals.

Preparing the Building Materials

The timbers for columns, crossbeams, wall panels, fences and window frames are taken from the abundant fir forests of the Dong region.[18] Cutting wood in the mountain is perceived as a dangerous activity for the craftsmen. Moreover, if the mountain spirits become annoyed, the timber-cutting might be unsuccessful. So an auspicious day and time would therefore be selected for cutting the timbers, so as not to conflict with the evil currents that pervade the mountains.[19] In the Dong view, ghosts exist within every day of human life. A legend of the Dong tells of a demon who is described as a ghost of the mountains, and its shape is similar to a monkey, but with backward feet (heels in front and toes behind) and invisible to people. Because the Dong believe in the existence of these demon ghosts, when they cut trees or quarry stones from the mountain, they would worship these hidden spirits to avoid injury or retaliation. The children are warned not to throw stones when they climb the mountains or play in rivers, to keep from annoying the spirits.[20]

The ridge pole is called the golden beam (*jin liang* 金梁), which supports the top roof of house, bridge or drum tower. The golden beam would be selected according to detailed criteria: the heavier the timber the better, for the golden beam symbolizes weighty gold or silver; the timber would be taken from one of a pair of twin trees—tall, thick and rigid; and once the timber is selected and cut, it would not be disturbed by anyone. Near the selected twin conifers would stand a third, smaller tree, possibly suggesting a family group that consists of two parent trees and a child. Timber that has been damaged by a thunderstorm is prohibited from use, because the homeowner that use it might otherwise be punished by the heavens.[21]

The golden beam is achieved by "stolen" from the other mountain in the early morning, before the date chosen for the setting up of the frames, instead of being harvested from the forest owned by the householder. A possible origin and legend about the ceremony is the story of Zhang Liang, who studied craft skill with Lu Ban and after three years thought his skill was better than that of his supervisor. He therefore decided to compete with Lu Ban to set up a house within three days. On the second day, Zhang Liang went to peep at his supervisor's work, and found that he had fixed all the frameworks and prepared for setting up the next day. If he was slower than Lu Ban, he would feel embarrassed. So he sawed and broke Lu Ban's middle beam secretly. In the middle of the night, Lu Ban went to check the frameworks, and discovered that one of the beams was cut and broke. He knew that it was done by Zhang Liang, and went quietly to cut another timber in the mountain to replace the damaged one. The next day, Lu Ban had set up his house at daybreak; however, Zhang Liang was still hurrying to fix the broken framework. He realized that he still needed to learn more from Lu Ban, and asked Lu Ban to teach him the skill how to connect the broken beam. Lu Ban laughed at him: "I don't know any skill of repairing the broken beam, where the one was another one stolen and swapped by me".[22] Actually, for the houseowner, the performance possibly means while borrowing some timber from another mountain, to which wealth from others is attached, further wealth and fertility are brought to the house and householders.

The event called 'stealing the golden beam' (*tou liang* 偷梁) implies that the piece of timber is made particularly valuable by being "stolen" from the other people's forest, which not only symbolizes that the wealth of the householder comes from a different source, but also means that the golden beam is infested by wild animals, and from the mountain spirits who try to keep it. The people who manage to secure the beam have taken risks, which makes the beam more special, more precious, and more auspicious.

The Stealing Beam ceremony is usually held in the middle of the night before dawn, and performed by four young men. The tree for the golden beam must be high and straight enough, and be one of the twin trees, which are named *yuan yang su* (male and female trees 鸳鸯树) and grow up close together, furthermore, beside them must be a small tree, which possibly means a family of trees. A lone tree will not suffice, even if it is high and straight enough. While the craftsmen go to the mountain, they have already found the tree and made themselves familiar with the road, and they carry with them the Lu Ban axes, lucky money package and a firework. Arriving at the tree, the foreman of carpenters burns incense and money paper under the tree, worshipping the mountain and tree spirits for *jin liang* (golden beam 金梁). The craftsman speaks loudly: "the tree is not an ordinary fir, and it is exactly set up as *jin liang*". The foreman of carpenters begins the first three cuts with an axe, and his activity is accompanied by loud speech from other people: "golden axe cuts first, and fortune arrives at the master's house", "golden axe cuts second, the master will get rich", "golden axe cuts third, wealth and fertility will arrive". Then, every other person cuts the tree continuously until it falls down. The golden beam needs to be felled in a special direction, and should not touch the ground. When they leave, they bring the timber with some of its leaves in their package, and this signifies that they bring the whole tree. A red string is tied in the middle of the tree carried by two young men. The other two persons put the lucky moneybag with 1 *yuan* 2 *jiao* or 12 *yuan* inside, on the stump of the tree, and send off the firework to thank the mountain owner and inform him to pick up the money. The mountain owner doesn't mind when he hears the firework, because he knows the 'stealing beam' ritual is being performed. The timber should be carried

The Rituals which Accompany the Construction of Dong Houses 211

on the same shoulders by two young men, and not changed. If they are tired and need to change, the other two persons should do this on their same shoulders, and they need to take it to the site as soon as possible and mustn't stop on their way home.[23] After preparing the middle beam, they begin to cut down fir trees according to the measurement and numbers provided by the foreman in the appointed areas by the head craftsman. They cut the trees, peel their bark and shape them, until they get enough fir elements for the building.

Cutting in the mountain is conceived as a dangerous event, which could harm the craftsmen or make the cutting unsuccessful if the mountain spirits are bothered.[24] According to the record in *Lu Ban Jing*, an auspicious day and hour must be selected for felling a tree, so that the work does not conflict with the evil currents pervading the mountains. When the carpenters enter the mountains to fell trees, they should, before they start working, first decide the number of trees, and usually odd numbers are perceived as auspicious and appreciated. When the timbers are delivered to the building site, they must not be piled up in the direction of the Yellow Current, nor must they be at variance with days controlled by the Eight Thrones of the Emperor or the Great Throne of the Nine Heavens.[25] Actually, arriving in the forest before the cutting, the head craftsman needs to make three axe-cuts in the first selected timber, since their work could possibly bother the mountain spirits and he must request the spirits' support: only then can the cutting begin. In their cutting work, the craftsman always announces their work by a knocking of three hammers on the tree, drawing the attention of the spirits, which is possibly related with the origins of Sa Sui in the Dong. Otherwise, it is believed that the mountain spirits would hurt the bodies of the working persons, and these persons would feel sick after working on the mountain. Feeling hurt by the spirits, they need to invite the priest to worship the mountain spirits at the home altar to request blessing in recovering from the hurt, and send them off to their places with the Inviting Spirits song:

> Get into the mountain,
> And step on the cliff.
> Climb on the trunk of big tree,
> And cross the small treetop.
> We would like to invite you twelve brothers,
> And name you twelve mountain spirits.
> Please go out of the mountain,
> And land on the cliff.
> Go out of the forest,
> And arrive in any place.
> Please take a seat around the table,
> And drink as much as you would like.[26]

While they hold up the Lu Ban axes, and recite the words inviting the spirit: "Lu Ban axes held in our hands, we are now welcoming the wood spirit. The spirit is invited to the splendid house as a ruler, and blesses the master's fortune. The master will be rich and noble with fertility".[27] The tree would be felled in a specific direction and cannot touch the ground. When the woodsmen leave, they transport the timber with some of its leaves still attached, symbolizing the notion that they have secured the whole tree. A red string is tied around the middle of the log, which is carried by two of the young men. The other two men place a lucky money bag on the stump of the tree, and set off fireworks in appreciation of the owner of the mountain, drawing his attention to retrieve the money. The timber would be carried on the shoulders of the same two young men. If they become exhausted, two other young men may relieve them, but dropping on the earth is not allowed, because the timber would be kept from being profane during the journey to the building site.[28]

Working on the Timber Elements

A three-story, three-bay house, erected from four frameworks (each of which has five columns) is about 300 to 400 square meters, and its construction requires hundreds of firs provided with appropriate mortises and tenons. After calculating the height, the width and the number of bays, the foreman marks in ink the timbers to be used for the beams and columns. For guidance, the Dong measuring rulers and the small structural models are applied.[29] When the mortises have been cut, the timbers would be piled in a special place where no one is allowed to enter; they are not bothered and only moved again in the stage of setting up the frameworks. Each carpenter in the construction team expects to become a foreman, the ink-marking craftsman and dreams most of all of being able to mark the timbers for the village's communal drum tower. Ink-marking craftsmen are held in the highest esteem by their families and villages.

The carpentry trestle would be set up at a favourable time and in a favourable orientation, with a ceremony called "inviting the trestle" (*qing mu ma* 请木马) (Figure 6.11). In the ritual, the foreman burns incense in front of the trestles, which he has set up on the site of the building with the help of the houseowner. Once the golden beam has been "stolen" and arrives at the building site, the master would set off fireworks and carefully place it on the trestles, awaiting the ink-marking stage (*fa mo* 发墨) (Figure 6.12). While marking the ink, the two ends of the ink-string are held by both the craftsman and the homeowner, snapping a line on the middle of the roof ridge pole. The foreman responsible for ink-marking begins this work with an auspicious speech to the golden beam: "*The jin liang* (golden beam), it is big and long enough. Measured with the *zhanggan*, not too long or not too short, it is the *jin liang* (golden beam) exactly. Supporting the whole house, it is secure and solid".[30] The craftsman meanwhile directs auspicious words to the houseowner:

> with the aromatic smell of marking ink and its long string, we mark ink on the golden beam, and the master's family would be fortunate, wealthy, and enjoy a long life; with the ink marking, the master's family would be rich and noble, enjoying fortune and fertility. The new house would be splendid and solid forever like the sunrise.[31]

While the carpenters mark ink with their *Zhanggan*, the length of the bay dimension of the main hall is first marked on the first principal rule, which is basis for the other dimensions, and the bay dimension of less important room is marked on the same rule. The second principal rule is marked with the bay dimension of the width. In relation to the distance between two columns, the dimensions of beams are also marked on this side. On the third principal rule is marked the height of columns, including the dimensions of principal columns and external columns, and the locations of mortises and tenons for the tie-beams. After the bay dimensions in length and width and height of column are finished, on the fourth principal rule are marked the projected dimensions of the eaves, from the centre of the external column to the edge of the rafter overlapping beyond the external column eaves.

Figure 6.11 The golden beam prepared on the trestle and waiting for the Raising the Golden Beam ceremony, Sanjiang, 2006 (photo: Ronald Knapp).

Figure 6.12 The craftsman marking ink on the golden beam of a new Wind and Rain bridge, Sanjiang, 1985 (photo: Mei ling).

While all the elements are ink-marked, the whole construction is processed only by the reminder of the simple building model, reminding the carpenters the number of storeys, bays and their collaborators in the structure. In the Dong view, after these timber elements are marked in ink, it is considered that the design stage for the building is complete.[32] All the constituent timbers would be prepared within half a month before the dates for constructing and setting up the frameworks (*shu wu* 竖屋).[33]

Setting up the Building Frameworks

Pai shan (fixing up the frame 排扇) occurs the day before *shu wu* (setting up house 竖屋), and each frame must be placed on the exact location on the ground (Figure 6.13). Fixing up the frame is not only the carpenter's job, but also needs the help of the whole kinship, the houseowner's relatives and friends and furthermore any families that ever receive help from the houseowner now come and help him. Setting up house is crucial not only to the family but also to the whole kinship. Before they fix the timbers together to make up a frame, a ceremony named *fa chui* (starting the hammer 发槌) is held by the ink-marking craftsman. The *fa* chui ceremony starts the building

The Rituals which Accompany the Construction of Dong Houses 215

construction, which aims to inform all spirits and the ancestors, particularly the carpenter spirit Lu Ban to pay attention to the house construction, praying for their help so that the building goes well, and seeking blessing for the master's fortune in the future. The mark ink craftsman sets up an altar, a square table with an incense burner and offerings on it, on the site of the golden beam. He burns the money paper to worship all the spirits, and then holds the hammer tied with red cloth, hammers the golden beam hard thrice and recites loudly:

> The golden hammer was passed down by Lu Ban,
> It seems of no use to the laity,
> But I use it for fazhui (starting the hammer).
> The hammer in my hand weighs more than a thousand jin (1 ji= 0.5 kg, here it means very important),
> And I wouldn't knock at the gate of heaven and hell,
> But only the golden beam of the new building,
> It sounds lucky.
> What we hear is only the sound of the golden hammer,
> The gigantic voice means flourish forever.
> One knock of the hammer means fertility,
> Two knocks of the hammer will be wealthy and noble,
> Three knocks of the hammer will be prosperous,
> With fortune and rich forever.[34]

Figure 6.13 The frameworks in proper location and the process of setting up the frameworks, Sanjiang, 1985 (photo: Mei Ling).

After the *fa chui* ceremony, the elements of the frame are put into their correct positions under the supervision of the mark ink craftsman, which is to fix beams, columns and short columns with crossing-beams, and it is similar to a 'fan'. *Pai shan* means to settle these frames on their exact positions. The house needs to be set up and supported with simple trestles, and erected at the auspicious time the next day. According to *Yang Zao Fa Shi*, the house structure is assembled by setting up the frames connected by the *chuanfang* (crossing-beam 穿枋), and the length or height of a frame, which is normally composed of five-column connected with the crossing beams, is usually more than 10 metres. If it could not be successfully set up at once, the master would be severely bothered, and the mark ink craftsman would be embarrassed. So before they set up the frames, a ceremony is held with the aim of ridding the house of evil spirits.[35]

The rite should be performed before daybreak on the day of setting up the structure by the mark ink craftsman. In this ceremony, the mark ink craftsman stands on a square table on the site of the main hall with a red cock held in his left hand and a Lu Ban axe in his right hand, and begins the ceremony. There is a dish of pork with three sticks of incense, and after burning the money paper, he speaks loudly: "the cock, which is a message from the mountain, is an ordinary cock with red crown on his head and flower dress on his body. The ordinary people don't know how to use it, but I use it as a message". Then, he kills the cock as a sacrifice with his Lu Ban axe, and walks around the ground of the house with the cock blood sprinkled everywhere. While he is doing this, he says: "evil spirits quickly leave, and the spirits must leave far away when the blood is sprinkled on the ground!" Meanwhile, he also spreads the blood on the ground beam. Finally, he goes back in front of the worship table, marks the blood on the table and says:

> With first mark, the master would be rich and fertile,
> With second mark, the master would be wealthy and noble,
> With third mark, the master would have many auspicious festivals,
> With fourth mark, the master would flourish in all four seasons,
> With fifth mark, the master's sons would be the best scholars,
> With sixth mark, the master would live without evilness.
> This is the urgent command carried by me from the spirit![36]

The favourable time for the Dong to set up their frameworks is in *yin shi* (寅时) (Figure 6.14).[37] It is said: "cocks sing at *yin shi* (寅时) and daybreak at *mao shi* (卯时),[38] and it is the most auspicious time for setting up the frameworks". It is dark, and they can only work under the light of torches. At the moment, every person gets to his location, and listens to the command from the mark ink craftsman. Firstly, the left frame of the main hall is set up. When the mark ink craftsman shouts: "Set up!" the working people answer: "Yes!" with the boom of fireworks and the shouting of people, the frame is set up. When the left frame is almost in its correct location, the mark ink

The Rituals which Accompany the Construction of Dong Houses 217

craftsman supports it with a wooden ladder and fork; secondly, the right frame is set up; and finally, when both sides' frames are set up, they are connected by the crossing-beams.

The second stage is the most difficult to connect and stabilize the frameworks with crossbeams. It is critically important to connect these frames, which are still unstable. Some workers need to climb to the tops of the columns and join the frameworks by inserting the tenons of the crossing beams into mortises. Raising each crossbeam requires three people. They stand on wooden ladders, and they lift the crossbeams with their hands. Getting ready, the head craftsman shouts, "opening the framework (*kai shan* 开扇)". The people on the ground pull the pair of frameworks, which are to be joined, in opposite directions with ropes. Those holding the crossbeam support it with one hand and rest their bodies on the frameworks. When the tenon of the crossing-beam is aligned with the mortise in the column, the head craftsman shouts, "connecting the frameworks!" (*he shan* 合扇), and the frameworks and crossing-beam are slowly mated, as the people shout "Yes!" Having secured the pieces well, the craftsmen knock on the column with wooden hammers to make the tenons engage fully with the mortises.[39] Feasting with oil tea, people have a break. And then, they continue to work until the three floors of the house are set up. By early morning, when the first

Figure 6.14 Setting up the new house structure, Sanjiang, 2006 (photo: Ronald Knapp).

sunshine sheds its light on the earth, the whole structure of the house is set up, symbolizing that the new house, similar to a new born baby, has been built up with fortune.

Raising the Golden Beam

Attention now turns to the most important structural ritual, which is Raising the Golden Beam ceremony (*shang liang* 上梁), when the ridge pole (golden beam) is set on the top of the house roof (Figure 6.15). The ceremony would also be practiced on the golden beams of the drum towers (Figure 6.16) and the bridges (Figure 6.17). Before the beam is raised in the *shang liang* ceremony by the craftsman, the important process named *kai liang kou* (open a mouth on the beam 开梁口) would be conducted. Having completed the work on mortises and tenons, the craftsman must especially open a 'mouth' on the golden beam. The 'mouth' is opened in the middle of the beam, about 10cm by 10cm; rice, silver coins, vermilion and tea are put in the hole, and it is closed with the same piece of timber block. Then the bamboo pen of the mark ink craftsman, a brush pen, and a piece of coloured thread wrapped in a piece of red cloth are nailed on top of the beam 'mouth', to represent a wish that the householder will be auspicious, fertile, intelligent and wealthy.

Figure 6.15 Shangliang ceremony in the new house, Sanjiang, 2006 (photo: Ronald Knapp).

The Rituals which Accompany the Construction of Dong Houses 219

Figure 6.16 Shangliang ceremony in the drum tower, Sanjiang, 1985 (photo: Mei Ling).

While the craftsman is doing this, he speaks auspicious words to the master: "the golden beam, which is wrapped in the red cloth, sheds splendid light; and when it is put up on the golden beam, the house will be full of fortune". He also needs to put a pair of chopsticks in the red package, which must come from a good business shop, whose purpose is to wish for richness and fertility.[40]

This ritual, in erecting the frames and hoisting the ridge-pole when building a house, is recorded in *Lu Ban Jing*. When a house is built, an auspicious day and a favourable hour have to be waited for the erection of the frames

220 The Rituals which Accompany the Construction of Dong Houses

Figure 6.17 Shangliang ceremony in the bridge, Sanjiang, 1985 (photo: Mei Ling).

and hoisting the ridge pole. At the auspicious time, a table is placed in the middle of the main hall, on which a portrait of the immortal master and incense are placed. Sacrificial money, fragrant flowers, candles, meat of the three sacrificial animals (chicken, carp and pork), fruits and wine are prepared. At the sacrificial ceremony, the foreman of the carpenter pays his respects to the Lord of the Earth, the second of the three Worlds, to the house gods of the five directions, to Lu Ban, the third squire and to the high and true worthies of the Ten Extremities. His *zhanggan* (the craftsman ruler), an ink marker and a square ruler are put on a rice barrel which is placed on the incense table, and everything is put in its proper place according to the compass of the geomancer. With the help of the Official's Tally and Three Noxious Currents, gods and evil currents are expelled. It is believed that the occupants of the house will lead a happy life forever.[41]

It is very interesting that, according to the craftsman Yang Shanren, the *shang liang* ceremony in building the Dong house is similar to the record of *Lu Ban Jing*. Before the 'raising the beam' ceremony is held, people need to worship it.[42] A table is set up on the site of the main hall with a pig's head, eight bowls, two dishes of sweets, five cups of alcohol and a litre of rice, and three bunches of incense with three sticks in a bunch are burned. In front of the pig's head, there is a pair of new shoes, which are prepared for the mark ink craftsman to perform the rite of 'stepping on the beam'. After the *jin liang* (golden beam) is 'invited' onto the trestles, with the offerings, such as a coloured, handmade brocade of Dong cloth, all hung on the beam, the worship ceremony is begun. The villagers and the relatives of the house-owner, who are waiting for the striking ceremony, surround the house. After the mark ink craftsman recites one auspicious sentence, everybody needs to answer: "Yes!" Normally, the favourite time for *shang liang* (上梁) ceremony is usually after *wu shi* (午时),[43] the auspicious time depending on the *ba zi* of the houseowner.

At the moment of the auspicious time, the mark ink craftsman shouts: "Wenqu Xing (the Civil Spirit) and Wuqu Xing (another Civil Spirit) go on the top of the house please!" Then, two selected young men climb to the top of the house quickly with the shouting of the craftsmen, and a rope is dropped down by them. People on the ground tie the rope on both ends of the golden beam quickly. And then, the craftsmen recite loudly again:

> At the fortunate time, the sky and earth open to welcome the golden beam to rise on the main hall, and with the golden rope tied firmly on both ends, the golden beam is raised to the sky. The mountains would create wealth and nobility with the rising of the left end, and the best scholar would be born from the master's descendants with the rising of the right end. Raise the beam![44]

The Wenqu Xing and Wuqu Xing, who are standing on the top of the frame, then drag the beam up and put it on the top of the golden beams, waiting for the mark ink craftsman to ascend to perform *an liang* ceremony (setting up the beam 安梁). At that moment, with three loud booms, the fireworks prepared by the householder and his relatives are set off to announce the start of the ceremony to all spirits and villagers. After the raising beam ceremony, the mark ink craftsman carries on *an liang* (setting the beam 安梁) and *chai liang* (stepping on the beam 踩梁) ceremonies with the new shoes. While climbing up, he sings:

> With first step on the ladder and two steps of walking,
> the shed is full of pigs, ships, cows, and horses.
> Thousands of animals go out in the daytime,
> and millions of them come back in the night.
> With second step on the ladder and three steps of walking,
> many auspicious festivals arrive.
> Thousands of guests present their gifts in the daytime,
> and millions of lights will shine in the night.
> With third step on the ladder and four steps of walking,
> the four directions belong to the wealthy spirits.
> Wealth comes from the east and treasure comes from the west,
> wealth is full in the house.
> With fourth step on the ladder and five steps of walking,
> the house would be higher than clouds in the sky,

> Dragon and phoenix would surround the columns towards the sun,
> and the lions play with kylin[45] in front of the house.
> With fifth step on the ladder and five steps of walking,
> every generation of the descendants are clever.
> Last generation is nominated,
> and this generation is named among the best scholars.
> With sixth step on the ladder and seven steps of walking,
> the grain would be harvested.
> It would be sold to Yunnan in the west,
> and to Beijing in the north.
> With seventh step on the ladder and eight steps of walking,
> the master would own thousands and millions of acres.
> The master would be rich from receiving gold and silver,
> and his sons would be famous for their high education.
> With eighth step on the ladder and nine steps of walking,
> the road in front of the house would lead to Beijing.
> The master would be rich when he goes out in the morning,
> and fertile after he comes back in the evening.
> Upstairs in the first floor,
> the descendants would be famous.
> Beautiful girls would be born,
> and scholar boys would be born in the house.
> Upstairs to the second floor,
> the civil and military spirits would arrive,
> Persons living here would be better than Bao Zhanxiang
> and Yang Liulang.
> Stepping on the stairs,
> the master would be wealthy after the house has been built.
> The granaries in front of the house and behind it would be full of grain,
> which is used to serve millions of people in June.[46]

Finally, he arrives at the top of the frame, and sits on the tenoned end of the *jin liang* (golden beam), which means '*an jin liang*' (setting the golden beam安金梁). He stops on the middle of the golden beam with the Lu Ban axe in one hand and the Lu Ban ruler in his other hand, and knocks at the golden beam gently. Then he continues:

> With a book in the middle of jin liang (golden beam),
> and the old people would live long, the young enjoy good fortune.
> There is a pair of chopsticks in the middle of jin liang,
> and the master would be rich and fertile forever.
> There is a bottle of ink in the middle of jin liang.
> and the descendants would get golden ranks in horse-racing.
> There is one chi cloth hanged on the middle of jin liang.
> and many millionaires would be created from the descendants.

The Rituals which Accompany the Construction of Dong Houses 223

Standing on the middle of the main hall,
I hope the master would enjoy good fortune.
The first hope would be for richness and fertility,
and the second for wealth and nobility,
The third hope would be many auspicious festivals in the house,
and the fourth would be to flourish within the four seasons,
The fifth hope would be awarded the scholar,
and getting promotion of the descendants for the sixth hope,
The seventh hope would be reunion of the family,
and the eighth hope would be to receive the presents from the eight spirits.
The ninth hope would be for the golden fish to become dragon,
and that the master would be famous is my last wish.[47]

Chai liang (stepping on the beam) ceremony is held soon after '*an jin liang*' (setting the beam) ceremony. He walks on the beam from left to right as if walking on the ground. While walking, he sings:

With first step, jin liang (golden beam) would shed the splendid light,
Which gets rid of the evil spirits, and blesses the master forever.
With second step, jin liang would be more solid.
It would bless the master with riches, and bring his descendants good fortune.[48]

The audience is impressed by the craftsman's songs, and praise him lavishly with loud shouting. The craftsman sings in more rhythm with the inspiration of the people. The ceremony named '*zhuo liang*' (sitting on the beam 坐梁) follows the stepping on the beam ceremony. Wenqu Xing and Wuqu Xing take their seats on opposite ends of *jin liang*. In front of them is a tray on *jin liang* with six bowls of foods and a bottle of alcohol. They sing auspicious songs to praise the beam and the house, while drinking a cup of alcohol.[49] At the end of the *An Jin Liang* ceremony, they throw the colourful sticky rice cakes prepared by the householder to the people. Usually, he must prepare enough cakes so that each person can have at least one. A container filled with cakes, silver coins and silver bangles is raised to the top of the beam. The craftsman chooses 12 bigger cakes and puts them on *jin liang* with silver coins, bangles and a lucky moneybag. The houseowner lays out a red cloth on the main hall ground to receive what is thrown from *jin liang*. The craftsman on the beam asks: "what does the master need? rich or noble?" the family answers: "both". Then, the silver coins, bangles, and lucky money are thrown from *jin liang* by the craftsman on to the red cloth while the craftsman recites: "It would bless the master's family rich and noble; their grain would be harvested every year; and would succeed in civil and military life". The houseowner is very happy to receive the blessing from the craftsman.

Then, the craftsman throws 12 cakes, which are received by the houseowner, and put on the family altar to worship. And finally, the mark ink craftsman takes out all of the cakes, and throws them to the people, while sending his blessing to all people:

> The cakes are thrown to the east,
> and heroes would be created from the descendants.
> The cakes are thrown to the west,
> and the family would not worry about food and clothing.
> The cakes are thrown to the south,
> and it would bless the family with luck, security, and reunion.
> The cakes are thrown to the north,
> and the auspicious sunshine would surround the house.
> Eating the white cake,
> you would get rid of illness.
> I throw the cakes to the house ground,
> and whoever gets it would try it.
> Senior people would get long life if they get it,
> and the middle-aged ones would be rich,
> Young woman would have a son if she gets it,
> and young girl would marry a good boy,
> Young man would have elaborate skills if he gets it,
> and little boy would do better than before.[50]

While he sings and throws the cakes, everybody tries hard to get them, and the ceremony fills with fortune and happiness. To the houseowner, the most important thing has been finished after the *shang liang* ceremony. When the house has been set up, if the owner has enough money, he would invite the craftsman to build the floors and separate the rooms with timber walls. However, this usually costs as much as setting up the house. Actually, the householders only move in after the hearth and one or two bedrooms have been built, although the whole house is not at all finished. They usually continue their building work and decorating work after they move inside.[51] After the ceremony, the housemaster must serve the mark ink craftsman, carpenters and all villagers who help him in building the house with a meal named '*shuwu jiu*' (the meal for setting up the house 竖屋酒),[52] which is usually held in the houseowner's old house. The feast is usually held on the outdoor ground with tens of tables, which are laid out straight, and all the kin of the master come to help, which is viewed as their duty. Because building a house is a special event for the Dong, the Dong song teachers and villagers come and express their congratulations to the houseowner with the singing of auspicious songs. Usually, people like to compete in their singing at the feast. The mark ink craftsman, carpenters and song teachers are respected as noble guests accompanied by the kin of the master. Having drunk *jian mian jiu* (drinking for greeting each other 见面酒), the song teacher begins to sing the songs expressing their appreciation, starting with songs of admiration to the carpenters:

> The kind and lucky master invites Lu Ban arriving into the world.
> The house is built higher and larger, with phoenix and dragon being carved.
> It is better than any houses in the neighbouring villages, and the elaborate technology will be famous in the world.
> Dragon and phoenix are carved by the way, the sky-high building would be settled down.
> People admire you carpenters' merits and skills, with your talent.[53]

Then they offer congratulations to the houseowner:

> The master builds the magnificent house, elegant and splendid.
> Its eaves support the sun and moon, with auspicious cloud around its beams.
> Today you build the house, and you would have long life.[54]

Meanwhile, the houseowner wouldn't miss the chance to express his gratitude to them:

> Lu Ban builds the house, which is high to the sky.
> You would be asked to build in the heaven, and the spirits would request you.
> The ground floor would be shed with the light from the first floor, and the aromatics from the east garden could be smelt in the west garden.
> Today I am very glad to feast the song teachers, which is similar to the stars' benefit from association with the moon.
> I am very appreciative of my noble friends' coming, and I feel much fortune in my heart.
> Many thanks for your help, I would remember you if I couldn't return my debt.[55]

At the end, people express their fortune wishes to each other by singing the Invitation of Drinking Wine songs

> Guest:
> Today we passed villages and houses,
> And arrived at your house with both feet,
> We only hope to congratulation to your longevity,
> Wishing you long life and good fortune.
>
> Host:
> The Yangzi River is long and never stops,

And the pine trees are green forever,
I receive congratulations from you,
The old people will enjoy longevity and you will have more fortune.

Guest:
Everybody is happy because of the longevity of one person,
Your relatives and friends are all coming,
Congratulating your longevity as long as the sky and the earth,
And peace as the everlasting sky and earth.

Host:
Today guests don't mind walking a long way,
And coming to my home in happiness,
Congratulation to us with your golden jade and lucky words,
Just because of you, we gain much fortune.

Guest:
The Yellow River should not dry but water flows forever,
Old person has longevity year after year,
The longevity star climbs on the 'yuan gu lao',
Living happily without any anxiety.[56]

In the final stage of the ceremony, the craftsmen throw coloured sticky rice cakes, prepared by the householder, to the participating people. A container filled with cakes, silver coins and silver bangles is raised to the top of the beam, and the head craftsman selects twelve bigger cakes and puts them on the *jin liang* with silver coins, bangles and a lucky money bag. The houseowner lays out a red cloth on the floor of the main hall to receive what the craftsman drops from the golden beam, symbolizing wealth received in the new house. After the ceremony, the lucky decoration is sent to the golden beam of new structure (Figure 6.18). The desirable decoration is hanged on the golden beam, which is the charm for the new structure, to protect them from the evil (Figure 6.19). To the homeowner, the most important thing has now been completed, and he would serve a meal to the ink-marking craftsman, carpenters and all the participants. The head craftsmen, carpenters and song teachers are respected as noble guests. The *shang liang* ceremony focuses on the ridge pole, indicating that it is the most sacred element in these buildings. The golden beam symbolizes the human backbone, supporting the whole body, the building roof, or heaven, and it must be firm and secure. To ensure this, the building would be set up in the proper order and at a favourable time (Figure 6.20). Through ceremonies, performances, recitations and the singing of auspicious songs by the villagers, the golden beam is enlisted in the campaign to eliminate evil, and its successfully raising is seen to ensure the security and good fortune of the whole building and its occupants.

The Rituals which Accompany the Construction of Dong Houses 227

Figure 6.18 The Dong brocade sent by the healthy and fertile family to the site of the new bridge, Sanjiang, 1985 (photo: Mei Ling).

Figure 6.19 The lucky decoration of golden beam of Chengyang bridge, Sanjiang, 2004.

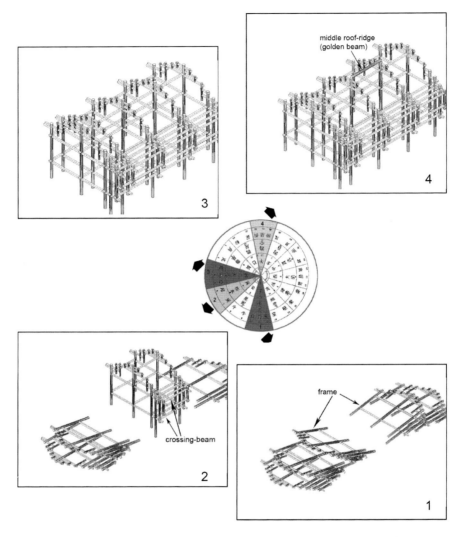

Figure 6.20 The chronological order of setting up a house (drawn by author):
1. The structural frames exactly located before 12am;
2. The structure started from the middle bay at 4am;
3. The whole structure completed on the *mao* clock at 6am;
4. The *shangliang* ceremony after *wu* clock of 12pm.

Opening the Door of Wealth

In the Dong house, the symbolic importance of the golden beam is rivaled only by that of the doors, and they, too, are associated with rituals. After the new house is built and ready to move in, a ceremony named Opening

The Rituals which Accompany the Construction of Dong Houses 229

the Door of Wealth (*kai cai men* 开财门) would be performed, celebrating the symbolic importance of the threshold. The entrance to the living room is especially important, which is called "the door of wealth". Dong doorways are distinctively decorated with two carved bosses or nodes attached to the lintel, named *da men chui* (door hammer 打门槌). The doorway of the Yang family house in Sanjiang is typical, marked with typical symbolism (Figure 6.21). Two cylindrical wooden nodes, approximately 15 centimeters in diameter, project about 30 centimeters from the top of the door frame. The left node, carved with a yang trigram image of three unbroken lines, stands for heaven, awareness and creativity; and the right node bears a yin trigram of three broken lines, symbolizing the earth, willingness and receptiveness.[57] In the Dong's view, the world wouldn't have vitality without humans. Thus, with people going through the door, the world is animated (*huo* 活). So, the door (*meng* 门) and the animate world construct the Chinese character '阔' (*kuo* 阔), which means 'wealth'.[58] And that is why the door is called Wealthy Door. The wealthy door would be built to particular measurements,

Figure 6.21 The *yin* and *yang* hammers on the top of the door frame of the living room in the house, Sanjiang, 2004.

230   *The Rituals which Accompany the Construction of Dong Houses*

for instance, the upper side of the main hall door should be wider than the lower, which means *tian kuan di zhai* (the sky is wide and the earth is narrow 天宽地窄), so that the wealth comes easily down to the house from the sky. Piece branches of beach tree are usually put on the pair of hammers, which are believed to protect the family from evil. The timber for the threshold is about 40 cm high, and as the highest threshold of the house, the timber must be 'stolen' similar to the golden beam. The threshold is viewed as 'door dragon', which is a protective spirit of the house. To prevent the 'dragon' escaping from the house, there is a bronze nail in the middle of the threshold, because it is said the 'dragon' is not scared of the fire burning from the heaven and the earth, just scared of the bronze nail breaking off its waist. Outside the threshold, there is a stair leading to the ground floor.[59]

Kai chai men (opening the wealthy door 开财门) ceremony is performed before the family moves in, while the door is first used (Figure 6.22).[60] On a favourable date, a skit is enacted with dialogue between two respected middle-aged men. One plays the role of a Spirit of Wealth outside the new house while the craftsman appears inside the door as Lu Ban. In this rite, a middle-aged man, who is not only good at speech but also has a fertile family with both sons and daughters, appears as a 'wealthy spirit'. He stands outside the new house door with a bag on his back and an umbrella in his hand. The craftsman stands inside the door and appears as Lu Ban. The 'wealthy spirit' knocks outside the door:

> there is a new scene in front of the master's new house with fortune sunglow and cloud surrounding the gate; and there are a cyan dragon and white tiger protecting the house on both sides of the door with the purple star shining on the middle of the house.

Then, he continues: "With the sky and the earth acting in cycle, at the auspicious date, I came here to present wealth to you. Please open your wealthy door!"

Lu Ban answers inside: "The golden door is made by the golden axe, and who is outside? Apart from the spirit from the heaven, we can't open the door".

The 'wealthy spirit': "I am a wealthy spirit from heaven, and I wouldn't come without business".

Lu Ban asks: "what are you going to do here"?

The 'wealthy spirit': "I am coming to open the wealthy door for the master".

Lu Ban: "What hat are you wearing, and in what clothing do you dress? What waistband are you tying, and what shoes are you wearing"?

The 'wealthy spirit': "I am wearing the black gauze hat, dressing in purple clothing, tying the golden waistband, and wearing dragon and phoenix shoes".

The Rituals which Accompany the Construction of Dong Houses 231

Figure 6.22 kai chaimen ceremony performed in front of the Yang's wealthy door, Sanjiang, 2004.

Lu Ban: "Where did you come from, the road or the river? How many mountains did you cross, and how many river banks did you pass?"

The 'wealthy spirit': "I came here without walking on the roads or crossing the rivers. I sped across the sky to here, and I couldn't see any mountain and river".

And ask: "Who are you, and what is your name? Which year, month and date is your birthday? What are you doing here for the master"?

Lu Ban: "I come from the country Lu, and Gong Shu is my surname and Ban is my first name. I was born in May 7th of *ren yi* (壬巳) year, and I make the wealthy door for the master".

The 'wealthy spirit': "How long are the four edges of the door frame together"?

Lu Ban: "1 *zhang* and 8 *chi* 8, the master wouldn't worry about food and clothing".

The 'wealthy spirit': "how tall and wide is the door? Where to open the door eye and fix the bolt? When and who will open the door"?

Lu Ban: "The door is 5 *chi* and 6 *cun* tall, and 4 *chi* and 3 *cun* wide. The door eye is opened at 4 *chi* and 3 *cun*, and the door bolt is fixed at 4 *fen* and 8 *li*. When the sun rises in the morning, the daughter in law would open the bolt".

Lu Ban: "I don't know which spirit would come first, who in the middle, and who in the last? Could you please tell me"?

The 'wealthy spirit': "in front of the house, there is '*Zhiwei* star' shining on the sky; in the middle, there are 'Wenqu Xing' and 'Wuqu Xing'. Today I just arrived, and speak directly to you".

Lu Ban: "What presents do you bring with you? Could you please tell me in detail".

The 'wealthy spirit': "in front of me, there are five boys and two girls, and behind me, I bring the gold and jade, which are presented to your new house. The heavy wealthy is brought in my left hand, and harvest grain in my right hand. I am coming today in particular to congratulate the master, and wish him fortune and health".

Lu Ban: "What is the present in your hand?"

The 'wealthy spirit': "The gold in one of my hands, and silver in my other hand".

Lu Ban: "Because the wealthy spirit is coming, I would be glad to open the door".

Lu Ban opens the door, and then the 'wealthy spirit' pushes both side of the door, and sings loudly:

> Push the door with my hands, which are made of golden fan and silver fan.
> Push the left fan with greeting of the golden cock, and right fan with singing of the phoenix.
> Bring in my left foot with thousands of treasures, and right foot with millions of silver.
> Congratulations to the master with fertility and richness,
> Meet fortune while opening the door, and flourish forever.[61]

As soon as he goes in, a red lucky money bag with 1 *yuan* 2 *jiao* from the package of the wealthy spirit is presented to the houseowner, and named *jin chai* (welcoming the wealth 进财). The Lu Ban craftsman would kill a cock, and sprinkle its blood on the door, which means protecting the house from evil. The houseowner would receive the lucky money bag, which is symbolic of wealth, and welcome both the 'wealthy spirit' and Lu Ban to take seats in the main hall, and serve them with tea and tobacco. Then they need to do the 'inviting the fire spirit in the hearth' ceremony. Before the rite, the houseowner has prepared cookers and firewood, and just waits for the 'wealthy spirit' to burn the charcoal. The fire kindling is from the old house hearth, and is put in a container. Finishing the tea, the 'wealthy spirit' and Lu Ban are invited by the master to stir up the fire. When the 'wealthy spirit' arrives at the hearth, he squats and blows on the wooden coal so as to light it up, and then puts it into the hearth with dry firewood. So the fire is then burning in the hearth. Then, the wealthy spirit sings auspicious songs:

> While the fire spirit is invited to the hearth,
> the master's house would have fortune.
> Burning the fire for thousands and millions of years,
> the master would cook food forever.
> There are lavish dishes and beautiful wine
> for every meal.
> The family would be rich and his descendants
> would flourish forever.[62]

After these ceremonies, the houseowner feasts people around the hearth. The 'wealthy spirit', the Lu Ban craftsman, the relatives of the family, and the family kin would drink the *fu gui jiu* (wealthy and noble wine 富贵酒) in the main hall. During the meal, people congratulate the master again with the auspicious songs.[63]

The dialogue in the Opening the Door of Wealth ceremony between the houseowner and the Spirit of Wealth reflects the strong awareness of boundaries among the Dong, whether at the village gate or at the house door. The door communicates between the inside and outside, providing the passageway through which both good energy and evil energy might go in and out. The ceremony shows the houseowner's desire to welcome fortune and security and block evil from the house. In return, the owner offers a meal to the "spirits" and the villagers who bring good fortune to him, expressing his appreciation and his hope to pray for further blessings.

Conclusion

It is interesting that the building procedure and techniques of the Dong are fulfilled with symbolic meanings and rituals, which celebrate the transition of material, measurement and building from the status of disorder or profane to order and sacred, to promise a new fortunate building born. A Dong building is regarded as secure not only because it serves its basic function as physical shelter, but also because rituals have empowered it to shield its occupants from the invisible energies responsible for human suffering. Arnold Van Gennep has stated that "every new house is taboo until, by appropriate rites, it is made secular or profane".[64] And Tony Atkin and Joseph Rykwert have added to this that, through sacrifice and ritual, a building becomes a model of the ordered world, of the cosmos.[65]

Human beings have to make sense of the world before they start building shelters, because the cognitive order is prior to the material one. While people are able to control available materials with craft in their buildings, construction is viewed more as the greatest of human activities, imbued with richly cultural symbolic meaning, rather than simply as building works. The structures not only have a practical aim, but also reassure their occupants, either in the building process or moving inside. This is analogous to the constants of social life for an individual, who is placed in various sections of society with a series of ceremonies performed from the day of his birth to that of his death, to guarantee the person passing from one category to another. According to Dumarcay in his account of Asian vernacular architecture, without these rites of passage in construction, the building is believed to have insecurity, and the householder would be seriously bothered.[66] Although these rituals are often very varied, they are based on the same purpose, with no other aim than to protect the house against the malignant forces disturbed by its construction and to integrate the building into the surrounding space. Furthermore, the ordering of the rituals presents and reinforces beliefs about the nature of the world, which in an oral culture are not held in other forms, and these signs also act as mnemonics and educational devices for the young people.

Time and space are usually experienced together in architecture, as they are in ritual, which can be described as formalized movement that occurs in both space and time. Dong building rituals are designed both to gain mastery over time by prediction and divination and to impose order on space.[67] Time has always been related to concepts of the cosmos, most specifically in the perennial human quest to identify fortunate or unfortunate times and dates, and rituals mark such time-specific events as changes in social status and milestones in human life.[68] Space-specific rituals such as those surrounding the construction of Dong houses are similar to rituals still evident in Western culture in the ground breaking, housewarming and cornerstone ceremonies that celebrate auspicious architectural beginnings. Among the most common of these rituals is the 'topping out' ceremony that celebrates the laying of the last concrete floor or the setting of the topmost steel beam in a high-rise building—the Western equivalent of raising the golden beam.

Notes

1 *Tailiang* and *chuandou* were two types of timber structural system used in traditional Chinese architecture. The tai liang system was used in buildings and houses in northern China. A tai liang beam-column network is defined by the width of the building; the main beam is supported by the principal column, and short pillars rest on the main beam, forming the frame that supports the big roof. In a chuan dou structure, the columns are set along the wide sides of the building, and roof purlins rest on the tops of columns directly. The columns are connected by crossbeams, forming a beam-column framework, and each frame is connected by crossbeams. Compared with tai liang structure, chuan dou structure is lighter and uses materials more economically. The diameter of a chuan dou structural column is usually 20 to 30 cm, and that of cross-beam is 6 by 12 cm, or 10 by 20 cm. Cf. Dunzhen Liu, Zhongguo Gudai Jianzhu Shi 1980. 中国古代建筑史† (*The History of Chinese Traditional Architecture*. Beijing: Zhingguo Jianzhu Gongye Press; Binjian Ma, Zhongguo Gujianzu Muzuo Yingzao Jishu

The Rituals which Accompany the Construction of Dong Houses 235

1991. 中国古建筑木作营造技术† (*The Techniques of Timber Structure in Chinese Traditional Architecture*). Beijing: Kexue Press, 1991; and Yuhuan Zhang *et al.* (eds.) 2000. Zhongguo Gudai Jianzhu Jishushi 中国古代建筑技术史† (The Techniques of Chinese Traditional Architecture). Beijing: Kexue Press.

2 Author's interview with Yang Shanren, in Sangjiang county in July of 2002, Yang Niankui in Nanning and Wu Hao in Liuzhou in August of 2004. Also see Li, Xuemei 2007. "The Life Bridge: An Anthropology of the Dong Wind and Rain Bridge in Southern China" PhD thesis, School of Architecture, University of Sheffield.

3 According to the Book of Rites, among all things by which men live, rites are the most important. Without rites, there would be no means of regulating the services paid to the spirits of heaven and earth; no means of distinguishing the positions of ruler and subject, superior and inferior, old and young; no means of maintaining the relationships between man and woman, father and son, elder and younger brother; and of conducting the communication between families related in marriage. See Wu, Hung, *Monumentality in Early Chinese Art and Architecture*. Palo Alto, CA: Stanford University Press, 1995, p. 20; also see James Legge, Li Chi. *Book of Rites* New York: University Books, 1967 [1885], 2: 261.

4 Ceremonies related to the construction of houses are extremely common in Southeast Asia, where they are believed to impart sacred status on the building. The house is regarded as a refuge from evil forces and influences, not only because it restricts the access of outsiders, but also because it has been cleansed of malign influences through the performance of religious rituals during its erection and upon completion. Cf. Turton, Andrew 1978. *Architectural and Political Space in Thailand* London: School of Oriental and African Studies; Kana, N. L. 1980. *The Order and Significance of the Savunese House*. Cambridge: Harvard University Press; Dumarcay, Jacques 1987. *The House in South-east Asia*, trans. and ed. Michael Smithies. Singapore: Oxford University Press; and Waterson, Roxana 1990. *The Living House: An Anthropology of Architecture in South-East Asia*. Singapore: Oxford University Press.

5 This was personally communicated by Wu Hao, Wu Shihua and Yang Shanren in 2004; and also Cf. Xian 1995; Yang 1983; and Geary 2003.

6 See Yu, Dazhong 2001. *Dongzu Minju* 侗族民居 (The Dwellings of the Dong). Guiyang: Huaxia Wenhua Yishu Press, pp. 108–10, translated by the author. Many rituals practised during building process, including stealing the beam, *shangliang*, opening the wealthy door ceremonies, and Dong songs, are collected in this book.

7 Interviewed with Yang Shanren in 2004.

8 Ruitenbeek, Klaas 1996. *Carpentry and Building in Late Imperial China: A Study of The Fifteenth-Century Carpenter's Manual Lu Ban Jing*. Leiden, New York, Koln: E. J. Brill; and Li, F. (ed.) 2003. *Lu Ban Jing*. Haikou: Hainan Press. Lu Ban Jing was written by Wu Rong in Ming dynasty (1368–644).

9 Li, F. (ed.) 2003. *Lu Ban Jing*. Haikou: Hainan Press. *Lu Ban Jing* was written by Wu Rong in Ming dynasty (1368–644), pp. 62–3.

10 See Ruitenbeek 1996: 168; and Li 2003: 38. In imperial China, although 1 to 9 can be selected as the number of house bay, only 9 bays or over can be used as the emperor palaces. The officials can select 3 to 7 bays depending on their rankings, and the public only can choose house bay numbers not more than 3.

11 See Yu 2001: 93.

12 *Ibid*. p. 123.

13 *Ibid*. pp. 117–8.

14 Oral information from interview with Shanren Yang in the summer of 2004; also see Yu 2001: 117–8.

15 Interview with Yang Shanren and Yang Yongqing in Ma'an village at Sanjiang county in August of 2004.
16 See Fan, C. et al. 1991. *Guangxi Minzu Chuantong Jianzhu Shilu* 广西民族传统建筑实录 (The Record of Vernacular Architecture in Guangxi). Nanning, Guanxi Kexue Jishu Press, p. 63.
17 Yang, Tongshan (ed.) 1983. *Dongxiang Fengqing Lu* 侗乡风情录 (The custom of the Dong), Chengdu: Shichuan Minzu Press, pp. 69–78.
18 The whole story of a house's construction was told to the author by Yang Shanren in the summer of 2004. Also see Yu Dazhong, Dongzhu Minju 2001. 侗族民居†(The Dwellings of the Dong). Guiyang: Huaxia Wenhua Yishu Press, 120–6.
19 Author's interview with Wu Shihua and Yang Shanren in Sanjiang county in 2004. Also see Ruitenbeek, Carpentry and Building, 155.
20 Author's interview with Yang Shanren in 2004. Also see Zhe Jun and Nian Haoxi (eds.) 1994. *Dongzu Minjian Wenhua Shenmeilun* 侗族民间文化审美论 (Aesthetics of the Dong Folk Custom). Nanning: Guanxi Renmen Press, pp. 112–3.
21 Author's interview with Yang Shanren in 2004.
22 See the whole story recorded in Yu, Dazhong 2001. *Dongzu Minju* 侗族民居 (The Dwellings of the Dong). Guiyang: Huaxia Wenhua Yishu Press, pp. 122–3.
23 Interviewed with Yang Niankui by the author in the summer of 2004.
24 Interviewed with Yang Shanren in 2004.
25 See Ruitenbeek 1996: 155; and Li 2003: 1–2. The direction of the Yellow Current refers to *wu* 午 (south direction), responding to Fire in the Five-phases.
26 See Wu, Hao and Zhang, Zhezhong 1991. *Dongzu Geyao Yanjiu* 侗族歌谣研究 (Research on the Dong Songs). Nanning: Guangxi Renmin Press, pp. 43–4, translated by the author.
27 Author's interview with Wu Hao in August 2004.
28 Author's interview in the summer of 2004 with Yang Shanren and Yang Niankui in Ma'an village at Sanjiang county, the second son of Yang Shanren, who used to be chosen to cut timbers for house building.
29 See Peter Blundell Jones and Xuemei Li, "What Can a Bridge Be? The Wind and Rain Bridges of the Dong," *Journal of Architecture* 13, no. 5 (2008), 565–84. The bridge model was made by the Dong carpenter Yang Shiyu in 2001 for the new drum tower of Sanjiang county.
30 Quotation from interview with Wu Hao in Liuzhou, August 2004. Author's translation.
31 Quotation from interview with Wu Hao in Liuzhou, August 2004. Author's translation.
32 Personal communication with Yang Shanren in the summer of 2004.
33 Author's interview with Wu Shihua in the summer of 2004.
34 Yu 2001: p. 121, the author's translation.
35 Interviewed with Yang Shanren in 2004.
36 Yu 2001: p. 124, translation by the author.
37 *Yinshi* 寅时 refers to 4am in the morning on the compass.
38 *Maoshi* 卯时 is 6am in the morning on the compass.
39 Interview with Yang Shanren in the summer of 2004, and also see Yu 2001: 120–6.
40 The auspicious amulet attached on the ridge in *shangliang* ceremony is described in a personal communication with Wu Hao in the summer of 2004. Also see Yu 2001: 123.
41 See Ruitenbeek 1996: 164; and Li 2003: 33–5.
42 Interviewed with Yang Shanren in the summer of 2004.

43 *Wushi* 午时 is located to the south on the compass, and refers to 12 pm on the clock.
44 Yu 2001: 127.
45 A pair of fortunate animals in Chinese legends, which are also named *qilin* 麒麟 in Chinese. The male is *qi* 麒 and the female is *lin* 麟.
46 See the record in Yu 2001: 128–8, the author's translation.
47 *Ibid.* pp. 129–30.
48 *Ibid.* p. 130. The author's translation.
49 *Ibid.* pp. 130–1.
50 *Ibid.* pp. 131–2. The author's translation.
51 Interviewed with Yang Shanren and Wu Hao in the summer of 2004, and the 'raising the beam' ceremony can also be found in Yu 2001: 126–33.
52 The feast is served in both afternoon and in the night, and the lunch is rather simple only with four dishes and one soup, but the dinner is more formal, normally with eight, twelve dishes or even fourteen dishes, and the number of guests is more than that for lunch. See Yu 2001: 132.
53 *Ibid.* p. 133. The author's translation.
54 *Ibid.* The author's translation.
55 *Ibid.* p. 133. The author's translation.
56 Wu 1991: 46–7, my translation.
57 Fieldwork by the author at the Yang house at Sanjiang county in 2004.
58 The story about the origin of 'Wealthy Door' was told by Yang Shanren to the author in the summer of 2004.
59 Yu 2001: 134.
60 The whole story sees the record of Yu: 2001: 135–8.
61 *Ibid.* pp. 136–7. The author's translation.
62 *Ibid.* p. 137. The author's translation.
63 *Ibid.* pp. 134–7.
64 Arnold Van Gennep 1960. *The Rites of Passage*, trans. Monika B. Vizedom and Gabrielle L. Caffee. Chicago: University of Chicago Press.
65 Atkin, Tony and Rykwert, Joseph 2005. *Structure and Meaning in Human Settlements*. Philadelphia: University of Pennsylvania Museum of Archaeology and Anthropology.
66 Dumarcay, J. 1987. *The House in South-east Asia*. Singapore: Oxford University Press, pp. 16–17.
67 Personal communication with Professor Peter Blundell Jones, Sheffield University, 2006.
68 See Van Gennep 1969. *Rites of Passage; Victor Witter Turner, The Ritual Process: Structure and Anti-structure*. New York: Aldine De Gruyter); and Maurice Bloch 1992. *Prey into Hunter: The Politics of Religious Experience*. Cambridge: Cambridge University Press.

7 Conclusion
Symbolic Meaning, Ritual and Architectural Order

> And the woman said to the serpent, Of the fruit of the trees in the garden we may eat,
> But of the fruit of the tree which is in the midst of the garden, God has said, You
> shall not eat of it, nor shall you touch it, lest you die.
> And the serpent said to the woman, You will not surely die.
> For God knows that in the day you eat of it your eyes will be opened, and you will
> become like God, knowing good and evil.
> And when the woman saw that the tree was good for food and that it was a delight to
> the eyes and that the tree was to be desired to make oneself wise, she took of its
> fruit and ate, and she also gave some to her husband with her, and he ate.
> And the eyes of both were opened, and they knew that they were naked; and they
> sewed fig leaves together and made loincloths for themselves.
> Genesis 3: 2–7[1]

The Dong's architecture is built evidently for rituals, and is constructed with rituals. The cosmos of the Dong villages is well-ordered with the drum towers that are central to the villages, and the Wind and Rain bridges that are peripheral and transitional. They constitute an essential complement, both as places of spiritual presences and ritual observance, built with the Dong' s pride and woven with the symbolic meanings based on the traditional cosmology. The Dong believe in reincarnation, therefore souls have to return from the realm of the dead to the realm of the living, and this transference takes special effect on the Wind and Rain bridge, as shown by one of its alternative names 'soul bridge' and by a number of customs. A bride should be carried across it on the night before her wedding, lovers may meet there to assure a happy union, barren women wanting children would quietly make offerings and pregnant women would pray there for a

DOI: 10.4324/9781003228837-7

safe delivery. The idea is that returning souls arrive down the river with the life-giving *qi*, and this is perhaps reinforced by the image in Dong myth that the realm of the dead from which they return lies high in the mountains at the river's source.

For the Dong, the measurement system is most essential technique in the Dong's carpentry, which is based both on the human body and geometric proportions. Shaped by this measurement rules, the Dong architecture has obtained a meaning relating to their lives. Protagoras, the Sophist philosopher of the fifth century BC, claimed that 'man is the measure of all things'.[2] On the one hand, we measure the building to build; and on the other hand, we are measured by the building as we enter it.[3] The human sense of architecture is both social and spatial, as Bourdieu declaims, "the human body is nothing other than a socially, informed body, with its tastes and distastes, its compulsions and repulsions ... all its senses are more than the traditional five senses".[4] The human body functions as a practical operator relating with the movements of left and right, up and down, and front and behind, which are endowed with meaning of social significance, because right, up and front of human body usually indicate positive sides, compared to left, down and back. Based on human sense of fortune and unfortune derived from the orientation, the measurement rules as the essential techniques of the Dong is scaled with symbolic meanings and made with rituals, in order to achieve a building with prosperity and promotion. So it is evident that building with the symbolic meanings and rituals in the Dong's architecture is to achieve a desirable order of the architecture. Why are the symbolic meanings and rituals essential to the architectural order?

The Classification of Order or Disorder by the Symbolic Meaning

The story of the Book of Genesis narrates the first man and woman created by God, Adam and Eve, in the Garden of Eden where they may eat the fruit of many trees, but are forbidden by God to eat from the tree of knowledge of good and evil. However, ignoring God's wisdom, the woman is seduced by the craftier serpent, she eats the forbidden fruit and gives some to the man who also eats it. They become aware of their "nakedness" and make fig-leaf clothes, and hide themselves when God approaches. God then curses the serpent, the woman then the man, and expels the man and woman from the Garden before they ate of the tree of eternal life. Since then, the first human beings have the knowledge of good and evil, sacred and profane, order and disorder, and so on.

In the *Oxford Learner's Dictionaries*, 'Order' means the way in which people or things are placed or arranged in relation to each other; or means the state of being carefully and neatly arranged; also means the state that exists when people obey laws, rules or authority. In the *Online Etymology*

Dictionary, 'Order' origins from Latin *ordinem* (nominative *ordo*) "row, line, rank; series, pattern, arrangement, routine," originally "a row of threads in a loom". The sense of order derives from the experience of human body, to identify balance and orientation of up and down, left and right and front and back of the perceived environment, and discover good (order) or bad (disorder) scene, smell and sound, by our eyes, noses and eyes. Experience is the only teacher to form human being's innate ideas. As Gombrich argues, nothing could enter this mind except through the sense organs, and only when these "sense impressions" became associated in the mind could we build up a picture of the world outside.[5] The mind would ever order such impressions in space and in time if space and time had first to be learned from experience. As Gombrich argues:

> It must be able to answer the questions 'what?' and 'where?' In other words it must find out what the objects in its environment mean to it, whether any are to be classified as potential sources of nourishment or of danger, and in either case it must take the appropriate action of location, pursuit or flight. These actions pre-suppose what in higher animals and in man has come to be known as a 'cognitive map', a system of co-ordinates on which meaningful objects can be plotted.[6]

Sense of order involves perception of meaning and the perception of order, which has been made and referenced as a rule in the world, and people have perceived the regularity of the natural world. People experience and enjoy the discovery and phenomenon of the natural environment, and try to understand it and interpret it within the perspective their cultural context. Thus, the phenomenon of natural world is endowed with symbolic meanings by the people from different culture.

In contrast, 'Disorder' means an untidy state; a lack of order or organization, and 'Chaos' means a complete lack of order. In the Cretan Labyrinth Myth, the wife of King Minos of Crete, named Pasiphae, fell passionately in love with a handsome bull. To satisfy her lust, master Daedalus who is an inventor of antiquity of the Athenian, built her a wooden cow covered with hides. Pasiphae climbed into the cow, mated with the bull, and conceived the Minotaur, a monster with the body of a man and the head of a bull. King Minos was shamed by this visible proof of his wife's lechery, and he commanded Daedalus to construct the confusing and inextricable labyrinth to imprison the Minotaur. While the animal concealed inside tried to find the way out, its energy would be exhausted to die.[7] The image of typical medieval labyrinth thus consists two important principles of order and disorder: the whole perfect circle implies the circular order of the cosmos, the shape of the world, eternity and seasonal repetition and renewal; the path inside illustrates confusion, torture and death, symbolizing a disruption of perfect order.[8] Thus, disorder and chaos symbolize abnormal, evil and profane, which lead to death.

Conclusion: Symbolic Meaning, Ritual and Architectural Order 241

The classification of order or disorder would derive from our collected memory and experience, which is essential to everything we do and think. Memory is engaged on a personal level in our interaction with everything, not only because of the experience and appreciation, but also because we tend to compare what we do now with what we did last time. As Blundell Jones argues, it would be further engaged on a social level, for the shared social activities that can be traced and learned.[9] With the previous experience and context, we would decide what to do next, and predict what to happen, and try to fit into the structure of relations in which we find ourselves.[10] As David Lowenthal puts it:

> The prime function of memory is not to preserve the past but to adapt it so as to enrich and manipulate the present. Far from simply holding on to previous experiences, memory helps us to understand them. Memories are not ready made reflections of the past, but eclectic, selective reconstructions based on subsequent actions and perceptions and on ever-changing codes by which we delineate, symbolize, and classify the world around us.[11]

Since human beings have the awareness of good or evil, order or disorder, fortunate or unfortunate, everything is classified and thus endowed with symbolic meanings. The anthropological theory has been developed to interpret the architectural space with its symbolic meanings.[12] A 'Symbol' is defined in *Symbolic Classification* by Rodney Needham as to something that stands for something else. For instance, an eagle stands for the United States although the nation has no bill, feathers, nest or eggs; artillery pieces are fired off in honour of a visiting statesman, though there is no target and there are no shells in the guns, and in each case symbolic, in that it enhances or marks the importance of the subject: the might of the nation, the diplomatic relationship with a foreign state.[13] Lakoff points out that symbolic meaning and metaphor are "pervasive in everyday life, not just in language but in thought and action", providing understanding of other subjects, governing a person's perception, and structuring a person's action, because symbolic meaning and metaphor have been woven into the person's conceptual system with his everyday experience.[14] With a metaphorical experience in life, as Eliade argues, oppositions are usually assumed by traditional societies between the natural world and the unknown or indeterminate place that surrounds it, such as 'this world' (our world, the cosmos) and a sort of 'other world' outside this world, meaning a foreign, chaotic space, peopled by ghosts, demons and so on.[15] The matter of practical hygiene, as Mary Douglas argues that pollution behaviour is always symbolic, and its rules vary from culture to culture. As she puts:

> Dirt is never a unique isolated event. Where there is dirt there is system.
> Dirt is a by-product of a systematic ordering and classification of matter, in so far as ordering involves rejecting, inappropriate elements.

This idea of dirt takes us straight into the field of symbolism and promises a link-up with more obviously symbolic systems of purity.[16]

She explains that it is a relative idea, because shoes are not dirty in themselves, but it is dirty to place them on the dining table; and food is not dirty in itself, but it is dirty to leave cooking utensils in the bedroom, or food bespattered on clothing drawing room; clothing lying on chairs; out-door things in-doors, upstairs things downstairs.[17] Thus everything is defined by the symbolic meaning endowed with it, and the classification of good or evil, fortunate or unfortunate and order or disorder depends on personal experience, world views and the cultural context.

Ritual as the Action of Transition

The word 'ritual' is defined in *The Concise Oxford* as 'a prescribed order of performing rites', and *The Random House Dictionary* adds that 'ritual' is a prescribed code of behaviour regulating social conduct, as that exemplified by the raising of one's hat or the shaking of hands in greeting; and 'rite' is any customary observance or practice, for example, the elegant rite of afternoon tea; and the white-collar rite of the 10 a.m. coffee break.[18] In this sense, ritual implies a connection between practiced and beliefs or views of the world, marked by repetition and rules. Most of the time it is positively social, dealing with how the connection works and what is to be regarded as primary in things done together and agreements about how to behave.

Ritual practice is linked with the daily life events, particularly in the critical life circle by Arnold van Gennep in his celebrated book of 1908 *Rite de Passage*, which for the first time brings in the idea that rituals function in the transition of personal status.[19] This book describes transitions in life such as birth, puberty, marriage and death, and he also discusses the parallel between these personal transitions and territorial transitions such as the crossing of frontiers, which firmly establishes the metaphor of passage. Rituals are used to be realized as practical actions among the generally understood 'rites of passage', where birth truly involves physical transition, marriage ceremonies across the world stress thresholds, and death ceremonies express in the metaphors 'passing over' and 'passing on', to the supposed destination necessarily remaining imaginary. But the idea of transition with ritual action or practice derives from our experience. It seems to be founded in the universal experience of bodily movement, as Pierre Bourdieu argues that the body as geometer.[20] How we learned to understand space is based on the experience of bodily movements in daily life that people learn to first encounter the world, recognizing what it meant to go back and forth, up and down, in and out, with particular marks and meanings in the ritual performance. These are the pairs of terms that appear in books intended to teach young children about 'opposites', as they struggle to classify the world, and the same sense of direction is reflected repeatedly in language. The pervasiveness of spatial metaphors is revealed

Conclusion: Symbolic Meaning, Ritual and Architectural Order 243

every day as we talk of 'entering into' an agreement, 'making progress' or 'coming out' of a depression. From all of the above we see that real movement and metaphorical movement complement and mirror one another, which is perhaps what makes Van Gennep's concept of the rite of passage so compelling.

The rituals of personal transitions in the life cycle, involving birth, puberty, marriage, reproduction and death, are defined as 'rites of passage' by Arnold van Gennep.[21] The life of an individual in any society is a series of passages from one stage to another and from one occupation to another. For the change of each stage, the ceremonies would be essential to enable the individual to pass from one defined position to another. Thus the metaphoric boundaries in between the 'passage' are indicated by Van Gennep as crossing doorways or thresholds. In the process of rites of passage, transitions between social statuses are marked by rituals which first separate people from their normal contexts and communities; then place them in a transformative state of liminality; and finally reincorporate them into the newly transformed status. All rites of passage or transitions are marked by the three phases, which are separation, margin or threshold and reunion, and people move from lower to higher states after each social transition. The pregnancy ceremonies focus on the role transformation of woman, but it aims on fertile delivery and prays for protection of mother and child from evil forces; the rituals of marriage not only constitute the transition of the married couple from one social category to another, but also celebrate that they establish residence in a new house; and the most extensively elaborated rites of funeral imply the separation of the deceased from the living world and reunion with another life in the dead world.

'Ritual' thus not only means a prescribed order of performing religious or other devotional service, as Turner argues, but also a series of actions compulsively performed under certain circumstances, which has to have somewhere to 'take place'.[22] Without the performance of ritual acts, people would experience tension and anxiety. More than this, ritual experience connects symbolic meanings with space, making metaphorical ideas visible. The imagery of the space, as the place of 'separation' from the past, 'crossing' the present, and 'reunion' to future, possibly makes these metaphorical transitions an essential requirement in defining and constructing an order space or world. As James Watson observes that ritual is about transformation—in particular, it relates to the transformation of one being or state into another, changed being or state, and rituals are "expected to have transformative powers, because rituals change people and things, and the ritual process is active, not merely passive".[23] The necessity of separation before the incorporation of another stage indicates the threshold-making. As Van Gennep argues, the rites of separation from a previous world are preliminal rites, executed during the transitional stage are liminal (or threshold) rites and the ceremonies of incorporation into the new world are postliminal rites.[24] This is similar to the metaphor of threshold as a part of the door, as the usual site for the rites of entrance, of waiting and of departure, in the rites of passage.

A change of social categories, such as from unfortune to fortune, disorder to order, and so on, needs actions for a change of position, ritually expressed with various forms of rites of passage. In Maurice Bloch's *Prey into Hunter*, he argues that the transformation takes place in an idiom which has two distinguishing features: first, it is accomplished through a classic three-stage dialectical process, and secondly it involves a marked element of 'violence of conquest', which is defined by him as 'rebounding violence'.[25] According to Bloch, the significance of the dramatic violence is a mark of the initial stage of separation and the return to the world. In his view, it needs to be violent, otherwise the subordination of vitality would not be demonstrated, and this final consumption is outwardly directed towards other species.[26] In his discussed examples, the animals as victim represent the violence against neighbours in transition rituals, which means the symbolical sacrifices are achieved through acts of symbolic violence.

Victor Turner's concern regarding pilgrimage and liminality undoubtedly produced important insights on the threshold or named 'ambiguous area'.[27] The 'ambiguous area' could be understood as the specific zone in an airport, after people check in to leave the boundary of this country and wait for permission to get in and travel to another country. Van Gennep's work deals with the ritual progression with movement, separation from community life, through a threshold state or limen into a ritual world, and then a re-entry into community life. It is defined by Turner as 'structure' and 'anti-structure', because the transformation of status is brought about and accompanied with ritually elaborated and challenged enactment. Turner focuses in the condition of liminality during pilgrimages, which is the liminal state between the condition of separation from, and re-entry into society life, and is concerned with the "apparent potential of separation experiences to evoke or generate transformative emotional states and social attachments".[28] As Turner puts it:

> The attributes of liminality or of liminal personae ('threshold people') are necessarily ambiguous, since this condition and these persons elude or slip through the network of classifications that normally locate states and positions in cultural space. Liminal entities ......are betwixt and between the positions assigned and arrayed by law, custom, convention, and ceremonial. As such, their ambiguous and indeterminate attributes are expressed by a rich variety of symbols in the many societies that ritualize social and cultural transitions.[29]

Thus the threshold-making in the rites of passage is essential, and to perform rites is to obtain a stable order on the threshold between the conditions of stability and instability. As Hay argues, the threshold-making of ritual in society is the construction of sacred space, which would be defined as a

Conclusion: Symbolic Meaning, Ritual and Architectural Order 245

'boundary-between': between place and space, the known and unknowable, the controlled and a threatened surrender of this control to external forces.[30] The purpose of producing thresholds is fundamental to such a ritual classification of propriety, which appears in a visibly expressive form, similar to walls with gates marking the permissible sites of transgression.[31] The differentiation between inner and outer is identified through a series of enclosure boundaries, and a social hierarchy is created and clearly indicated with the creation of the boundary. Among the transformation rituals, as Abrahams argues in the foreword to *The Ritual Process*, that "the all-important confrontation of everyday norms took place through socially subversive and ritually intensive acts".[32]

Turner observes the essential signification of boundary-making in the *Isoma* ritual of the Ndembu. Among the Ndembu, a woman who has suffered from a series of miscarriages or abortions would experience a ritual translated as 'women's rituals' or 'rituals of procreation'. The ritual is performed in three stages—the first, separates 'the candidate from the profane world'; the second, 'partially secludes her from secular life'; and the third, 'is a festive dance, celebrating the removal of the shade's interdiction and the candidate's bearing a child and raising it to the toddling stage'.[33] Before performing the *Isoma* ritual, a temporary tunnel must be specially built, which is dug by the doctor and his assistants, and connected by two entrance holes named life hole and death hole. The *Isoma* rite involves a passage from the cool (dead hole) to the hot hole (life hole). At the cool hole the doctor splashes the cold medicine which symbolizes that any witches or curse layers must remove their evil effect from the woman. When she return to the hot hole, she is splashed with the hot medicine by the doctor's assistants.[34] The woman goes down from the death hole and through the tunnel and up through the life hole, symbolizing that she is separated from the living world and goes into the death world: then through the tunnel she returns to the living world. It is believed that, through the ritual of *Isoma*, the effects of misfortune or illness due to the offensive ancestors is removed, and the woman is healed to extend the marriage lineage fruitfully. In the preparation of sacred site for the *Isoma* rite, only when the symbolic path from death to life is completed can the rite be brought through. The ordered realm created with its visible structure, as Turner argues, is "a set of evocative devices for rousing, channelling, and domesticating powerful emotions, such as hate, fear, affection, and grief".[35]

The Order of Architecture

Architecture would support the order and rituals of daily life related to religious and cosmological ideas. The ritual features order the space with such symbolic meanings as natural and supernatural, this world and other world, profane and sacred, low status and high status, living and dead and so on, ordering buildings in a set of metaphysical discriminations. As Blundell

Jones points out, "architecture meshes with a series of social rules and beliefs, each sustaining the other".[36] Architecture, involving buildings and even landscapes, used to be built and modified by the users, traditionally endowed with the spiritual, social and cultural meanings and thinking, rather than from a narrow material or technical point of view. Architecture is distinguished, for as Rapoport argues, people with very different attitudes and ideals would respond to varied physical environments, responses varied from place to place because of changes and differences in the interplay of social, cultural, ritual, economic and physical factors.[37] In his view, "a house is a human fact", and even the most physical constraints and limited technology in construction involve 'cultural values'.[38] So Rudofsky, in his *Architecture without Architects*, points out that the original integration of buildings to the natural surroundings, is constructed by the ingenuity of untaught builders with a special 'humaneness'.[39]

It is however recent that indigenous or vernacular architectures have become the subject of a growing literature by both architects and anthropologists, with the common goal not only recognizing the typology of architecture but also understanding them within their local context.[40] Rapoport's classic book *House Form and Culture* concerns the relation between humans and their buildings, demonstrating that architecture is determined by socio-cultural factors: man within a specific social complex.[41] He argues that meaning resides not only in things but in people: people want their environment to mean certain things, including almost everything built by man since first built. Rapoport defines the factors, such as climate, materials, construction, techniques, economy, as physical modifying factors of the socio-cultural factors that he takes as fundamental.[42] Initial inspiration forms Levi-Strauss's analysis of the symbolic meanings in the settlement patterns in his important paper *'Do Dual Organizations Exist?'*,[43] which says that there has been a slow growth in anthropology of spatial organization.[44] In *Domestic Architecture and the Use of Space*, the architecture and space are investigated from historical and cross-cultural perspectives, and the fundamental role of culture is explored as expressed in technology, symbolism, socio-political organization and economics, with the cases in a wide range of areas, such as North America, South America and Africa.[45] Roxana Waterson in her pioneering book, *The Living House*, focuses on the house within the social and symbolic worlds of Southeast Asian peoples, with a wide field of sources of information from both architects and anthropologists, as well as the author's own first-hand research. She reveals new insights into kinship systems, gender symbolism and cosmological ideas, relating with houses and householders' lives.[46] It provides a vivid picture of how people shape buildings and buildings shape people with the uses of space. Carsten and Hugh-Jones in their *About the House* reveals how the houses in Southeast Asia and South America stand for social grounds and represent the surrounding world, where they bridge the disciplines of anthropology and architecture, and mark a major step in understanding

Conclusion: Symbolic Meaning, Ritual and Architectural Order 247

the relations between material culture, sociality, kinship and the body.[47] As Blundell Jones argues, 'the effect of anthropologists' studies is both more indirect and more essential, provoking fundamental questions about issues such as the organization of social life, the function and significance of art, the origins of architecture, the relation of people to buildings, and the role of the architect, and also in his view, "anthropologists can help us to understand how the relationship between buildings and society worked before it became so complicated, and they can also help to trace the stages of the complication".[48]

Ordering a building is similar to the organization of a cosmic world in varied cultural contexts, embodied with a cosmological symbolism of the society. Space in a way is closely related with every aspect of ritual, particularly as the shelter for ritual performance. The daily ritual performances would take place anywhere, including buildings, paths, forests, rivers and even bridges, and everyday rituals are also held everywhere inside buildings, such as entrances, thresholds, family altars and so on.[49] Because people often pray for blessings to the personal desire of fertility, wealth and fortune, the buildings as ritual places are often constructed with symbolic meanings. In the Atoni of Timor of eastern Indonesian society is a ritual centre for prayer, sacrifice and feasts. The daily rituals of life cycle are conducted normally at the house of those immediately involved, and prayers would be directed from the house to the divinity, the powers, the ancestors and to special tutelary spirits.[50] In building the Berber house, threshold defined the house, separating the inside world from the outside world, and crossing the threshold is meaningful to a newborn son on seventh day, where the mother needs to perform the rite to across the threshold, and sets her right foot upon the carding comb that symbolizes a fight with the first boy she meets, in order that her son be courageous.[51] The order of Kabyle House is dominated by the metaphor that man is the lamp of the outside and woman that lamp of inside, where man is the sun providing the light of the day and woman the moon shining on the night. For, the simple two-room structure of Kabyle House maintains as a microcosm organized by the opposition between the world of female life and that of the male. It is set along symbolic polarized axes reflecting the revised world between unfortunate and fortunate, outside and inside, dark and light, high status and lower status, wet and dry, female and male, corresponding to the classification of properties, which are substantiated with rituals. The inversion of space starts at the threshold of the house; in this ritual a person who enters the house and faces the wall of light has the highest status, and yet leaving the house must face east, the propitious direction.[52]

Myth serves to carry a necessary cultural message, which would be manifested in architecture in the absence of a literary record. Myth helps to explain how man and the world have their origin, as Guidoni argues that they give "solidity and significance to the presence of a group in some particular area by providing them with a historical and existential justification for their own presence there, for their relationship with their neighbours and with natural resources, for the relationship between their clans, and so forth".[53] The myths and legends of the Dogon society provide an imagine of the world-system of the society, as the rules to order the village plan, the large family house, the granary and the sanctuary, which are built up through the connection with their eight ancestors. In the record of M. Griaule, the front elevation of Dogon architecture is twelve cubits wide and eight cubits high, which is pierced by ten vertical rows of eight square niches, measuring a handbreadth. These niches extended from ground level to a horizontal line of swallows' holes, which lay under the shelter of a roof, and the whole façade is finished by a series of slender columns like sugar loaves, each one topped by a flat stone intended to catch the rain.[54] According to the Dogon, the paired holes on the two surfaces of the front wall are particularly occupied by the one of the eight ancestors, Lébé, who is subsequently reincarnated in the form of a serpent, and the front façade, with its eight rows of ten niches, represents the eight ancestors and their descendants, numerous as the fingers on their hands. The height of niches shows the ranks of the ancestors, which occupy them in order of birth beginning with the highest row, and the niches would never be closed, for the ancestors need to breathe the outdoor air.[55] From a purely practical viewpoint, these decorations on the façade of the Dogon house seem unreasonable and irrelevant to their structural techniques. However, in the Dogon's view, the buildings, which embody the myth and the religious beliefs they hold in common, link the various groups of Dogon with their mythic ancestors in the cultural domain, and provide them with the functions not only of physical shelters but also of sanctuaries of living and dead souls.

The Dreamtime myth of the Australian Aborigines tells the story of how they order the landscape and construct small temporary huts for the society. According to the myth, the mythical ancestor-snake and the imitation movement of a real snake cross a sandy terrain in the Dreamtime ritual, and the mythological heroes appear and disappear from 'holes' on the surface of the earth and go through serpentine paths, and thus the landscape is created on a featureless world, involving mountains, watercourses, the areas for the livings and so on. The ritual plan is constituted by circles and straight lines, locating the site for temporary huts and ceremonial routes. While the Australian Aborigines in the rituals wander through the landscape and follow the path of the Dreamtime events, the mythology born in their minds also becomes the map of the territory, explaining the creation of landscape by the mythical heroic creatures of the Dreamtime, which sustain the power of their clan structures. The myth serves to order both the architecture and the world of landscape, marking out place, and indicating the differences between places, some of which are more significant than others, and thus the physical structure and natural features of the landscape are conducted with the local context.[56]

Conclusion: Symbolic Meaning, Ritual and Architectural Order 249

The built forms are never free of symbolic meanings, carried either in 'modern' industrial societies or 'traditional' and non-industrial ones, building up the relationship between habit and the socially structured environment. Thus, building as a model of the cosmos reflects the perception, attitudes and behaviour of a society in shaping and ordering their cognitive world. Cosmological and ritual diagram are usually woven in a building when it is constructed to serve rituals. Rituals frame human activities by establishing a setting that acts as a mnemonic for the repeated actions, and they need special space to practice them in the ritual performance. The participants seek to establish an identity between man and the ritual objects, between ritual objects and the world, and so between man and the world. The experience of ritual makes possible the founding of sacred space, which the sacred manifests itself into space, and the ordered world comes into existence. As Mircea Eliade argues, a house is not an object or a "machine to live in", but it must be animated and receive life and a soul possibly through the transfer of the ritual of a blood sacrifice, and every construction implies a new beginning of life with every inauguration at dawn with the first light shining on the world.[57] Hence the sacred character of space locates the building in the role not only as the ritual space but also involved in countless sacrificed rites, which attribute to frame the world within the limits and establish the order of the world. As Blundell Jones puts:

> Rituals involve both practices and beliefs, which reinforce each other. Grace before a meal is a shared acceptance of divine providence, a social agreement about the order of things, as well as setting a necessary punctuation in time and place. Ritual practices always reflect shared ideas and are hedged about with rules, many of which are implicit. Because they occur in space, they usually require a specific location, and the definition and embellishment of that location is arguably among architecture's primary tasks. When created for or adapted to ritual processes, buildings reinforce their efficacy, carry memories of them in their organization, and both guide and encourage their repetition. This depends on interaction between the structures laid out in physical space and the accompanying structures of ritual, along with the beliefs and states of mind that sustain them.[58]

The promise of function of architecture attributes to both the users and memory. As Blundell Jones argues, architecture is usually viewed as 'architectural texts' as an aid to memory.[59] House is one of the greatest repositories of the thoughts, memories and dreams of the users, because the remains of occupation, whether desired or compromised by the space, and signs of the people who have been using them, are never removed, precisely because people want them to remain. This has inspired a tendency in the view of philosophy, literature and poetry to 'write a room', 'read a room' or 'read a house'.[60] Although factors such as climate, site choice, construction, materials and techniques, would be considered in the structural process, they never explain the jumps from the structural materials to the shaping of building and linking artefacts to mentality on architecture, the users' thinking behind its construction.[61] As Blundell Jones points out, the appearance of a building not only tend to become associated with the activities that go on inside it, however, its organization would also reflect the roles and relationships of those who use it, frame human activity, and often imply a certain role.[62]

Thus, what could be a more powerful confirmation of the idea of symbolic passage to sustain the local culture than the Dong's architecture, particularly the 'Wind and Rain' bridge? While the Dong cross the bridge, it reminds how and why to cross the threshold with their experience, and the repeated activity of daily rituals is essential to establish both the order between bridge space and ritual actions, and the meanings attached to the bridge. The bridge combines real safe passage across the river with a site for numerous ritual observances connected with all three main rites of passage—birth, marriage and death. It not only links the end and beginning of life as the place where returning souls are supposed to enter new mothers, but also is the frontier and gate to the village, holding an equal and opposite role to that of the drum tower—the community centre and focus—for as the site of the blocking ceremony it is the threshold of welcome and departure. In additional, the ideology of fengshui enhance its status as a container of *qi* and controller of the watercourse mouth. It houses different gods in the altars underneath the pavilions, and carries icons including representations of calabash, birds and fish, supposedly indicating fortune, fertility and abundance. Each construction process is accompanied with auspicious rituals to promise a sacred and fortunate building born. As Blundell Jones argues, the establishment of traditions handed down by the rituals allows people to get on with building without much conscious reflection, simply as part of 'the order of things", and there need be no difficulty for the people who build and use it, because the building process automatically and strongly reflects their beliefs and values.[63]

Notes

1 Full Recover Version Bible, Genesis 3:2–7.
2 Arthur Klein, H. 1974. *The World of Measurements: Masterpieces, Mysteries and Muddles of Metrology*. New York: Simon and Schuster, p. 23.
3 Richard Padovan 1999. *Proportion: Science, Philosophy, Architecture*. London: New York: E & FN Spon, p. 200.
4 Pierre Bourdieu 1977. *Outline of a Theory of Practice*, trans. by Richard Nice. Cambridge: Cambridge University Press, p. 124.
5 Gombrich, E. H. 1979. *The Sense of Order: A Study in the Psychology of Decorative Art*. Oxford: Phaidon Press Limited, p. 1.
6 *Ibid*. p. 1
7 Doob, Penelope Reed 1990. *The Idea of the Labyrinth: from Classical Antiquity through the Middle Ages*. Ithaca and London: Cornell University Press, p. 11–3.

Conclusion: Symbolic Meaning, Ritual and Architectural Order 251

8 *Ibid.* p.103.
9 Jones, Peter Blundell 2016. *Architecture and Ritual: How Buildings Shape Society.* London, Oxford, New York, New Delhi, Sydney: Bloomsbury Academic, p. 4.
10 *Ibid.* pp. 4–6.
11 Lowenthal, David 1985. *The Past is a Foreign Country.* Cambridge: Cambridge University Press, p. 210.
12 Cf. Cunningham, Clark E. 1964. 'Order in the Atoni House', *Bijdragen tot de Taal-, Land-en Volkenkunde,* 120: 34–68; and Bourdieu, P. 1973. 'The Berber House', in Mary Douglas (ed.), *Rules and Meanings: The Anthropology of Everyday Knowledge.* Harmondsworth, Middlesex: Penguin.
13 Needham, Rodney 1979. *Symbolic Classification.* California: Goodyear publishing Company, p. 3.
14 Lakoff, George and Johnson, Mark 2003 (first published 1980). *Metaphors We Live By.* Chicago and London: the University of Chicago Press, pp. 3–6.
15 Eliade, Mircea 1987 (first published 1957). The *Sacred and the Profane: The Nature of Religion,* translated from Franch by Willard R. Trask, San Diego, New York, London: A Harvest Book, p. 29.
16 Douglas, Mary 1966. *Purity and Danger.* London: Routledge and Kegan Paul, p. 35.
17 *Ibid.* pp. 35–6.
18 See Jones, Peter Blundell 2016. *Architecture and Ritual: How Buildings Shape Society.* London, Oxford, New York, New Delhi, Sydney: Bloomsbury Academic, p. 8.
19 Gennep, Arnold Van 1960. *The Rites of Passage,* trans. Monika B. Vizedom and Gabrielle L. Caffee. Chicago: The University of Chicago Press.
20 Bourdieu, Pierre 1977. *Outline of a Theory of Practice,* trans. Richard Nice. Cambridge; New York: Cambridge University Press, p. 90.
21 Gennep, Arnold Van 1960. *The Rites of Passage.* trans. Monika B. Vizedom and Gabrielle L. Caffee. Chicago: The University of Chicago Press, p. 25.
22 See Turner, Victor 1995 (first published 1969). *The Ritual Process: Structure and Anti-Structure.* New York: Aldine De Gruyter. And Bloch, Maurice 1992. *Prey into Hunter: the Politics of Religious Experience.* Cambridge: Cambridge University Press.
23 Watson, James L. 1988. 'The Structure of Chinese Funerary Rites: Elementary Forms, Ritual Sequence, and the Primary of Performance', in J. L. Watson and E. S. Rawski (eds.), *Death Rituals in Late Imperial and Modern China.* Los Angeles: Berkeley, p. 4.
24 Van Gennep, Arnold 1960. *The Rites of Passage.* trans. Monika B. Vizedom and Gabrielle L. Caffee, Introduction by Solon T. Kimball. Chicago: The University of Chicago Press, pp. 20–2.
25 Bloch, Maurice 1992. *Prey into Hunter: The Politics of Religious Experience.* Cambridge: Cambridge University Press, p. 4.
26 *Ibid.* p. 7.
27 Turner, Victor 1995 (first published 1969). *The Ritual Process: Structure and Anti-Structure.* New York: Aldine De Gruyter.
28 Quote from Stafford, Charles 2000. *Separation and Reunion in Modern China.* Cambridge: Cambridge University Press, p. 20.
29 Turner, Victor 1995 (first published 1969). *The Ritual Process: Structure and Anti-Structure.* New York: Aldine De Gruyter, p. 95.
30 Hay, John 1994. *Boundaries in China.* London: Reaktion Books Ltd, p. 9.
31 *Ibid.* p. 17.
32 Victor Turner 1969. *The Ritual Process: Structure and Anti-structure.* New York: Aldine De Gruyter, in the foreword by Roger D. Abrahams.

33 *Ibid.* p. 14.
34 *Ibid.* p. 33.
35 *Ibid.* pp. 42–3.
36 Blundell Jones, Peter 1985. 'Implicit Meanings', in *Architectural Review*, 6: 34–9.
37 Rapoport, Amos 1960. *House Form and Culture.* Englewood Cliffs, N. J.: Prentice-Hall, p. 46.
38 *Ibid.* p. 48.
39 Rudofsky, Bernard 1973 (first published 1964). *Architecture without Architects: A Short Introduction to Non-pedigreed Architecture.* London: Academic Edition, Preface.
40 Cf. Rapoport, Amos 1960. *House Form and Culture.* Englewood Cliffs, N. J.: Prentice-Hall; Rudofsky, Bernard 1973 (first published in 1964). Architecture without Architects: A Short Introduction to Non-pedigreed Architecture. London: Academic Edition; Knapp, Ronald G. 1989. *China's Vernacular Architecture: House Form and Culture.* Honolulu: University of Hawai'I Press; Knapp, Ronald G. 1999. *China's Living Houses: Folk Beliefs, Symbols, and Household Ornamentation.* Honolulu: University of Hawai'I Press; and Waterson, Roxana 1990. *The Living House: an Anthropology of Architecture in South-East Asia.* Singapore: Oxford: Oxford University Press.
41 Rapoport, Amos 1960. *House Form and Culture.* Englewood Cliffs, NJ: Prentice-Hall.
42 *Ibid.* p. 105.
43 Levi-Strauss, C. 1963. 'Do Dual Oganizations Exist?' in his *Structural Anthropology.* Harmondsworth: Penguin, pp. 132–63.
44 Cf. Cunningham, Clark E. 1964. 'Order in the Atoni House', Bijdragen tot de Taal-, Land-en Volkenkunde, 120: 34–68; Bourdieu, P. 1973. 'The Berber House', in Mary Douglas (ed.), *Rules and Meanings: The Anthropology of Everyday Knowledge.* Harmondsworth, Middlesex: Penguin; and Hugh-Jones, Stephen, and Carsten, Janet (eds.) 1995. *About the House.* Cambridge University Press.
45 Kent, Susan 1990. *Domestic Architecture and the Use of Space: An Interdisciplinary Cross-cultural Study.* Cambridge: Cambridge University Press.
46 Waterson, Roxana 1990. *The Living House: an Anthropology of Architecture in South-East Asia.* Singapore: Oxford University Press.
47 Carsten, Janet and Hugh-Jones, Stephen 1995. *About the House: Levi-Strauss and Beyond.* Cambridge: Cambridge University Press.
48 Blundell Jones, Peter 1996. 'An Anthropological View of Architecture', in *Architectural Design Profile*, No. 124: 22–5, p. 22.
49 Cf. Eliade, Mircea 1987 (first published in 1957). *The Sacred and the Profane: The Nature of Religion*, trans. Franch by Willard R. Trask, San Diego, New York, London: A Harvest Book; Cunningham, Clark E. 1964. 'Order in the Atoni House', *Bijdragen tot de Taal-, Land-en Volkenkunde,* 120: 34–68; Griaule 1965 Griaule, Marcel 1965. *Conversations with Ogotemmeli: An Introduction to Dogon Religious Ideas.* Oxford: Oxford University Press; Bourdieu, P. 1973. 'The Berber House', in Mary Douglas (ed.), *Rules and Meanings: The Anthropology of Everyday Knowledge.* Harmondsworth, Middlesex: Penguin; and Waterson, Roxana 1990. *The Living House: An Anthropology of Architecture in South-East Asia.* Singapore: Oxford University Press.
50 Cunningham, Clark E. 1964. 'Order in the Atoni House', *Bijdragen tot de Taal-, Land-en Volkenkunde*, 120: 205.
51 Bourdieu, P. 1973. 'The Berber House', in Mary Douglas (ed.), *Rules and Meanings: The Anthropology of Everyday Knowledge.* Harmondsworth, Middlesex: Penguin, p. 106.

Conclusion: Symbolic Meaning, Ritual and Architectural Order 253

52 Bourdieu, P. 1973. 'The Berber House', in Mary Douglas (ed.), *Rules and Meanings: The Anthropology of Everyday Knowledge*. Harmondsworth, Middlesex: Penguin, pp. 106–8.
53 Guidoni, Enrico 1975. *Primitive Architecture: History of World Architecture*. New York: Electa/Rizzoli. p. 13.
54 Griaule, Marcel 1965. *Conversations with Ogotemmeli: An Introduction to Dogon Religious Ideas*. Oxford: Oxford University Press, p. 91.
55 *Ibid*. pp. 92–3.
56 Rapoport, Amos 1975. 'Australian Aborigines and the Definition of Place', in Paul Oliver (ed.), *Shelter, Sign & Symbol*. London: Barrie & Jenkins, p. 49.
57 Eliade, Mircea 1987 (first published 1957). *The Sacred and the Profane: The Nature of Religion*, translated from French by Willard R. Trask, San Diego, New York, London: A Harvest Book, pp. 55–7.
58 Peter Blundell Jones 2016. *Architecture and Ritual: How Buildings Shape Society*, London, Oxford, New York, New Delhi, Sydney: Bloomsbury Academic. p. 10.
59 Blundell Jones, Peter 1996. 'An Anthropological View of Architecture', *Architectural Design Profile*, No. 124: 22–5.
60 Bachelard, Gaston 1969. *The Poetics of Space*, translated from the French by Maria Jolas. Boston: Beacon Press, pp. 10–4.
61 Rapoport, Amos 1960. *House Form and Culture*. Englewood Cliffs, NJ: Prentice-Hall, pp. 3–4.
62 Blundell Jones, Peter 1996. 'An Anthropological View of Architecture', *Architectural Design Profile*, No. 124: 22–5.
63 Blundell Jones, Peter 1996. 'An Anthropological View of Architecture', *Architectural Design Profile*, No. 124: 22–5.

Bibliography

English Sources

Arnold, Dana 1999. 'London Bridge and its Symbolic Identity in the Regency Metropolis: The Dialectic of Civic and National Pride', *Art History*, 22 (4): 545–66.

Bachelard, Gaston 1969. *The Poetics of Space,* translated from the French by Maria Jolas. Boston: Beacon Press.

Baker, Hugh D. R. and Feuchtwang, Stephan (eds.) 1991. *An Old State in New Settings: Studies in the Social Anthropology of China in Memory of Maurice Freedman*. Jaso: Oxford.

Barth, Fredrik 1969a. *Ethnic Groups and Boundaries: the Social Organization Culture Difference*. Bergen-oslo: Universitetsforlaget.

Barth, Fredrik 1969b. 'Pathan Identity and its Maintenance' in Barth, Fredrik (ed.) *Ethnic Groups and Boundaries: The Social Organization of Culture Difference*. Bergen-oslo: Universitetsforlaget, pp. 117–134.

Baynes, Cary F. 1951, *I Ching* (Book of Changes), the Richard Wihelm Translation rendered into English. London: Routledge & Kegan Paul Ltd.

Bellwood, Peter S. 1978, *Man's Conquest of the Pacific: The Prehistory of South-East Asia and Oceania*. Auckland: Collins.

———. 1985. *Prehistory of the Indo-Malaysian Archipelago*. Sydney (N.S.W.); Orlando, Fla.: Academic Press.

Benjamin, G. 1979. *Indigenous Religious Systems of the Malay Peninsula*. New Jersey, Ablex Publishing Corporation.

Bloch, Maurice 1992. *Prey into Hunter: The Politics of Religious Experience*. Cambridge: Cambridge University Press.

Blundell Jones, Peter 1985. 'Implicit Meanings'*, Architectural Review*, 6: 34–9.

——— 1987. 'The Social Construction of Space', *Space & Society*, No. 40: 62–71.

——— 1990. 'The Sustaining Ritual', *Architectural Review*, 11: 93–5.

——— 1996. 'An Anthropological View of Architecture', *Architectural Design Profile*, No. 124: 22–5.

Blundell Jones, Peter and Li, Xuemei 2008. 'What Can a Bridge Be? The Wind and Rain Bridges of the Dong', *Journal of Architecture*, 13 (5): 565–584.

Bourdieu, P. 1973. 'The Berber House', in Mary Douglas (ed.), *Rules and Meanings: The Anthropology of Everyday Knowledge*. Harmondsworth, Middlesex: Penguin, pp. 84–97.

——— 1977. *Outline of a Theory of Practice*, translated by Richard Nice. Cambridge; New York: Cambridge University Press.

256 Bibliography

Boyd, Andrew 1962. *Chinese Architecture and Town Planning 1500B.C.-A.D. 1911.* London: Alec Tiranti.

Bray, Francesca 1997. *Technology and Gender: Fabrics of Power in Late Imperial China.* Berkeley; London: University of California Press.

Carsten, Janet and Hugh-Jones, Stephen 1995. *About the House: Levi-Strauss and Beyond.* Cambridge: Cambridge University Press.

Chang, K. C. (Kwang-chih) 1983. *Art, Myth, and Ritual: The Path to Political Authority in Ancient China.* Cambridge, MA; London: Harvard University Press.

Chao, Paul 1983. *Chinese Kinship.* London, Boston and Melbourne: Kegan Paul Instauration.

Clay Trumbull, H. 1896. *The Covenant Threshold: Or the Beginning of Religious Rites.* New York: Charles Scribner's Sons, pp. 184–96.

Cullen, Christopher 1996. *Astronomy and Mathematics in Ancient China: The Zhou Bi Shuan Jing.* Cambridge: Cambridge University Press.

Cunningham, Clark E. 1964. 'Order in the Atoni House', *Bijdragen tot de Taal-, Land-en Volkenkunde*, 120: 34–68.

Dall, G. 1982. *The Traditional Acehnese House.* Melbourne: Monash University Centre of South-East Asian Studies.

Douglas, Mary 1966. *Purity and Danger: An Analysis of the Concepts of Pollution and Taboo.* London and New York: Ark Paperbacks.

Doxtater, Dennis 1983. 'Spatio-symbolic Oppositions in Ritual and Architecture', *Design Study*, 4 (2): 124–32.

Dumarçay, Jacques 1987. *The House in South-East Asia*, translated and edited by Michael Smithies. Singapore: Oxford University Press.

Eliade, Mircea 1954. *The Myth of the Eternal Return*, translated from the French by Willard R. Trask. New York: Bollingen Foundation.

────── 1987 (first published in 1957). *The Sacred and the Profane: The Nature of Religion*, translated from Franch by Willard R. Trask, San Diego, New York, London: A Harvest Book.

────── 1959. *The Sacred and the Profane: The Nature of Religion*, translated from French by Willard R. Trask. San Dieo, New York, London: Harcourt Brace & Company.

Errington, S. 1983. '"Embodied Sumange" in Luwu', *Journal of Asian Studies*, 42 (3): 545–70.

Faure, David and Sui, Helen (eds.) 1995 *Down to Earth: The Territorial Bond in South China.* Stanford: Stanford University Press.

Fei, Xiaotong 1939. *Peasant Life in China: A Field Study of Country Life in the Yangze Valley.* London: Routledge & Kegan Paul.

Feuchtwang, Stephan 1992. *The Imperial Metaphor: Popular Religion in China.* London: Routledge.

────── 2001. *Popular Religion in China: The Imperial Metaphor.* Surrey: Curzon Press.

Fisher, Marshall and Fisher, David E. 2000. *Mysteries of Lost Empires.* London: Channel 4 Books.

Forth, G. 1981. *Rindi: An Ethnographic Study of a Traditional Domain in Eastern Sumba.* The Hague: Nijhoff.

Fox, J. J. (ed.) 1980. *The Flow of Life: Essays on Eastern Indonesia.* Cambridge, MA and London: Harvard University Press.

Freedman, Maurice 1966. *Chinese Lineage and Society: Fukien and Kwangtung.* New York: Humanities Press.
────── 1969 "Geomancy", in *Proceedings, Royal Anthropological Institute of Great Britainand Ireland, 1968*, pp. 5–15. London: Royal Anthropological Institute.
────── (ed.) 1970. *Family and Kinship in Chinese Society.* Stanford, CA: Stanford University Press.
────── 1979. *The Study of Chinese Society*, selected and introduced by G. William Skinner. Stanford, CA: Stanford University Press.
Fu, X. *et al.* 2002. *Chinese Architecture.* New Haven, CT and London: Yale University Press.
Geary, D. Norman *et al.* 2003. *The Kam People of China: Turning Nineteen.* London: Routledge Curzon.
Gennep, Arnold Van 1960. *The Rites of Passage*, translated by Monika B. Vizedom and Gabrielle L. Caffee. Chicago: The University of Chicago Press.
Griaule, Marcel 1965. *Conversations with Ogotemmeli: An Introduction to Dogon Religious Ideas.* Oxford: Oxford University Press.
Guidoni, Enrico 1975. *Primitive Architecture: History of World Architecture.* New York: Electa/Rizzoli.
Guo, Qinghua 1995. *The Structure of Chinese Timber Architecture: Twelfth Century Design Standards and Construction Principles.* Sweden: Chalmers University Press.
────── 1998. '*Yingzao Fashi*: Twelfth-Century Chinese Building Manual', *Architectural History*, 41: 1–13.
────── 1999. 'The Architecture of Joinery: the Form and Construction of Rotating Sutra-Case Cabinets', *Architectural History*, 42: 96–109.
Hay, John (ed.) 1994. *Boundaries in China.* London: Reaktion Books.
Hugh-Jones, Stephen, and Carsten, Janet (eds.) 1995. *About the House.* Cambridge: Cambridge University Press.
Humphrey, Caroline with Onon, Urgunge 1996. *Shamans and Elders: Experience, Knowledge, and Power among the Daur Mongols.* Oxford: Clarendon Press.
I Ching (Book of Changes), the RichardWihelm Translation rendered into English by Cary F. Baynes 1951. London: Routledge & Kegan Paul Ltd.
Jing, Jun 1996. *The Temple of Memories: History, Power, and Morality in a Chinese Village.* Stanford, CA: Stanford University Press.
Kana, N. L. 1980. *The Order and Significance of the Savunese House.* Cambridge, MA: Harvard University Press.
Kent, Susan 1990. *Domestic Architecture and the Use of Space: An Interdisciplinary Cross-cultural Study.* Cambridge: Cambridge University Press.
Kohl, D. G. 1984. *Chinese Architecture in the Straits Settlements and Western Malaya: Temples, Kongsis and Houses.* Singapore: Heinemann Educational Books (Asia) Ltd.
Knapp, Ronald G. 1986. *China's Traditional Rural Architecture: A Cultural Geography of the Common House.* Honolulu: University of Hawaii Press.
────── 1989. *China's Vernacular Architecture: House Form and Culture.* Honolulu: University of Hawai'I Press.
────── 1999. *China's Living Houses: Folk Beliefs, Symbols, and Household Ornamentation.* Honolulu: University of Hawai'I Press.
Izikowitz, K. G. and Sørensen, P. (eds.) 1982. *The House in East and Southeast Asia: Anthropological and Architectural Aspects.* London: Curzon Press Ltd.

Bibliography

Lakoff, George and Johnson, Mark 1980. *Metaphors We Live By*. Chicago and London: the University of Chicago Press.

Levi-Strauss, C. 1963. 'Do Dual Organizations Exist? in his *Structural Anthropology*, Harmondsworth: Penguin, pp. 132–63.

Li, Xuemei 2005. 'Architecture, Myth, and Ritual: Origins of "Wind and Rain" Bridges in Southern China', in *Cultural, trade and geography in East Asia*, New York Conference on Asian Studies.

——— 2007. 'An Anthropology of Vernacular Architecture', in *Traditional Way of Building in the East and the West*, a Seminar of East and West in Architectural School of Sheffield University.

Li, Xuemei and Smith, Kendra Schank 2011. Time, Space, and Construction: Starting with Auspicious Carpentry (开工大吉) in the Vernacular Dong Dwelling', *Journal of the Society of Architectural Historians*, 70: 7–17.

Li, Xuemei Li, Li, Weiye, Smith, Kendra Schank, and Smith, Albert C 2019. 'Hidden from the Wind and Enjoying the Water (藏风得水): Fengshui and the Shaping of Dong Villages in Southwestern China', *Journal of Landscape Research*, 44: 614–627.

Liang, Sicheng 1984. *A Picturial History of Chinese Architecture*. Cambridge, MA; London: MIT Press.

Liu, Laurence G. 1989. *Chinese Architecture*. London: Academy Editions.

Marcel Mauss in Collaboration with Henri Beuchat 1979. *Seasonal Variations of the Eskimo: A Study in Social Morphology*, translated and with a forward by James J. Fox. London, Boston and Henley: Routledge & Kegan Paul.

Needham, Joseph 1956, with the research assistance of Wang Ling. *Science and civilization in China*, Vol. 2: History of Scientific thought. Cambridge: Cambridge University Press.

——— 1959, with the collaboration of Wang Ling. *Science and Civilization in China*, Vol. 3, Mathematics and the Sciences of the heavens and the earth. Cambridge: Cambridge University Press.

——— 1962. *Science and Civilisation in China*, Vol. 4: Physics and Physical Technology. Cambridge: Cambridge University Press.

——— 1971. 'Civil Engineering and Nautics', in *Science and Civilization in China*, Vol.4: Physics and Physical Technology, Part 3. London: Cambridge University Press.

Needham, Rodney 1979. *Symbolic Classification*. California: Goodyear publishing Company.

Oliver, Paul 1990. *Dwelling: The House across the World*. Austin: University of Texas Press.

——— 1997. *Encyclopedia of Vernacular Architecture of the World*. Cambridge: Cambridge University Press.

Rapoport, Amos 1960. *House Form and Culture*. Englewood Cliffs, NJ: Prentice-Hall.

——— 1969. 'The Pueblo and The Hogan', in Paul Oliver (ed.), *Shelter & Society*. London: Barrie & Jenkins, pp. 60–79.

——— 1975. 'Australian Aborigines and the Definition of Place', in Paul Oliver (ed.), *Shelter, Sign & Symbol*. London: Barrie & Jenkins.

——— 1982. 'Sacred Places, Sacred Occasions and Sacred Environments', *AD*, 9–10: 75–82.

Rossi, Gail and Lau, Paul 1991. *A Hidden Civilization: The Dong People of China*. Singapore: Hagley & Hoyle.

Ruan, Xing 1996. 'Empowerment in the Practice of Making and Inhabiting', *Journal of Material Culture* (editors include James Clifford and Nicholas Thomas), 1 (2): 211–38. London: Sage.

Rudofsky, Bernard 1973. *Architecture without Architects: A Short Introduction to Non-pedigreed Architecture*. London: Academic Edition.

—— 1977. *The Prodigious Builders*. London: Secker & Warburg.

Ruitenbeek, Klaas 1996. *Carpentry and Building in Late Imperial China: A Study of the Fifteenth-Century Carpenter's Manual Lu Ban Jing*. Leiden, New York, Koln: E. J. Brill.

Smith, Kendra Schank, Li, Xuemei and Smith, Albert C 2013. *A Human Measure: Structure, Meaning and Operation of the Lu Ban Foot-rule (鲁班尺) of the Dong Carpenters*. Architectural Research Quarterly, Vol. 17, pp.227-236). Cambridge University Press.

Stafford, Charles 1992. 'Good Sons and Virtuous Mothers: Kinship and Chinese Nationalism in Taiwan', *Man* 27: 363–78.

—— 1995 *The Roads of Chinese Childhood*. Cambridge: Cambridge University Press.

—— 2000. *Separation and Reunion in Modern China*. Cambridge: Cambridge University Press.

Sterckx, Roel 2002. *The Animal and the Daemon in Early China*. Albany: State University of New York.

The Book of Odes (*Shi Jing*), transcription and translation by Bernhard Karlgren1950. Stockholm: The Museum of Far Eastern Antiquities.

The Book of Songs (*Shi Jing*), translated from Chinese by Arthur Waley 1937. London: George Allen & Unwin Ltd.

Turner, V. 1967. *The Forest of Symbols: Aspects of Ndembu Ritual*. Ithaca and London: Cornell University Press.

—— 1969. *The Ritual Process: Structure and Anti-structure*. New York, Aldine De Gruyter.

—— 1974. *Dramas, Fields, and Metaphors: Symbolic Action in Human Society*. Ithaca, NY and London: Cornell University Press.

Turton, A. 1978. *Architectural and Political Space in Thailand*. London, School of Oriental and African Studies.

Tu, Wei-ming 1994 'Cultural China: The Periphery as the Centre', in W. Tu (ed.), *The Living Tree: The Changing Meaning of Being Chinese Today*. Stanford: Stanford University Press, pp. 1–32.

Twitchett, Denis and Fairbank, John K. (eds.) 1986. *The Cambridge History of China*. Vol. 1: The Ch'in and Han Empires, 221 B.C.-A.D. 220. Cambridge: Cambridge University Press.

Van Gennep, Arnold 1960. *The Rites of Passage*, translated by Monika B. Vizedom and Gabrielle L. Caffee, Introduction by Solon T. Kimball. Chicago, IL: The University of Chicago Press.

Waley, Arthur (translated) 1937. *The Book of Songs*. London: Allen & Unwin.

Waterson, Roxana 1990. *The Living House: An Anthropology of Architecture in South-East Asia*. Singapore: Oxford University Press.

Watson, James L. 1982. 'Of Flesh and Bones: The Management of Death Pollution in Cantonese Society', in Maurice Bloch and Jonathan Parry (eds.), *Death and the Regeneration of Life*. Cambridge: Cambridge University Press, pp. 155–86.

Watson, James L. and Rawski, Evelyn S. (eds.) 1988. *Death Ritual in Late Imperial and Modern China.* Berkeley, Los Angeles, London: University of California Press.

Watson, Rubie S. 1985. *Inequality Among Brothers: Class and Kinship in South China.* Cambridge: Cambridge University Press.

—— 1994. 'Introduction' and 'Making Secret Histories: Memory and Mourning in Post-Mao China', in R. Watson (eds.), *Memory, History, and Opposition Under State Socialism.* Sante Fe: School of America Research Press.

Watson, Rubie S. and Ebrey, Patricia Buckley (eds.) 1991. *Marriage and Inequality in Chinese Society.* Berkeley: University of California Press.

Wheatley, Paul 1971. *The Pivot of the Four Quarters.* Edinburgh: Edinburgh University Press.

Wu, Hung 1994. 'Beyond the 'Great Boundary': Funerary Narrative in the Cangshan Tomb', in John Hay (ed.), *Boundaries in China*, London: Reaktion Books Ltd, pp. 81–104.

Yan, Yunxiang 1996. *The Flow of Gifts: Reciprocity and Social Networks in a Chinese Village.* Stanford: Stanford University Press.

Yang, C. K. 1967. *Religion in Chinese Society: A Study of Contemporary Social Functions of Religion and Some of Their Historical Factors.* Berkeley and Los Angeles: University of California Press.

Yang, Mayfair Mei-hui 1994. *Gifts, Favors and Banquets: The Art of Social Relationships in China.* Ithaca: Cornell University Press.

Zito, Angela 1994. 'Silk and Skin: Significant Boundaries', in Angela Zito and Tani E. Barlow (eds.), *Body, Subject & Power in China.* Chicago: The University of Chicago Press, pp. 103–30.

Chinese Sources

Bai, Hemin 1995. *Fengshui Luopan Zucheng Xiangjie* 风水罗盘组成祥解 (The Explanation on Each Ring of Fengshui Compass). Hongkong: Juxian Press.

Cai, Ling 2004. *Dongzu Jujuqu De Chuantong Cunluo Yu Jianzhu Yanjiu* 侗族聚居区的传统村落与建筑研究 (Traditional Villages & Architecture Research of Dong Nationality's Habitation Region). PhD dissertation, Department of Architecture, South China University of Technology, Guangzhou.

Census Office of the State Council 1991. Zhongguo Dishici Renkou Pucha De Zhuyao Shuju (Main Data from the Fourth Population Censes in China). Beijing: Zhongguo Tongji Press.

Chen, Jianjun 1991. *Zhongguo Gudai Jianzhu Yu Zhouyi Zhexue* 中国古代建筑与周易哲学 (Chinese Primitive Architecture and *Zhou Yi* Philosophy). Changcun: Jilin Jiaoyu Press.

—— 1999. *Zhongguo Fengshui Luopan* 中国风水罗盘 (Chinese Fengshui Compass). Nanchang: Jiangxi Kexue Press.

Chen, Jianjun and Shun, Shangpu 1992. *Fengshui Yu Jianzhu* 风水与建筑 (Fengshui and Architecture). Nanchang: Jiangxi Kexue Jishu Press.

Chen, Mingda 1981. *Yingzao Fashi Damuzuo Yanjiu* (Research on the Major Carpentry of *Yingzao Fashi*). Beijing: Wenwu Press.

Chen, Zhihua 1999. *Xiangtu Zhongguo: Nanxijiang Zhongyou Gucunluo* 乡土中国：楠溪江中游古村落 (Chinese Vernacular Architecture: the Villages of Nanxijiang). Beijing, Shanghai, Guangzhou: Sanlian Press.

Bibliography 261

Chen, Zhijun 2000. Yun Qi Jianzhu Kongjian: 'Nei Jing' Wuyun Liuqi Xueshuo Jiqi Zai Yangsheng Jianzhuzhong De Yingyong Tantao 运气建筑（空间）：《内经》五运六气学说及其在养生建筑中的应用探讨 (The Transmissions of *qi* in Architectural Space: Research on the Five Movement and Six *qi* Theory of Huangdi Neijing and its Application on the Design of Ecological Architectural Space). Thesis for Master degree, Department of Architecture, South China University of Technology, Guangzhou.

Compilation Group of Annals of Liping County 1989. *Liping Xianzhi* 黎平县志 *(Annals of Liping County)*. Chengdu: Bashu Shushe Press.

Compilation Group of Annals of the Nationalities in Sanjiang County 2002 (first published 1946). *Sanjiangxian Minzuzhi* 三江县民族志 (Annals of the Nationalities in Sanjiang County). Nanning: Guangxi Minzhu Press.

Compilation Group of Local Gazette of Guangxi Province 1996. *Guangxi Tongzhi Jiaotongzhi* 广西通志:交通志 (General Gazette of Guangxi Province: Traffic Section). Nanning: Guangxi Renmin Press.

Compilation Group of Local Gazette of Guangxi Province 1992. *Guangxi Tongzhi Minsuzhi*, 广西通志: 民俗志 (General Gazette of Guangxi Province: Custom Section). Nanning: Guangxi Renmin Press.

Compilation Group of Survey of the Longsheng Nationalities' Autonomous County 1985. *Longshengxian Minzuzhi* (Survey of the Longsheng Nationalities' Autonomous County). Nanning: Guangxi Minzhu Press.

Compilation Group of Survey of the Qiandongnan Miao Dong Autonomous Prefecture 1986. *Qiandongnan Miaozu Dongzu Zizhizhou Gaikuang* 黔东南苗族，侗族自治州概况 (Survey of the Qiandongnan Miao Dong Autonomous Prefecture). Guiyang: Guizhou Renmin Press.

Compilation Group of Survey of the Sanjina Dong Autonomous County 1984. *Sanjiang Dongzu Zizhixian Gaikuang* 三江侗族自治县概况 (Survey of the Sanjinag Dong Autonomous County). Nanning: Guangxi Minzu Press.

Compilation Group of Survey of the Tongdao Dong Autonomous County 1986. *Tongdao Dongzu Zizhixian Gaikuang* 通道侗族自治县概况 (Survey of the Tongdao Dong Autonomous County). Changsha: Hunan Renmin Press.

Compilation Group of Survey of the Zhijinag Dong Autonomous County 1987. *Zhijiang Dongzu Zizhixian Gaikuang* 芷江侗族自治县概况 (Survey of the Zhijinag Dong Autonomous County). Changsha: Hunan Renmin Press.

Dai, Wusan (ed.) 2003. *Kaogong Ji Tushuo* 考工记图说 (The Illumination of *Kaogong Ji*). Jinan: Shandong Huabao Press.

Deng, Minwen and Wu, Hao 1995. *Meiyou Guowang De Wangguo: Dongkuan Yanjiu* 没有国王的王国：侗款研究 (The Kingdom without King: Research on Dong *Kuan*). Beijing: Zhongguo Shehui Kexue Press.

Deng, Qisheng 1985. 'The Conceiver of Repair of Xiangzi Bridge', in The Institute for History of Natural Sciences at Chinese Academy of Sciences (ed.) *Chinese Ancient Architecture Technology*. Beijing: Zhongguo Jianzhu Press, pp. 43–6.

Fan, C. *et al.* 1991. *Guangxi Minzhu Chuantong Jianzhu Shilu* 广西民族传统建筑实录 (The Record of Vernacular Architecture in Guangxi). Nanning: Guanxi Kexue Jishu Press.

Fu, Xinian *et al.* 2002. *Chinese Architecture*. New Haven, CT; London: Yale University Press.

Gao, Shouxian 1995. *Xingxiang, Fengshui, He Yundao* 星象，风水和运道 (Horoscopy, Fengshui, and Divination). Nanning: Guangxi Jiaoyu Press.

Guxi, P. 2001. *Zhongguo Jianzhu Shi* (The Chinese Architectural History). Beijing: Zhongguo Jianzhu Press.

Guangxi Museum (ed.) 1991. *Guanxi Tonggu Tulu* (Pictures of Bronze Drum in Guangxi). Beijing: Wenwu Press.

Guangxi Wenwu Guanli Weiyuanhui (ed.) 1978. *Guangxi Cutu Wenwu*. Beijing: Wenwu Press.

Guangxi Zhuangzu Zhizhiqu Wenhuachu, Guangxi Zhuangzu Zhizhiqu Wenwu Guanli Weiyuanhui Bangongshi (eds.) 1997. *Guangxi Zhuangzu Zhizhiqu Guanchang Wenwu Zhenping Mulu* (The Catalogs of Collections in Guangxi Zhuang Museum). Nanning: Guangxi Minzhu Press.

Guo, Hanquan 2004. *Gujianzhu Mugong* 古建筑木工 (The Carpentry Techniques in Traditional Buildings), Beijing: Zhongguo Jianzhu Press.

He, Qiang 2002. 'Introduction and Analysis of Peach Blossom Patterns of the Yao in Xiaoshajiang, Longhui County, Hunan Province', in Yasuda Yoshinori (ed. 安田喜宪主编), *Myths and Rituals of the Yangtze River Civilization* (神话祭祀与长江文明). Beijing: Wenwu Press, pp. 101–115.

He, Rong-an 2002. *Yijing Yizhi* (The Introduction of *I Jing*). Beijing: Huawen Press.

He, Xiaoxin 1990. *Fengshui Tanyuan* 风水探源 (The Origins of Fengshui). Nanjing: Dongnan University Press.

Hu, Guosheng (Qing Dynasty). *Luojing Jieding* 罗经解定 (The Explanation of Compass). Taiwan: Xuanxue Press.

Huai Nan Zi (Compendium of Learning Assembled under the Patronage of Liu An, Prince of Huai Nan), completed by 139 BC, *Sibu congkan* (ed.).

Huang, Shouqi and Zhang, Shanwen 2005. *Zhou Yi Yizhu* 周易译注 (The Explanation of *I Jing*). Shanghai: Shanhai Guji Press.

Huangdi Neijing: Su Wen 黄帝内经：说文 (Yellow Emperor's Classic of Internal Medicine: Basic Questions), Complied first century B.C. or A.D. Shanghai: Kexue Jishu Press, 1983.

Huitu Lu Ban jing (Illustrated canon of Lu Ban) 1808. A late Qing edition of the Ming text of the *Lu Ban jing* (q.v.), in the collection of the Needham Research Institute, Cambridge.

I Jing (Book of Changes), originally a manual of divination, with later accretions dating as late as W. Han, *Sibu congkan* (ed.).

Jiang, G. 1997. *The Dwelling Culture of Yunnan Nationalities*. Kunming: Yunnan Minzu Press.

Jiang, Tingyu 1999. *Gudai Tonggu Tonglun* 古代铜鼓通论 (Research of Ancient Bronze Drums), Beijing: Zhijincheng Press.

Kuang, Lu (1604–50). Chiya (Records of minority nationality customs in Guangxi and Guizhou during the Ming dynasty).

Long, Yaohong and Zhen, Guoqiao 1998. *The Dong Language in Guizhou Province, China*. Arlington, Dallas: Summer Institute of Linguistics and University of Texas.

Li, Changjie (ed.) 1990. *Guibei Minjian Jianzhu* (Vernacular Architecture in Northern Guangxi). BeiJing: Zhongguo Jianzhu Press.

Li, Dingxin 1990. *Ganzhou Yang Jiupin Fengshui Shu Rumeng* 赣州杨救贫风水术入门 (Introduction to the Fendshui School of Yang Jiuping). Hongkong: Tianma Tushu Youxian Gongshi Press.

―――― 1997. *Zhongguo Luopan 49 Ceng Xiangjie* 中国罗盘 49 层祥解 (The Explanation of 49 Scales on the Chinese Compass). Hongkong: Juxianguan Wenhua Youxian Gongshi Press.

Li, F. 2003. *Xinjuan Jingban Gongshi Diaozhuo Zhengshi Lu Ban Jing Jiangjia Jing* (The Canon of *Lu Ban Jing*). Haikou: Hainan Press.

Li, Guohao et al. (eds.) 1991. *Jianyuan Shiying—Zhongguo Gudai Tumu Jianzhu Keji Shiliao Xuan* 建苑拾英 (A Compilation of Classic Texts about Traditional Chnese Building). Shanghai: Tongji University Press.

Li, Jie, *Yingzao Fashi*, completed 1100, first edition 1103, second edition 1145. Shanghai: Commercial Press, 1925.

Li, Xi 2001. 'Fengshui *Qiao*' 风水桥 (Fengshui Bridge), in Zhang Zhezhong (ed.), *Dongzu fengyuqiao* 侗族风雨桥 (The 'Wind and Rain' bridge of the Dong). Gui*yang*: Huaxia Press, pp. 23–8.

Li, Xiaodong 2002. 'The Aesthetic of the Absent: The Chinese Conception of Space', *Journal of Architecture*, 7 (Spring 2002): 10–20.

Liang, Shicheng 1981. *Qingshi Yingzao Zeli* 清式营造则例 (The Architectural Manual of Qing Dynasty). Beijing: Zhongguo Jianzhu Press.

Liang, Shicheng 1983. *Yingzao Fashi Zhushi* (The Notes of *Yingzao Fashi*). Beijing: Zhongguo Jianzhu Gongye Press.

Liu, Dunzhen 1957. *Zhongguo Zhuzhai Gaishu* 中国住宅概述 (Introduction to Chinese Dwellings).

―――― Liu, Dunzhen 1962. *Lu Ban Yingzao Zhengshi* (The Carpenter's Manual *Lu Ban Jing*), in *Wenwu* 2, pp. 7–11.

―――― 1980. *Zhongguo Gudai Jianzhu Shi* 中国古代建筑史 (The History of Chinese Traditional Architecture). Beijing: Zhingguo Jianzhu Gongye Press.

―――― 1984. *The History of Chinese Ancient Architecture* 中国古代建筑史 (*Zhongguo Gudai Jianzhu Shi*) under the general editorship of Liu Dunzhen.

Lu Ban Jing 鲁班经 (Lu Ban Jing), which was written by Wu Rong in Ming dynasty (1368–1644 AD), in Li Feng (ed.) 2003. Haikou: Hainan Press.

Lu, Yuanding 1978. *"Nanfang Diqu Chuantong Jianzhu De Tongfeng Yu Fangre"* (Ventilation and Heat Insulation of Traditional Architecture in South China). *Architectural Journal*, 4: 36–41.

Lu, Yuanding and Yang, Gusheng 1988. The *Vernacular Architecture* volume as one of the six volumes on Chinese architecture encyclopedic *Zhongguo Meishu Quanji* (Arts of China series).

Lu, Yuanding and Wei, Yanjun 1990. *Guangdong Minju* 广东民居 (Vernacular dwellings of Guangdong).

Luo, Ying and Tang Huancheng 1985. *Zhongguo Shigong qiao Yanjiu*. Beijing: Renmin Jiaotong Press.

Ma, Binjian 1991. *Zhongguo Gujianzu Muzuo Yingzao Jishu* 中国古建筑木作营造技术 (The Techniques of Timber Structure in Chinese Traditional Architecture). Beijing: Kexue Press.

Ming Lu Ban Yingzao Zhengshi: Tianyi Ge Cangben (The Carpenter's Manual of Lu Ban Jing in Ming Dynasty: Collected by *Tianyi Ge*), with an Introduction by Chen Congzhou 1988. Shanghai: Kexue Jishu Press.

Pan, Guxi (ed.) 2001. *Zhongguo Jianzhushi* 中国建筑史 (Chinese Architectural History). Beijing: Zhongguo Jianzhu Gongye Press.

Bibliography

Qi, Heng and Fan, Wei 1992. 'Gucheng Langzhong Fengshui Geju: Qianshi Fengshui Geju yu Gucheng Huanjing Yixiang' 古城阆中风水格局: 浅释风水理论与古城环境意象 (The Fengshui Pattern of Langzhong City), in Wang Qiheng (ed.), *Fengshui Lilun Yanjiu* 风水理论研究 (Research on the Theory of Fengshui School). Tianjin: Tianjin University Press, pp. 41–68.

Ruan, Yuan (1764–1849), *Kaogong Ji*. Kaogong Ji Chezhi Tujie written in 1803, in Huang Qing Jingjie (ed.) 1860, Vol. 1055, 1056.

Shi, Kaizhong 2001. *Dongzu Gulou* (The Drum Towers of the Dong). Guiyang: Huaxia Wenhua Yishu Press.

Shi, Ruoping 1984. *'Qiantan Dongzu de Zuyuan He Qianxi'* (A Brief Discussion of the Origin and Migrations of the Dong Nationality). *Guizhou Minzu Yanjiu (Journal of Guizhou Nationality Research)*, 4: 75–88.

Shi, Ruoping and Wu, Shancheng 1989. *Sanjiang Dongzu Zizhixian Minzu Zhi* (Records of the Nationalities of Sanjiang Dong Autonomous County). Nanning: Guangxi Renming Press.

Sun, Yingkui and Yang, Yiming 1998. *'Liushisi' Gua Zhong De Rensheng Zheli He Moulue* '六十四卦'中的人生哲理和谋略 (The Philosophy and Tricks in the Sixty-four Hexagram). Beijing: Shehui Kexue Wenxian Press.

Wang, Hongqi 2003. *JingDian TuDu Shan Hai Jing* 经典图读山海经 (Picture and Explain of the Classic Canon of Mountains and Seas). Shanghai: ShangHai ChiShu Press.

Wang, Qiheng (ed.) 1992. *Fengshui Lilun Yanjiu* 风水理论研究 (Research on the Theory of Fengshui School). Tianjin: Tianjin University Press.

Wang, Wenguang 1999. *Zhongguo Nafang Minzu Shi* 中国南方民族史 (The Nationality History of Southern China). Beijing: Minzu Press.

Wang, Xiuwen 2002. 'The Supernatural Force of Gate of Hell and Peach and the Worship of Sun', in Yasuda Yoshinori (ed.), *Myths and Rituals of the Yangtze River Civilization*. Beijing: Wenwu Press, pp. 134–145.

Wang, Yude 1991. *Shenmi De Fengshui – Chuantong Xiangdishu Yanjiu* 神秘的风水—传统相地术研究 (The Secret of Fengshui: Research on Traditional Geomancy). Nanning: Guangxi Jiaoyu Press.

Wei, Yujiao 1999. *Guangxi Sanjiang Dongzu Cunzhai De Dili Huanjing He Jianzhu Tese* 广西三江侗族村寨的地理环境和建筑特色 (The Villages and Buildings of the Dong in Guangxi). Master degree thesis, Architectural Department of Guangxi University, Nanning.

Wu, Hao (ed.) 1987a. *Zhongguo Geyao Jicheng: Sanjiangxian Juan* 中国歌谣集成: 三江县卷 (Collection of Nationality Folk Ballads, Volume from Sanjiang County). Sanjiang: Sanjiang County Office Press.

—— 1987b. *Dongzu Kuanci, Yege, Jiuge* 侗族款词, 耶歌, 酒歌 (Collection of Chinese Folk Ballads, Volume from Sanjiang). Sanjiang: Sanjiang County Office Press.

—— 1989. *Sanjiang Gezu Minge*, in *Zhongguo Geyao Jicheng Guangxi Fenjuan: Sanjiang Dongzhu Zhizixian Zhiliaoji (3)*. 三江各族民歌 (Collection of Nationality Folk Ballads of Guangxi, Volume from Sanjiang). Sanjiang: Sanjiang County Office Press.

—— 1995. *Gulou, Taiyang, Yueliang* 鼓楼, 太阳, 月亮 (The Drum Tower, the Sun and the Moon). Guangzhou: Guangdong Renmin Press.

—— 2001. *'Qiaoqu'* 桥趣 (The Legends and Custom of the Bridge), in Zhang Zhezhong (ed.), *Dongzhu Fengyuqiao* (The 'Wind and Rain' Bridge of the Dong). Guizhou: Huaxia Wenhua Press, pp. 45–53.

Wu, Hao and Zhang, Zhezhong 1991. *Dongzu Geyao Yanjiu* 侗族歌谣研究 (Research on the Dong Songs). Nanning: Guangxi Renmin Press.
Wu, Nengfu 2001, 'Fu Qiao' (Good Fortune Bridge), in Zhang Zhezhong (ed.), *Dongzhu Fengyuqiao* (The Wind and Rain Bridge of the Dong). Guizhou: Huaxia Wenhua Press, pp. 9–13.
Wu, Tingdong 1993. *Dongzu Shi Baiyue Yizhi Fazhan Qilai De Tuzhu Minzu* (The Dong Nationality are Aboriginals Who Developed from a Branch of the Baiyue People). *Guizhou Minzu Yanjiu* (Journal of Guizhou Nationality Research), 2, pp. 66–74.
Wu, Zhao 1999. *Dianguo De Yinyue Yu Jisu* 滇国的音乐与祭俗 (Retracing the Lost Footprints of Music). Taiwan: Dongfang Press.
Xian, Guangwei 1995. *Dongzu Tonglan* 侗族通览 (A General Survey of the Dong Nationality). Nanning: Guangxi Minzu Press.
Yang, Fan 2002. 'The Origin and Date of the Bronze Civilization in Dian and its Religious Beliefs', in Yasuda Yoshinori (ed.), *Myths and Rituals of the Yangtze River Civilization*. Beijing: Wenwu Press, pp. 80–100.
Yang, Guoren and Wu, Dingguo 1981. *Dongzu Zuxian Nalilai* (Where Did the Dong Ancestors Come From). Guiyang: Guizhou Renmin Press.
Yang, Quan et al. 1992. *Dongzu* (The Dong Nationality). Beijing: Beijing Minzu Press.
Yang, Shengzhong and Yang, Zaihong 1989. *Liping Xian Minzuzhi* (Annals of the Nationalities of Liping County). Guiyang: Guizhou Renmin Press.
Yang, Tongshan et al. 1982. *Dongzu Minjian Gushi Xuan* (An Anthology of Dong Folktales). Shanghai: Shanghai Wenyi Press.
Yang, Tongshan et al. 1983. *Dongxiang Fengqinglu* 侗乡风情录 (The Customs of Dong). Chengdu: Shichuan Minzu Press.
Yang, Tongshan et al. (eds.) 1987. *Dongzu Pipage* 侗族琵琶歌 (Collection of Chinese Nationality Folk Ballads: Dong *Pipa* Songs). Sanjiang: Sanjiang County Office Press.
Ying Zao Fa Shi 营造法式, which is written by Li Jie in Song dynasty (960–1279 AD), in *Siku Quanshu* 四库全书 1987, Vol. 673. Shanghai: Shanghai Guji Press.
Yu, Dazhong 2001. *Dongzhu Minju* 侗族民居 (The Dwellings of the Dong). Guiyang: Huaxia Wenhua Yishu Press.
Zang Jing 葬经 (the Canon of Bury), written by Guo Pu in Ji Dynasty (256–316 AD).
Zang Jing (The Book of Burial), by Guo Pu (276–324), translated with an Introduction by Juwen Zhang 2004. Lewiston, NY; Lampeter: Edwin Mellen Press.
Zhang, Min 1983. '*Qiantan Dongzu Yu Geling He Ling*' (A Brief Discussion of the Relations between the Dong and the Geling and Ling Nationalities). *Guizhou Minzu Yanjiu* (Journal of Guizhou Nationality Research), 1: 86–93.
―――― (ed.) 1985. *Dongzu Jianshi* 侗族简史 (A Concise History of the Dong Nationality). Guiyang: Guizhou Minzu Press.
Zhang, Shishan and Yang, Changsi 1992. *Dongzu Wenhua Gailun* 侗族文化概论 (A Survey of Dong Culture). Guiyang: Guizhou Renmin Press.
Zhang, Yuhuan, et al. (eds.) 2000. *Zhongguo Gudai Jianzhu Jishushi* 中国古代建筑技术史 (The Techniques of Chinese Traditional Architecture). Beijing: Kexue Press.
Zhang, Zhezhong (ed.) 2001. *Dongzu Fengyuqiao* ('Wind and Rain' Bidges of the Dong). Guiyang: Huaxia Wenhua Yishu Press.
Zhang, Zhimo et al. 1993. *Guilin Wenwu Guji* 桂林文物古迹 (The Heritage of Guilin). Beijing: Wenwu Press.

Zhe, Jun and Nian, Haoxi (eds.) 1994. *Dongzu Minjian Wenhua Shenmeilun* 侗族民间文化审美论 (Aesthetics of the Dong Folk Custom). Nanning: Guanxi Renmen Press.

Zhou Li (Ritual of the Zhou Dynasty), late Warring States, with commentaries and subcommentaries in *Shisan Jing Zhushu*, repr. Taipei 1972 from edition of 1815.

Zhou, Xing 1998. Jingjie Yu Xiangzheng: '*Qiao He Minsu*' 境界与象征: 桥和民俗 (Boundary and Symbol: Bridge and Folk Custom). Shanghai: Shanghai Wenyi Press.

Index

Note: *Italic* page numbers refer to figures and page numbers followed by "n" denote endnotes.

About the House (Carsten and Hugh-Jones) 246
Abrahams, Roger D. 245
American Museum of National History 121
an jin liang (setting the beam) ceremony 222–223
an qiao (Setting up Bridge) ceremonies 59–60
architecture: Asian vernacular 234; 'Austronesian' style of pile-built 18; Blundell Jones on 249; Chinese vernacular 147; Dong 12, 21–22, 29, 104, 154, 174, 189, 238–239, 248, 250; and human body 153; human sense of 239; indigenous 246; local vernacular 22; of northern Guangxi Province 22; Order of 245–250; vernacular 246
Architecture without Architects (Rudofsky) 246
Atkin, Tony 233
Australian Aborigines, Dreamtime myth of 248

'*bao ye qiao*' (guardian father bridge) 63
Barth, Fredrik 104
ba sha huang quan pan (Eighth Evil Spirit of Hell Scale) 143
Batuan bridge 9, *11, 185*
bazi (birthday in Chinese calendar) 36, 66
Bei shi·Liao zhuan (*liao* people) 15–16
Bellwood, Peter S. 19
Bible 132
bing (illness) 164, 169
Bing Fire Qi 142

bing huo qi (*bing* and fire pattern) 142
Bloch, Maurice 244
Blundell Jones, Peter 241, 245–246, 247, 249, 250, 252n36, 252n48, 252n62, 252n63
Boerschmann, Ernst 22, 26n56
Book of Rites 235n3
Bridge festivals 4
bridges: family rituals of worshipping on 59–67, *61–62, 64–66*; personal rituals of worshipping on 59–67, *61–62, 64–66*; physical 49–59, *50, 54–55, 57–58*; symbolic 49–59, *50, 54–55, 57–58*; as symbolic crossing 36–48, *40–43, 45–46*; Wind and Rain 5–14, *5, 7–8, 10–14*
Bronze Age Culture of Dongson in North Vietnam 18
building materials, 166, 175; Dong house 209–212; preparing 209–212
building structure, setting up 206, 214–218, *215, 217*
Buyi ethnic group 3, 4, 15
Buyi language 4

cai (Wealth) 164, 169
cai-fen modular system 154, 157–158, *158*
cai ge tang (stepping on the singing stage) ceremony 93–94
calabash 92, *93,* 186, 250
Carpentry and Building in Late Imperial China: A Study of the Fifteenth-Century Carpenter's Manual Lu Ban Jing (Ruitenbeek) 191n8
Carsten, Janet 246

268 *Index*

ceremonies: *an jin liang* (setting the beam) ceremony 222–223; *an qiao* (Setting up Bridge) ceremonies 59–60; around drum tower 91–99, *93–94, 97*; *cai ge tang* (stepping on the singing stage) ceremony 93–94; *fa chui* (starting the hammer) 214, 216; *nuan qiao* (Warm the Bridge) ceremony 65; Opening the Door of Wealth *(kai cai men)* 228–233, *229, 231*; Raising the Golden Beam ceremony *218–220*, 218–228, *227–228*; related to construction of houses 235n4; *shangliang* 236n40; *tai guan ren 99–100*, 99–103
chai liang (stepping on the beam) 221, 223
cha sha (investigating attitudes and flourishing plants of the hills or mountains around) 129
Chengyang bridge 9, *10, 14*, 28, 30, 37, 39, *40*, 41, *41*, 46, 47, 49, 51, 54, *54*, 56, 69n2, 69n3, *110*, 137, *137*, 138, 142, 180, *181*, 184, 188–189, *227*
Chen Yongqing 27, 137, *137*, 138
Chen Yongzhang 55, 56
Chinese architecture 161; and carpentry 6; traditional 155, 159, 161, 188, 194n62, 234n1
Chinese New Year 4, 133
Chinese vernacular architecture 147
Chinesischer Architektur (Boerschmann) 22, 26n56
chuan dou (timber structural system) 194n62, 234n1
chuandou shi (cross-beam structure) 180
chuan fang (crossbeams) 206, 216
Chu King 81
communal meals and *tai guan ren* ceremony *99–100*, 99–103
The Concise Oxford 242
cosmology: and culture 148; defined 148; traditional, of Dong people 30–36; of vital energy *qi* 112–116; of *yin* and *yang* 32–36, 155–156
culture: and cosmology 148; Dian 19; Dong 15, 63, 75, 133; Han 18, 106n18, 113, 145; Homudu 17; Neolithic 18
customs: of the Dong 2–5; of Dong marriage 80; of the *liao* people 16; *mai liang dui* 208; *zuo mei* 208; *zuo ye* 208

Dai language 4
da mu xiao shi 157

da mu zuo (major structural carpentry) 157, 162
Dao de Jing 133
Daoism 22
Dian culture 19
Di Li Ren Zi Xu Zhi 127
Di Li Shu 141
Di Li Wu Jue (Five Transmitted Teachings in Geomancy) (Zhao Jiufeng) 151n51
Di Li Zhuo Yu Fu (Precious Tools of Geomancy) (Xu Zhimo) 151n51
di mai long shen (the pulse of earth and the spirit of dragon) 131
Disorder, and symbolic meanings 239–242
'*Do Dual Organizations Exist?*' (Levi-Strauss) 246
Domestic Architecture and the Use of Space (Kent) 246
Dong architecture 12, 21–22, 29, 104, 154, 174, 189, 238–239, 248, 250
Dong carpenters 163–166
Dong 'Conference of the ninety-nine elders' (Yuezhai) 106n20
Dong culture 15, 63, 75, 133
Dong house: building materials, preparing 209–212; building structure 214–218, *215, 217*; construction of timber house 197–199; fortunate location of 199–209, *200–201, 203–205, 207–208*; Opening the Door of Wealth *(kai cai men)* 228–233, *229, 231*; organization of 199–209, *200–201, 203–205, 207–208*; orientation of 199–209, *200–201, 203–205, 207–208*; Raising the Golden Beam ceremony *218–220*, 218–228, *227–228*; rituals and construction of 196–234; timber elements 212–214, *213–214*
Dong language 4
Dongliang Chen 71n33
Dong measurement system 191n8; meanings of 166–172; structure of 166–172
Dong people: bridges as symbolic crossing 36–48, *40–43, 45–46*; Dong 'Conference of the ninety-nine elders' 106n20; family rituals of worshipping on bridges 59–67, *61–62, 64–66*; personal rituals of worshipping on bridges 59–67, *61–62, 64–66*; rituals on physical bridges 49–59, *50, 54–55*,

57–58; rituals on symbolic bridges 49–59, *50, 54–55, 57–58*; traditional cosmology of 30–36
Dong society: construction as an event in 197; and *The Kam People* 74; and *kuan* laws 83–84; order of 84; and shamanism 59
Dong songs 51, 70n16, 84, 94–96, 235n6
Dong villages: bridges as symbolic crossing 36–48, *40–43, 45–46*; carpenters 163–166; Chinese cosmology of vital energy *qi* 112–116; custom of 2–5; dragon den *(long xue)* 132–137; dragon vein *(long mai)* 127–132; drum towers 5–14, *5, 7–8, 10–14*; *fengshui* compass linking time with space 116–127; *fengshui* practice and Ma'an Village 137–147; *ganlan* structure in 14–21, *15, 21*; hills *(sha)* 127–132; language of 2–5; measurement system 166–172; rituals and timber house construction 197–199; typology of 2–5; water *(shui)* 132–137; watercourse mouth *(shui kou)* 132–137; Wind and Rain bridges 5–14, *5, 7–8, 10–14*
Douglas, Mary 241, 251n16
Dragon Boat Festival 5
dragon den *(long xue)* 132–137
dragon vein *(long mai)* 127–132
Dreamtime myth of Australian Aborigines 248
drum towers 5–14, *5, 7–8, 10–14*, 106n12; ceremonies around 91–99, *93–94, 97*; communal meals *99–100*, 99–103; *kuan* (Dong regulation) and *kuan* alliance 81–83; *kuan* laws 83–86; Mapang drum tower as ritual space *86–87*, 86–91, *89*; *tai guan ren* ceremony *99–100*, 99–103; *tang wa* and *tang sa* 77–81
Duan Mu Qi 163
dui gua 142, 145
Duke Liu (ancestor of Zhou tribe) 125
Duke of Lu Ding 163
Duliu river 3
duo ye ji sa (singing and dancing ceremony for worshipping Sa Sui) 93

Eating New Rice festival 5
Eat New Festival 63
Eight-trigrams system 141, 142, 145, 164, 189

Eliade, Mircea 69n4, 71n48, 241, 248

fa chui (starting the hammer) ceremony 214, 216
Fang Wei School (school of *fengshui* compass) 116, 125
fengshui (wind and water): compass *89*, 92–93, 116–125, *141, 144*; encyclopaedia 113; as 'geomancy' in West 114; ideal resident site in *126*; *long xue* 136; master crossing symbolic bridge *57*; master crossing temporary bridge *61*; and mountain ranges 128; practice on arrangement of Ma'an Village 137–147, *140*; in shaping the Dong villages 109–148; tree *78, 91*
Fengshui bridge 149n8
fengshui compass: linking time with space 116–127; origins of 116–127
Fengshui Compass School 88
Feuchtwang, Stephan 73n78, 73n79
Fireworks Day festivals 5
five-colour yarn (cyan, blue, red, yellow and white) 65
Five Movement and Six *Qi* theory 149n14
Fourth National Census 2
fu gui jiu (wealthy and noble wine) 233

ganlan structure in Southern China 14–21, *15, 21*, 196, 206
Geary, D. Norman 22, 74
Genesis 132, 239
God of Foundation *(diji zu)* 45, *46*
God of Rebirth (Hualin Spirit) 44
god tablet 71n37
Gombrich, E. H. 240, 250n5
Gong Liu 125
Gong Shu 163
'good start and perfect ending' *(you tou you wei)* 103
'good start but no ending' *(you tou mei wei)* 103
Gua (Earth Mother) 165
Gua (Heaven Father) 165
Guan Di (King of War) 41, *42*, 43–44
Guan Gong 47
Guan Shi Di Li Meng 127
Guan Zi 133
'Guidelines of Green' *(yue qing)* 83
'Guidelines of Yellow' *(yue huang)* 83
Guidoni, Enrico 247, 248
Gui Gu Zi 118
Gui Hai Yu Heng Zhi 4

gu lou ping (drum tower square) 75
Guo Moruo 1, 149n8
Guo Pu 114, 126

Han culture 18, 106n18, 113, 143
Han Dynasty 15, 43, 121, *121*, 149n13, 151n67, 169; Chinese Language Etymology in 169
Han Fei Zhi 14
Han Fei Zi 24n28, 118
Han Long Jing (Manual of Moving Dragon) 126
Hao Wu 70n17, 70n20
Hay, John 244
Heaven Pool *(tian chi* or *tai ji)* 125
Helong bridge 11, *13,* 145
Heng Mountain (Shanxi) 150n37
Hen Mountain (Hunan) 150n37
he Zhong sheng (inviting celestial gods) 59
hills *(sha)* 127–132
Homudu culture 17
House Form and Culture (Rapoport) 246
Hou Tian system 123, 150n42
Huai river 149n19
Hua Lin 47
Hualin God 32, 55, 60
Hua Mountain (Shanxi) 150n37
huang (yellow) 164
Huangdi Neijing 114–115, 149n13, 149n14
Huang Di Zai Jing 123, 128
huan qiao wang yuan (worshipping god of bridge) ceremony 59
Hugh-Jones, Stephen 246
huo ju (fire pattern) 141

in chai (welcoming the wealth) 232

Ji dynasty 126
Jielong bridge 11
jin liang (golden beam) 209, 212, 220, 222–223, 226
Ji river 149n19
Jiuwan Mountain 3
Johnson, Mark 148
Judge God (God of Rebirth) 41

Kam language 4
The Kam People (Geary) 74
Kam-Shui languages 3–4
Kam-Tai languages 3–4
Kaogong Ji 115–116, 149n16
kuan (Dong regulation) 81–83
kuan alliance 81–83
Kuan institutions 4, 74, 75, 81–82, 84, 100
kuan laws 83–86
kuan organization 107n37
kuanping 75, 105n9
Kui Xing (God of Scholar) 41–43, *43,* 44, 47

Lakeoff, George 148
language(s): Buyi 4; Dai 4; Dong 4; of the Dong 2–5; English 190n3; Kam 4; Kam-Shui 3–4; Kam-Tai 3–4; Maonan 4; Mulao 4; Shui 4; Tai 3–4; Thai 4; Tibeto-Burman 3; Western 190n3; Zhuang 4; *see also specific language(s)*
Lao Zi 145
Le Corbusier 153–154, 171, 190n5, 191n8
Levi-Strauss, C. 246
Liang Changzhong 37, 70n30
Liang Tongyun 70n17
Li Jie 155, 191n9, 192n14
Linxi river 37
The Living House (Waterson) 246
Li Xi 22
Locality God (God of Locality) 41, 43, 45–46
Lowenthal, David 241
Lu Ban (Chinese architect or master carpenter) 163–164, 209, 210, 212, 215, 220, 230–233
Lu Ban Chi 163–166
Lu Ban foot rule 166, 167, 168, 169–173, 177, 190, 222
Lu Ban Jing (carpenter's manual) 6, 22, 163–164, 166, 169, 199, 211, 219–220
Luo Shu magic square 150n42
Luoyang river 45
lu sheng (musical instruments) 16, 32, 51, 53, 72n53, 92, 100–101, 103
lu sheng Day 5

Ma'an Village: Chengyang bridge in *10, 110; fengshui* practice on arrangement of 137–147; layout of *140,* 142; location of 27; watercourse mouth of *144*
Major Carpentry *(da mu zuo)* 154–163
Maonan language 4
Mapang drum tower 27, *76;* door of 87; location of 75; origins of 74; plan and orientation of 87, *89;* as ritual space 86–87, *86*–91, *89;* Sa Sui altar inside *79;* stairs accessing to 87

Mapang village: *fengshui* tree and Locality God *78*; gates of *88–89*; location of *75*; Mapang drum tower in 74; personal or family bridge found in *62*; plan of *76*; ritual routine of *86*; viewed from east bank of Wuluo river *75*
Material Modular System *(Cai-fen zhi)* 154–163
Meng Xi Bi Tan (Shen Kuo) 120
Miao ethnic group 3, 15
Miaolin Mountain chain 3
Miao-Yao languages 3
Mid-Autumn Festival 5
Ming dynasty 78, 163
Minor Carpentry *(xiao mu zuo)* 154–163
Molao ethnic group 3
mu gong (Tomb Palace) 141–143, *143*
Mulao language 4
Mushroom Song 93

Natural Philosophy 190
Needham, Joseph 22, 26n57, 116–117, 119, 121–122, 126, 149n11, 149n21, 150n35, 150n42, 150n43, 150n46, 151n51, 154, 191n11
Needham, Rodney 241, 251n13
Neolithic culture 18
New Year festival 101
New Year's Day 65
niu tui qing (Dong music instrument) 99
nuan qiao (Warm the Bridge) ceremony 65

Online Etymology Dictionaries 239–240
Opening the Door of Wealth *(kai cai men)* 228–233, *229, 231*
Order: of architecture 245–250; classification by symbolic meanings 239–242
Oxford Learner's Dictionaries 239

pai zhanggan (rule making) 173–178, *174, 175*
personal rituals of worshipping on bridges 59–67, *61–62, 64–66*
physical bridges, rituals on 49–59, *50, 54–55, 57–58*
Pingyan bridge 138
pipa songs 70n16
Planting Cotton Day 5
Prey into Hunter (Bloch) 244
Pueblo Indians 104

Pumpkin Day and Cultivating New Land ceremonies 5

qi (vital energy): Chinese cosmology of 112–116; Five Movement and Six *Qi* theory 149n14
Qian Han Shu 118
Qiao Wang (bridge god) 60
Qin dynasty 14, 20
Qing architectural regulation 159
Qing dynasty 80, 160, 163
Qing Nang Ao Yu 126
Qing Nang Hai Jiao Jing 127, 129
Qing river 3
Qing Shi Ying Zao Ze Li 159, 160, 185
Qingshui river 3
Qin Nang Ao Yu 139
Qushui river 3

Raising the Golden Beam ceremony *218–220,* 218–228, *227–228*
The Random House Dictionary 242
Rapoport, Amos 104, 148, 246
rebirth, belief in 69n4
Relph, Edward 147
Research on the Dong Songs *(Dongzu Ge Yao Yan Jiu)* 74
rice cultivation 18
Rite de Passage (Van Gennep) 242
The Ritual Process 245
rituals: accompanying construction of timber house 197–199; as action of transition 242–245; and construction of Dong house 196–234; defined 242; family 59–67, *61–62, 64–66*; Mapang drum tower as ritual space *86–87,* 86–91, *89*; personal 59–67, *61–62, 64–66*; on physical bridges 49–59, *50, 54–55, 57–58*; *shengmu ye* 107n31; on symbolic bridges 49–59, *50, 54–55, 57–58*
ritual space, Mapang drum tower as *86–87,* 86–91, *89*
Rudofsky, Bernard 246, 252n39
Ruitenbeek, Klaas 167, 191n8
Rykwert, Joseph 233

Sa Gaoqiao (guardian spirit) 88
Sa Jingmei (ancestor spirit) 88
San Hai Jing 90
Sanjiang gazette 4
Sa Tudui (locality spirit) 89
Science and Civilization in China (Needham) 22, 26n57
self-perpetuating groups 104

272 *Index*

self-preservation 4
sexual activities 60
shamanism 59
Shang dynasty 16, 117
shangliang (raising the beam) ceremony 181, 218, 220–221, 224, 226, 236n40
Shanren Yang 69n2, 70n30
Shanshenpo Mountain 3
shan tang ye 108n62
sha qi (evil power) 64
Shen Kuo 120
Shi Lin Guang Ji 119
shi nan 118
Shiping Yang 69n3
Shizhai Mountain 19
Shui ethnic group 3, 4
shui ju (water pattern) 141
shui kou (watercourse mouth) 139, 141–142
Shui language 4
Shu Jing 123
'*shuwu jiu*' (meal for setting up the house) 224
Si Ku Quan Shu 191n9
Song dynasty 120, 154, 155, 163
Song Shi 4
southeast *(xun)*/earth gate 87
Southern China: bronze drums in 19; Dong minority in 2; *ganlan* structure in 14–21, *15, 21*; Neolithic cultures of 18; pile-building in 18
southwest *(kun)*/ human gate 88
space: *fengshui* compass linking time with 116–127
Stafford, Charles 67
Sui dynasty 4
Sun Spirit 107n34
Sweet Rice Cake 4
symbolic bridges, rituals on 49–59, *50, 54–55, 57–58*
Symbolic Classification (Needham) 241
symbolic crossing: Dong's bridges as 36–48, *40–43, 45–46*
symbolic meanings: and architectural order 238–250; classification of Order by 239–242; and rituals 238–250

tai guan ren ceremony *99–100, 99–103*
Tai languages 3–4
tai liang (timber structural system) 194n62, 234n1
tailiang beam-column network 194n62, 234n1

tai liang structure 196
Tai Mountain (Shandong Taian) 150n37
Tang dynasty 4, 81, 123, 126, 163
tang sa 77–81
tang wa 77–81
Ta Ssu Thu 118
The Ten Books on Architecture (Vitruvius) 153
Thai language 4
Thompson, D'Arcy Wentworth 190
Three-harmony Principle 142
Tibeto-Burman languages 3
'tilt-hammer' 4
timber elements: Dong house 212–214, *213–214*; working on 212–214, *213–214*
timber structural system: chuan dou 234n1; tai liang 234n1
time: *fengshui* compass linking space with 116–127
Ting Yu Jiang 19
Ti Shun 16
traditional building techniques: Dong measurement system 166–172; *Lu Ban Chi* and *Zhanggan* (the carpenter's rule) of Dong carpenters 163–166; Major Carpentry *(da mu zuo)* 154–163; Material Modular System *(Caifen zhi)* 154–163; Minor Carpentry *(xiao mu zuo)* 154–163; *pai zhanggan* (rule making) 173–178, *174, 175*; Wind and Rain bridge, constructing *179,* 179–189, *181–189*; *Ying Zao Fa Shi* 154–163; zhanggan 173–178
traditional Chinese architecture 155, 159, 161, 188, 194n62, 234n1; chuan dou system 234n1; tai liang system 234n1; *see also* architecture
traditional cosmology of Dong people 30–36
"Treatise on Architectural Methods" 154
Tuan, Y.-f. 148, 152n100
Tudi Gong (Locality God) 42, 47, 77
Tujia ethnic group 3
Turner, Victor 244–245, 251n22, 251n27, 251n29, 251n32
typology, of the Dong 2–5

Van Gennep, Arnold 104–105, 108n76, 108n78, 233, 242–244, 251n19, 251n21, 251n24
Vitruvian Man 154
Vitruvius 153, 190n2

Wang Anshi 191n12
'Wang Anshi Reform' 155
Wanshou bridge 11, *13*
Washing Water-Buffaloes 5
water *(shui)* 132–137
Water-Buffaloes' Birthday 5
watercourse mouth *(shui kou)* 132–137
Water Dragon pattern 136
Waterson, Roxana 246
Watson, James 243
'wealthy spirit' 230–233
Wenchang Xing (God of Scholar) 41, 44, 47
Wenqu Xing (civil spirit) 221, 223, 232
Wenqu Xing (God of Scholar) 42
Wen river 149n19
Wen Wang 150n42
Western Chou period 125
Wind and Rain bridges 5–14, *5, 7–8, 10–14*, 72n53, 149n8, 191n7; constructing, with traditional techniques *179*, 179–189, *181–189*
Worship yin Bridge 50
Wu Changhong 75
Wu Changren 70n20
Wu Changyuan 75
Wu Hao 22, 27, 168, 193n44, 193n47
Wu Hongmiao 84–85
Wu Jing Zhong Yao 120
Wu Liang tomb 120
Wulin Mountain 3
Wu Luo river 105n6
Wu Main 81
Wu Mountain 3
Wuqu Xing (civil spirit) 221, 223, 232
Wu Rong 163
Wu Shihua 27
Wu Shilin 75
Wu Shilu 75
Wushui river 3

Xia dynasty 16
xiao mu zuo (non-structural carpentry) 162
Xing Shi School (school of form and attitude) 116, 125–126, 139
Xuefeng Mountain 3
Xun river 3
Xu Zhimo 151n51

Yang Shanren 12, 27, *29*, 30, 37, 46, 70n31, 74, 113, 135, 138, 167, 191n7,
193n44, 193n47, 194n52, 194n53, 194n54, 194n55, 194n56, 194n57, 194n60, 220
Yang Tangfu 30, 46, 70–71n31
Yang Tangzhen 46
Yang Tongshan 74
Yang Yunsong 126, 139, 141
Yang Zao Fa Shi 216
Yangzi river 195n68
Yan Wang (King of Hell) 44
Yanzhai bridge 28, *45*
Yao ethnic group 3, 15
Yellow Emperor 149n13
Yi-Fu Tuan 112
yin and *yang* 32–36, 155–156
Ying Zao Fa Shi (Li Jie) 154–163, 180, 185, 191n9
Yin Yang Er Zhai Quanshu (Complete Treatise on Siting in relation to the Two Geodic Currents) 151n51
Yin/Yang river 36–37
Yin/Yang song 32
Yi Zhi 163
Yongji bridge 38
Yuanbao Mountain 3
Yuanshui river 3
Yuechenlin Mountain 3
yue ye ceremony 91

Zang Jing (The Book of Burial) (Guo Pu) 113–114, 116, 125–126, 129, 134
Zhangган (the carpenter's rule) of Dong carpenters 163–167, 173–178, 200, 212–213, 220
Zhang Liang 60, 186, 209–210
Zhang Mei 60, 186
Zhang Zhezhong 22
Zhao Jiufeng 151n51
Zhe Zhong, Emperor of Song 155
Zhou dynasty 16, 163, 170
Zhou Li (Ritual of the Zhou Dynasty) 118
Zhou tribe 125
Zhuang ethnic group 3, 15
Zhuang language 4
zhuque 151n67
Zong ba (Eating sweet rice cake) Festival 5
zuo mei (young people playing and singing with *pipa,* weaving and drinking oil tea) 208
zuo ye (lovers talking and drinking oil tea overnight) 208

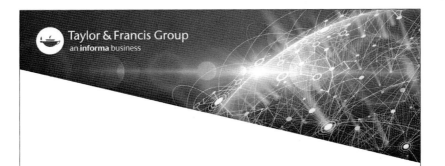